From Smartphones
to Social Media

From Smartphones
to Social Media

How Technology Affects Our Brains
and Behavior

Mark Carrier

An Imprint of ABC-CLIO, LLC

Santa Barbara, California • Denver, Colorado

Library of Congress Cataloging-in-Publication Data

Names: Carrier, Mark, author.
Title: From smartphones to social media : how technology affects our brains and behavior / Mark Carrier.
Description: Santa Barbara, California : Greenwood, [2018] | Includes index.
Identifiers: LCCN 2018016450 (print) | LCCN 2018017344 (ebook) | ISBN 9781440851797 (e-book) | ISBN 9781440851780 (hard copy : alk. paper)
Subjects: LCSH: Information technology—Social aspects. | Information technology—Psychological aspects. | Internet addiction.
Classification: LCC HM851 (ebook) | LCC HM851 .C367 2018 (print) | DDC 303.48/33—dc23
LC record available at https://lccn.loc.gov/2018016450

ISBN: 978-1-4408-5178-0 (print)
      978-1-4408-5179-7 (ebook)

22 21 20 19 18   1 2 3 4 5

This book is also available as an eBook.

Greenwood
An Imprint of ABC-CLIO, LLC

ABC-CLIO, LLC
130 Cremona Drive, P.O. Box 1911
Santa Barbara, California 93116-1911
www.abc-clio.com

This book is printed on acid-free paper ∞

Manufactured in the United States of America

Contents

Acknowledgments

This three-year adventure of planning, organizing, writing, and finalizing the text for this book began in late 2015 after being contacted by ABC-CLIO. At first, I wasn't sure if there was a place for the book among all of the other books on the topic, but after doing market research and identifying the niche for my book, a contract and plan were put into place quickly. Researching existing books took place in September 2015 and I had signed a contract by the end of November 2015. Although I did the writing, my home institution—California State University, Dominguez Hills (CSUDH)—and my colleagues from CSUDH made the most essential contributions to this effort. In the 2016–2017 and 2017–2018 school years, CSUDH granted me financial resources and paid time off to work on the book. My school gave me money to hire paid research assistants during the 2016–2017 academic year, as well as to hire an experienced interviewer. The paid assistants helped to gather much of the materials for the initial chapters that I wrote, getting me off to a great start on the book. The interviewer, Dr. Larry Rosen, used his professional connections to provide access to the top researchers in the field of the psychology of technology. A sabbatical leave for the Fall of 2017 was the most generous resource provided by my campus. The leave released me from my teaching and service duties, enabling me to write the bulk of the manuscript. I also took full advantage of the library resources available at the campus. CSUDH maintains an extensive set of online library resources that include electronic copies of journal articles and, in many cases, digitized versions of entire books. Through the library's inter-library loan program, I was able to receive physical copies of texts from other libraries when local print or digital versions were not available.

My colleagues at CSUDH assisted in several ways. Students from the George Marsh Applied Cognition Laboratory (GMAC Lab) helped to do the background research. On several occasions, the students had discussions with me about the substance of the chapters; these discussions clarified my thoughts and provided new issues to include that I hadn't already thought of. These students are Natalie Liberman, Kaitlin O'Brien, Jonathan Pedroza ("JP"), and Elise Han, though the entire GMAC Lab is noteworthy in this process. I was absent from a lot of our biweekly lab meetings over the course of the last two years because I was working on the book manuscript. In my absence, the lab members carried out my responsibilities, such as running the meetings, mentoring students, and managing the day-to-day operations of the lab. It was very helpful that Dr. Nancy Cheever ran the lab meetings during this time, Dr. Tom Norman assisted with lab presentations and mentoring, and the graduate students—Ryan Butler, José Franco, and Enya Valentin—pitched in when needed. At Dominguez Hills, I also thank the University administration for indulging me, letting me write when I needed to. Initially, Dr. Ellen Junn—then my Provost—formally provided the time to work on the book through my contract as Director of Assessment at CSUDH, and Dr. Gitanjali Kaul— Vice Provost and my direct supervisor—let me maintain my autonomy via setting my own work schedule. Later, Dr. Rod Hay, the Interim Provost, and Ken O'Donnell—Interim Vice Provost and my second supervisor—graciously accepted and renewed the prior contractual arrangements. Ken, most notably, never said no to me when I kept altering my work schedule as the book deadline grew near. Further, I thank Craig Geber and Dr. Dorota Huizinga from the Office of Graduate Studies and Research, for their willingness to let me spend the grant money from the Research, Scholarship, and Creative Activity grant in the way that benefitted me most, and I thank Khanh Vanpetten ("Van") and Christina Luu for managing the grant funds for me.

I thank the 10 interviewees—all prominent researchers and scholars—for giving their time to answer my questions: Dr. Laura L. Bowman, Dr. Jeanne Brockmyer, Dr. Nancy A. Cheever, Dr. Michelle Drouin, Dr. Robin Kowalski, Dr. Megan A. Moreno, Dr. Beverly A. Plester, Dr. Larry D. Rosen, Dr. Kaveri Subrahmanyam, and Dr. Kimberly Young (and I apologize to two researchers whose interviews were not included). Of the many people who helped me, two people stand out in particular. One of the standouts is Maxine Taylor, Senior Acquisitions Editor at ABC-CLIO. Maxine read all of my drafts, issued helpful feedback, checked on me regularly to see how things were going, and guided me through the entire process of planning and constructing the book. Maxine's flexibility regarding the scope of the work and specific deadlines was crucial to me. She also positively reinforced my writing effort along the way, and I appreciate that immensely. Finally, Maxine taught me what makes a good case study, something that I thought I already knew, but apparently did not. The other standout is Dr. Larry Rosen, my colleague and frequent co-author. In addition to conducting the interviews, Larry lent to me his entire reference collection of research articles in PDF form, opening the door to the personal library of a premier researcher in the field. Further, Larry made himself accessible to me for the entire three-year process. His advice, feedback, answers to my questions, and emotional support were invaluable.

I estimate that I read about 1,000 references in order to write this book, about 100 per chapter. During the long hours that I spent reading, taking notes, and converting my notes to sentences, my dog "Bones," and my music—thanks to iTunes and Pandora—were my faithful companions. I did nearly all of the writing at home, which meant that I was able to spend a lot more time with my wife and son than I normally get to do. They left me to my own devices for long periods of time but also indulged me when I wanted to share an exciting piece of information that I learned from my research. Thanks Arleen and Michael!

Introduction

Everyone seems worried about addiction: addiction to our cell phones, addiction to our computer games, addiction to Facebook, Instagram, and Snapchat. The media routinely run stories on individuals whose lives suffer due to their technology use, and news commentators regularly warn us about how our computer- and Internet-based devices need to be regulated, turned off, or altered. There is a pervasive rumor that computer and phone manufacturers, along with the software companies, have conspired to keep us looking at and using our devices 24 hours a day. This is the so-called attention economy, with the real goal of businesses supposedly being to get people to pay attention to their information and communications technologies (ICT) as much as possible. (The more that consumers use their technologies, the more that they click on advertisements, they more they make in-app purchases, and the more they sign up for subscription-based services, so the extended rumor goes.) According to people who write books on the topic for the general public, even workers in the technology industry are aware of this conspiracy, and they actively take steps to lessen the impact of it on their own families. Steve Jobs, the famous former head of Apple, Inc., purportedly maintained control over his child's technology consumption. At the same time, psychologists, sociologists, anthropologists, and other scientists have been examining the effect of the Internet and our devices upon society for several decades now, using the research tools of their professions. A large body of scholarly work has been amassed, although the constantly changing nature of ICT means that there is always some new phenomenon to be investigated. So how much of what we hear in the media or read about in popular books matches what scientists have learned? Is it true that we are all addicted to our technologies? If so, then what are the downsides of it? Should parents be worried about their children? The scientific, scholarly record provides answers to these questions, based on objective, empirical (i.e., based on data) studies—not just media hype, rumors, and conspiracy theories.

There is no doubt that addiction to technology is perceived to be a real problem by many people. In South Korea, for example, the government pays for Internet addiction therapy. But establishing Internet addiction as a real phenomenon through scientific research has been extremely difficult. Another theme out there in the media is that we are losing our ability to interact with other people because our faces are constantly behind a digital screen. Especially disconcerting is the widespread fear of the loss of empathy—the ability to feel compassion for another person. Yet the scientific evidence does not conclusively link declines in compassion to the advent of computer technology and the Internet. In fact, empathy appears to be alive and well online. Another recent perspective among the general population was that online dating was for, well, losers—people who could not find dates in real life. However, there is now considerable research on the topic, and the research shows that it is possible and common for people to be successful in online romance. In fact, about one-third of all romantic relationships in the United States now start on the Internet. An especially popular topic for theorizing in the media is the use of social media, especially by adolescents. For a brief while, Facebook depression was the scary phrase that made headlines. There are other social-media–related concerns too, like Facebocrastination (using Facebook to avoid school-work). Unfortunately, there is credible scientific evidence to support connections between social media use and negative emotions and connections between social media use and poor academic performance. A final example—one of many that could be given here—is the case of violent video gaming. Every time there is another mass shooting in the United States, commentators look for links between the shooter and a personal history of playing violent video games. But the scientists who study violent video gaming are not in agreement that the effects of violent video gaming are meaningful. Even those scientists who argue that violent video gaming is bad for kids acknowledge that it is impossible to conclusively put the blame for one person's real-life violent behavior on that person's video gaming habits.

While the general public is fascinated with how technology is impacting society, and with extreme cases of technology gone wrong—such as violent video gamers supposedly turned mass shooters—there are other real, deep reasons to scientifically study the effect of computer-based technologies upon people's brains and behaviors. First, for a particular, gigantic segment of the technology-using populace, there is some reason to think that any changes in their thoughts and behaviors due to technology use may be permanent. This gigantic segment of the populace is children, adolescents, and young adults. The human brain is not fully developed until the late twenties, meaning that the brains of these young people are changing at the same time that they are engaging in thoughts and behaviors never before seen in human history—personal technology use. A significant number of scientists are concerned about the potential changes in brain development, and there is some research on the topic. Second, many deleterious effects of technology use are now well-established. The delay of sleep onset caused by the blue light from computer screens, the development of a technology addiction, and the ease of cyberbullying are just a few of these. Objective, science-based research into these topics may provide insight into steps that can be taken to reduce or eliminate these problems. Third, to flip the perspective, there are many beneficial effects of personal technology use that are well-documented. Educators are using gamification to turn traditionally boring learning tasks into game-like scenarios. Computer camps—as well as numerous online sources—are providing young people with opportunities to learn computer programming, perhaps one of the most important skills for young people who will be entering the workforce. Manufacturers are creating wearable devices that monitor and track our physical status and help us keep to our exercise regimens. And ICT is allowing family and friends who are physically apart from each other—even in opposite places around the world—to stay in touch in ways that were never possible a few decades ago. Perhaps serious scholarly investigations into new technologies will provide information that can be used to maximize the positive uses of technology.

THE 1990s AND ONWARD

This book focuses on the most recent five to ten years of research into new ICT. Obviously, the computer and Internet eras reach further back in time. The problem is, technology changes rapidly. Trying to write a book that covers the entire period of the introduction of personal electronics into people's lives would probably have to contain three times as many pages of information as are contained in this book, meaning thirty chapters instead of ten! For present purposes, the 1990s are a good point in time to start some reflection. During the nineties, email ruled as a communications form, smartphones were neither available nor widespread, and video games were played in video arcades and on home console systems. The first electronic storybook was published on CD-ROM in the mid-nineties, opening the door to the combination of text and images in ways that print books could not provide. Television content was "aired" in ways similar to its historical pattern: episodes of shows were released and available to view at a specific time on a specific day of the week. Recordings of shows and theatrical movies were available on storage media (i.e., DVDs) that could be purchased or rented at retail establishments. In the mid-nineties, online dating became possible, opening up the ability to find dates with people who were not part of one's immediate social circle, but the software was limited and clunky compared to contemporary dating websites.

The current state of affairs with respect to ICT and personal electronics is quite different than merely twenty years ago. Devices are mobile, with the best examples being the cellular phone—now, smartphone—and the laptop computer, which went through a metamorphosis and became the tablet computer. In the early 2000s, along with the mobility of devices, came the ability to access the Internet from the devices and the expansion of software that is installed on those devices (i.e., the apps). The most famous tablet computer in America—the Apple iPad—was launched in April of 2010. The advent of data plans for cell phones led to the creation of the smartphone that contains numerous applications for playing games, keeping personal records, checking email, and—perhaps most importantly—accessing online social networks. In fact, the number one place that American college students access their social networks is their smartphone. The text messaging app, or more simply the messaging app—formerly known as Short Message System that started in 1992—is a key tool for communication between individuals and spawned its own form of language known as text-speak, among many other labels. Even dating has become mobile, with the rise of dating apps on the phone. In the academic world, students of all ages are given access to, and required to use, computer-based and online resources for studying, doing assignments, and even taking exams. Aside from computer gaming, this academic need puts students "behind a screen"—in this case, a laptop or desktop screen—for more hours per week than ever before. Television content is available anywhere, anytime, due to online streaming services, making it easy for people to "binge-watch" their favorite productions. This describes a mostly United States-based view; in other countries, the history and trajectory of personal electronics may be different. For instance, Singapore put significant effort into bringing the Internet to its citizens, with a goal of giving everyone access to the Internet starting in the early nineties. In fact, several Asian countries show much higher and faster rates of adoption of new technologies than the United States. These countries include South Korea, where rates of Internet gaming addiction may be the highest in the world. The research literature summarized in this book mostly centers on studies in the United States, but scientists around the world are contributing to the body of scientific knowledge on the topic. And through the reports of studies done in various countries, it can be seen that the general pattern of technological development and personal use is the same in nations around the world.

In the research world, the nineties to the present witnessed the seminal investigations into the effects of technology upon people's behaviors and brains. In one example, the study of Internet addiction began with the first publications on the topic in the late nineties. These publications exposed other scientists to a phenomenon that had not been reported before. In a second example, by the early 2000s, researchers were acknowledging that the Internet was a place for people to express themselves sexually. The concepts of sex-based technology addictions and Internet pornography were introduced. In the mid-2000s, scientists started studying online social networks intensively, with a very popular (among scientists) formal definition of a social networking site (SNS) being published in 2007. In the early 2010s, studies of cyberbullying appeared in scientific journals, leading to a robust research effort that continues to today. Scientists have learned that, in many ways, the specific forms of hardware and software are irrelevant to understanding people's behavior when it comes to ICT. After all, the fundamental motivations that people have for using these devices are biological and psychological in nature. For instance, when humans become sexually mature, they seek out romantic and sexual relationships with others. This has been true since the dawn of time, but the means for identifying and forming those relationships have changed immensely. In the 1980s, would-be suitors used video dating services and old-fashioned classified advertisements in newspapers to make romantic connections outside of their immediate physical social network. In the 1990s and 2000s, romance-seekers could now use online dating services that presented hundreds, if not thousands, of potential mates. In the 2010s, people can do all of this on their phones at home, at work, on the train, anywhere and anytime. And once a romantic relationship has been initiated, the phone can be used as a tool for maintaining the relationship through text messaging and—when a relationship is far enough along in its development—through sexting.

SUMMARIZING THE RESEARCH LITERATURE

It is a hopeless endeavor for scientists to try to keep up with studying technology at the rate that it is changing. The scientific process is a slow one. It is not atypical for a research study to take two to three years for completion, and another one to two years for publication in a research journal. (A research project is not considered "science" until is published in a scientific journal.) Therefore, the latest and greatest technology trends receive only limited coverage in the scientific body of work. A great example is Instagram. Although the social media application has been around since 2010, there are not many published research studies that examine it. This book's contents are based as much as possible on published scientific studies, so the book will not touch upon all of the newest innovations in personal technologies. However, the book attempts to meet a different important goal: to translate the scholarly literature into prose that is understandable by educated persons who are not trained as scientists. There are several other recent publications in book form that come close to meeting this goal, but do not quite get there. The *Oxford Handbook of Internet Psychology* (2009) contains valuable information about what scientists know about the Internet and people's attitudes, thoughts, and behaviors, yet scholarly handbooks tend to be written for, well, scholars—not non-scientists. The same can be said of the *Oxford Handbook of Media Psychology*, the *Oxford Handbook of Internet Studies* (2013) and *the Wiley Handbook of Psychology, Technology, and Society* (2015). To be fair, there is a relatively large set of insightful and interesting books written for lay audiences by scholars or science journalists on the topic of the present book. Many have emerged in the last five to ten years. This set includes, along with many other titles, *Always On: Language in an Online and Mobile World* (2008), *Rethinking Education in the Age of Technology: The Digital Revolution and Schooling in America* (2009), *The Shallows: What the Internet Is Doing to Our Brains* (2010), *Alone Together: Why We Expect More from Technology and Less from Each Other* (2011), *iDisorder: Understanding Our Obsession with Technology and Overcoming Its Hold on Us* (2012), and *iGen: Why Today's Super-Connected Kids Are Growing Up Less Rebellious, More Tolerant, Less Happy—and Completely Unprepared for Adulthood—and What That Means for the Rest of Us* (2017). The present book attempts to distinguish itself from this second set of books by presenting the scholarly literature as-is: the scientific work is described in a way that matches the work as closely as possible without putting a "spin" on it, and without drawing conclusions that go beyond the original publications. A second aspect of the present book is that it focuses on the personal use of technology. It is concerned with research on how regular people use technology and are affected by it in their everyday lives. Although people in the workplace are also affected by technology use, the issues that arise in that setting are often different ones than those that come about in people's everyday experiences. And much of the research on workplace technology use is driven by the needs of businesses, namely to maximize efficiency, minimize distractions and irrelevant behaviors, and maximize profits.

One problem that comes up when writing a book about personal technology use is that the writer—in this case, a heavy technology user, like most professors—will have his or her own experiences with technology that may bias the writing. To reduce the influence of these prior experiences (after all, the point of the book is to present the research without interpretation), the writer attempts to maintain an open mind. As a scientist, one learns that real data do not always match one's expectations for what those data should look like and that real data are not always intuitive, meaning they do not always match one's gut feeling for how the world should be. Rather, the writer's beliefs should be guided and informed by the data and evidence that are encountered as a result of doing research for the book. As much as possible, the narrative contained in the following chapters lays out the evidence as encountered without injecting personal experiences into the text. Sometimes, this approach leaves questions unanswered; this only reflects the state of the research on the various sub-topics. Thanks to the Internet, most professors have access to nearly the whole of the scientific body of knowledge through the online libraries at their home institution. The current book benefitted from this, as well as the extensive personal libraries of research articles from the writer and colleagues (thanked in a different part of this book). Sticking to the published scientific research is the backbone of the present approach. That backbone is formed from a rigorous evaluation process called peer review, which all publications in high-quality journals must go through. After completing a research project, a scientist writes and sends a manuscript to a journal's editor, who sends the manuscript out to two to four other scientists who evaluate the manuscript. Often, manuscripts are rejected based on the comments by the scientist reviewers. The manuscripts that are accepted for publication have passed this screening test for quality, relevancy, and currency. One downside of the scientific literature on a topic is that it tends to be numbers-oriented, quite dry, and impersonal. To add a sense of color to the chapters, the scientific literature is supplemented by information gleaned from news articles from leading news outlets.

ORGANIZATION OF THE BOOK

The table of contents presents the ten chapters of this book in a particular order, but it is not required that the chapters be read in that order. Each chapter stands alone to a large degree. Within each chapter, the reader will find the main narrative, along with an interview and a case study. The interviews were conducted with leading researchers in the field of the psychology of technology; each interviewee provides a personal perspective on a particular topic and provides a glimpse of current thinking on the topic. The case studies are designed to be interesting and to make a connection between real life and the topic of the chapter. The back matter of the book gives more information to the reader that enables a full understanding of each chapter. The glossary provides alternative definitions of a key set of terms and phrases that predominate the book. The list of resources provides references to additional information that allows the reader to learn more about the various sub-topics of the chapters.

The chapters roughly are grouped into sections. The section on social relationships includes Chapters 1 (Social Relationships) and 4 (Dating and Sexual Behavior). Clearly, romantic and sexual relationships qualify as social relationships, but the sheer amount of material that has been published on the former warrants a separate chapter. The section on aggression includes Chapters 2 (Physical Aggression) and 3 (Electronic Aggression). Both of these chapters involve aggression, but Chapter 2 only covers aggression related to violent media, while Chapter 3 covers mass and interpersonal forms of aggression that occur exclusively online. Several chapters discuss the workings of our mental and intellectual processes and how these are affected by personal technology use. Thus, the section on cognitive processes includes Chapter 5 (Information and Attention), Chapter 6 (Higher-Order Processes), Chapter 7 (Reading and Writing), and Chapter 8 (School Learning). Chapters 5 and 6 are oriented to understanding the fundamental cognitive processes, while Chapters 7 and 8 deal with narrowly defined intellectual tasks like reading comprehension and school learning. There are two more chapters that address the separate issues of how emotions are affected by the Internet (Chapter 9, Emotions) and effects on personal health (Chapter 10, Health).

Many interesting topics had to be left out of the book for space reasons. On most of these topics, there is not much published research compared to other topics. Some of these include electronic health records, links between Internet use and substance abuse, interventions to reduce Internet and digital media consumption, delivering mental health therapy through the Internet, and in-depth analysis of different "tech" generations (e.g., iGen). (If all goes well, then these could be included in future editions of the book!)

1

Social Relationships

Case Study: When the Internet First Visited Home

In 1995 and 1996, 93 families in Pittsburgh, Pennsylvania, were given computers, software, telephone lines, and free Internet access by researchers at Carnegie Mellon University. The study participants were Internet novices and they did not know many other people who were using the Internet. Known as the HomeNet study, the researchers aimed to evaluate what happened when regular families added the Internet to their lives. The researchers assessed family members across a range of variables between 52 and 104 weeks of having access to the Internet. The researchers learned that interpersonal communication was the main reason that people used the Internet, but for many of the assessment variables, the outcomes were negative. Not only did family members talk to each other less than they had before having Internet access, but there were also increases in loneliness, depression, and stress. People who were lonely at the start of the study did not use the Internet more than others, but people who used the Internet more ended up being lonelier over time. The study authors argued that this showed that using the Internet caused people to become lonely. They found that talking to others online could replace talking to people face-to-face, especially if online relationships are somehow weaker than offline relationships. This is referred to as the social displacement hypothesis. Another important finding was that spending more time communicating with somebody via email did not make a participant feel psychologically closer to that person. In contrast, time spent talking to a person face-to-face increased the psychological closeness that was experienced. In publishing their work, the research team described the phenomenon as an Internet paradox. On the one hand, the Internet is a social technology; on the other hand, the Internet reduces social involvement.

This first part of the HomeNet study received national attention. When reporting on the study results, the front page of the New York Times on August 30, 1998, read, "Sad, Lonely World Discovered in Cyberspace." However, most of the effects seen in the study were minimal. For example, the decline in the average size of a person's nearby social network was 1 person—decreasing from 24 to 23 people. Later results from the HomeNet study suggested that the negative effects on social outcomes were temporary; three years after receiving access to the Internet, the loneliness and depression in affected individuals dissipated. The researchers began to formulate a new hypothesis: Communicating with others online can expand a person's existing social network, thus increasing a person's set of social resources. This hypothesis is known as social augmentation. Possible factors for the new results were that users spent less time online as the novelty of the Internet wore off, people stopped spending time visiting uninteresting websites, and individuals stopped making superficial online relationships that did not provide real social support. The range of activities that people could engage in online from 1995 to 1998 pales in comparison with what Internet users can do now. During the early part of the HomeNet study, it's likely that participants were visiting websites and communicating with people that they did not know. Over the course of the study, new services such as Instant Messenger and ICQ (chat services) were unveiled that made it easier for Internet users to connect with people that they already knew (in other words, people with whom they had deep relationships). Plus, more and more of people's friends and family members were also getting online access. And of course, nowadays there is widespread Internet use, which includes rampant use of social networking sites (SNSs).

Nonetheless, the later HomeNet results revealed other interesting effects, namely with regard to personality. Extroverts—people who routinely seek out social interactions—showed different behaviors online than introverts—those who do not seek out social interactions. While extroverts using the Internet showed decreased loneliness, introverted Internet users showed increased loneliness. The HomeNet study results, and the flurry of scientific research done during the late 1990s, generated a wealth of valuable information to the study of the Internet. Also, a number of hypotheses were formulated about how social relationships change online—hypotheses that would later be tested and reformulated as the research on the Internet advanced. For instance, the "rich-get-richer" hypothesis argues that people who already have advanced skills in one way or another, such as extroverts, gain extra benefits by using the Internet. Conversely, the "poor-get-poorer" hypothesis argues that people who are less advanced in certain areas, such as introverts, experience decreased psychological well-being when going online. Further, the research following the HomeNet study began to show an important aspect of studying the psychology of the Internet: The crude measure of how much time people spend on the Internet is generally not as informative as carefully assessing what people are doing when they are online, and what type of person is doing it.

INTRODUCTION

Elizabeth Barrett Browning famously asked, "How do I love thee? Let me count the ways." With the rise of computer-mediated communication (CMC) over the last 30 years, we can similarly ask, "How do I *express* my love to thee?" And there are numerous ways. In addition to talking with someone face-to-face, they include electronic mail (email), chat, short messaging service (SMS)—more commonly known as text messaging—video chat (for example, Skype), cell phone calls, and posts on social networking websites. Email was available to many people in the 1980s, but further use of CMC skyrocketed during the 1990s and 2000s. The design and deployment of software that allows people to interact "behind a screen" has led to the widespread adoption of various kinds of programs and applications that let people strengthen existing relationships, build new friendships, and find like-minded individuals. However, there may also be costs associated with the great movement to socialize online.

Young people are caught in the currents made by the rapid changes in personal technologies. Adolescence and young adulthood are times of reaching out and making connections with people. From a psychological perspective, much of adolescent activity is driven by the need to establish an identity in the world, to figure out who one is, and how one wants to be portrayed to everyone else. Social needs are paramount. Texting is one of the most recent phenomena. Texting is king among adolescents right now; they prefer to use it, and do use it, as a primary communication channel. There may be several good reasons for doing so, which is supported by research. CMC has provided comfortable alternatives to talking face-to-face for fulfilling those social needs. Five factors have been proposed for why texting is so popular among teens. These are cost, privacy, ease, disinhibition, and language play. (Note that these factors make texting appealing to people of other ages, too.) Regarding cost, many cell phone plans in the United States and other Western countries include free, unlimited text messages. Regarding privacy, messages are usually sent to one individual and, since they are not spoken aloud as in face-to-face communication, it is possible to keep their contents private even when other people are around. When it comes to ease, text messages are fast to type; in fact, many teens have learned to type them without even looking at their phones. Disinhibition means that a person can feel comfortable expressing their true opinion through a text because he or she cannot see the potentially negative nonverbal reactions of the person receiving the message. Finally, language play involves the fun of creating new expressions and using text enhancements like emojis. As early as 2010, it was established through surveys that U.S. teenagers preferred and used text messaging over all other communication channels, including face-to-face communication. The five factors driving the popularity of texting have been found to influence teens' adoption of text messaging as a key form of communication around the world, although not every factor is equally important in all countries. In Kuwait, for instance, very few teenagers mention wordplay as an important reason to use text messaging. The differences between the use of texting in different countries may be due to differences in cultures, which may affect the manner in which people use text messaging.

TALKING FACE-TO-FACE AND FRIENDSHIPS

People choose communication channels to suit their purposes and motivations, and they actively switch between channels. It is preferable for some types of interactions to be done online. Within communication channels, people may use different tools for different communication purposes. Researchers in the field of Communications have refined an approach to understanding why people choose certain communication channels. The approach is called uses and gratifications; it aims to connect people's self-reported motives for using technology to their actual technology choices. Research has uncovered multiple different motivations that shape how people connect to others. These include social coordination (planning to get together), impression management (wanting to look good in the eyes of others), regulating closeness and distance (how deep of a relationship you want), and managing arousal and anxiety (for example, avoiding others to reduce negative thoughts). When people want to have communications that involve a more personal focus, provide immediate feedback, have complete information about emotions being experienced, and allow for full emotional expression, they will prefer "rich" communication channels, such as talking face-to-face. In contrast, there may be times when these features are not preferred; in those cases, people will want to use "lean" communication channels, such as texting or chatting. Also, there are often two ways to do things in the contemporary world, the offline way and the online way. Take, for example, looking for casual work. Finding work usually requires an interview, but interviews can be conducted face-to-face or via CMC (such as a Skype interview). When asked, most young people say that they prefer to do things offline, face-to-face—the old-fashioned way; but, introverts may prefer to conduct their social relations online. In Singapore, for instance, it was found that young adults who were introverts had a greater preference for online interactions than young adults who were extroverts. Further, for some people the Internet is used as a substitute for face-to-face interactions, whereas for other people it is used to extend social circles. Examples of the former situation would be having Internet-only friends and establishing new relationships with friends online. Examples of the latter would be maintaining long-distance relationships and supporting daily social interactions. Again, the uses appear to correlate with personality type: people who identify as extroverts tend toward social extension, while people who identify as introverts tend toward social substitution. Introverts seem to want to be able to express their "real me"—defined as a sense of presenting oneself in an authentic way—online because they have difficulty doing so offline.

People have wondered whether using personal technologies is taking away from face-to-face interactions, and the data show that the answer is both yes and no. There is no doubt that using personal technologies can displace face-to-face interaction in the moment. Consider when you are seated next to a stranger on a train. If you spend time scrolling through your Facebook page instead of talking to the stranger, then you are losing out on face-to-face interaction that could build your social skills, lead to new social connections, and bring on a positive mood. Or consider dinner time at home. If you check Instagram on your phone instead of talking to your spouse, then you may be losing out on strengthening your relationship with your loved one, learning about the goings-on of a family member, and getting feedback on issues of concern to you. But data from studies on people doing everyday tasks at home show that people are often not just doing one thing at a time; they are not just, for example, sending text messages on their phone and doing nothing else. In fact, people are often multitasking; that is, when they use personal technology, they also talk face-to-face at the same time. Young adults in the United States have been found to surf the World Wide Web (the web), send and receive emails, use instant messaging or chat, send and receive text messages, and even watch television and talk on the phone while they are talking with another person in the room. In the long run, rather than displacing face-to-face interactions, online communication may be enhancing face-to-face relationships. Young adults in the United States who spend more time engaging in use of their devices to communicate with other people also spend more time engaging in face-to-face interactions than other young adults. Rather than displacing face-to-face interactions, going online enhances them.

The interaction and merging of face-to-face interactions with CMC has led to perhaps the ultimate evolution of social relationships: the mixed-media relationship

(MMR). An MMR is a relationship that takes place across a combination of communication channels. For example, it is now completely normal that conversations with friends unfold during a typical day across a mix of voicemail, text messages, and face-to-face meetings. Another example occurs after friends have gathered for a party and then go off in their own directions but share and discuss pictures of the gathering through social media.

The choices made by the companies and computer programmers who create information and communication technologies (ICT) influence the social activities that users engage in while socializing online. Online discussion forums, virtual locations where users can interact with each other about particular topics or concerns, are said to be independent of time and place. With respect to time, these forums are known to be asynchronous; that is, the built-in tools for having a discussion with someone do not require that both parties having the discussion are online at the same time. With respect to place, the parties having the discussion can be anywhere in the world where they can gain Internet access. Both of these forms of independence are radically different from face-to-face interactions, which require two people to be in the same physical location at the same time. Yet rather than diminishing the relationship, discussion forums are known to foster relationships that would not otherwise be possible in the real world. Since many discussion forums center around topics of needs and concerns (for example, breast cancer discussions), it is possible for the forums to help people find peer support and empathy.

SNSs, such as Facebook, are usually coded by programmers in a way that requires users to create a profile of themselves that is at least partially open to the public. These public profiles serve two purposes when it comes to interacting with others: on the one hand, they serve as support for private correspondence with friends and family members; on the other hand, they serve as broadcasts of a person's life to a mass audience. This situation affects how socializing unfolds on social media platforms. In addition to the creation of a public profile, the design of social media sites allows for many socially relevant actions on the part of users, such as starting new relationships, maintaining existing relationships, and altering the nature of some relationships. Forming relationships requires only that a user send a friendship invitation to another user; when the other user accepts the invitation, the two users are linked together in a social network. Communicating with other users is easy and usually involves sending a message to another person with a profile. These tools help users keep in touch with real-life friends and family, as well as new people they meet online. Crafting messages that are posted on the site allows for self-expression, an important activity to young people who are in the process of forming their identities and gauging how other people react to those identities. Other activities, while not directly involving communication, contribute to the building of social relationships and networks. For instance, SNSs usually allow a way to access the profiles of other users, even when they are out of one's friendship network; this provides the opportunity for social research that can help users find other people with shared interests.

While not the first, Facebook is the most famous of the social networking sites. Facebook was founded in 2004 as a social networking site for students at Harvard University. It was originally designed to help students living in residence halls identify students living in other residence halls. Facebook is no longer only for college students, but it is limited to users who are at least 13 years old. Like all social networking sites, Facebook has grown rapidly in the last 15 years. By 2011, researchers were reporting that over 90% of U.S. college students used Facebook. At the time of writing this book, it seemed like virtually every adolescent and young adult in the United States was using Facebook. In fact, a national survey in 2015 found that more than 71% of 13- to 17-year-olds use Facebook. In 2005, only 8% of American adults used social networking sites at all; in 2013, the percentage of American adults using SNSs had grown to 72%. It's not just younger people who are attracted to social networking. In 2013, it was reported that about 60% of Americans aged 50 to 64 used social networks; among older adults aged 65 years or older, the percentage was 43%.

Facebook has dominated worldwide social networking usage. By 2008, it had reached the milestone of 100 million users. It reached another milestone—500 million users—in 2011. A year later, in 2012, it had reached 1 billion users. While the company that owns Facebook knows best what people are up to when they use the site, scientific researchers have learned through interviews and surveys that the average user spends about 30 minutes per day on the site. Using the site inspired a new word—Facebooking—that covers such activities as updating one's status (inspired by the perpetual phrase that appears when a user logs into the site: "What's on your mind?") and "friending" other users. On Facebook, communicating with other profile owners happens in multiple ways. For one, users can send private messages to other users, whether or not they are personally linked in the network. Second, users can post messages on the public "walls" of other users. Third, a user can post a message on his or her own wall that is immediately shared with a set audience within the network. All of the design factors going into games and social media platforms, as well as other types of software that allow socializing, feed into basic human needs for social interaction. When it comes to social media sites, passively viewing material from a site—such as scrolling through other users' profiles—might not provide any social interaction, but active viewing—involving posting comments, replying, and adding new content—contributes to a person's sense of social connectedness.

Similar design factors and software occur in games. In the olden days of video arcades, whether only one or more than one person could play a game depended upon whether the game designers and builders had constructed ways for multiple people to play at the same time. Some games allowed the users to specify how many players would participate, then the machine would allow the players to take turns playing. Other games had physical controls for multiple players so that groups could play the game simultaneously. Fast forward to today's games, played mostly at home, and not only can people play with friends who are present in the room (for example, on a gaming console), but also that one can play online with many people at the same time. Often, these other players are strangers from around the world. Subtle design and coding decisions have a big impact on socializing in games. If a person is playing a game that takes place in an online virtual world, but other people in the virtual world are not represented on the game screen, then there is no possibility of social encounters. More directly, some game designers choose not to add tools that allow for interactions with other people playing the game at the same time. *Pokémon Go*, a worldwide phenomenon in 2016, did not provide social tools such as chat. Neither was there an indirect route to in-game interactions between players. For instance, there was no way for players to alter the content of the game—as is possible in many other popular games, such as Minecraft—which would increase interactivity between users. At the same time, the design of *Pokémon Go* and other hybrid reality games—games that blend virtual life with real life—forces people to get outside into the physical world. This action creates opportunities for face-to-face social connections, which *Pokémon Go* became famous for.

Examples of places online where people can socialize include websites; message boards; online gaming; social networking sites such as Facebook, Twitter, and Instagram; and information sharing sites like You Tube. This variety of venues available for socializing using ICT came about rather rapidly over the last several decades. The rise of mixed-media relationships has occurred within a growing tide of software applications for socializing. The innovations around online socializing of the late 1990s and early 2000s were built upon earlier revolutions in computing. One of those revolutions was in desktop computing during the 1980s. Individuals were able to purchase home computers that allowed them not only to employ a computer in the conduction of their personal business, work, and schoolwork, but also to use a modem and a telephone line to access remote computer systems where they could interact with other people. The original virtual social communities in the late 1980s and 1990s were based on shared interests of their members. By some accounts, the very first social networking site was SixDegrees in 1997. It was based on the concept of each person being socially connected to every other person by no more than six personal connections; hence, six degrees of separation. The establishment of the Internet, widespread access to the World Wide Web, and the increased portability of computer-based devices, such as cell phones and hand-held computers, increased the amount of personal communication via screens. From 2005 to 2015, everyday people flooded onto social networking sites, dating sites, and other types of social sites. One of the main differences between virtual meeting sites from the past and social networking sites of the present is that SNSs are egocentric; that is, they revolve around individuals creating profiles of themselves and their own characteristics. In the earlier type of site, individuals rallied around a central theme or shared interest.

Many of the statistics that are gathered refer to teens and their behaviors with technology. A national survey of teens and young adults in the United States in 2008 showed that, already, 89% of teens and 90% of young adults had profiles on a social networking site. Reading and writing blogs were gaining popularity, with 25% of teenagers and 34% of young adults writing or updating their own blogs. And texting was already rampant in these age groups, with 84% of teens and 88% of young adults sending and receiving texts. Teenagers were displaying high levels of texting behaviors by 2010; more than half of the teens with cell phones were texting with friends daily and about one-third of them were sending more than 100 texts per day. By 2011, in the United States alone, more than 2 trillion text messages were being sent each year. Among U.S. college students, 88% of women and 84% of men were texting daily, while 30% of women and 37% of men were also contacting people through instant messaging. In 2012, it was learned that U.S. adolescents were sending an average of 60 text messages per day. The numbers of older Americans using social networking sites has gone up too, with 34% of Americans 65 years old or older using them, a slight rise from the 27% using them in 2013. In the last few years, Instagram—a platform allowing for the quick distribution of personal messages—gained a large following; in 2014, it was reported that Instagram was the preferred social media platform for most American adolescents.

With its displacement of traditional social ties, early researchers argued that the Internet was leading to a weakening of our social fabric. Electronic communications might not be as effective as face-to-face interactions; not only can spending time behind a screen take time away from speaking with another person in the flesh, but it also might alter socializing so that it is electronic and not physical. In the mid-1990s, there was concern among researchers that relationships conducted online would either replace real-world relationships or would supplement them. Either way, this would alter how people interact with each other and how people manage their identities. Especially damaging to socializing would be the use of technology that does not involve socializing, such as television viewing. A key question is, how important is physical proximity in having a social relationship? Since electronic communications do not require physical proximity, can they provide the same benefits to a person as a face-to-face social relationship? If electronic communications lead to a decline in a feeling of being socially connected with others, then they also might lead to an increase in loneliness and a decrease in social support—the ability to rely on others for assistance with emotional and other needs. Further, withdrawing from events in the real world, say, by visiting an online tour of a museum instead of the physical museum, might decrease the number of physical interactions between people within a community. These interactions play a crucial role in building social ties in a community, a concept known as social capital. At the same time, other negative outcomes for individuals using the Internet have been identified. Frequently connecting to other people in one's life has been made easier by electronic devices. For some, the extreme salience of one's entire social network being accessible through a device may have bad side effects. Among university students, anxiety over social ties predicts increased cell phone use. Additionally, a few researchers have attributed phantom phone vibrations—those annoying feelings that one's phone is buzzing when it is not—to people becoming more socially anxious than in the past.

Nevertheless, especially for teenagers, the time spent online in relationships with other people, known or not known in real life, is intertwined with real life. For adolescents, relationship issues are paramount. Online social interactions serve an important function in the minds of adolescents, as do face-to-face social interactions. The same holds true for people as they enter young adulthood. Scholars have recognized that face-to-face social worlds bleed into online social worlds for these age groups. As one recent paper put it, "adolescents are living their social lives online" (Underwood & Ehrenrich, 2017). There is no doubt that people can use electronic communications to build strong relationships; the software tools exist for doing so. And the crossover into the real world exists as well, with, for example, people using software tools to arrange face-to-face meetings. There may be a trend toward Internet users focusing on people they already know in real life when they spend time socializing online. One survey found that 40% of Facebook users friend all of their offline friends. For anyone, the information contained in other people's profiles may enhance face-to-face interactions. One study done in a research laboratory showed that having access to the Facebook profile of a person made talking to that person more enjoyable. Also, through the many mechanisms already discussed, online relationships can build social support and social capital, not just detract from them. The Internet and cell phones, specifically, give people increased access to their loved ones, from whom they derive emotional benefits.

TRENDS IN EMPATHY

Empathy is a basic human activity that is critical for effective social experiences. Empathy is a set of mental experiences and social skills that allow us to feel and respond to the emotions of others. Without empathy, people passively react to the negative emotions in others, as when witnesses to online bullying do nothing to support the victim. This is a real phenomenon. A study in Belgium with preteens and teenagers aged 9 to 16 years old showed that youths who had relatively low levels of empathy were more likely than other youths to remain passive when viewing cyberbullying.[1] According to some scientific descriptions of empathy, it takes two emotional skills to be considered an empathetic person: an ability to recognize the feelings of others and an ability to feel the same feelings as others are feeling. It is well documented that females experience higher levels of empathy than males; recent data from young adults in the United States confirm the long-standing pattern that females have higher levels than males in both aspects of empathy. But both sexes experience empathy via a set of brain pathways that are wired to react to aspects of face-to-face interactions with other people. Upon seeing or witnessing the negative or positive emotional experiences of other people, most people have immediate internal reactions involving thoughts, feelings, and judgments of the other person's state. However, for people with high empathetic skills, those thoughts, feelings, and judgments remain private—they are not expressed outwardly. Only through carefully controlled and crafted reactions does an empathetic person react to other people's experiences. Critically, a particular area of the brain—the frontal lobe—is responsible for inhibiting these initial reactions to avoid upsetting other people. And, within the frontal lobe, various regions are involved in coordinating outward behaviors so that they match an individual's goals and intentions. The orbitofrontal cortex is one of the regions involved in this executive control process, and it helps people shape empathetic responses to others. Additionally, when we interact with others in face-to-face situations, our social interactions involve directly looking into other people's eyes. Gazing into other people's eyes activates parts of the brain that enhance our processing of socially

---

1. Low empathy was not the only factor that was linked to passively responding to cyberbullying.

relevant information and thus our abilities to recognize and share other people's feelings. Thus, direct eye gazing is key for human empathy.

Empathy does occur in online settings, however. Virtual empathy is empathy expressed or experienced in an online setting or when behind a screen, such as in a text message. Certain online settings naturally evoke empathy from others. More generally, empathy has been described and documented in a range of settings behind a screen, and it is facilitated by the features of the Internet and by the actions that people take while online. One advantageous feature of the Internet is the ease of making online friends. Having friends available in the online world should raise the chances of finding an empathetic listener when a person needs some empathy. In fact, research shows that people with more friends in online social networks have fewer signs of serious depression than those with fewer friends. This suggests that empathetic ability is actualized in virtual environments (hence, virtual empathy) and exists among networks of friends. Interest-based places in the virtual world can foster and facilitate virtual empathy. It is easy—and popular—for Internet users to visit sites or participate in social media groups that are centered around a par-ticular topic. By seeking out people interested in a similar topic, Internet users are more likely to find other people going through the same experiences that they are going through. Sixth through 12th graders in the United States were tracked for a year as they engaged in online interactions. The students, all African-American adolescents, were monitored for the types of interactions they engaged in, includ-ing interactions with other African Americans and gathering information about being African American. The results showed that empathy improved in those stu-dents who had race-related interactions, as long as they also did not experience online racial discrimination. Additionally, even general Internet use benefitted empathy in girls (but not boys). Computer-mediated communication allows for expressions of empathy in mostly written ways. Here is an example of an empa-thetic post made in an online forum for people going through the heartache of a romantic breakup: "Losing a best friend and a partner in one fell swoop is . . . well . . . f*** miserable!" (McKiernan, Ryan, McMahon, & Butler, 2017). And another: "I can totally understand where you're coming from on this. It[']s frustrating when you feel like the person you're with doesn't really know you" (McKiernan et al., 2017). An additional setting where it is well documented that virtual empathy exists is online health support groups. For example, scientists have documented the cultural aspects of breast cancer support groups, analyzing how women read and write about the disease. A theme of the interactions in these groups is the fostering of a sense of connectedness among the participants; this is partially achieved through empathetic interactions online. People with particular health issues, such as chronic illnesses or disabilities, are known to find each other online in virtual discussion sites, where they can find empathy, support, friendship, and so on.

However, outside of special settings where people seek out empathetic experi-ences, contemporary personal technologies may be degrading empathy. There is an apparent trend in which empathy is declining in the world. Studies of college students over several decades show that empathy levels are on the decline. Specu-lation over the causes of the decline have drifted toward CMC as the culprit. There are good logical reasons to anticipate that being online and using personal technology are linked to this decline. Although rich in features that make it easy to connect and communicate with people anywhere in the world, CMC has a long history of being criticized for lacking many features associated with face-to-face conversations. When people interact with others via their devices, some features that are present in face-to-face interactions are no longer present. Direct eye contact is one of those features. It was learned from studying the effects of television that the social interactions that play out on a screen rarely involve the user looking directly into the eyes of someone with whom the user is conversing. Because children's brains are developing through childhood, it is important for children to receive stimulation related to social skills and, perhaps especially for empathy, social stimulation that involves eye gaze and the parts of the brain that direct eye gaze activates. There are other lost characteristics in CMC, such as non-verbal cues and voice inflections. When mobile phones started to catch on with the general public, it was a common feeling to experience some negative emotions when a person who was with you would take a call or respond to a text message in the middle of a conversation. Not only does this type of discomfort persist as mobile phone penetration is nearing 100% in many countries, but it may also signal a detrimental impact on important social skills such as empathy. Some observers have noted that high school and college students—who tend to be the groups with the highest usage of mobile phones—seem to be experiencing a lack of empathy that has been called empathy deficit disorder. To the degree that the lack of rich detail in CMC impacts emotional aspects of interactions, the ability to experience and express empathy could be impaired. A reduction in empathy has also been connected to taking "selfies." When people take selfies—either in the moment or over a long period of time—they must focus time and energy on themselves and away from other people. This could temporarily decrease empathy for others, or perhaps even represent a long-term reduction in empathy.

Another possible reason for a reduction in empathy due to technology is problems that people might have extracting important information from an online conversation. Irrespective of age, it might be harder for people to recognize the emotions of others online or behind a screen because the complete context of the emotion is not easily determined. If a person posts "I'm sad:-(," it is impossible to know why the person is sad. When face-to-face, however, other information is conveyed through the whole setting, and this would include information about the person's full facial expression, body language, tone of voice, place or location, and other aspects. Further, as you look at your cell phone screen and read a Tweet—a message on Twitter—from a famous celebrity that you follow, your mind thinks of the message as coming from a real person. But there is not a physical person present with you—only a few words on a screen. In this context, the "people" that you interact with through CMC are not real, in the sense that they would be in a face-to-face situation. If these people are not real, then how could you feel empathy for them? This explanation has been put forward for how viewing online pornography leads to subhuman treatment of women. In a study of this topic, one woman, a former entertainer in an online sex show membership club, put it this way: "One member wrote a letter, he said he couldn't accept that we were real people. We were just little people who lived in the computer. Sometimes, I look at them that way. I have a hard time thinking of them as real people" (Hughes, 2004). And there may be deeper issues related to the fact that online social partners are not, technically, real people. Online disinhibition is a phenomenon where people are more likely to express (mostly negative) emotions and information online compared to being offline. It is one of the well-accepted truths of the psychology of the Internet that people experience online disinhibition. What keeps people from being disinhibited in real-life settings is the executive control that is provided by the frontal lobe, as discussed earlier. Without effective executive control, people may engage in impulsive reactions online, displaying a lack of empathy.

Displacement is another possible mechanism for reductions in empathy. The more time a person spends online in superficial social interactions or any other online activity, the reasoning goes, the less time a person spends interacting face-to-face with others. The displacement of face-to-face time gives people, especially children and youths, less practice at being empathic, along with less practice at other social skills. However, the idea that going online displaces face-to-face time was not supported in a U.S. study of more than 1,000 young adults. In fact, the opposite was shown: going online is linked to an increase in the amount of face-to-face interactions with other people when the online activities involve communication with others. Nonetheless, some studies provide data that support a link between technology use and lowered empathy. Despite the clear existence of virtual empathy and the tools available to express it, it may exist at only low levels online. When university students in Germany were asked to describe the emotions and experiences that they have when they use social media sites, they were able to describe how they felt compassion, pity, sympathy, and empathy when they viewed posts by other users. But only about 8% of the students reported these types of experiences. In a study of virtual empathy among young adults in the United States, it was found that online empathy is weaker than regular, offline empathy. This was discovered by giving people two versions of the same empathy measure: one measured empathy in the real world and the other measured empathy in online settings. Virtual empathy occurred at lower levels than real-world empathy, and when compared to real-life feelings of social support, virtual empathy gave one-fifth to one-sixth the feeling of social support that real-life empathy provides. As the authors of the study put it, "to gain the same feeling of social support that you get from, say, one hug or empathic conversation with someone in the real world you might need between five and six empathic comments online" (Carrier, Spradlin, Bunce, & Rosen, 2015). Also, research studies have found at least a temporary reduction of empathy when cell phones are present during face-to-face conversations. When two strangers have a conversation, the mere presence of a cell phone makes the two people less trusting of each other, lowers how emotionally close they feel to each other, and impacts the empathy they feel from the other person. The same effects did not occur when a notebook—the same size as a mobile phone—was present. If one of the strangers held his or her mobile phone during the conversation or had his or her phone on a table within view, the conversation was rated as less satisfying and involving less empathy. Whether this "iPhone effect" has a long-term impact on people is yet to be established.

Video gaming is one of the most studied technologies with regard to empathy. Because there have been longstanding concerns about the impact of violent video games on youth, much research has been conducted over the last couple of decades on the topic. While measuring and documenting the impact of video game violence, scientists have formulated credible explanations of how video gaming could affect empathy. Part of a normal, healthy reaction to witnessing violent events is to feel negative emotions, and to experience physiological arousal that is connected to fear or disgust. With repeated exposure to violent events—such as what might happen when a person plays violent video games—this normal reaction might become blunted, a phenomenon known as desensitization. The next step in this problematic process would be having diminished emotional responses to violence, which could also interfere with the ability to recognize and/or to sympathize with others, leading to reduced empathy. A significant body of work shows an association between extensive violent video gaming and reduced empathy in people—though not every individual study has found a link. For example, one study used functional magnetic resonance imaging (fMRI), a type of sophisticated brain imaging, to compare people who play violent video games excessively to people who were similar on all other dimensions but do not play violent video games. All participants abstained from gaming for at least 3 hours prior to the study in order to eliminate any short-term effects on empathy. In that case, no differences in how the brain was used to respond to empathetic situations were found between the groups, suggesting that there are no long-term effects of violent video gaming (VVG) on empathy.

However, across studies, there is a general pattern of short-term and long-term effects in this regard. A famous 2010 paper on the effects of violent video gaming used a technique called meta-analysis to synthesize the results of many individual studies done up to that point in time. Selecting only the highest-quality research that was available, the paper's authors performed analyses on studies that examined changes in empathy or desensitization due to violent video gaming. By combining the results of several studies, the statistical analyses were effectively performed on a sample of more than 8,500 subjects from different countries. In the end, violent video gaming was consistently linked with reduced empathy or increased desensitization. This occurred both in short-term game playing contexts and over long periods of time. Short-term reductions in empathy occur soon after people play violent video games. These reductions also are linked to increased aggressiveness (discussed in Chapter 3). When researchers representing the American Psychological Association (APA) did a follow-up meta-analysis in 2017, they also found a connection between VVG and reduced empathy or increased desensitization. Using only those studies that had been conducted after the 2010 meta-analysis, the APA group showed a similar impact of VVG upon empathy as was found in the earlier study. Further, they found that seven out of the nine studies that they focused on showed some sign of reduced empathy with VVG. Finally, it also has been shown among young adults in the United States that the amount of video gaming done on a typical day is related to levels of empathy. People who video game more frequently show lower levels of empathy than other people. Despite these data, there is an ongoing debate about the importance and meaningfulness of the relatively small sizes of these effects. The effects of VVG on outcomes are often discussed in terms of "effect sizes," such as estimates of how strongly VVG and negative outcomes are related. While meta-analyses have found that there is a consistent negative effect of VVG on empathy, the effect sizes are not large. This has prompted some critics to argue that the effects of VVG on negative outcomes may be small and negligible.

PROSOCIAL BEHAVIOR

Despite evidence that empathy is declining in the United States, civic involvement—a form of prosocial behavior—is rising in young people. For instance, the Girl Scout Research Institute in the United States has documented a growing number of young girls participating in community-based activities. According to the Institute, 10th and 12th grade girls were active in community affairs or volunteer work more in 2014 than in 2007. When it comes to young adults, typical prosocial behaviors include saying nice things to others, offering to help others, cheering others up, and letting others know that they care. A classic measure of prosocial behavior used by scientists is the pen-drop task. It's a real-life situation where the experimenter pretends to accidently drop a set of pens on the ground in front of a study participant; the gauge of performance is whether the participant volunteers to help pick up the pens. Prosocial behavior is an important offshoot of empathic responses. People with high levels of empathy also have relatively high levels of prosocial behavior, including civic engagement. Brain-based mechanisms underlie prosocial behaviors that are measured in laboratories as well as real-world activities such as civic involvement. For example, when people play prosocial videogames, brain activity—assessed using sensors of electrical activity on the scalp—is different than when people play games that are neither prosocial nor violent.

Young adults who are prosocial in face-to-face settings also tend to be prosocial online. With the high penetration of Internet use in the world, it is not surprising that people's offline and online worlds are interconnected, especially for youths, and this may explain why face-to-face prosocial behavior is correlated with online prosocial behaviors. As preteens become teenagers, and teenagers become young adults, they are inundated with issues related to growing and getting older. These developmental issues pervade their real lives and their online lives, partially because the Internet allows for people to not only consume information but also to create information that is used by themselves and others. The theoretical perspective that describes this entanglement between real and virtual worlds for young people is called co-construction theory. There are basically two types of activities that preteens and teens engage in: non-technological activities that include regular daily activities and technological activities like TV viewing and social networking. Non-technological activities, like helping others, playing outside, playing sports, and hanging out with others, are part and parcel with prosocial behavior. Since these two categories of activity are normally done at the same time, some researchers have suggested that technology-based activities can displace prosocial behaviors.

Prosocial behavior is affected both positively and negatively by what people do when they are online and when using specific media. What a person does online will affect how he or she behaves offline. This can benefit offline prosocial behavior through careful construction of avatars (online representations), online actions and activities, and online experiences, but it can also be to the detriment of offline prosocial behaviors through displacement. Researchers who study the links between the online world and face-to-face prosocial behaviors have demonstrated that there is a psychological pathway between playing an online game and prosocial behaviors that follows along the virtual representation of a person online. In one example of this, game players who were allowed to customize their own avatars engaged in more prosocial behaviors after the game than players who either used a generic avatar or used an avatar based on a photo of the player. Virtual reality environments—experiences created by immersing users in an online world through the use of three-dimensional presentation, enhanced audio and video, and realistic input devices (e.g., with sensors attached to hands and feet)—have been shown to be places where certain experiences can facilitate later prosocial behaviors. For example, using a virtual-reality-game-like environment, players who were represented as superheroes flying through a city to find a missing child later engaged in more prosocial behaviors than players represented riding in a helicopter through the city. Another example of a short-term effect on prosocial behaviors is a virtual-reality–based study that showed that chopping down a tree in a virtual world caused people to reduce their paper usage in the real world. Long-term effects also occurred, as in the case of switching media content for boys away from violent media toward educational and prosocial media; this improved the behaviors of the boys.

Due to their particular features, television, gaming—especially violent video gaming—and smartphones all have been examined for their connection to reduced prosocial behaviors. Smartphones are known to affect how a person interacts with others, including their empathy, as discussed earlier. In a study in Canada, college students were asked to find an unfamiliar building on their college campus, either with or without the use of a smartphone. Not surprisingly, using the smartphone made the task easier to complete. But, in parallel, the smartphone made a person more socially disconnected: smartphone users talked to fewer people while traversing campus and felt less socially connected than those who did not use a phone. However, this lack of social connection did not translate into decreased prosocial behaviors as measured by the pen-drop task.

For gaming, individual studies on gaming and prosocial behaviors have mixed results, but meta-analyses have shown that there is a broad pattern of decline in prosocial behaviors with violent video gaming. Science progresses by an accumulation of findings across a variety of studies, not by one research study alone. The reason for this is that not every study will agree on the answer to a research question. Each study is set in a particular time period, under particular circumstances, with a particular set of participants from a particular culture. These and other variables influence the outcome of a study. Therefore, scientists look for patterns across a range of studies; they look for commonalities and assess the differences in the outcomes. Scientists also seek tools to help them synthesize the results of many studies simultaneously. One such tool is the meta-analysis. The effects of video gaming on prosocial behavior is one of those research areas where there are many studies showing a mixed set of results. For example; on the one hand, it has been found that adolescents with high levels of electronic gaming engage in less prosocial behavior than adolescents with moderate amounts of gaming. On the other hand, it also has been found that there is no connection between screen time (gaming and television) and prosocial behavior in seven-year-olds in the United Kingdom, and that playing a violent video game did not affect people's reactions in the pen-drop task, a charity donation task, and a task in which people choose the level of difficulty of a problem that another person will receive.

One of the earliest attempts to apply meta-analysis to the video gaming research was in a now-famous publication from 2001. Prosocial behavior, along with aggressive behavior, aggressive thoughts, aggressive emotions, and bodily arousal were all studied as potential outcomes of violent video gaming. Meta-analysis produces a measure of the strength of the relationship between violent video gaming and the outcome variable. This measure, r, is considered small when it is around .10, medium-sized when it is around .30, and large when it is around .50. The meta-analysis of the eight known studies looking at prosocial behavior (involving a total of 676 participants) produced an r of -.16, indicating that prosocial behaviors become less frequent when exposure to violent video gaming goes up. Since that time, other meta-analyses—incorporating new studies as they were published or performed—have found varied results, with one meta-analysis finding very small effect sizes when looking at children and adolescents, especially when only studies that are considered methodologically sound are included. One of the most recent meta-analyses done on the topic, which looked at scientific papers published between 2009 and 2013, found that seven of the nine studies found decreased prosocial behaviors with violent video gaming. However, most of these studies were done with young adults. Logically, those researchers who believe in the negative effects of violent video gaming say that the negative effects would be expected from social cognitive theory. Social cognitive theory is a theory of how environment and experiences affect behaviors. Social cognitive theory says that our experiences shape elements of our psyche, which in turn influence the behaviors that we perform. In the case of violent videogaming, it is suggested that the exposure to violence decreases a player's sensitivity to violence; this makes the person less likely to engage in prosocial behavior.

Further, in children and youths, parenting behaviors play a role in how technology affects prosocial behavior. There are two behaviors that parents can use to affect prosocial behavior in their children: active media monitoring and co-viewing. Parental monitoring of their children's media use can involve assessing the amount of time spent online or in video games, setting limits on how much and what types of media can be consumed, and enacting penalties for poor behavior or rewards for good behavior. These parenting behaviors appear to be effective in affecting prosocial behaviors. Prosocial behaviors in young children can be measured by asking teachers to evaluate how helpful a child is to his or her peers. Restricting the amount of time spent with media, especially with elementary-school-aged children, reduces how much time youths spend behind a screen, which in turn improves sleep, improves school performance, reduces aggressive behaviors, and increases prosocial behaviors—in this case, helpfulness. Co-viewing is when a parent watches or views a message on a medium (for example, a television show) with a child. Co-using is when the parent uses an interactive medium with the child (for example, playing a video game together). Research shows that parental co-viewing of television can increase a child's prosocial behaviors. Parent-youth co-use of technologies also improves youth's prosocial behaviors.

EFFECTS WITH SPECIAL POPULATIONS

Effective socializing through ICT requires well-developed social skills; however, people with weak social skills—those who are socially anxious, lonely, depressed, shy, or introverted—may be attracted to ICT socializing for various reasons. Although there may be short-term gains for those individuals, there is evidence that these people may suffer negative, long-term consequences unless they improve their social skills. Any technology that allows for sending and receiving messages to others and reveals information about both the sender and the receiver could qualify as a Socially Interactive Technology (SIT). SITs include social networking, texting, and instant messaging. There is a conflict between how SITs want people to manage social relationships and how deep, meaningful relationships are formed and maintained. Take text messaging, for instance. Sending a text message may require less "brain power" in the sense that the sender has to worry only about crafting a small number of characters into a message, and the sender does not have to worry about their facial expressions and tone of voice. Emotionally, the reactions of the receiver of the message do not have to be dealt with right away as there usually is at least a small pause before getting a response. The emotional reaction of the receiver may also be blunted because it is transmitted via CMC, so there is less emotional information for the sender to process upon receiving a reply. More broadly, with SITs it is often not necessary to respond immediately to messages posted online (as in, say, a Facebook post on your wall), but it would be expected for a person to react immediately if the same message were given in a live setting. General aspects of the software that shape relationship management include the fact that there is greater control of self-presentation online than offline, that relationship communications often are spread out over time (i.e., not immediate, as in face-to-face communication), and that messages are often shorter and less rich than when carrying out face-to-face conversations. Because of their implied anonymity, SITs may encourage self-disclosure, an invaluable social skill. Defined as, "any message about the self that a person communicates to another" (Wheeless & Grotz, 1976), self-disclosure builds trust, helps to reveal common interests, and increases the depth of relationships. Skilled socializers use self-disclosure to achieve these goals without disclosing irrelevant, excessive, or negative information that would damage a relationship. But blind or careless self-disclosure, as may happen online, can be damaging to one's relationship and to one's social network as a whole. For these reasons, people who come to the Internet already possessing effective social skills can thrive, and people who do not have these skills may be attracted to CMC but suffer. SITs lack features from real life that trigger shyness or social anxiety, for example, so shy or socially anxious people may see the Internet as a safe place for communicating with others.

Social anxiety is debilitating worry over interacting with other people. People who are socially anxious may avoid real life social situations in order to reduce or avoid anxiety. If online contact with other people helps socially anxious individuals build effective relationships, then this would represent a benefit of going online compared to interacting face-to-face with others. This is called the social compensation hypothesis. There are indications that socially anxious people prefer and use ICT for socializing more than people who are not socially anxious. In research studies, people who were identified as socially anxious indicated a preference toward using online communication for building and maintaining social relationships. A well-cited research study from 2009, conducted with California teenagers, uncovered the motivations of socially anxious adolescents at a point in time when SITs were becoming common. The adolescents—280 high school students—were technology-savvy: 83% of them owned cellphones and 65% texted on a regular basis. Ninety-eight percent of them had an email account and 74% had a social networking profile. Social anxiety was assessed in a very simple way—students were asked how comfortable they felt when talking to a person face-to-face. The findings showed that social anxiety correlated with greater comfort in talking with others through SITs and in greater amounts of texting. Importantly, students who did not show social anxiety made more friends online. Not only do socially anxious people prefer to use the Internet for social relationships, but they are also more likely than non-socially-anxious people to actually form social relationships online, supporting the social compensation hypothesis. However, using SITs may have adverse consequences, like a risk of problematic Internet use (PIU), for these people. Scientific studies have found that online communication motivated by social anxiety is linked to negative outcomes, such as poor relationships. One of the main risks of spending a lot of time online is addiction to technology. Social anxiety has been associated with smartphone addiction, texting addiction, and general Internet overuse. Social anxiety might also be correlated with other negative outcomes in the online world. As noted earlier, some researchers link Internet use with loneliness and depression. One possible mechanism for that link is that it is socially anxious people who want to go online a lot.

Having relatively few social relationships can lead to a feeling of loneliness, which is often associated with depression. When a person is lonely, he or she will not be getting the positive feelings that other people get when they socialize. Using SITs, such as social networking sites, may give lonely people those positive feelings as they interact with others online. At least temporarily, socializing online eases loneliness in lonely people. And, sure enough, loneliness and depression, like social anxiety, are states that sometimes are linked with an increase in ICT use. But, as with the case of social anxiety, using the Internet for socializing comes with possible risks for lonely and depressed individuals. Online relationships may not have the richness of in-person relationships because of the way the online software tools work and because of the absence of effective social skills. So, instead of addressing the problems underlying their loneliness, going online to find relationships might actually make a lonely person's situation worse. A serious possible risk for lonely and depressed people, just as with socially anxious people, is the risk of developing a technology addiction. Research has shown that addictions to technology are linked to negative moods, depressive symptoms, and loneliness, along with stress and lower satisfaction in life and in relationships. It is quite possible that for depressed individuals—who have significant negative moods—going online produces temporary lifts in mood, which contributes to further Internet usage—a pattern that, when repeated, can develop into problematic Internet use (also known as Internet addiction).

Satisfying social interactions involve being able to achieve one's "real me," that sense of opening up to another person that leads to positive feelings. There is also a feeling of comfort involved. Introverted people tend not to socialize with others. Being introverted is a long-lasting trait; it's part of one's personality and is considered the opposite end of a personality dimension from extraversion. Introverts like to keep their information—including their opinions, feelings, and beliefs—private. They do this by withholding information from others. Introversion and shyness are used interchangeably to describe people with the same characteristics. In contrast to socially anxious, lonely, and depressed people, introverts may be able to compensate for their personality by going online. There are benefits of going online that make up for being shy in real life. Online, introverts are able to develop relationships and, by doing so, to improve their own well-being. Self-disclosure is one of the social skills that is improved by going online. Since introverts and shy people will withhold information about themselves in social settings in real life, the way that being behind a screen encourages self-disclosure can help these types of people. Further, when shy people and introverts connect with other people through online communications like Facebook, they receive an increased sense of belonging to a greater social network. One scientific study revealed an important difference in how introverts and extroverts interact with other people online. After identifying who was an introvert and who was an extrovert, it was found that extroverts tended to find their "real me" through face-to-face communications, while introverts tended to find their "real me" through online interactions like chatting. Thus, shy and introverted people may be able to reach the level of a "real me" online, even when they find it difficult to do so offline. As a research subject in one of the relevant research studies stated, "I'm shy in social situations, but am more open on the net, in chat rooms" (Greenfield, 1999).

The relationship between the different personality types and other user characteristics is complicated, although there are clearly established connections between personality and cell phone use. For instance, when Canadian college students were asked to fill out measures of social anxiety, proneness to addiction, and cellphone use, the results showed that both social anxiety and addiction proneness predicted cellphone use. This was a correlational study, so while the results show that social anxiety and cell phone use are linked, the results cannot be interpreted to show in which direction the causal link goes. However, the researchers offered the possibility that social anxiety causes increased cell phone use. Of course, the obvious reason why this might be so could be that people with social anxiety seek out ways to communicate with their friends and acquaintances that don't involve talking face-to-face. Regarding personality and texting, researchers in the United Kingdom learned that socially anxious people prefer to text other people rather than call them on the phone. In contrast, lonely people prefer to call people over sending a text to them. Both types of communication have reduced richness compared to face-to-face communication, but text messaging has fewer of the features that might trigger social anxiety, like messages requiring immediate feedback and cues to one's emotional state (e.g., tone of voice). Therefore, socially anxious individuals—actively avoiding richer types of communication—would avoid telephone calls, and lonely individuals—actively seeking social contact—would embrace phone calls.

The connections between personality and social networking are more intriguing. The research looking at how personality is correlated with social networking has frequently focused on Facebook usage. There appears to be a somewhat complicated relationship between Facebook usage and personality dimensions like social anxiety, introversion, and shyness, among others. People with high social anxiety will be attracted to social networking sites because of the impression management functions built into the sites. Remember that people with social anxiety may want to control how they appear to others, a task that is much more difficult when speaking to a person face-to-face than when communicating online. Thus, it is not surprising to find that Facebook users who are motivated by the opportunities to manipulate one's image are less interested than other Facebook users in building up existing social relationships and in communicating with friends. Unfortunately for socially anxious users, this may also reduce the positive social outcomes of being online. Regarding other personality dimensions, an Australian study of many personality dimensions and Facebook usage asked young and middle-aged adults to fill out an online questionnaire of multiple personality dimensions that included extroversion, open-mindedness, conscientiousness (rule following), agreeableness, neuroticism (mood stability), narcissism (a focus one oneself to the exclusion of others), shyness, and loneliness. The study authors compared Facebook users to non-users to see what the typical characteristics of both groups were. Facebook users were more extroverted and more narcissistic than non-users. In other words, introverts did not use Facebook as much as extroverts, and people with a desire to promote and focus on themselves were more likely than other people to use the social network. Non-users were more likely than users to be conscientious and shy. Interestingly, loneliness showed a subtle pattern, where non-users were more socially lonely (i.e., lacking friends) than Facebook users, but Facebook users showed more family loneliness (feelings of loneliness with one's family despite physical closeness). Other studies have found that shyness is associated with more Facebook use, even though the friendship social circles for shy people are smaller than for others. The same pattern has been found for people with low self-esteem. As with most scientific research, it can be difficult to reconcile the results of multiple studies that seem to conflict with each other. In some cases, research is planned in a way that makes it methodologically superior to other research studies. For example, prospective research designs track a group of individuals from one time period to another. The investigators look to see how individuals with particular features at one time (say, high Internet use) are faring at a later time (with, say, problematic Internet use). This type of research is more powerful than many of the studies that are typically done in the field because it lends credibility to the idea that events at time one caused the events at time two, although it is not definitive in that regard. With that said, many of the studies on personality have been of the less-powerful, correlational variety. When researchers carried out a prospective study with American college students, looking at how depression, general anxiety, and social anxiety at one point in time predict changes in social networking 3 weeks later, they found that there was no connection between these variables. Thus, it appears that depressed and anxious individuals do not adjust how much time they spend on SNSs, however they may be changing what they do online. For instance, they may be having more difficulties carrying out deep and meaningful relationship building activities. Other differences exist between socially anxious individuals and lonely individuals. Socially anxious people are not as likely as lonely people to self-disclose information about their past, their current relationships, and intimate information.

Looking more deeply at how personality is associated with the negative outcomes of Internet use, one finds research that bears on the negative consequence of PIU and the direction of causality involving negative consequences. Researching the impact of depression, stress, and loneliness upon problematic Internet use, scientists in Holland tracked nearly 400 adults for 5 years in a prospective study. While the results showed that these negative indicators of well-being were correlated with PIU, the more sophisticated design revealed more detail about whether depression, stress, and loneliness can cause PIU. In fact, these three factors did not predict what happened to the Dutch individuals later, in terms of PIU; rather, levels of PIU predicted depression, stress, and loneliness, supporting the assertion that PIU causes a reduction in a person's well-being, not the other way around. Interestingly, the study found that people who experienced increased happiness at one point in time had less PIU at a later point in time. Similarly, it has been shown that loneliness can be the result of using social media too much. Further, the Internet might exacerbate existing differences between different personality types, rather than eliminate them. An alternative to the social compensation hypothesis is the rich-get-richer hypothesis. This hypothesis states that people with certain attributes, such as loneliness and social anxiety, go online and behave in the same way that they do in real life. In other words, lonely people communicate with others relatively less when they go online while non-lonely people communicate more (the rich getting richer). Indeed, some studies have found that this holds true for socially anxious and lonely adolescents.

CONCLUSION

Social relationships certainly have been affected by the widespread use of information and communication technologies. Scholars have raised several possible scenarios, starting with the social displacement hypothesis that Internet-based relationships replace stronger, face-to-face relationships. However, research over the last 20 years has shown that people can indeed create deep relationships in the virtual world, and that social relationships now are not restricted to any one communication medium, as with mixed-media relationships. At the same time, one's personality and other characteristics interact with using computer-mediated communication, especially for lonely, depressed, socially anxious, shy, and introverted individuals—albeit in sometimes complicated ways.

In reviewing how socializing has been affected by the explosion of the Internet, several important themes were uncovered. These themes cut across different aspects of the psychology of technology and permeate the other chapters of this book:

Compensation: The Internet and computer-mediated communication may provide a way for people who are at some disadvantage (e.g., weak social skills) to make up for that disadvantage.

Diminished cues: Computer-mediated communication leaves out important information about the person with whom you are interacting, like facial expressions and tone of voice.

Disinhibition: When people are behind a screen, there is a natural tendency to become more open to sharing information about themselves, including private thoughts and emotions.

Displacement: Using electronic devices, including computers and smartphones, can replace other activities that may be healthier for a person (for example, engaging in face-to-face conversations).

Identity development: Preteens and teenagers naturally work to establish and maintain a social identity (and sexual, work, and other identities) as part of normal psychological development. This can drive online behaviors.

Personality: Personality is the tendency to behave and think in the same way over time. One's personality interacts with how personal technology is used and affects the outcomes of using that tech.

Research design: In psychology and the larger set of social sciences, there is a progression of research designs from weaker designs to stronger ones (for instance, interviews compared to longitudinal studies). The stronger ones give greater confidence in the conclusions of the researchers.

There are a few other themes in the following chapters, which have yet to appear in this chapter. These are:

Gender differences: There are times when men and women behave differently and react differently to what happens online. Often, these differences are understood with respect to the theory of evolution.

Neural correlates: Much of what people do online, and how going online affects them, can be understood with reference to what is going on in different systems in the brain.

Reinforcement: People will repeatedly engage in activities that provide a reward of some kind. Similarly, people will repeatedly engage in behaviors that put an end to distasteful or unpleasant experiences.

Interview with an Expert: Dr. Kaveri Subrahmanyam

There's no better group to study scientifically than children and youth if one wants to understand the effect of technology on society; after all, they are avid users of personal technology and several important psychological forces are at play when they go online. As a researcher and educator, Dr. Kaveri Subrahmanyam, a professor of psychology, investigates key questions about the effect of ICT upon the public and shares her knowledge through scientific publications, presentations, and media coverage. She is the associate director of the Children's Digital Media Center at LA, a research organization whose mission is to "study children, teens, and emerging adults' interaction with the newer forms of interactive digital media and to see how these interactions both affect and reflect their offline lives and long-term development." Dr. Subrahmanyam regularly contributes to media coverage of events related to technology and has been interviewed by the New York Times, USA Today, and many other news organizations. As a developmental psychologist, Dr. Subrahmanyam has scientifically studied a range of topics related to children and technology, including digital gaming, social networking, and interactive media. Her work has culminated in articles in scientific journals, special issues of journals, book chapters, and a book on media effects on youth.

Q: Over the past few decades we have gone from one-to-one, face-to-face communication to email, texting, and social media. How do you see these communication modalities differentially impacting social relationships?

A: First and foremost, it seems to be transforming how we are interacting with others. Digital communication platforms seem to promote exaggerated public interactions that are multimodal involving audio, text, video, and icons. They also seem to be leading to much wider networks. So daily diary work suggests that the positive feelings from high quality face-to-face interactions last longer than digital interactions. I suspect that we may be moving towards having more social relationships that could be less intimate compared to a time when we only interacted via face-to-face communication. I am not saying that we are not interacting face-to-face anymore, but I do think digital means are dominating for informal peer interactions. I haven't really studied empathy, but I think emoticons and images can certainly add tone and emotion. I think they can also definitely lead to misunderstandings. There is some evidence that screens may [get] in the way of detecting emotions, but we need a lot more research!

My own observation and some recent research does seem to suggest that practice with short messaging systems may spill over into formal and informal writing. I wonder what is *true communication* anymore. I certainly think that even sips of connections can be helpful...whether they are enough to sustain an individual through his or her life course is what I am not sure. I see social media as a quick and dirty way of keeping up with a large and wide network of friends and acquaintances. So, in that sense, they can be helpful, given how busy and harried everyone is. The drawbacks, of course, [are] that it could lead to over sharing, compromise privacy, and lead to bullying, harassment, [and] digital footprints that never go away. I think it is too early to say for sure, but anecdotal evidence suggests that youth definitely prefer digital means of communicating, especially with adults outside their immediate social circle. I think these days youth interact online with offline peers. So [it's] hard to say that they have online friends separate from offline ones. Of course, some do, and these are likely individuals in special populations.

Q: Are there any special populations that might actually benefit from online communication more than face-to-face communication? How are they helped in developing and maintaining social relationships and building their social identity?

A: I think on this point, it has helped individuals who may have been marginalized or who did not have resources in their offline lives. But, of course, when online lives are completely disconnected from offline ones, it may lead to individuals creating fake identities and living in alternate realities. For most people though, online self-presentation seems to be related to identity development, although we cannot say for sure that it is all good or bad. I think disabled individuals, shy young people, introverts, and minorities within minority (e.g., gay youth in a community of color) may also benefit from digital communication. There is evidence that gay youth are coming out at earlier ages, likely because of the opportunities to meet others like them via digital venues. Youth with cancer and other illness similarly have found social support online. But online context can also make problematic behavior (e.g., cutting) seem normative.

Q: What are some of the unanswered questions in your field of research?

A: Oh wow, where to begin!!! When can text messaging be beneficial and when is face-to-face better? How do personality variables moderate the effects of multi-tasking? What are the positive and negative effects of visual-content social media on problematic behavior such as drinking? How does parents' digital media use relate to children's language and cognitive development?

I was very positive about these technologies until a few years ago. I worry now that smartphones are very disruptive—they are so efficient that they have come to permeate all aspects of our lives. The information overload, the easy access of information—how is all that impacting our learning, memory, critical/deep thinking, and creativity? So, I am a bit concerned, but I am an eternal optimist. The technology is still young, and I think we will figure out when and how to best use [it]!

2

Physical Aggression

Case Study: The Debate over Violent Video Gaming and Mass Shootings

Mass shootings were rare before the 1960s. Defined as four or more people shot at once in a short time period, they became a topic of national concern after one particular event in the 1960s. In 1966, Charles Whitman climbed to the top of the tower at the University of Texas at Austin campus and shot 16 people with a rifle. While television and movie violence existed at that time, violent video games (VVGs) were yet to be invented. The 2013 Washington Navy Yard shooting is one of the much more recent cases of mass murder where video gaming has been interwoven into the story. Taking place in September of that year, it was not the first mass shooting to generate speculation about video games, but the case—involving a young man obsessed with guns—is illustrative of the issues surrounding research on VVGs. Aaron Alexis, the shooter, was a Buddhist who habitually attended a local temple in the Texas town where he was living. At temple, he meditated regularly, perhaps upon some of the most basic aspects of contemporary Buddhism, including the way to find a spiritual path between the opposing forces of positivity and negativity that tear at the souls of all people. Yet Alexis, a 34-year-old man, was known always to carry a gun with him. On September 16, Alexis traveled to the Washington Navy Yard in southeast Washington, D.C., and climbed above an atrium, giving himself a good view of people below. He shot at everyone who was within sight, killing 12 people, and was eventually killed in a shoot-out with emergency officials.

The link between video gaming, especially violent video gaming, and mass shootings had already been in the public's mind for a while, and Alexis's rampage seemed to fit the pattern. Just the year before, two wildly shocking mass shootings had taken place, and in both cases, there was discussion in the media about video game playing in the shooters' histories. In Newtown, Connecticut, Adam Lanza was a fan of mass murders, keeping detailed notes on 100 years of incidents. He was trained to shoot guns; he practiced regularly with his mother, whom he eventually murdered. Lanza, after killing his mother, went to Sandy Hook Elementary School, fatally shooting 20 children and 6 adults. Lanza was 20 years old. During the investigation of the shooting, agents found VVGs in his game room, including a game called *School Shooting*, in which the player shoots students in a school. Lanza's game collection included first-person shooters, games in which the player sees the world from the perspective of the shooter/main character, as did the game collection of the shooter in the Aurora, Colorado, shooting in the same year. On July 20, James Eagan Holmes, the Aurora shooter, murdered 12 people in a movie theater showing *The Dark Knight Rises*, a movie based on the Batman literature. Twenty-seven years old at the time of the shooting, he had routinely played video games with a group of fellow students in high school.

Alexis's connection to video gaming was a strong one. He immersed himself in VVGs, reportedly spending up to 16 hours at a time in a gaming session. He played *Call of Duty*, a first-person shooter set in military contexts and described by the Entertainment Software Ratings Board (ESRB) as involving blood and gore, intense violence, and strong language. One VVG researcher suggests that playing this game can train a person to become a better shot in real life. Obviously though, factors other than video gaming must play a role in individuals becoming mass shooters. Even though recent shootings appear to have video gaming as a connection, many prior shootings had occurred before VVGs existed. Also, tens of millions of people play VVGs, and these people do not commit violent crimes, so playing VVGs is not sufficient by itself to lead to a mass shooting. Virtually all mass murderers have been males; the majority come from the dominant white culture in the United States and are in their 30s or 40s. In some cases, mass murderers are enamored with former killers and think of those earlier murderers as heroes. Alexis showed signs of another characteristic associated with some mass shooters: problems with mental health. In the month prior to the shootings, he exhibited signs of paranoid thinking, a symptom that can be part of schizophrenia. He believed people were trying to steal his belongings; hence, he carried his .45-caliber handgun with him at all times.

The mass media seem to put their own spin on these cases. Many members of the media explicitly drew attention to the violent video gaming backgrounds of the shooters in the Aurora theater shootings, the Sandy Hook massacre, and the Washington Navy Yard shootings. Often in media reports, the association between VVGs and committing crimes is a direct, causal connection (i.e., that playing VVGs creates mass murderers) or an indirect relationship where the games provide a training platform for becoming a skilled killer. The media coverage most likely echoes the same concerns that regular citizens share after they hear of another mass shooting involving a young man. In a few instances, the media may be influenced by other, more political forces in society. The National Rifle Association, a long-standing U.S. organization that promotes gun rights, has been accused of trying to refocus the public's attention away from the guns used in shootings and toward alternative explanations, like VVGs. While the media plays up the connection between VVGs and mass shooters, scientists continue to uncover evidence of only a weak connection. Sometimes, the facts themselves do not support a clear link. For example, Lanza's preferred type of video game was nonviolent: he frequently played *Dance Dance Revolution*—a landmark game involving whole-body motion—and *Super Mario Brothers*. The investigators of the Sandy Hook shooting concluded that Lanza had not viewed the attack as a video game-like experience. Specific causal mechanisms have been proposed by scientists; one way to link VVGs to mass killings is through scripts, learned memories of how to kill people, which might be created when people play the games. But there is agreement that the VVG/mass-murderer connection is only a small part of the phenomenon of contemporary mass shootings. Other factors—among the potentially hundreds—that might contribute to a young person committing a mass shooting include social isolation and a history of being bullied. In the long run, it might not be scientifically possible to ever prove that a connection exists. For one, mass shootings are so rare—despite society's feeling that they are happening all the time—that it is nearly impossible to study them systematically, the way that other events might be studied. The relationship between VVGs and mass shootings is unclear enough that some scientists even have referred to it as a myth.

INTRODUCTION

While scientific research into TV violence is decades old, much of the current work in media violence centers on VVGs. The most interesting and dramatic question about these types of games is whether playing them causes the player to become more physically aggressive. Is he more likely to commit an aggressive act right after playing the game? ("He" is appropriate here, since most VVG players are men or boys.) Is he more likely to commit an aggressive act in the future due to his experiences playing video games now? Over the past 20 to 25 years, there has been extensive research conducted to help answer these questions. This research has used a wide variety of games, including online games and first-person shooters, and a wide variety of methods and measures. The field has been dominated by one continuously developing theoretical model—the General Aggression Model (GAM)—but not without controversy among the researchers themselves.

The GAM explains how playing a VVG or witnessing violent media affects a person's thoughts and emotions that, in turn, might lead to aggressive behavior. According to the GAM, being exposed to violent media can lead to a series of effects inside of our psyches. The GAM incorporates psychological processes known to affect behavior in a wide variety of contexts. In the model, these processes have been identified as contributing specifically to aggressive behavior that is the result of being exposed to violent media. These effects include changes in our thoughts, changes in our feelings, and changes in our arousal levels, and they each are part of different potential pathways for instigating aggressive behavior. The processes—cognitions, emotions, and arousal—constitute a person's internal state at any given moment in time. These three processes are linked to each other. For instance, when a person is having aggressive thoughts, then it is likely that they also are experiencing elevated arousal like an increased heart rate.

EFFECTS OF VIOLENT MEDIA ON OUR PHYSIOLOGY

It seems that almost everywhere you look, there is an outlet for media violence in contemporary life. In addition to TV shows and movies, it could appear in video games and online videos. And these types of media can appear on many different types of screens, which includes television screens, but also smartphone screens, handheld gaming device screens (e.g., Nintendo DS), laptop computer screens, desktop computer screens, tiny movie screens mounted in the back seats of automobiles, etc. While much research was done in the past looking at the effects of movie and TV violence on audience reactions, the way media content is presented nowadays is different than in the past; it has become highly interactive. With the advent of electronic games, video games, and computer games, people can participate in media-based violence, rather than passively view it. These activities not only contain violent content, but they are often competitive and occur at a fast pace—additional elements that could cause a player's arousal levels to increase.

In portrayals of the Old West on television and in films, it is not uncommon for a mean-spirited gunslinger to challenge a town newcomer to a gunfight, while the public spectacle of two fighters about to engage in a gun battle prompts the townsfolk to quickly hide and shutter themselves. In the TV and film-viewing audience, this scene can cause tension, fear, and suspense based on what is about to happen. Inside the body and mind of the viewer, the emotional reaction can be divided into two parts, based on what is known as the two-factor model of emotion. The first part is the level of arousal produced by the event; the second part is the brain's decision as to what is causing this arousal, also known as the attribution. The gunfight in the street might lead to a high level of arousal that is experienced as a jump in one's heart rate, heightened blood pressure, and sweaty hands. In a laboratory, researchers have tools that can measure these reactions in a person. Heart rate can be measured by devices attached to the chest or to the ear (using beams of light through the skin to determine the heart rate); blood pressure can be determined using a blood pressure cuff; the sweat generated on your skin, or rather the electric changes in your skin associated with sweating, can be detected using techniques such as the galvanic skin response. Arousal can even be indicated in our brain waves. The P300 is an event-related potential (ERP), an electrical pattern detected on the scalp, which is considered to reflect the processing done by the brain when viewing or reacting to the situation or stimulus. Assessing ERPs is said to be non-invasive, meaning there is no harm done to the subject's body during the experiment or study. Rather, the electrode sits firmly on the outside of the skull, usually held in place by a contraption called a skull-cap. The P300 is usually correlated with surprise, making it a marker of the brain's involvement in arousal.

The brain, knowing that you are sitting in front of a screen showing a film or show, would correctly attribute this arousal to the excitement of the gunfight. The involvement of the body, in this case the cardiovascular and nervous systems, in the reaction to the scene is referred to as the physiological effect of the event. Since this attribution is correct, your brain tells you that you do not have to run and hide, like the townsfolk are doing on the screen. However, what could happen if you leave the room or theatre, continue on with your life for a few minutes, but your arousal level stays high? And, what if you temporarily forget why your arousal level is so high? According to the process of excitation transfer, the high level of arousal that you are experiencing could be misinterpreted, or misattributed, to another cause. If you were provoked, even accidentally, by another person, you could misattribute the elevated arousal to this provocation, leading to aggressive behavior as a result of seeing the gunfight minutes earlier on the screen. This might happen even though you are not aware of it.

As adults, most people have mastered the abilities to become aware of, reflect upon, and control arousal levels. A typical adult, having just viewed the riveting gunfight scene in the TV show described above, would recognize her elevated arousal levels, correctly attribute them to the fictional scene, and take measures to calm down (e.g., breathing slowly). Yet children may be less likely to control themselves and might be more susceptible to the perils of excitation transfer. The processes involved in self-control, collectively called self-regulation, are slow to develop in humans and require repeated experiences, both successes and failures, in order to be refined. Because of this, they are not well developed in children. In fact, many of the psychological processes of self-regulation depend upon the brain's frontal lobe, especially the prefrontal cortex, an area that takes as long as 30 years to mature in healthy adults.

Having high arousal levels in response to viewing violence is not necessarily bad. It might reflect a normal sensitivity to scenes involving blood and gore and, appropriately attributed, it might help us to avoid, minimize, or resolve violent situations or scenes in our lives. Therefore, it is of concern to researchers that repeatedly watching violence is associated with decreased arousal over time. The initial increased arousal from watching violence lasts four to nine minutes after the violence is viewed, while the lowering of arousal over time may last much longer, perhaps months. Researchers call the long-term form of changes in arousal habituation or desensitization. Further, another form of arousal, sometimes referred to as anger arousal, has an emotional component and leads to relatively long states of anger that may fueled by rumination, persistent thinking on an issue that drives the anger.

Typically, arousal studies are done in research laboratories, usually on college campuses. Studies bring people, known as participants, into the laboratory to be under the watchful eyes of the experimenters, and usually scientific devices are attached to participants. Luckily for the participants who enjoy playing video games, there often are one or more sessions of playing games that vary in the level of violence. In some cases, the games are played on commercial video game platforms such as PlayStation 3 (PS3); in other cases, the experimenters might create and code their own games in order to exert greater experimental control over the game elements. Other studies focus on media violence more generally—they don't use video games but perhaps movie clips or immersive environments like 3D films. Physiological arousal can be measured with a heart rate device or a blood pressure monitor. Changes in emotional arousal (anger, hostility, aggression) can be measured with questionnaires given to the participants before, during, or after game play. The experimenters do not want to tip off the participants to the true purposes of the experiments, as any advance information about the studies might cause the participants to change the way that they behave or the way that they react to the games. Cover stories are concocted that provide a reasonable explanation of why the participants are viewing media without giving away the true meaning of the study. For example, one study used the cover story that participants were helping to choose video games for a future study, rather than revealing the true purpose of assessing reactions to violence in the games.

When commercial video games are used to present media violence in the laboratory, the experimenters often choose one violent game and one or more comparison games that are either nonviolent or are less violent. The game *Myst* has been used as a nonviolent game. *Myst*, first released in 1993, is a first-person video game, meaning that the graphics depict the world in a way that authentically reflects how a person would see an imaginary world as she moves through it. In the game, the player solves puzzles in order to advance through the game levels. *Myst* was purposely designed to be nonviolent and does not contain much of a competitive aspect. Other off-the-shelf games that might be used include sports games and games that might have brief episodes of violence. In contrast, *Wolfenstein 3D* has been used as the violent game in some studies. In *Wolfenstein 3D*, blatant violent content is depicted in a realistic way. The goal of the player is to use weapons to kill others and advance through the levels. There are bloody scenes, and screams and groans from victims. Other violent games that might be used—sometimes called killing games by researchers—include *Mortal Kombat, Street Fighter, Doom, Medal of Honor, Halo,* and *Call of Duty.* Games are generally rated by non-profit boards of reviewers based on their content and game features, such as the ESRB, an industry-funded, self-regulatory agency in the United States and Canada. Using the ESRB system, *Myst* is rated E (everyone) on the PS3 video game console, while *Wolfenstein 3D* and *Mortal Kombat* are rated M (mature 17+; intended for players 17 years old and older).

Sony PlayStation is a popular platform for video game playing. The platform has been updated and improved several times by the manufacturer, with the latest version being PlayStation 4 (PS4). Like other game consoles, a variety of games are available with differing types of content. Users can play violent, fast-paced games; action/adventure games; sports games; and other types of games, as well. Playing games on this and other consoles can elevate a player's heart rate and blood pressure, signs that the body is experiencing physiological arousal. Interestingly, some physiological reactions become lessened over time. For instance, a study of PS3 players found that physiological reactions to playing games *decreased* over three game-playing sessions during a three-week period. Researchers labeled this phenomenon cardiovascular desensitization, and found that the effect did not depend upon what type of game was played.

New devices are available to home game players that increase the realism of game playing. Headsets or goggles that contain dynamic, sometimes 3D graphics can be purchased by anyone and used in conjunction with commercial video games. Using these devices appears to contribute to physiological arousal. This was shown in a study where American college students played violent or nonviolent versions of the same video game. In this case, the video game was created and programmed by the researchers. In some cases, the players used a head-mounted display that allowed the graphical view to be synchronized with the player's head movements. This immersive virtual environment technology (IVET), coupled with the violent version of the video game, caused the players' heart rates to be elevated in a way that signaled physiological arousal.

The number of studies that have been done on how violence in the media affects arousal are useful in being able to put all of the study results together and estimate the overall impact of media violence on arousal. Scientists have developed a statistical technique that allows for combining the results of many studies, as long as they are done similarly and are of high quality. The technique, meta-analysis, gives a measure called effect size, that can be anywhere between −1 and +1, with −1 representing reductions in arousal and +1 representing increases in arousal. In 2001, American researchers used meta-analysis to put together the results of many studies that had been published in the scientific literature up to the year 2000. The researchers included only those studies in which children or adults actually played video games, rather than watching someone else play. With these requirements, they found seven studies that tested a link between video game violence and physiological arousal; these seven studies involved 395 participants in total. The statistics gave an average effect size of .22, meaning that playing video games raised arousal levels; in addition, the effect size was statistically significant, in that it was not due to randomness or chance. According to experts in scientific research, this effect size is in the small to medium range. As more studies have been done over the years, these researchers and their colleagues have continually updated the meta-analysis, adding new studies, refining the statistical techniques, and addressing criticisms from scientific peers. In 2002, the average effect size of violent video gaming upon arousal was estimated to be about .15. The general outcome that there is a small to medium effect on arousal was confirmed again in 2004.

There are many kinds of computer and video games that cause people to become aroused. They do not necessarily have to be violent games. For example, an exciting treasure hunting game with lots of action might trigger high levels of physiological and emotional arousal. However, scientists know that it is the violent content, and not just the arousing properties of violent media, that affects later aggressive behavior. When they have compared games with similar arousing effects on laboratory participants, only violent games triggered aggressive reactions. Exposure to the violence in violent media may trigger several different kinds of thoughts and emotions. The emotional and cognitive reactions that people have to the violent content in violent media are important for how those people respond to events afterward.

EFFECTS ON AGGRESSIVE THOUGHTS AND EMOTIONS

With respect to our thoughts, or cognitive processes, our knowledge of the world is presumed to be contained in a network of information located in the brain, such that related information (e.g., the image of a gun and the image of a gunshot wound) is connected to each other. Because the neurons of the brain—the cells that work to send and receive electrical messages—share information with the other neurons they are connected to, activating the information and neurons related to one piece of information will also activate the information and neurons associated with related information. In other words, the image of a gun will also activate the memory of the image of a gunshot wound. This process, which does not last very long—seconds or minutes at most—is called priming, and it is one of the cognitive pathways from violent media to aggressive behavior. When knowledge is primed, it becomes more accessible, and thus more likely to lead to a related behavior. An example would be the case of playing a game in which a stranger suddenly appears in your view and surprises you. If the knowledge of a gun had been primed earlier in the game, then the player would be a bit more likely to use the in-game gun to respond to the appearance of the stranger. A long-term version of priming might occur when a person plays violent games many times over an extended time period; in this case, there may be chronic activation of the violence-related knowledge in memory.

Priming can lead to the hostile expectation bias. A bias is a systematic tendency to interpret events in a particular way. In this case, you might encounter an ambiguous situation but interpret the situation as violent, even though it is not necessarily so. What if you are walking in a hallway, for example, and a stranger going the opposite ways bumps into you forcefully? You might wonder, why did the stranger do it? People experiencing the hostile expectation bias will perceive the bump as an aggressive act. Emotions and thoughts operate through an appraisal process. If you are slapped in the face—literally—then you will immediately have an emotional reaction via an automatic appraisal process, an emotion that is generated according to how we interpret the slap in the face. Most likely, you will feel angry or scared; these are emotions triggered by our body's fight-or-flight system to keep us safe. But if you wait a few seconds, then your brain will generate another interpretation of the slap in the face, one that is based on a cognitive analysis called the controlled appraisal process. You might think, "Oh, I provoked this person and I deserve the slap in the face."

Another impact of violent gaming upon knowledge relates to our beliefs about violence. While it is natural to believe (and to hope) that serious conflicts can ultimately be resolved through peaceful means, habitual players of VVGs may have developed an alternative belief system in which violence is a more successful path to resolution than peace. After all, VVGs seem to reward violent behavior more than peaceful behavior. These belief systems—developed through interactions with video games—might become indistinguishable from belief systems from real life, possibly allowing the violent beliefs to affect real-life behavior. Repeated exposure to violent media may lead to people taking the aggressive strategies portrayed in the media and internalizing them as memorized actions to take when certain situations are encountered in life. Scripts are sets of actions learned through repeated experiences that a person takes in order to achieve an outcome. A situation where a script might be helpful would be getting into a parking lot fight over a parking space. This is an upsetting experience for most people, and there are many different options for resolving the fight. Our natural reactions to avoid anxiety- or fear-inducing situations would cause us to try out scripts for a peaceful resolution, such as letting the other driver take the space and consoling ourselves with the thought that being nice to people will pay off for us in the long run. However, a person with chronically active violence-related scripts might feel that the situation calls for an aggressive reaction such as honking their horn or yelling at the other driver. Not only might violence-related scripts be stored in memory as a result of playing VVGs, but also the scripts might become part of the associative network of memories, allowing them to become primed though exposure to violent media. A final form of aggressive thought is a perceptual schema—a memory of a frequently occurring visual element of violent media, such as a particular type of gun or knife. After perceptual schemas have been formed during repeated violent media exposure, the schemas may become activated and influence a person's internal state—the collection of thoughts, emotions, and arousal levels that are currently active in one's psyche. Stored scripts and interpretations of events become triggered during violent media exposure through priming.

The hallmark emotion that might be triggered by violent media is anger. Feeling angry after playing VVGs could affect later behavior and make it more aggressive than it would have been naturally. Further, empathy is a psychological process through which normal people react to other people's emotions. In violent media, victims of violent acts may show pain, suffering, and negative emotions. A healthy reaction to other people's suffering is to have empathy, such as to experience the suffering as if you yourself were suffering. This empathic response lessens the likelihood that you will commit an aggressive act. However, repeated exposure to violence in media may lead to a blunted empathic response. The normal reaction to other aspects of violence, such as emotional reactions to the sight of blood and gore, may become diminished over time through desensitization as well. Emotions that would normally occur in response to violence, things like fear and disgust, may wane with repeated exposure to violence in VVGs because the violence is rewarded in a game (e.g., with a high score), there is no negative repercussion of witnessing violence (i.e., players are not literally hurt when attacked or attacking), or other emotions such as excitement and glory are reinforced through gameplay. The waning of the normal emotional reaction to violence is referred to as emotional desensitization. The problem is that normal emotional reactions to violence are useful in preventing people from committing violent acts. Emotions can be primed, as well, and can prime other parts of the memory network. Therefore, exposure to violent media can prime thoughts and emotions and behavioral tendencies (scripts) so that later situations are interpreted and acted upon in certain ways. Spreading activation is the process by which one unit in the brain's neural network activates other nearby or connected units, resulting in priming.

Scientists have clever ways of measuring aggressive emotions and aggressive thoughts in laboratory settings. The questionnaire method is often used to study aggressive feelings. After encountering violent media (e.g., video games), psychologists ask participants questions and the responses are used to quantify the level of aggressive feelings. In most cases, the questionnaires measure state aggression, meaning that the questions are designed to assess the person's current levels of anger (or hostility, frustration, etc.), rather than their usual levels of the emotion, known as trait aggression. In one study of violent video gaming, for instance, participants played a video game, then were asked simple questions about the emotions that they experienced. The participant responded on a scale from 1 to 5. One question was, "How enjoyable did you find playing the video game today?" Another question was, "How frustrating did you find playing the video game today?" Two ways that aggressive thoughts are measured in the laboratory are through the lexical decision task and through interpretation of ambiguous stories. In the lexical decision task, participants are asked to respond as quickly as they can to sets of letters that appear on a computer screen. Some sets of letters form words; some do not. The task is simple: press one key if the letters form a word, press a different key if the letters do not form a word. While people rarely make an incorrect response, the task reveals priming through how long it takes people to make each decision, also known as the reaction time. Words that already are active in a person's memory (primed), take less time to respond to. If a person's aggressive thoughts include primed concepts of weapons, for example, then they will take a relatively short time to respond to words like "cannon," "weapon," and "knives." With the approach that uses ambiguous stories, the experimenters give participants a fictional narrative in which a character takes an action that could be interpreted as either aggressive or not aggressive. For participants who have just played a VVG, and who might be experiencing the hostile attribution bias, the ambiguous actions will appear to be violent acts. In another version of the ambiguous story approach, participants are asked to immerse themselves in a fictional situation and to say what they would do next in the situation if they themselves were part of the story. One such story describes how a woman, Jane, orders food in a restaurant and waits a long time for her food. After an hour of waiting, Jane is just about to leave the restaurant when the waiter arrives with the food. The measure asks, if you were Jane, what would you do? Various forms of aggression can be detected in this experimental paradigm. Subtle aggression would be indicated if, for example, you said that you would "leave without tipping the waiter"; serious aggression would be indicated, if for example, you said that "I just want to punch him." Other stories include getting hit by another driver when you are driving your car, and a friend who decides at the last minute not to go on a trip that you have been planning with her for a long time.

Across many studies, there is a small but consistent effect of violent video gaming upon thoughts and feelings. In several scientific papers, the meta-analysis technique of combining the results of several research studies into one super-study was used to look at the typical effect of violent media upon aggressive thoughts and aggressive emotions. In one of the first applications of meta-analysis to violent video gaming studies, published in 2001 by researchers at Iowa State University, the pattern of results that would be found in later analyses was first established. There was a small effect across several studies of violent video gaming upon aggressive emotions ($r = .18$) and a larger effect upon aggressive thoughts ($r = .27$). An updated meta-analysis from the early 2000s showed that exposure to VVGs increases aggressive thoughts and affect in adults and children. The relationship between VVGs and aggressive emotions was a little over .1, meaning that exposure to the games predicted less than 5% of the changes in aggressive mood. The relationship between VVGs and aggressive thoughts was larger, with an effect size of about .25. This showed that exposure to violent games was responsible for between 5% and 9% of the changes in aggressive thoughts. A few years later, in 2004, a revised meta-analysis verified the pattern from the earlier meta-analyses.

AGGRESSIVE BEHAVIOR

There are several proposed ways that arousal could lead specifically to aggression. The connections between arousal and aggressive behavior are modeled in the laboratory using different setups, one of which is the hot sauce paradigm. In the hot sauce paradigm, a person is told that they are part of a study on food and personality. As part of the study, the person must choose some hot sauces for another person—the taster—to try. (In reality, there is no taster.) The person gets to choose the level of heat and the amount of sauce. If the task is done shortly after playing violent or highly competitive video games, then the total intensity of the prepared taste tends to be higher than in other types of games. Another setup is the noise blast task, a simulation of real-world violence. Two people play a game; the winner gets to blast the loser with a noise and the winner sets the intensity and duration of the noise. More aggressive players choose more intense and longer blasts than less aggressive players. (Think of the noise blast as a weapon wielded by the experimental participant.) Unbeknownst to the winning participant, the other player is fictitious; therefore, no one is actually receiving loud and long noise blasts.

Even though having a high arousal level may lead to a violent act, being aroused is not the only important factor. In the case of a naturally violent person, arousal may cause a person's normal behavior tendencies to become more evident. This will mean that the person will be more likely to be violent when aroused. Also, there is a known psychological mechanism of excitation transfer, in which the arousal must be interpreted as being related to conflict or violence. Excitation transfer has been demonstrated in the laboratory as a way to bring about aggressive behavior, and it does not necessarily have to come from violent media. A classic psychology experiment, Milgram's electric shock paradigm, involved asking experimental participants to give electric shocks to other participants. The original research examined how much shock a person was willing to deliver when an authority figure asked him or her to do so. (As with any psychology experiment, the participants were deceived; they were tricked into believing that they were shocking another person.) In the excitation transfer version of this experiment, the electric shock paradigm is used as the laboratory measure of aggressive behavior after the experimental participants viewed violent or neutral media. Violent media led to more shock being given, as did highly arousing erotic media. But, as stated above, high levels of arousal do not directly cause aggressive behavior; as one researcher has pointed out, pornography users do not "riot in the streets" after viewing explicit materials (Giles, 2003).

People who play VVGs will recognize the experience of still feeling highly aroused even after the game is over. But to what does a player attribute this postgame arousal? If he attributes it to the game, then behavior will be normal. However, if he attributes it to another event—say, another individual making a rude comment—then this misattribution of arousal could lead to an aggressive act. So not only is arousal involved in the process of making an aggressive act, but also the arousal must activate internal thoughts and emotions related to violence; this is known as cross-modality priming. Cross-modality priming is a feature of the GAM. By influencing the contents and values in our internal state, exposure to violent media may increase the likelihood that a person will commit an aggressive act. Not all types of arousal are always equal when it comes to being aggressive. If two video gamers play two equally arousing games—as measured by heart rate and blood pressure—but only one game involves violence, then only the violent-video-game player has an elevated chance of carrying out an aggressive act in a laboratory measure of aggression like the noise blast task. This is probably because only the violent game primes the aggressive thoughts in a person's mind.

There is an additional path from arousal levels to aggressive behaviors. We may become desensitized to surprising events in some circumstances, which can lead to later aggressive acts. It is presumed that the surprise and arousal associated with a violent event is a very negative experience. This is natural, since humans appear to want to avoid or reduce violence when possible. When a person becomes desensitized to violence, the alerting and arousal responses become weaker, showing that the person is no longer as surprised as before. Researchers have shown that this reduction in alerting to violence occurs with interactive, technology-based games. Another name for this reduction in alerting is habituation, as when a person's heart rate becomes habituated to game-based violence. Seeing violent events over and over again might bring about a habituation of these negative responses, ultimately ending in callousness toward violence. Scientists can measure the desensitization to violence in the brain as well, by placing electrodes on a game player's skull. The scientists examine the brain's electrical response to violence, the P300, which decreases as the player becomes desensitized. When the P300 is diminished, it can be inferred that the experimental participant was not surprised. Violent-video-game players show a weaker P300 response to violent images than nonviolent-video-game players, which means that violent-game players may have experienced desensitization to violence. Interestingly, people who show the diminished P300 are later more likely to show aggressive behavior in the laboratory. The violent-video-game players—those with the diminished P300s—show relatively high aggression levels in the noise blast task. Both short-term and long-term desensitization have been found. Short-term desensitization is a reduction in arousal that occurs over a matter of minutes, for example in the hour after a video game is played. Long-term desensitization occurs over much longer time spans, say weeks or months. Even people without much experience at playing VVGs can suffer from short-term desensitization. In one study, people without much VVG experience played a VVG that resulted in a small P300 response compared to people who played nonviolent games. Later in the study, these same people showed more aggressive behavior in the laboratory than the nonviolent game players. Old studies of violence in television and films showed similar effects, with desensitized individuals becoming more aggressive in the laboratory after viewing violence, although the results somewhat depended on whether the violence was real or fictional.

There is considerable evidence from the research laboratory to support the model. Two of the pathways to aggression—changes in cognition and changes in emotions— can be demonstrated in laboratory settings. Consider a situation in which the interpretation of another person's behavior is unclear. For example, you are walking along a pathway when you hear a rush of footsteps approaching from behind. What is going on? If you get the immediate feeling that someone is about to accost you, then you are experiencing the hostile expectation bias, because it is also possible that a person is rushing toward you because they need help of some kind. These sorts of ambiguous situations may also lead to an expectation that another person is having aggressive thoughts, or that they are experiencing aggressive emotions; both cases represent variations of the hostile expectation bias. The hostile expectation bias has been observed in people of many different ages. Elementary, middle, and high school students all show a pattern such that those children who play more VVGs are more likely to interpret ambiguous situations as hostile. Further, the thoughts that other people are being hostile are made worse by playing a range of VVGs and by playing games in relatively short sessions spread out over time. The latter pattern of game playing matches a familiar pattern known among scientists who study academic learning. Called distributed practice, it is well known to lead to better learning than getting exposed to material in one, mass block of time, or massed practice. Distributed practice at violent video gaming enhances the hostile attribution bias. One set of scientists concluded that VVGs are "exemplary teachers of aggression" (Gentile and Gentile, 2008). The same effect occurs in college students. When college students perform the noise blast task after playing a VVG, their blasts become more aggressive (louder and longer) when they have relatively high levels of hostile expectation bias. Interestingly, the pattern is stronger for men than for women. Hostile expectation bias has been described as viewing the world through "blood-red tinted glasses" (Hasan, Bègue, and Bushman, 2012).

The GAM predicts that the amount of change in aggressive cognitions and aggressive emotions will affect how much aggressive behavior is likely to occur after being exposed to violent media; so other factors that make a person feel like they are "in the game" or mentally engaged in a medium should cause more violent media effects. In fact, laboratory studies have found that these other factors do increase the effect of violent media, although not every study has found the effect. The sense of being "in the game" is known among scientific researchers of virtual experiences as presence. Many different factors can affect presence, including how realistically a situation is portrayed in the virtual world. The realism of the virtual environment involves not only how the environment looks to the user (e.g., authentically looking blood and a first-person perspective) but also how the environment sounds (e.g., blood-curdling screams). When presence is intensified through these techniques in a VVG, players also experience higher levels of aggressive emotions. However, the level of presence is not always related to the effect of violent media upon aggressive thoughts and feelings. The quality of the graphics in a gaming platform, assumed to impact the realism of the events depicted in the video game, do not relate to how the violence in a game impacts thoughts and emotions. An even higher level of involvement in a virtual world is thought to take place when users achieve a state of flow. Being completely absorbed psychologically, game players in a state of flow are said to not be consciously attending to their own thoughts and emotions because they are totally engaged in the action in the virtual world. Players in a state of flow may be so caught up in what they are doing on the screen and in the game that they are not aware of what is going on around them in the real world. They might not answer when someone in the room talks to them. Some scientists worry that this higher level of presence may make the effects of violent video gaming worse.

However, there also is evidence that goes against the model. Data supporting the model are weaker for the emotional pathway than for the cognition pathway. In the case of the emotional pathway to aggressive behavior after violent video gaming, research results that this pathway may be weak or nonexistent, or at least not as important as the cognitive pathway. For instance, one study with U.S. college students found that playing a VVG for 15 minutes in a research laboratory did not cause more hostile feelings than playing a nonviolent game for 15 minutes. Further, increasing the time spent playing to 45 minutes did not change the results. More evidence that the emotional pathway might be weaker than the cognitive pathway comes from a three-year longitudinal study—one that tracked more than 2,000 elementary, middle school, and high school students in Singapore. Each year, students completed measures of aggressive behavior, aggressive thoughts, and aggressive emotions. The measures of aggressive thoughts included assessments of students' beliefs about the appropriateness of violence, their fantasies of committing violent acts, and their hostile attribution bias. The measure of aggressive emotions was an empathy scale, with lower levels of empathy presumed to be linked to higher aggressive emotions. The results showed that the effect of violent video gaming upon aggressive behavior was related to the amount of aggressive cognitions that a student experienced, but not to the amount of aggressive emotion. Plus, the GAM has been criticized for being too general, and other explanations for the effects of violent media have been put forward. The GAM, being an accumulation of many different psychological effects that might impact aggressive behavior, has been described as a "kitchen-sink" theory, making it difficult to test and difficult to disprove. Treating science as a linear process, where each new result is added to the old results and the theories are adjusted each time to encompass all of the prior results, is not the only available approach to learning and understanding in the world of science. In fact, many scientists believe that science is non-linear, where each theory will eventually be displaced by a new theory, and then another new theory, and so on. Sometimes, there will be setbacks and reversals, but this is all normal. One alternative to the GAM is a motivational model. A motivational model assumes that people engage with violent media in order to satisfy basic human needs, borrowed from a more general explanation of human behavior called self-determination theory. A person, for example, might play a VVG in order to satisfy the competence need—the need to feel that you are good at something. Other possible reasons to play a VVG might be to satisfy the relatedness need—the need to interact with other people—or an autonomy need—the need to be independent. Changes in emotions can occur when a game does not satisfy these needs for various reasons. Perhaps the gaming interface is too difficult to learn or there is no opportunity to practice within the game in order to get better. In this model, even nonviolent games might produce aggression-related emotions.

There may be particular effects for children and adolescents when playing VVGs. Children and adolescents might not have enough life experiences to know how to regulate their arousal in highly arousing situations. Certainly, the violent content of video games would make arousal levels higher in children and adolescents than in adults, but there is also the factor of the competitiveness of certain games. When adolescents play competitive violent games, an additional boost in arousal levels is observed. As mentioned earlier, the aggressive cognitions can include violent scripts and hostile thoughts. The aggressive affect can include anger and frustration. People's arousal may change through an elevated heart rate or increased blood pressure. There is laboratory evidence that there is a pathway from exposure to violent games to violent behavior through changes in cognition. College students were asked to play video games under the cover story that these would help the students develop their motor skills. Two games were played that were matched for their levels of arousal and emotions that happen when playing the games. The games were *Myst* and *Wolfenstein 3D*. Playing *Wolfenstein 3D* increased the players' aggressive thoughts and their aggressive behavior in a lab-based task, but playing *Myst* did not. Another way to conceptualize this process is to think of each exposure to violent content—especially violent video gaming—as a learning opportunity for becoming an aggressive person. One learning mechanism that has been proposed is imitational learning. This is when players have a desire to copy the behaviors that they witness in the gaming world or that they play out in digital form.

The impact of violent video gaming on lab-based aggression occurs in young adults and children, in different types of research designs, and in females and males. Not only are aggressive behaviors increased after playing VVGs, but helpful, prosocial behaviors are decreased. While meta-analyses of laboratory-based aggressive behaviors show a small but consistent impact of violent video gaming, not all studies of real-world aggression show an effect. In the real world, the effects of gaming are varied, and the studies are diverse in their participants and methodologies. On the one hand, some studies of young people and violent video gaming have found a connection between gaming and real violence. Aggressive behavior in elementary and middle schoolers might include hitting other kids. When studied over three years, this time in Singapore, children at these ages were more likely to exhibit aggressive behavior if they played violent games at the beginning of the study. Further, if they changed their amount of video game playing over that time period, then their aggressive behavior changed as well. In this particular case, the game playing and aggressive behaviors were connected to aggressive thoughts held by the children. Another study of children, this time 3rd, 4th, and 5th graders in the United States, showed that parents can influence aggressive behaviors at school by monitoring their children's media usage and exposure to media violence. On the other hand, there are studies that find no effect. In Germany, a study found that teenage gamers who played VVGs were not more likely to commit physically aggressive acts one year later. In fact, the reverse was found. Adolescents who committed violent acts were more likely to play VVGs a year later. This shows that there is a selection effect where violent teens choose to play VVGs. In young adults who were older than 17, neither effect was found. The selection effect, also called a selection bias, is commonly used to explain how violent video gaming might be linked to aggressive acts. Scientists have developed a statistical method of correcting for selection bias by exactly matching gamers and non-gamers on many other personal characteristics. Using this method, called propensity score matching, a study of eighth graders in Delaware showed that playing M-rated video games was not linked to several violent outcomes that included hitting someone, taking a weapon to school, or carrying a gun when not in school. And video gaming in general—not just VVGs—does not cause a person to commit more copycat crimes. Copycat crimes are crimes inspired by the events that occur in violent media (e.g., in movies). This was shown by studying U.S. inmates; inmates who played video games are not more likely to copy these crimes than non-gaming inmates. Finally, using national statistical data in the United States does not help to show an effect of violent video gaming. Swings in violent crimes over time do not show an overall link to video game sales. Instead, the crime statistics show hints that VVGs are related to *less* violent crime. Monthly sales of video games are linked to reduced numbers of aggravated assaults (especially violent attacks); Internet searches of gaming guides for violent games are linked to reductions in aggravated assaults and homicides, and homicides tend to become less common following the release of a popular M-rated video game.

CONTROVERSY OVER VIOLENT MEDIA EFFECTS

Whether there is a small effect of violent video gaming upon aggressive behavior in the laboratory is not in doubt; there is serious debate, however, about the quality of the research conducted and the implications of the laboratory research for real-life violence. On these latter points, the scientists are divided. Some scientists have complained that VVG research suffers from particular methodological flaws that can lead to an overestimate of the effect size. According to the critics, several actions could be taken to improve the VVG research. For one, the measures of aggression used in laboratory studies could be refined. As it stands now, different researchers use different measures and this makes it difficult to compare the effects of media violence across the many studies. Also, there is the third-variable problem. This is, when two values appear to be related, for example, hours spent playing a VVG and aggressive behaviors, but there is not a direct causal link. While it may appear that hours spent playing VVGs causes aggressive behaviors, there may be another variable—the third variable—that causes both. One example third variable is the home environment of the player. Kids who live in stressful home environments may retreat to video games for escape while at the same time showing aggression due to the disturbing home environment. The researchers' use of the technique of meta-analysis—normally thought of as a way to solve disagreements within psychological research—has also come under attack. Instead of estimating the size of the impact of VVGs from one study, meta-analysis combines many studies into one analysis to generate one overall effect size. The researcher doing the meta-analysis must decide which studies are included in the analysis, because the choice can influence how the results come out. Careful screening of potential studies to include is key, usually done with a precise description of what counts as a VVG research study. But what about research that was done but never published? Unpublished research, if included in meta-analyses, may alter the results. Critics of the major meta-analyses on VVGs have argued that those analyses suffered from this publication bias by not including all of the relevant studies, or in some cases that the analyses were damaged when these unpublished results were included.

Critics cite national-level statistics and data that are relevant to the general research program. The main counterevidence to there being a link between VVGs and violence comes from national crime statistics in the United States. As crime rates in the United States have declined, video game playing has taken off, with multiple different measures showing that video game playing is very common. One possible reason for the relationship is that VVG playing provides a neutral way for people to express their negative emotions from real life. Also, youth violence rates have been declining in the United States over time, coinciding with the rise in sales of VVGs. In fact, one research team calculated the correlation between video game sales and youth violence as $r = -.95$, meaning that every increase in video game sales is associated with a decline in youth violence. Based on this fact, and others, the critics have asked, "Is psychology inventing a phantom youth violence crisis?" (Ferguson & Kilburn, 2010).

As noted earlier, the effect sizes for VVG effects are not large; they are in the .1 to .3 range. These are considered small- to medium-sized effects by many researchers in psychological science. One camp argues that small effects are irrelevant, while another camp argues that small effects can have big and important effects in society. Complex behaviors like aggression are probably caused by a multitude of psychological factors. Quantitatively, the small effect sizes mean that very little of actual aggressive behavior is explained by VVG playing. Even when the effects are statistically significant (meaning that they can be replicated reliably in a laboratory), the predictability of violent media may only be around 1% of total aggressive behavior. If there is concern about aggressive behavior in youths, then factors other than VVGs should be investigated, like poor-quality home environments, drug abuse, and school problems. Many psychology researchers, who in their own research discover effect sizes this small, would say that they have found negative or inconclusive effects. Instead, the critics argue, proponents of the VVG/aggression link put a positive spin on the effect sizes and often claim that there is causality: that playing VVGs causes aggression. On the other hand, within the larger context of many different causal factors, any one causal factor that has a .1 to .3 effect size might be interpreted as important. This has been one of the arguments of the camp that argues for the importance of the VVG/aggression link. Another way to look at the small effect size is in the realm of society as a whole. If millions and millions of youths play video games in the United States in any given year, then even a small effect upon aggressive behavior or a decrease in prosocial behavior could impact a large number of players.

The scientists do not even agree on whether they agree. Before widespread video game playing, television violence was a key concern of scientists and the public in general. A 1984 survey of researchers who study violence found 80% agreement on the claim that media violence causes aggression. However, more recently there is debate about whether scientists agree on the effects of VVGs. In addition to questioning the existence of a consensus on the topic among researchers, accusations of foul play in the world of science have been made. One research team claimed to have observed that ". . . some scholars actively and aggressively attempt to quell dissenting views, disparage skeptics, question the motives of those who disagree with them, and enforce a highly ideological view of this field" (Elson & Ferguson, 2014). And the national organization of psychologists has changed its stance over the years. The leading society of practicing psychologists in the United States—the American Psychological Association (APA)—has had inconsistent views with respect to the topic. When media violence came before the U.S. Supreme Court, the APA declined to get involved on the basis that the research did not give a clear picture. Years later, in 2017, the APA published work from a task force on violent video gaming. The task force, after conducting their own meta-analyses of recent research studies (published between 2009 and 2013), came to the conclusion, among others, that VVGs decreased empathy and desensitized people to violence. As with other meta-analyses, the task force found small but statistically significant effect sizes.

The in-fighting among scientists has led to interesting intellectual attacks, such as levying a list of psychological insults against each other. The pro-VVG/aggression link camp wonders why critics do not accept that VVGs are a factor in youth aggression. After all, there are clear, statistically significant, effects from the meta-analyses, and there is a logical and compelling understanding of how VVGs could cause aggression (the GAM). That camp concludes that there must be psychological reasons for the researchers' absence of belief in the link, or what this camp calls "denial." Two such reasons offered are a need for cognitive consistency and desensitization. The psyche wants to maintain a consistent set of beliefs (cognitive consistency), so evidence that goes against one's views or one's behaviors will be denied. For instance, researchers who grew up playing video games—even violent ones—might not want to accept that video games are damaging. Also, as years of violent media have been generated for consumers and as the media—not just video games—have become more violent, the public (including scientists) may have become unable to perceive the actual violence in violent media. The other camp has countered by pointing out the hostile behavior of their opponents, asking if media violence research can cause aggression.

CONCLUSION

There are ICT-related activities other than VVGs that might cause someone to engage in violent behaviors. Internet addiction (IA) occurs when a person is no longer able to control his or her online or phone-based activities; the uncontrolled activities lead to problems in home life, relationships, work, or school. When a person is afflicted with IA, that person also is likely to be more aggressive than non-afflicted individuals. In one study of young people showing problematic use of the Internet (another label for Internet addiction), persons who suffered from IA also were found to be likelier than others to get into serious fights and to carry a weapon with them. The relationship with getting into serious fights occurred for both boys and girls; the relationship with carrying a weapon occurred for boys only. Researchers have found that several factors overlap between Internet addicts and aggressive people. For one, both are more likely to be males than females. Another is that Internet addicts and aggressive people have tendencies toward depression. A third common factor is that both groups are on the low end of the dimension of self-esteem. A fourth common factor is that both groups are linked to having poor family functioning. The association between IA and depression and aggression occurs in other studies outside of the United States, for instance in Taiwan. Interestingly, research shows that depression affects executive function—our ability to control our thoughts and behaviors—negatively. Part of the responsibility for the connection may be the emotional rewards that an addict gets when feeding his or her addiction. Intense emotions are known to overwhelm the cognitive control mechanisms in the brain, possibly leading to an inability to suppress urges to act aggressively. The ability to suppress emotional reactions—known as inhibition—is a key function within the set of executive functions. It's not just IA; the connection with aggressive behaviors also includes compulsive shopping.

But most of the recent research on violent media revolves around VVGs. VVGs are arousing, an effect that could possibly contribute to later aggression. Arousal may be experienced as an increase in heart rate, respiration rate, or raised electrical conductance in the skin. Aggressive thoughts and emotions also occur when VVGs are played. Aggressive thoughts include the creation of scripts for solving disputes through violence and priming of internal mental representations associated with violence, such as knowledge of guns, while the key aggressive emotion is anger. The three components of arousal, emotion, and thoughts (cognition) form the internal state. And people whose internal state indicates hostility or aggression may be more likely than other people to carry out aggressive acts or to interpret other people's acts as aggressive. Most of this research is done in the laboratory where aggressive acts include sending noise blasts to other people and choosing the spice levels of hot sauce given to other individuals. In the hostile attribution bias, one's internal state may lead to the interpretation of ambiguous situations (such as getting into a car accident that is the other driver's fault) as aggressive, despite their also being a neutral or benign reason for the situation. These processes that lead from exposure to media violence to actual aggression are captured in the GAM. The model is a leading explanation of the effects of VVGs and captures the emotional, cognitive, and behavioral components of the link between violent media and violent acts. However, these effects are disputed by some scientists on several levels, including the sizes of the effects, the methodology used in the studies, and the practical implications of the research.

The connection between technology and aggression is not limited to physical aggression. Aggression can occur online, as well, and can take many forms in the online world. Aggression in that context is the subject of Chapter 3.

Interview with an Expert: Dr. Jeanne Brockmyer

Dr. Jeanne Brockmyer is professor emeritus of psychology at the University of Toledo. As a child clinical psychologist, she has been active in the study of the effects of video games for nearly 30 years. She has been scientifically studying video games since the early 1990s, when console gaming was booming in popularity. Through her extensive research program, Dr. Brockmyer, among other achievements, has developed key tools for researchers who study the effects of video games. With her colleagues, she has published scientific measures of empathy, attitudes toward violence, and game engagement. One of those tools, the Game Engagement Questionnaire, assesses video game players' psychological involvement with games. People who take the questionnaire must evaluate statements like, "If someone talks to me I don't hear." As a result of her knowledge in the research field, she acknowledges the connection between VVGs and negative outcomes. Regarding the effect of VVGs on people's emotional responses to violence, she says, "Initially, people are horrified by things they see, but we can't maintain that level of arousal. Everyone gets desensitized to things." (Brockmyer, 2014; in Bilton, 2014). Additionally, Dr. Brockmyer contributes to important, collaborative research-related efforts in the field of gaming research. She participates in efforts to move the findings from video game effects research out of the laboratory and into the public eye. She was a member of the Internet Gaming Disorder working group at the 2015 National Academy of Sciences Sackler Colloquium on Digital Media and Developing Minds. The working group activities culminated in an important paper in the journal *Pediatrics* in 2017 that assesses the state of the scientific knowledge on the disorder and provides recommendations for moving forward on the topic. Dr. Brockmyer also has spent time advocating on behalf of psychological research with members of the U.S. Congress.

Q: The literature seems to be controversial when examining the impact of violent or aggressive video games. What happens in the brain regarding video games, and where do you stand on this controversy?

A: The brain is truly fascinating! We are just starting to understand the effects of experience on the developing and developed brain, thanks, at least in part, to huge advances in technology. We do not have clear evidence as to whether exposure to a video game has a bigger impact on the developing or fully developed brain, keeping in mind that the brain may continue to develop well into a person's early 20s. Individual differences in brain structure and function, as well as life experience variabilities, complicate our ability to make specific predictions about the impact of video game play on any particular person. Brain responses identified through advanced technology suggest both temporary and long-term desensitization to violence while individuals are playing a violent video game. Playing other types of video games can have positive effects when used for a targeted therapy.

Actually, this is a pretty one-sided "controversy." Most well-established researchers agree that exposure to violence in video games increases the relative risk of aggression and desensitization to violence. This is based on a convergence of evidence from laboratory-based experiments, correlational research, and a small amount of longitudinal research. Relative risk is a very important concept: established researchers are not claiming a direct effect, rather that exposure to violence in video games is one risk factor for future aggression or failure to act to help others. There are obviously other important risk factors, including poverty and childhood maltreatment, but exposure to video game violence is the factor that may be most easily changed.

Q: Why do some people seem to be addicted to video games and what is the prevalence of addiction that you see in current international research?

A: At the present time, there is no such thing as "video game addiction," at least according to the American Psychiatric Association. However, researchers across the world are studying groups who spend excessive time gaming on a variety of platforms. Addiction is being operationally defined as a preoccupation with gaming that leads to some type of impairment. There are several specific types of impairment including jeopardizing significant relationships in the real world. Prevalence estimates of addiction vary greatly, due in part to lack of a common definition. Internationally, reports range from 1.2% to 8.5% of gamers studied, across a variety of age groups. These numbers may seem small, but when one considers the overall prevalence of game-playing (over 90% of U.S. children and youths by one estimate, plus four out of five young adults and over 50% of all American adults), the problem becomes critical. We have a long way to go in understanding what drives gaming addiction although pre-existing anxiety, depression, and social isolation are reasonable candidates.

Q: What do you see as the impact of emerging game types like augmented reality games such as *Pokémon Go*, virtual reality games, and "prosocial" games?

A: Augmented reality games are fun! In addition, unlike traditional video games, they most likely get participants up out of a chair and out of the house. On the negative side, they can be so immersive that people lose track of their surroundings. There are reports that players have continued to play while driving and caused car accidents and even some fatalities. It will be very interesting to see what happens with the next *Pokémon Go*! As virtual reality games become more cost effective they are likely to become an important part of the field. A decent virtual reality headset can be purchased for about $100, with even cheaper (and of course also more expensive) options available. What was once an extremely costly research tool is now an accessible option. Because virtual reality is an emerging technology, little is known about how its increased availability will play out. Some fear that the attraction of virtual reality will lead to increased social isolation for players, and there are those who experience a form of motion sickness when trying to play. It seems likely that any negative effect of prolonged exposure to negative messages, such as "violence is fun," could be heightened within a virtual reality context. However, there is great promise in adapting virtual reality for a variety of therapies. But, the jury is still out on the overall impact of totally immersive games.

Prosocial games have had a bit of a struggle. It is very expensive to develop a video game and profit depends on game popularity. Relatively speaking, there is not much money to be made in prosocial games, at least at this time. Prosocial games are often used as a form of cognitive stimulation or therapy. For example, "brain games" seem to have a market for adults, for individuals with traumatic brain injury, and for children with attention issues. Games for Change is a movement that produces games that promote social change. This group encourages collaborations between game designers who want to develop issue-driven games and those who can promote commercial success. Educational games, which have considerable promise, have had variable acceptance in schools. Although most children and youths are in favor of in-school games and teaching aids, a recent literature review suggests that teachers are resistant to using video games due to several factors, including personal video game experience and availability of technical support. Cost also continues to be a limiting factor.

One of the most important unanswered questions is the long-term effect of exposure to video game technology. Well-designed longitudinal research is needed to answer this question, and this will require a major funding commitment. As noted above, the issue of video game and Internet addiction is just beginning to be addressed. The impact of new approaches to gaming and new technologies such as augmented reality and virtual reality is essentially unknown. The promise of prosocial games is yet to be fully developed. This is an exciting time in the field and we need to keep moving forward, utilizing all available resources to minimize negative player impact and maximize benefits.

3

Electronic Aggression

Case Study: What Is Koobface?

What is Koobface? It's an anagram for Facebook. Also, it's a history-making computer worm that worked so well that Facebook and investigative groups put considerable effort into tracking down the perpetrators. Computer worms are sometimes called by the name of Internet worms, but the two phrases are essentially interchangeable. Computer worms are subtly different than computer viruses, and—as in the case of Koobface—can be used to create botnets. Experts describe computer worms in varied ways, but the core feature of a worm is that it can spread on its own with limited or no human behaviors required. A computer virus requires the intervention of a human in order to spread. For instance, a virus might attach itself to a Microsoft Word document. In order to spread, the computer user must open the document. This could occur if the user downloads the document from a website and opens it on her computer. A worm, in contrast, can get into a user's computer system, access the user's email address book, and send messages to all of the other users in the address book. This is a common replication method of worms. When a worm replicates itself across a group of computers, it may also install software that allows the computers to be controlled remotely from a central control system. The resulting network of hijacked computers is called a botnet, where "bot" refers to the robotic behavior of the hijacked computers. Another phrase that refers to the hijacked computers is "zombie" computers. Becoming part of a botnet can be prevented by using anti-virus software, installing a firewall, and behaving safely while browsing the web; however, cybercriminals count on sloppy practice by computer users to achieve their goals. Although computer worms can be a form of malware and often are used to commit cybercrimes, the world's first worm was not intended to be malicious. In 1988, a Cornell University student named Robert Morris wanted to know how large the Internet was. He created a computer program that moved from computer to computer, counting as it went. A side effect of his worm was that it sometimes crashed people's computers because of a bug in the computer code. Despite not trying to be hurtful in his efforts, Morris was prosecuted for his behavior and expelled from the university.

Starting in the late 2000s, an innovative social engineering method led to Koobface's effectiveness. Although a computer worm does not require human intervention in order to spread, the method of insertion of the malware does require an initial behavior from the computer user. Not-so-devious tricks are used by the designers of malware to convince computer users to take that initial action. These tricks are not so devious because it takes only a little inspection or reflection for a computer user to prevent the infection; yet many people fall prey to these tricks because of an inherent desire to trust messages from other people. These tricks—lumped together as a group of activities referred to as social engineering—are put to use for maximum effectiveness by cybercriminals. With Koobface, these tricks were used to convince people to willingly click on a link that would start the process of installing malware. If you received a message from a friend that purported to contain a "secret video," you certainly would be interested and curious to know the contents of the video. If you then clicked on the link associated with the video, the worm would then present a message saying that your Flash Player (software commonly used to watch video clips in a web browser) is out of date and needs updating. The key action here occurs when the user accepts the truth of the message by clicking on a button. The malware proceeds to install the Koobface worm. If you are not duped by the promise of seeing a secret video, then perhaps you would be enticed to click on the link that is associated with this message: "You look just awesome in this movie." As with the secret video, clicking on the link prompts the user to update their video player software, eventually leading to infection. And, if you are savvy enough to resist the temptation to watch a secret video or a video in which you look "awesome," you might still be unable to stop yourself from clicking on the link in a message from your friend that contains a funny or sexy video. If you did click on it, the result would be the same as before. Once the computer is infected with the worm, and Koobface is installed, your computer is now part of the worldwide botnet.

In August 2008, the computer worm was noticed by some users. By December of that year, 120 million Facebook users had been targeted. MySpace, a social networking platform popular with an earlier generation, also was affected. MySpace was attacked before Facebook, and the administrators put measures into place to prevent the worm's spread. The proliferation of the worm established a large, worldwide botnet that was very profitable for the criminals. The three-year stint of Koobface saw it infiltrate Facebook, Twitter, and other social media platforms. The growth of the botnet was estimated to be rather large, with anywhere between 400,000 and 800,000 computers being part of it. The computers could be located anywhere in the world and still remain under control by the cybercriminals. One research group decided to test the effectiveness of Koobface by creating a fake version that had no detrimental effect on people or their computer systems. The Koobface emulator was posted in Facebook and the researchers observed what happened. According to the researchers, the social media platform was able to block the spread of the worm, but only in 27% of the cases. Further, it would take the system four days, on average, to respond to the worm.

No one knew who had created and activated the worm. Early on, people who studied the worm were alarmed by its potential for wreaking havoc. With its sophistication, experts perceived that the worm would be able to do all sorts of bad things, including stealing people's private information, which could lead to identify theft and credit card fraud. But as knowledge of the worm was gained, it was clear what the criminals were up to. The perpetrators sold advertisements to other criminals who pitched bogus anti-virus software in the botnet. The advertisements were used to collect money from unsuspecting users. Additionally, web browsers were altered to send users to pharmacy websites of questionable reputation. Records of the websites that a user had visited were stolen from computers. These records are valuable. They can be sold to marketers, and marketers can use them to improve their advertising campaigns. Although it can't be known for sure, it was estimated that the cybercriminals behind Koobface could have been earning $2,000,000 per year during the three and one-half year run of the worm. While not much money was made compared to other cybercrimes, the criminals were able to live luxuriously while other groups tried to figure who and where they were. Facebook was a significant player in the search for the criminals. As the Facebook and other investigators began to figure out the identities of the perpetrators, they learned that the criminals had used their illegal profits to fund luxury vacations around the world. Two of these locations were Monte Carlo, Monaco, which is world famous for its casinos, and Bali, Indonesia, a place known for its beaches. The criminals had not attempted to hide all of the worldwide exploits, posting images of themselves in these exotic locations in their own online social media networks.

Frustrated with the lack of progress by law enforcement officials, Facebook resorted to publicly naming the criminals. When doing a thorough tracking of the worm, Facebook employees discovered that the criminals had made some technical mistakes. These mistakes allowed the employees to learn the nicknames of the perpetrators. The group of five men, collectively known as the "Koobface gang," included the usernames KrotReal, leDed, PsViat/PsychoMan, PoMuc, and Floppy. Once the nicknames were known, the true identities were found. As if to address the initial fears of the experts who characterized Koobface early on, the group of criminals—who called themselves "Ali Bab & 4"—left an electronic Christmas card inside infected computers in 2009. In the card, they explained to Internet security researchers that they would never steal credit card or bank information from victims. Amidst the search for these individuals, Facebook also obtained other important clues. One was a photo posted on social media that still had the metadata attached, meaning the location that the photo was taken was embedded in the photo file. The location was St. Petersburg, Russia. Another clue was a check-in on the social media application Foursquare that revealed a very particular spot within St. Petersburg. Even though Facebook had learned the names of the criminals and publicly posted those names, no law enforcement authorities were known to be investigating the individuals. In the end, the Facebook team was able to eradicate Koobface from the social network. By March 2011, the worm was gone from Facebook. Confidence in the feat was boosted after nine months had elapsed without an infection.

INTRODUCTION

Chapter 2 showed how violent media are suspected of making people commit aggressive acts in real life. The virtual world also has properties that make it a breeding ground for electronic acts of aggression. One-on-one attacks, such as cyberbullying and online romance scams, target victims with various backgrounds and characteristics; mass attacks, such as phishing, take advantage of inherent human tendencies.

CYBERBULLYING

It's very common for people who use social media to witness meanness and cruelty online. Cyberbullying is a subtype of general aggression that carries significant negative consequences for its victims. By 2011, less than 10 years after online social media took off, one national study in the United States found that 88% of social media users had seen this kind of behavior online. Cyberbullying might be considered a subset of the mean interpersonal behaviors seen online. Cyberbullying has been hard to define by researchers, partly because it can take so many forms, but also because it keeps changing its nature as the technology changes. Similar problems occur for cybervictimization, the state of being a victim of online bullying. Aggression comes in many forms, as does bullying. The different forms of aggression are defined by the behaviors that are associated with them. One big distinction between types of aggression is the difference between overt aggression and relational aggression. In the physical world, overt aggression includes physical acts like hitting someone and pushing someone, as well as threatening someone with physical acts. Overt victimization can be physical or verbal; obviously, it's the verbal form that translates into online aggression. In contrast, relational aggression includes social acts meant to inflict harm. Examples of relational aggression include excluding someone from a social event, manipulating a friend through words or deeds, and gossip.

Cyberbullying occurs in a variety of online settings. Cyberbullying takes place in social media sites (e.g., Facebook), instant messaging apps and programs, and chat rooms. On Facebook, for example, college students report that other users show bad behaviors like flaming, trolling, complaining, and attacking other people. Additionally, cyberbullying occurs through other forms of ICT, such as text messaging. Flaming is a relatively old term for negative statements made online that are directed at an individual or group. One research team defined flaming this way: "the use of hostile expressions toward others in online communication" (Lapidot-Lefler & Barak, 2012). Trolling is harmless or harmful posts and messages online that irritate and provoke others. Two aspects of trolling that can heighten its impact on others is intentionality (i.e., purposeful attacks on others) and repetition. The goal of Internet trolls is to post comments and make statements online that aggravate and annoy other people. Bloggers are frequent victims of trolling and flaming, so much so that one respected researcher in the field of cyberpsychology recommended that bloggers "better develop a tough skin" (Suler, 2014; in Rosenbloom, 2014).

When a person goes online to interact with other people, the normal circumstances of face-to-face communications are disrupted. In textual exchanges, as in instant messaging and social media posts, there is no eye-to-eye contact. There is another physical factor that contributes to people being mean to each other online: the actual distance between two people interacting online; or, more precisely, it's the fact that the two people are not in physical proximity to each other. This provides a safe environment for carrying out aggressive acts without physical repercussions. The affordances of technology also come into play. Contemporary communication technologies have allowed people to have access to the Internet—and thus their entire social network—all day long and through the night, every day of the week. In-person communications require that a person waits to give messages to another person when the two people are in the same physical location. Internet- and phone-based communications remove this hindrance to communication. Doing so, it becomes easier to troll, to flame, etc. and to do it more frequently than would have been done in person.

It is clear that cyberbullying is partly a result of the psychological effects of being behind a screen. The person may be using a username that does not reflect their real name and identity, also known as a pseudonym. And if the person is communicating with strangers or others who are not close relationships, then there will be little information to indicate anything about the person's background. These factors conspire to induce a phenomenon known as online disinhibition—the willingness to disclose or to act in a way that the person might not do in real life. Online disinhibition is said to occur in two forms. In the benign form, it may help a person communicate, or act in a way that is beneficial. For example, benign online disinhibition might compel a person to reveal personal feelings to another individual that help to deepen the relationship between the two people. However, a mean form of disinhibition exists. Known as toxic online disinhibition, this form of disinhibition occurs when the person is more willing than normal to say, post, or do things online that are negative, critical of other people or groups, hateful, irritating, etc. Even seemingly normal interactions online can become toxic, as was found in a study where people solved problems by interacting online with strangers. The feeling of anonymity, the feeling of invisibility (not being seen by the other person), and the lack of eye contact led to measurable flaming in the online dialogue. Another purported factor that contributes to toxic online disinhibition is the lack of authority relationships in the online world. In most online discussion spaces, such as social media sites, all users are equal to each other in power and authority. This fact removes one of the barriers that prevent people from being mean in real life. For example, the presence of a parent in a room will normally prevent two kids from making mean remarks about each other. Lack of awareness of tracking can be one of the factors that impact people's willingness to make negative statements online. Many people are not aware of how much tracking of personal information occurs online. Tracking can also be done on one's personal posts and comments. Posts and comments might be picked up by Internet search engines, and later appear in another person's search results.

Not all online settings may be alike when it comes to interpersonal behaviors. Researchers who study online gaming find that the specific aspects of gaming combine with online disinhibition to make drastic outcomes. Games are often varied, exciting, and fast-paced, which causes arousal in the players, can lead to sensory overload (the inability to process all of the information that is available in the environment), and presents novel situations for which players do not possess previously learned standard reactions. Mixed with the other characteristics of being behind a screen, these may lead to very aggressive online behaviors.

Although the online world precludes direct physical acts, overt aggression through statements or threats is possible. And relational aggression is possible, too. For example, one friend can start an online conversation with other friends and purposefully exclude another friend as a form of punishment. Relational aggression happens relatively frequently among friends and thus is a form of peer victimization. Peer victimization has been studied quite a bit among adolescents. In the early 2010s, 20% of young people in the United States felt that their peers were mostly unkind online. (Only 5% of adults felt that their peers were mostly unkind.) Among teens in the U.S., outcomes of being insulted online include having face-to-face arguments, ending a friendship, causing problems with parents, experiencing anxiety about going to school, getting into a physical fight, and getting into trouble at school. At the time, 15% of teenagers had been the recipients of mean comments online. In order from most frequent to least, the rates of the most common negative outcomes were 25% for face-to-face arguments, 22% for ending a friendship, 13% for problems with parents, 13% for anxiety about school, 8% for a physical fight, and 6% for getting into trouble at school.

While bullies may use varied types of aggression to achieve their goals, they broadly share a common goal. Their acts represent ". . . repeated assaults by a more powerful individual or group of a less powerful individual with the intention to cause harm or distress" (Boulton, Lloyd, Down, & Marx, 2012). Often the media are interested in reporting the most egregious cases of online bullying, when the victims eventually take their own lives, partly as a result of the bullying. While the news media make spectacles of particular cases of online bullying, researchers have attempted to determine actual prevalence rates. It is clear that the worst cases—when the victims injure themselves or commit suicide—are rare. Cyberbullying is an international phenomenon and measured prevalence rates show wide variation. Data from the United Kingdom show that one-third of 9- to 19-year-olds there have been bullied through online comments in social media. And online aggression in Asian countries has been documented. In China, questionnaire surveys of college students show that 18% to 43% have attacked other people online. These attacks included sending hate messages through email and flaming in social media. When it comes to cyberbullying, there is significantly more research being conducted among youths than other age brackets. Cyberbullying is more common than being the victim of sexual predation online. Across many countries, one expert review of the cyberbullying literature found that the typical rate of being a cyberbullying victim is in the range of 10% to 40% for children and teenagers. Another review of the literature estimated the rate of youth cybervictimization to be in the range of 4% to 39%. As far as college students go, the rate was estimated to be in the range of 9% to 43%. In the early 2010s, being cyberbullied was reported by 19% of American teenagers, while 21% reported having participated in cyberbullying.

There are intense, negative psychological consequences of being bullied online that researchers measure in various ways. Important negative consequences of being cyberbullied include emotional and mental health problems, but there are other bad outcomes, too. Emotionally, victims may suffer distress. In terms of mental health, they may develop social anxiety. Additionally, it has been noted that victims might suffer reductions in self-esteem and may act out through delinquent behaviors. Another emotional and mental health outcome associated with cyber-victimization is developing symptoms of depression. The sad, ultimate outcome of extreme depression is sometimes suicide. In extreme cases, the cyberbullying victims suffer intense psychological distress, leading to suicide. Around the world, cases of victims who kill themselves make headlines. In the United States, for example, 12-year-old Mallory Grossman was a popular athlete who was tormented by schoolmates in electronic media. Eighteen-year-old Conrad Roy III, from Massachusetts, was encouraged to commit suicide through text messages sent by a friend. In Italy, a 14-year-old girl who used the nickname "Amnesia" jumped to her death after being cyberbullied. And, Tiziana Cantone, a 31-year-old woman, committed suicide after a secret sex video with her in it went "viral." While experts agree that cyberbullying alone does not cause suicide, cyberbullying may make depression worse and facilitate suicide. One research study with young people found that, all other things being equal, having been a cyber-victim was associated with a nearly 200% increase in the chances of having attempted suicide. Prevention efforts are warranted. Cyberbullying is a common topic in education programs for youths, and the programs often give young people tips for avoiding victimization. One way that the reader might think to prevent cyberbullying is for parents to monitor their children's behavior online, but parental monitoring at home may not be very effective, and parental monitoring has been found in some studies to be unrelated to the chances that a child will experience cyberbullying.

The chances of being a perpetrator and being a victim are affected by psychological and other factors. The factors that affect cyberbullying—both carrying it out and being the recipient—include one's attitudes toward bullying, having trouble regulating Internet use, one's age, biological sex, and culture. One of the main findings with respect to being a victim is that people who are victimized offline—in the real world—also have an increased chance of being victimized online. Being an impulsive person, known as trait impulsivity, is linked to both being a cyberbully and being the victim of a cyberbully in high school. With respect to attitudes toward bullying, college students tend to have negative attitudes toward any form of bullying, but especially so against traditional physical bullying. The least negative attitudes are held against traditional verbal bullying; this is not seen as bad as other forms of bullying, either real-life bullying or cyberbullying. While female college students see bullying as less acceptable than male college students, men particularly do not have positive attitudes toward bullying victims. Male college students are less likely than female college students to feel sorry for victims and to think that victims need help and support. They are more likely than females to think that bullying victims are weak and should stand up for themselves. College students with more accepting attitudes toward bullying via social media are two-and-a-half times more likely than other college students to engage in bullying themselves. Having a more accepting attitude toward bullying via texting is associated with a threefold increase in the chances of being a bully. Finally, those students who have an accepting attitude toward physical bullying are three times more likely than others to be bullies themselves. While most people can control how much time they spend online or on their devices, some people may be suffering from an inability to regulate their use. In concrete terms, this may mean that some people spend more time online than they planned, cannot stop using the Internet when they want to, or may impulsively use the Internet. In adolescents, this may lead to problematic Internet use, which is Internet use that becomes associated with negative outcomes like declines in school performance and/or loss of friends. Studies have found that adolescents who suffer from problematic Internet use are also at more risk for being the victim of cyberbullying.

There are a few additional factors that increase a person's chances of being a victim. A victim's gender may impact the type of bullying that they are involved in. Females are known to engage in more relational bullying than males. For youths, the rates of being cyberbullied ascertained by researchers show that girls are more likely than boys to be victims; however, the details are complex, with some types of bullying not showing a difference between girls and boys. One of the additional factors relates to femininity, but it's not about whether a person is biologically a woman or not; rather, it's about whether a person—man or woman—has feminine tendencies like warmth, sensitivity, nurturing, and interdependence. For those with strong feminine tendencies, the chances of becoming a cyber-victim appear to be connected to how independent from others they are. If they feel that they are unique, autonomous, and separate from the people around them (known as having an independent self-construal), then they are less likely to experience cyberbullying than other people with feminine tendencies.

ONLINE PRIVACY AND RISKY ONLINE BEHAVIORS

Due to cyberbullying and other threats, it is natural that computer users want to feel safe when they are online. True safety, in the context of using computers, has been defined as "freedom from unacceptable risk" (Hollnagel, 2011). In other words, Internet safety means being able to carry out online behaviors without concern for negative outcomes. Online privacy is an important part of online safety. Privacy is a right to control one's personal data. A more formal definition is, "the claim of individuals, groups, or institutions to determine for themselves when, how, and to what extent information about them is communicated to others" (Westin, 1967). Of course, this is a big issue in today's online world, because many online organizations ask users to submit personal data as part of an enrollment process. People who do not secure their online data or who share too much private information online are vulnerable to various problems. A few of these problems that might be encountered by sharing private information are unwanted advertising (say, an online organization sells your personal information to a marketing firm), phishing attacks (designed to trick you into providing even more personal information), criminals using your location information (for instance, to rob your house while you are on vacation), and people in relationships taking advantage of you. Many experts believe that being online—behind a screen—makes people feel anonymous. That is, using the Web makes people feel that they cannot be identified by other computer users. Unfortunately, this increases the amount of sharing of personal information, also known as online self-disclosure.

Widespread tracking of private information also presents a problem. Web searches and web browsing present two opportunities for tracking of your private information by others. Cookies are small computer files that your browser creates while you navigate the World Wide Web. Cookies are very helpful in many cases. When you visit a website several times in a row, the website can behave as if it remembers you because information about your earlier visits is stored in cookies on the computer. If you are using the website to do some shopping, then the online shopping cart will retain your prior items because of the cookies. But, at the same time, cookies constitute a way of tracking your online behaviors. The tracked information also could be used to make you the victim of unwanted advertisements. It's not an uncommon experience for the following to happen. A computer user visits a website, pokes around a bit, then leaves that website to visit a different website. Surprisingly, an ad appears on the new website that promotes products or services from the previously visited website. This experience is partly attributable to cookies. Also, web searches are stored by the company offering the search service, unless the computer user changes settings to prevent it. At first, it may seem that your web searches are harmless, meaningless information to anyone else, but the web search history can be revealing. For instance, people may use the search functions to help them pursue their romantic interests. Thus, the search history might provide a clue to a person's romantic status. In one study, it was found that 17% of Internet users who were single and actively searching for a romantic partner had used the Internet to find a partner or date. Not only are your search keywords part of your personal, private information, but they can also be used to draw conclusions about you and to find even more private information about you. Thus, people's web search data are valuable to other groups, especially marketers. A real-life example of this phenomenon occurred in 2006 when the Internet service America Online (AOL) released a large set of web search data for researchers to use. The data had been anonymized, meaning that the names of the individual users had been removed. Yet bloggers and other computer users showed how they could use the anonymized data to learn the personal information of the original users. The ability to do so came as a great shock to AOL, who subsequently removed the data from the Internet. The person held responsible for the mistake was the company's chief technology officer, who was forced to resign.

Measures of concern over online privacy have revealed several interesting facts. First, most people seem to know about threats to online safety and are afraid. Regular people were becoming concerned about their online privacy fairly early on in the Internet revolution. By the late 1990s, it was reported that 80% of the people using the Internet had concerns. Parents were also very concerned for their children's privacy. One national study done in the United States in the late 1990s found that more than 75% of parents were worried. (Another concern of parents was that there was so much sexually explicit material online, a topic addressed in Chapter 4.) While parents were concerned for their children, there was much less concern coming from the children themselves. One report showed that while more than 80% of parents in the late 2000s were worried about online privacy for their children, only 29% of teenagers were concerned. The discrepancy between parental worry and child worry might be related to fact that teenagers are very likely to disclose their full names, their school names, their contact information, and their participation in social events in online venues. A great example of the outcomes of the heightened fears over personal information in the web is the development of Snapchat. Snapchat is an application that displays pictures and video messages and makes them available for only a very short time—usually 10 seconds or less—and was developed partly in response to people's concerns about private information being left online for others to see or use.

In a perfect world, people would disclose private information only to the extent that they receive benefits in return for doing so, and only when the benefits outweigh the risks of doing so. However, it is clear that the typical Internet user does not follow this rational model. People tend to disclose too much information online and they do not take the steps necessary to secure their information. For example, privacy agreements between users and organizations contain clauses that show what the organizations are legally allowed to do with the users' private information. But it is a fact that the privacy agreements provided by online organizations are in flux. Most people who use the Internet regularly receive periodic statements of changes to privacy agreements. Large, well-established organizations tend to require that users and account holders agree to these changes before their account is reactivated.

Thus, it is almost guaranteed that the privacy agreement that one initially agrees to will not be the same privacy agreement over time. Despite this, individuals willingly disclose their private information to organizations, or within social media sites like Facebook. Another case of irrational behavior relates to the anxiety or fear of being duped online. Since most people experience some anxiety about putting their private information online, it would be logical for them to act on that feeling and to employ privacy settings and very selective disclosure of information. However, very few people do this.

One of the contexts in which online disclosure has been studied is the realm of business transactions, also known as e-commerce. When consumers go online to make purchases or to shop for goods and services, they are often asked to disclose personal information. For instance, Internet vendors commonly require a user to make an account in order to complete an online purchase. Establishing a user account often necessitates entering one's legal name, residential address, and email address. Researchers have repeatedly shown that people are willing to disclose personal information in these cases, even when they are aware of the risks. The conflict between becoming a victim and enjoying online services has been characterized as moving along a range from Absolute Willingness to Disclose (AWD) information (despite the risks) to Absolute Perceived Risk (APR) (i.e., fear of disclosing information). Users in the AWD state of mind will share just about any information in order to make gains or to receive benefits. Users in the APR state of mind will very rarely share personal information. One interesting point along the continuum occurs when the willingness to share is equal to the perceived risk. This point, referred to as Maximized Disclosure Consciousness, freezes the user so that she takes no action whatsoever; she neither discloses personal information nor takes steps to protect her personal information. Perhaps rationally, prior experiences with online purchases make people more likely to disclose information in the future, thus moving those people along the range toward AWD. When people have experience making purchases, they have hopefully learned how to disclose information without negative consequences. In other words, they learn from their prior experiences and from their prior failures. These experiences reduce how much people see their chances of being negatively affected by shopping online, so experience reduces the perceived risk of disclosing personal information.

One group of Internet users that willingly discloses private information is bloggers. A significant portion of bloggers reveal their names and other demographic information on their websites and posts, maybe to increase their credibility. One-half of bloggers share their age, sex, and other vital characteristics. About one-third of bloggers share their full names and about one-third share their first names. One way that many people reduce their risks due to disclosing private information is to use pseudonyms, altered or entirely fabricated names that do not reveal one's full personal identity. Bloggers use pseudonyms to reduce their risk 29% of the time. Using pseudonyms may be a partial solution to the problem of the risks of going online. In one comprehensive set of interviews with experts who study technology, pseudonymity emerged as a potential theme in the future of the Internet. Another group of Internet users that has been studied is people who disclose illegal activities online. Disclosing one's illegal behaviors to others online is a very risky behavior. In some online discussion forums about drug use, this behavior is occurring at a measurable rate. Reddit is an online discussion forum about almost any topic. Investigators studying the content of Reddit users' posts discovered that users are willing to admit illegal behavior. For example, one post read, "I'm 19, smoke 1 gram a day, and work at a call center." Another post read, "I'm ignorant about street prices. How much should a 5 mg vicodin cost me?" It's clear that discussion group users use the discussion to gain information about illicit drugs; that's the benefit of disclosure. But the risk is very high. In analyzing the details of the messages between users, the investigators learned that there was a preponderance of "small talk" between users. Referred to as phatic communication by researchers, this small talk appears to facilitate social bonds between the forum users, giving people an increased sense of togetherness that contributes to a willingness to disclose private information.

Scientists have learned some of the additional factors that influence people's willingness to disclose and their likelihood of engaging in safe online practices. The factors that influence users' willingness to disclose and their engagement in safe online practices include personal characteristics, website characteristics, and social aspects. For instance, people with higher levels of education are less willing to disclose personal information in e-commerce than people with lower levels of education. Also, the appearance of websites influences decisions. The reader may have visited websites that look very polished and professional. The appearance of these websites should increase a person's confidence that the website can be trusted with personal information. Yet experiments show that people are less likely to disclose personal information on nice-looking websites than on sloppy-looking ones. Researchers interpret this as irrational behavior: websites that are not well constructed are probably more likely than others to lead to abuse of personal information. In addition, trust is an important factor that affects people's likelihood of revealing their private information in online settings. Trust is the sense of how much private information can be disclosed to a person without risk. So, naturally, when a computer user has a high level of trust for another individual, there will be more self-disclosure. Trust can also occur between a person and an organization, or a person and a website. In the case of a website, trust is the feeling that the website will not misuse the private information of the person. When people do not trust a website, then self-disclosure will be low. Trust can be thought of as a gatekeeper for private information. When trust is high, the gate is open and private information is disclosed. When trust is low, the gate is closed and little private information makes it through to another person or organization. The way that trust operates makes good sense for humans, generally, because sharing private, potentially damaging, information should be made only to those who will not abuse the information. Yet there is another aspect to trust that can be a problem when people go online. Scientists have found that humans are naturally trusting of other humans. This might be an advantage in the long run for the human race as a whole, because humans will tend to trust each other, tend to disclose to each other, and tend to benefit from the disclosure. Thus, natural trust provides an advantage in evolution, making the survival of the species more likely than not. But online, where many potential threats exist, having a naturally high level of trust can put a person at risk. The high level of trust in others, without knowing much else about the others, might lead to unnecessary self-disclosure in situations like responding to emails from strangers.

Being fearful may be a good thing when it comes to online self-disclosure. People who are afraid of the risks of disclosing information perceive a high level of online threats. Having a high level of online threat assessment is linked to practicing safe online behaviors like disclosing as little private information as possible and using privacy settings to control private data. People who have negative experiences online end up having higher levels of threat assessment than people without those experiences. People who have not had negative experiences might not think much at all about the risks of being online when they are traversing the Internet or using their smartphones. In contrast, people who have heightened levels of threat assessment will be directly involved in preparing themselves for the negative outcomes of self-disclosure. By putting people into the appropriate mindset, their disclosure behaviors can be curbed. The appropriate mindset includes an awareness of online risk and being alert to people or organizations trying to deceive. For instance, it is possible to bring people's attention to online risk, and this reduces how much information is disclosed. One way to focus attention toward online risk occurs in the context of responding to emails. When people respond to emails, it may be important to actively consider whether each email message represents an attempt to deceive. Email messages that contain requests to input private information such as a bank account number could possibly be "phishing" attempts. Phishing brings the user to an illegitimate website that collects the private data and uses it for criminal or other nefarious purposes. Asking email users to judge each email message on whether it could be a phishing attempt produces positive results. People who make this judgment before responding end up disclosing less information. In other words, priming people to think about phishing causes them to be more careful when responding to email messages.

Another important factor is one's sense of feeling connected to other people. When a computer user feels a sense of social connectedness to others, he is more likely to self-disclose than when there is no feeling of connectedness. Having discussions with other people can build this sense of connectedness, so online behaviors that involve discussions may contribute to self-disclosure. Instant messaging, for instance, often used for casual conversation among peers, may contribute to social connectedness that then may contribute to self-disclosure. People are sensitive to privacy policies, too. Privacy policies contain the agreement between a website user (or an app user) and the organization which provides the website. The agreement usually contains language regarding how the organization will use the private information of the user. Websites with weak privacy policies may not specify how private information will be used or may not give the user much control over her private information. When privacy policies are weak, and when the user is aware of this, the user is less likely to disclose private information than in other cases. Finally, in general, women are more likely to disclose private information than men, and not just in online settings. However, in other cases, people appear to use privacy settings to their advantage. On dating websites, most users follow the rules of the website and comply with the posted regulations. However, occasional users violate the rules or fail to comply with regulations in ways that irritate or annoy other users. For instance, online daters complain about other users who are rude, angry, or who lie about their profile information. In these cases, technologically savvy online daters will use their privacy settings to filter out these individuals. One way to do so is to set one's user profile so that it can only be seen by other individuals who have paid to have the highest level of membership at the site.

THE PERILS OF YOUTH

As with other topics in the study of technology use, much of the research on online disclosure is focused on the group perceived to be most vulnerable to technology's negative effects: youths. Youths are driven to use social media, and they show distinct behavioral patterns due to their age. Further, they are open to particular online threats for which they are targeted. Adolescents are highly likely to feel the need to know what is happening with their peers. This need is commonly referred to as the Fear of Missing Out (FOMO). Aside from being in the same physical location as one's peers, participating in an online social media platform is perhaps the best way for adolescents to keep abreast of what is going on with their contemporaries. Not only does FOMO drive youths toward social media, but social media give youths another benefit: they provide a venue for self-regulation, actions that help a person stay calm and emotionally stable. A young person can, as an example, post messages on Facebook that share the young person's current emotional state. When the young person's online friends see the post, they will reply with positive comments. These replies can give an emotional boost to the poster. (Using social media for self-regulation also has a downside: it can lead to negative emotions. This situation is discussed in Chapter 9.) Building friendships also occurs on social media. Adolescence is a time when young people actively trying to understand themselves. They want to know their places in the world and in society, they want to refine their values, and they want to know their roles with respect to other individuals. Known as identity formation, this psychological process compels young people to interact with others, representing another factor driving social media use. A big part of building friendships and interacting with other people is phatic communication, the small talk that appears to serve no real purpose, but does contribute to relationship depth.

While some youths appreciate that there is risk in online self-disclosure, young people as a whole tend to self-disclose a lot. By the late 2000s, almost all teenagers who went online were interacting with other people (83%). Although a sizeable portion of them were concerned about privacy (27%), the majority of them were willing to give out private data (62%) in order to register for a social media platform. Those teenagers who were concerned about sharing their private information were learning to use software controls and privacy settings to reduce how much information was shared. Additionally, they were beginning to create falsified information and use this in place of real information. Not only were teens interacting with other people, but a large number of them were being contacted by strangers. A nationally representative study in the United States in 2007 found that almost one-third of teenagers who used the Internet had been contacted by someone that they did not know. In that study, the amount of fake information submitted by teenagers was high; 46% of teenagers with social media profiles admitted having some false information in the profiles. Protecting themselves from online risks was one of the reasons that teenagers had for using fake information. (Another was to be playful or silly.) The teenagers with profiles were revealing a bunch of personal information that was real. Online profiles contained first names (82%), photos of the user (79%), photos of friends (61%), or the name of the city or town in which the user lived (61%). At the time, the typical teenager felt that it was never agreeable to post one's address, social security information, passwords, or medical information. Teenage bloggers have tendencies to disclose their first names. The next most likely piece of information that is disclosed is their ages, followed by their contact information and their locations. All of these types of private data are disclosed more than 50% of the time. As young people, they are vulnerable to particular types of cybervictimization, including becoming the target of sexual predators or the focus of a cyberstalker.

Some of the factors for youth self-disclosure have been identified by researchers. Being behind a screen promotes general factors that affect self-disclosure in youths. One of these general factors is disinhibition. As described earlier, the visual cues—like other people's eyes as they look at you—that might normally prevent the disclosure of sensitive information are not present online. This increases the chances of self-disclosure. In addition, quite a few youths—especially adolescents—feel the need to be popular within their peer groups. This need can lead to self-disclosure. The act of revealing personal information can build friendships, increase trust, and increase cohesion with others. In fact, youths who feel a need to belong to a social group are more likely than others to post personal information in their status updates on Facebook. Interviews with U.S. high school students show that they are concerned about being safe online, but that they have their reasons to share private information. One of these reasons is peer pressure, a sense of unease that occurs when one does not follow along with what one's friends are doing. If all of a teen's friends are making social media profiles and sharing private information, then there is peer pressure to do the same. According to teenagers, another factor that causes them to share their personal information is the design of websites and applications. When setting up a personal profile, the systems often prompt the user to provide significant amounts of private information.

Across all ages, scientific models of risky online disclosure link one's personal history of being a cyber victim to one's concerns about privacy. These concerns drive one's assessment of risks and benefits which, in turn, influence behaviors. One such model is the antecedents, privacy concerns, and outcomes (APCO) model. The model predicts when a person is likely to disclose private information online. The antecedents are the factors that contribute to a person's privacy concerns. (Earlier, privacy concerns were also described as one's level of threat assessment.) Negative online experiences, for instance, are expected to increase a person's privacy concerns. Trust is expected to decrease a person's privacy concerns. Privacy concerns affect a person's assessment of risk, as well as of the benefits, of any particular encounter online. The assessment is done using internal, mental calculations called the privacy calculus. The results of the privacy calculus determine how a person will behave, such as whether the person will disclose private information. In one study, it was shown that having been the victim of an online scam raises a person's privacy concerns. As a consequence, the victims show an increased rate of changing their passwords in order to prevent future victimization.

Experts have made recommendations on how people of all ages can avoid the negative consequences of risky online behaviors. A study done regarding online posts revealed a potential software fix. The experimenters forced users to wait momentarily before submitting a post to an online public space. This short delay decreased how much private information was shared by users. From the perspective of software developers, the U.S. government issues recommendations for website operators that relate to user privacy. A few of the recommendations include posting information about the kind of private information collected by the organization, giving users an option to turn off data collection, and allowing users to verify the information that has been collected by the organization. However, organizations are not required to follow the recommendations, and there are few ways that the government can enforce them. Website operators have two main approaches to privacy policies available to them. The "opt-in" policy requires that the organization get explicit permission from the user before collecting the user's data. The "opt-out" policy assumes that the organization is permitted to collect the data unless the user requests that the data collection not proceed. Many companies can benefit from the collected information, including marketing and advertising firms. Therefore, these types of companies may prefer that policies be of the "opt-out" type.

OTHER AGGRESSIVE BEHAVIORS

All of the factors that influence online self-disclosure put people at risk for a variety of cyberattacks or other online aggressive behaviors. Some attacks are aimed at large masses of people, while other attacks are aimed at individuals. Most researchers in the field of the psychology of technology agree that individuals should be given an expectation of online information privacy, or "the ability of the individual control information about one's self" (Stone, Gardner, Gueutal, & McClure, 1983). By the mid-1980s, researchers who studied the field of computers and society were considering people's information privacy one of the top issues of the day. Based on the growing prevalence of computer databases since the 1960s, many people in society were becoming aware of how their personal information could be collected and used in unacceptable ways. People's worry about their information privacy— referred to as privacy concerns—focuses on companies or criminals compiling databases containing private information that can be traded, sold, exposed, or used for manipulation. These concerns started long before the Internet was widely available. Before then, people began to realize that companies (or governments) could accumulate large amounts of information about individuals and easily organize and search this information with powerful computers. For instance, one of the concerns about information privacy in the 1980s and 1990s was that the information that was collected would be inaccurately recorded. One questionnaire item used by researchers to assess people's level of privacy concerns asked people to rate their agreement with this sentence: "All the personal information in computer databases should be double-checked for accuracy—not matter how much this costs" (Smith, Milberg, & Burke, 1996).

The advent of the Internet made the problem worse. By the mid-2000s, more than half of Internet users in the United States were worried about becoming the victim of online abuses such as phishing attempts. However, worry does not translate into taking appropriate precautions. In the same time period, more than 80% of adult Internet users had downloaded files onto their computes or devices without knowing what was in the files, and almost 75% of users had publicly posted personal information like email addresses, names, and birthdays. Nearly one third of users had responded to a phishing attempt through email. As one researcher put it, "awareness of the potential risks in itself does not mediate the user's willingness to put personal details online" (Ibrahim, 2008). Contributing to this phenomenon is humans' natural trust in others. Because people have a natural trust in other people, messages that appear online—like in email—from other people may be highly trusted automatically, even when the messages are from strangers. In contemporary times, having many privacy concerns makes people more suspicious and less likely to want to share their information when asked to do so online. So even though humans are fundamentally trusting of other humans, having a high level of privacy concerns decreases a person's trust in others. In the case of interacting through computers and smartphones, this could be a beneficial outcome. It was discussed earlier how being trusting might lead to becoming the victim of a cyberattack. Privacy concerns also impact how a person sees risks. As a person becomes more worried about online privacy, he also sees more risks of being online and sharing information. Thinking that there are many online risks to sharing information could be a beneficial outcome, too. It turns out that individuals who perceive there to be a lot of online risks are less likely than others to plan to share their private information.

Social engineering is used to reduce people's information privacy, leading to unwise online disclosure. Social engineering involves the manipulation of individuals due to their psychological tendencies. A formal definition of social engineering done in online or computer-based contexts is, ". . . using social interaction as a means to persuade an individual or an organization to comply with a specific request from an attacker where either the social interaction, the persuasion or the request involves a computer-related entity" (Mouton, Leenen, Malan, & Venter, 2014). A complex model of social engineering suggests that a variety of factors and influences cause a person to become the victim of nefarious manipulation. The recently proposed susceptibility to online influence model of social engineering assumes that the perpetrators of social engineering, or scammers, do not feel guilt or fear when manipulating other people because being online—and not face-to-face—reduces those feelings. For instance, online anonymity means that it is difficult for potential victims to check the identity of a scammer or to check the details of a scammer's message. The factors that influence victimization can be grouped into two categories: individual differences and contextual factors. Individual differences are variables that make some people different than others. Level of trust in others would be an individual difference. Other individual differences are having low self-control, low self-awareness, being a risk taker, and having a high need to have friends. Contextual factors are variables that relate to the setting or type of scam being carried out. For example, messages sent by scammers might imply a time limit on an offer or request that puts time pressure on the victim. Additionally, the individual differences and the contextual factors can interact: certain individual differences may be important in some contexts but not in others. The kinds of psychological manipulation used by scammers during social engineering include, among other tricks, authority (impersonating an authority figure), liking (using similarity to the victim), conformity (social pressure), and reciprocity (getting something in return for a free gift).

MASS ATTACKS

College students, known to be the most avid users of social media across age groups, will often post their relationship information, their personal interests, their addresses, and even their class schedules. Disclosure of private and personal information on Facebook and other social media opens people up to becoming victims of phishing and other attacks. Data mining on social media sites—using software to rip copies of users' personal, but public, information—can be used by companies, marketers, and even criminals to improve their activities and achieve their goals. Ethical phishing experiments show that personalizing malicious messages by adding scraped private data gets people to become victims in scams. In the United States, college students have been known to have their Facebook profiles hacked—that is, accessed by other individuals—leading to various sorts of attacks. One possibility is that the hacked profile can be used for cyberbullying. Hackers can change the profile data of a user, perhaps in an embarrassing way that leads to conflict with the user and her friends, family, or workmates.

There are many different types of cyberattacks and other online aggressive behaviors. The goal of many cyberattacks is to commit crimes. As examples, phishing attempts and hacking often are used to commit identity theft. One study by a large telecommunications firm estimated that nine personal records are exposed to criminals every second through cybercrimes. It should be noted that not all breaches of user privacy are committed by external criminals; it has been estimated that about a quarter of all breaches are done by people who work for an organization or who have authorized access to its records. One very common type of mass cyberattack is the phishing attempt. Phishing is an online scam with a relatively high success rate. Phishing is often done as a mass attack; the same message will be sent to thousands or tens of thousands of email account holders. Email messages that appear to be from eBay, PayPal, or the victim's own university or bank can look like official correspondence even though they are not. One common technique is for the email to contain a message that the user's account information— like a password—needs to be updated. If the account is not updated quickly, the message warns, the user may be locked out of it. Phishing can also be personalized. Scammers will personalize the email messages by embedding a little information about the recipient. This information can be gleaned by searching the Internet prior to creating the messages. This kind of phishing is referred to as spear phishing and makes the email messages look more authentic than they might otherwise look. Aside from coming from a friend, spear phishing attempts might also arrive from the official websites of well-known organizations. One telecommunications company calculated that 23% of people who receive phishing emails actually open the email messages. Across many studies, roughly 20% to 30% of people who get phishing emails respond to them. But fewer individuals actually suffer serious consequences. One estimate puts the percentage of people who lose money due to phishing as 3.3% of those who receive the messages.

Scientists have created artificial phishing scams in order to test hypotheses about what makes people willingly share their private information with strangers. The artificial scams created by scientists are called ethical phishing, because there is not any intent to swindle individuals. Rather, the goal is to discover how phishing scams operate socially and psychologically. When college students receive ethical phishing email messages, there are several factors that appear to work against them, making them more likely to respond to the messages. The top factor is using the Internet a lot. Other factors are being curious, knowing the name of the sender of the message, and having a risk-taking personality. Students who have Internet anxiety (i.e., worry about what they do online) are less likely than others to respond to the messages. Not only are details from people's profiles used to enhance phishing attempts, but the setting of the social media site leads users to lower their guards when it comes to scrutinizing messages from others. Phishing messages posted within the social media site—or from the social media site through email—are more likely to be accepted than in other settings. Perhaps the first and most-cited ethical phishing attempt was done in the mid-2000s. The researchers sent messages with the subject, "Hey, check this out." Unbeknownst to the recipients, who were Indiana University students, the scientists had "scraped" information from the students' online social networking profiles using freely available software. This allowed the research team to craft messages that appeared to come from a user who was a friend of the student. The team also used a comparison email that did not take advantage of the scraped information, so that the messages appeared to come from a stranger. The chance that a student recipient of the message from a stranger would click on the embedded link and enter their personal information was 16%, a significant response rate. However, the social message improved the response rate dramatically: the chance that a student responded with private information was 72%. The scientists summarized their results this way: "Sometimes a 'friendly' email message tempts recipients to reveal more online than they otherwise would, playing right into the sender's hand." (Jagatic, Johnson, Jakobsson, & Menczer, 2007). In another case, researchers approached people at a shopping mall in Holland, asking them to provide the researchers with personal information. The randomly approached individuals were very willing to provide this information. Eighty percent to 90% of the participants disclosed their email address, prior shopping habits, or store shopping histories. One particular piece of information was intended to push the limit of the kind of information that people would provide to strangers. In this case, the researchers asked mall-goers to provide part of their bank account number to the experimenters. Forty percent or more of the people were willing to do so, apparently due to the truth bias that people have when they trust other humans. However, being warned about cybersecurity reduces the likelihood that people will disclose information. Also, being primed about cybersecurity by asking some questions related to security affects how likely people will disclose information. Priming also lowers the chances of disclosing one's personal information.

Another type of mass attack is fake computer updates, as exemplified by Koobface in the case study. Koobface took advantage of victims by giving false warnings that the computer software needed to be updated. In the case of Koobface, victims were tricked into installing malware. Since the time of the Koobface outbreak—and others like it—researchers have discerned some factors that influence a person's likelihood of falling prey to warnings that pop up on the computer screen. Often, these fake computer updates rely on the fact that people make quick judgments based on fear or panic; this is called the affect heuristic. For instance, some computer users may become alarmed at this message (used in a real study):

> An update to Abode Flash Player is available. This update includes critical improvements to online security and stablity. Updates will run in the background and your system will continue to operate as normal. Please press accept to download these updates. (Accept) button, (Cancel) button. Further support can be found at http://abode.com/support (Williams, Morgan, & Joinson, 2017)

Would you click on the Accept button? This message contains typographic errors designed to represent how an attacker's message might appear. When people have the luxury of carefully attending to the messages, then they are less likely to click on the button compared to a genuine update message. But when people are put under mental pressure, the outcome changes. If people are engaged in a simultaneous, demanding task—like using their memories—they are just as likely to click on the accept button in the fake message as they are in the genuine message. In other words, the pressure induced by doing something else at the same time made people switch from careful attention to using the affect heuristic to respond to the message.

INDIVIDUALIZED ATTACKS

Providing personal information on social media sites can lead to individualized attacks. For example, cyberstalkers use personal information, posted publicly, to locate their victims in real life. Grooming is often a fundamental part of individualized online attacks. On the one hand, social grooming serves an important, positive role in everyday life. An example of social grooming in healthy relationships is a statement of love from one person to another. Messages of love can be transmitted in various electronic forms, including text messages and instant messaging. In a study of text messages sent and received in Norway, one example grooming message was the message, "Good that it went so well with your math exam. You are smart, Love grandma" (Ling, 2005). One way to recognize grooming messages on SMS is to notice that they do not involve some of the typical topics seen in text messaging communications. They do not involve planning of events or meetings, they do not involve coordinating activities between two people, and they often do not involve any replies. As one researcher describes them, grooming messages are ". . . in essence small gifts from one person to another" (Ling, 2005). One research team defines social grooming as ". . . communication attention to ties that serves to reinforce social bonds" (Bayer, Ellison, Schoenebeck, & Falk, 2016), while another team defines it as, "activities that signal attention, build trust, and create expectations of reciprocal attention" (Ellison, Vitak, Gray, & Lampe, 2014). The positive, uplifting messages that are part of social grooming represent only one aspect of the process. The frequency of interactions and the lengths of the messages also promote social bonding. In other words, stronger relationships are associated with positive, frequent, and relatively long communications between two people. Social grooming can be used to build close relationships with other people, and also to maintain far relationships at minimal levels, such as keeping in touch with old friends. Social networking sites make excellent venues for social grooming. The tools that are built into social networking sites allow users to craft, send, and receive messages that are part and parcel with social grooming. It is easy to find one's friends and family members, making it a quick place to send a positive, uplifting message. The newest technologies are used by people to socially groom. Snapchat, for example, allows short, transitory messages between individuals that are perfect for social grooming.

On the other hand, this may benefit strangers or acquaintances who are doing social grooming for illicit purposes. Attackers and criminals can use social grooming to effectively achieve goals that require long-term contact with victims. For instance, sexual predators—people who target other people online for sexual victimization—may have the ultimate goal of obtaining semi-nude or nude pictures and videos of the victims. Pedophiles are sexual predators who prey on children. As soon as the Internet reached widespread levels of use in the general population in the 1990s, pedophiles began using it to form relationships with children. Scientists started labelling this activity in the research literature in the early 2000s and looking for the characteristics of the Internet, of young people, and of cultural and social settings that contribute to social grooming by pedophiles. Through a long social grooming process, pedophiles may initiate sexting—exchanging messages that contain explicit text, photos, and videos—with the child victims. And sexual predators can use sexting as part of the social grooming process. Social grooming is a slow process that builds from small gifts and favors to much larger, and possibly reprehensible, acts. After setting up a sexting relationship with a youth, a predator might then move on to initiating actual, physical sexual acts with the child.

Loneliness would seem like a risk factor for becoming prey for malicious social grooming. Wouldn't a lonely person be desperate for online contact from other people, even strangers? People who are socially isolated, feel alienated from others, or who are lonely may be more likely than others to become victims of nefarious social grooming because of their need for attention from others, though, in fact, loneliness is not found to be a risk factor in all studies. Research with young people shows that a big risk factor for online social grooming is having a history of prior sexual abuse. In a very extensive review of the published literature by researchers in the United Kingdom, it was found that certain factors increase the chances that a young person will be the victim of online social grooming. Some of the factors are fixed: being a female, being an adolescent, and having a disability. Other factors may change over time: questioning one's sexuality, having low self-esteem, and having mental health problems. The home environment and parenting also can make a difference. When parents monitor what their children do online, the chances of victimization are reduced. Additionally, having a supportive relationship with one's parents promotes safety, while having conflict with one's parents increases the risk level for victimization. Young people who have high levels of Internet access, little parental involvement, and engage in risky online behavior (e.g., excessive self-disclosure) are making themselves more likely than others to be victims of social grooming. In summary, there may be two broad types of people, especially young people, who are potential victims of social grooming. One type is confident and extroverted, engaging in a lot of online social activities. They also are risk takers, posting information about themselves online and sharing that information in public forums. The other type includes people who have low self-esteem and low self-confidence. The latter group also may suffer from some kind of loneliness.

Human traffickers also use the Internet to find victims. The goal of traffickers is to find individuals, mostly young people and women, who are forced or sold into slavery, indentured servitude, or prostitution. Online social grooming is a technique known to be used by the traffickers. So people who have the risk factors for being groomed online also have risk factors for become the victim of human traffickers. And the online romance scam is one well-studied type of individualized attack. Like the catfishing described in the next chapter (Chapter 4), perpetrators of online romance scams use social grooming to build relationships with their victims over time. The relationships are often built upon faked information. Unlike catfishing, online romance scams are designed to trick victims into turning over money or other resources to the perpetrators. The profile photo of the perpetrator—the very first piece of visual information that a victim will see—is one kind of faked information. Online scammers steal photos from the Internet, often using attractive and flattering images of other people. The pleasing effect of the photos is the initial step in building trust with the victim. And these scammers are patient. It can take six to eight months of social grooming to build a relationship before the scammers start to profit from the relationship. There are different levels of trust that these relationships pass through. Initially, the criminal may make flattering statements, post additional pleasing photos, and provide small gifts to the victim. As trust deepens, the relationship becomes more personal, with the victim sharing more and more private information. At its deepest point, the relationship may make the victim feel comfortable enough to share secrets with the perpetrator. This is the point at which the relationship has become hyper-personal, and the point at which the victim is most vulnerable. The recurring pattern in many online romance scams has allowed researchers to build a model of the typical scam. The scammers persuasive techniques model includes several stages. In the early stage, the scammer declares his or her love for the victim and moves the online discussions from public forums to private channels (for example, instant messaging). As the relationship becomes deeper, and as the victims start to tell secrets about themselves, the scammer tests the strength of the relationship by asking for small gifts from the victim. If the relationship passes this test, then the scammer is free to execute one of several different criminal activities. In one kind of activity, the scammer will have a co-conspirator call the victim asking for money because a loved one is in the hospital. In another kind, the scammer will manipulate the victim into handling illegally obtained funds, that is, they will get the victim involved in money laundering. Asking the victim for naked pictures or to perform sexual acts in front of the webcam is another potential kind of activity. These images and videos can then be sold online or can be used in a second level of victimization by blackmailing the victim into even more activities. The scammers and cybercriminals are not lone individuals carrying out online crimes. They can be part of large, well-organized criminal gangs that operate worldwide. Researchers who study online romance scams have shown that there are large scam networks within which many individuals each have different roles in the criminal acts. Executors speak foreign languages and write flirtatious messages; these individuals carry out the main contacts with victims. Enforcers use emotional blackmail and extortion to ensure that the victims do the acts that are asked of them. If a victim refuses to comply, the enforcer might respond with messages like, "You don't have any feelings for me," "I thought we had a real relationship here," or "You're heartless." Money movers collect the money from the victims, and money mules physically go to wire transfer stations (e.g., Western Union) to pick up delivered funds.

CONCLUSION

Unfortunately, humans have a natural affinity for being cruel or mean to others. The Internet and other forms of modern technology opened the door for new forms of aggression, between individuals and toward large groups of people. Being behind a screen provides anonymity and psychological distance that contributes to cyberbullying, cyberstalking, phishing, online romance scams, and other undesirable behaviors. These aggressive behaviors can have catastrophic consequences for the victims, including suicide or loss of substantial amounts of money. At the same time, there are behaviors and attitudes like trust and distraction—as well as psychological characteristics like loneliness—that increase the chances of becoming a victim. Young people can be the most vulnerable because they are very likely to want to share their personal information online or with strangers as part of the natural course of psychological development. The effectiveness of social engineering in bringing about online scams and the natural human susceptibility to social grooming demonstrate how social relationships are an inherently important part of all humans' existence, even when we risk being taken advantage of. There is perhaps no more important type of social relationship than the romantic one—intrinsically tied to sexual relationships—for humans. And the subset of humans that includes adolescents and young adults are most actively engaged in pursuing romantic and sexual relationships, even in the virtual world and through other ICT such as phones. These types of relationships are explored in Chapter 4.

Interview with an Expert: Dr. Robin Kowalski

Dr. Robin Kowalski is a professor of psychology at Clemson University who holds a PhD in social psychology. She does scientific research into the topic of aversive interpersonal behaviors. Her research areas include the subtopics of complaining, teasing, and bullying. She garnered significant attention in the media for her research on complaining. Her research recently has focused on cyberbullying. In addition to publishing numerous articles in scientific journals, Dr. Kowalski has authored or co-authored five books on issues related to her research area. One of the products of her work in the area of cyberbullying was the book *Cyberbullying: Bullying in the Digital Age*. Dr. Kowalski does significant outreach into the community regarding online bullying. Part of her outreach efforts involves a website she authored with two other professionals in the field of cyberbullying. At CyberBullyHelp (cyberbullyhelp .com), visitors can get assistance at a Help Center, arrange for training and presentations by cyberbullying experts, and access several important resources about cyberbullying. The website defines cyberbullying as ". . . the use of information or electronic communication technologies to bully others." It calls for parents, educators, and students to be involved in the prevention of cyberbullying.

Q: What got you interested in this field?

A: For years, I had done research on prosocial teasing, cruel teasing, and bullying. A little over a decade ago, the realization hit that bullying was beginning to assume a new form (electronic aggression), so it was only natural that my research move in that direction. Combined with that, I have twin sons who have developed along with both the technology and the field of cyberbullying. So much of what we learned as researchers (e.g., don't share your passwords), I, of course, passed along as a parent. It's fascinating to see the application of research to the real world, particularly within my own home as I have tried to educate my own children on the costs and benefits of being online.

Q: Where and why does cyberbullying occur?

A: There is clearly a relationship between time spent online and the probability of being involved in cyberbullying (although other risk and protective factors are involved as well). The most likely locations for cyberbullying to occur depend on the most popular technology in use by individuals of a particular age group at a particular time. For example, currently, elementary school youth are more likely to be victims of cyberbullying via online games. Middle and high school students, however, are more likely to experience cyberbullying victimization on social media platforms, such as Facebook and Instagram. There is nothing magical about these locations. They are simply the "places" where people are spending their time online and, thus, where they are most likely to be cyberbullied and to cyberbully.

There are many methods and venues by which people can engage in cyberbullying. Nancy Willard has created a very useful taxonomy that reflects the most common methods by which cyberbullying can occur including flaming, outing and trickery (getting someone to disclose information that they would not like shared with others and then disseminating that information online), exclusion (e.g., blocking people online), harassment, denigration, and impersonation. The venues by which cyberbullying can occur include any technological medium including emails, instant messaging, chat rooms, websites, social media, and cellular phones. Which venue is used depends largely on the age of the sample being discussed.

Q: In your research, how often do you find incidences of cyberbullying? Does the prevalence rate differ depending upon the population being studied?

A: Even within my own research, the prevalence rates have varied, depending on the gender, racial, and age composition of the sample being investigated. The same is true for the field more broadly. On average, however, prevalence rates of victimization are around 15 to 20 percent and rates of perpetration 8 to 10 percent. I've been surprised that prevalence rates aren't higher than they are. I'm happy that they are not, but I'm also a little suspicious and wonder if perhaps some respondents are not properly identifying the behavior as cyberbullying.

Q: What do you think is the connection between online bullying and suicide?

A: I don't believe that any suicide is singly determined. I believe that all suicides stem from multiple factors and those that are related to cyberbullying are no exception. We hear a lot about this issue because of the media attention that is directed toward cyberbullying cases that involve suicide. And, indeed, some instances of cyberbullying do result in a suicide. But rather than viewing cyberbullying as the immediate cause, I would view cyberbullying as more of the tipping point. Many individuals who commit suicide after having been cyberbullied have also had a long history of having been traditionally bullied, and also often have a history of psychological problems.

Q: Where will the field be in 5–10 years?

A: What I would say is that we still have so much to learn and clarify about the topic. For example, prevalence rates are highly variable across studies, depending on so many different variables such as the definition of cyberbullying provided, the composition of the sample and the liberal versus conservative criterion used to determine whether electronic aggression has actually occurred. Coming up with a more universally accepted definition of cyberbullying would facilitate the entire research endeavor. Second, a more thorough understanding of the relationship between traditional bullying and cyberbullying would elucidate the unique contributions of each type of bullying to the negative outcomes that accompany both. This is important when discussing prevention and intervention efforts.

Initially, I believe research (my own and that of others) will expand into age groups that have received insufficient attention, namely elementary school age youth and working adults. In addition, as technology changes, so will the research on cyberbullying. So, the field will have to be ever ready to adapt to technological advances. Finally, I believe we will see increasing collaboration across fields, such as psychology and computer science, as people in those respective fields combine their expertise to try to develop methods of cyberbullying detection.

Q: What practical advice would you give to a person going online?

A: Think before you act. Don't send any type of online communication or respond to any online communication without thinking about that communication first.

4

Dating and Sexual Behavior

Case Study: When You Accidentally Hook a "Catfish"

Meeting people online for dating and romantic purposes is now rather common. However, that does not mean that there are no pitfalls associated with it. The normal pattern of online dating is to engage in a short period of online interactions that lead to a real, face-to-face date. But what if the online interactions go on and on, never leading to that first in-person date? Could the person on the other end of the interactions be lying about who he or she is, and avoiding a face-to-face meeting for that reason?

The answer, of course, is yes, and the experience of being fooled into believing that an online relationship is with an individual personified in the online interactions is called "catfishing." The term itself has made it into the Oxford dictionary as to "lure [someone] into a relationship by means of a fictional online persona." Other key components of catfishing are that the recipient of catfishing is tricked, the relationship is of an emotional or romantic nature, and the relationship extends over time. To understand more fully what catfishing is, it is instructive to review the story of Yaniv "Nev" Schulman, an American photographer whose online relationship experience brought the phenomenon to light and gave it a name.

Nev received an online request from an admirer who wanted to make a painting from one of his photographs. Through online exchanges, Nev eventually met the older sister of the admirer and fell in love with her. As the relationship continued, Nev began to suspect that something was not quite right about the older sister, Megan. Through small signs and gut feeling, the persona of Megan did not appear to be entirely authentic and material used in the online exchanges pointed to being fabricated or manipulated. In one case, for example, a recording of Megan singing at home was suspected to be the voice of a well-known pop star. At the same time, Nev's brother and a colleague started to film Nev's life and eventually turned the images and recordings into the documentary, *Catfish*, released in the United States in 2010.

Nev endeavored to get to the bottom of the story, finally discovering the truth about Megan. In Nev's own words: "It turns out she was not the 'hot,' 19-year-old girl she presented herself to be, and was actually, sort of a, troubled, 40-year old mom, instead." When Nev was able to meet the lady pretending to be Megan, he also met the lady's husband, a fisherman. The fisherman told a story of how catfish used to be put into containers of live fish to keep the live fish active while being transported over long distances. As Nev retells the words of the fisherman, "life would be droll, boring, and dull if we didn't have someone nipping at our fins." Thus, the "catfish" is the person pretending to be someone else online. The story resonated with people around the world, since it tapped into the fears of everyday Internet users as online relationships became more common. Over the next two years, the movie was released in Canada, Europe (Finland, Ireland, Luxembourg, Netherlands, Norway, Poland, Sweden, UK), Israel, Russia, and Taiwan.

Online relationships take many forms and serve many different purposes, but online dating is an area of relationships that is important to many people around the world. Online daters are keen to the trickery used by others, for example in their online profiles, as shown in research that found that 54% of online daters believe that there is fake information in profiles. With the perception that misrepresentation in online relationships is rampant, people everywhere are looking for deeper insight into how to recognize, avoid, or overcome deceptive social encounters on the Internet. After *Catfish*, the movie, Nev created *Catfish*, the television series, as a way to explore these types of relationships in a public venue. Each episode of the TV show follows the story of a person who has been in an online relationship for a long time without having met their online partner in person. Nev aids in resolving the mystery behind the relationship, moving step-by-step through the process for the TV viewers' consumption.

Often the featured person has a gut feeling that something is not right with the relationship. Nev's clever mix of straightforward logic, wisdom gleaned from other cases, and technological know-how frequently uncovers deceptive elements of the relationship. In some cases, the real catfish looks nothing like their online photograph, is pretending to be a different age, or even sex, or is in a relationship with another person. Along the way, viewers learn how easy it is to be duped. Nev aims to provide valuable, educational information to other teens and young adults, who are the primary viewers of the show. As the show tells it, the person featured is now able to enter into a healthy relationship with another individual. With impressive skill, Nev remains non-judgmental throughout the episode. He defers to the wishes and desires of both the victim and the catfish about what will happen to the relationship now that the truth has been revealed. There even are times when the two decide to stay together to start a new relationship.

INTRODUCTION

People around the world use the Internet to find dates, romantic partners, and sexual partners. Additionally, the widespread availability of sexually explicit material (SEM) online gives Internet users access to entertainment material, as well as provides opportunities for learning about sex and sexual behavior. Educational information about sex is online too. Romantic and sexually related activities online are often motivated by the formation of one's sexual identity and sexual orientation. One of the main challenges in psychological development is to form an "identity." Identity formation has several facets, including religious orientation, political orientation, sports involvement, and hobbies. It also includes sexual identity. Adolescence is the prime period of one's life when an identity begins to take shape. There are other important tasks for adolescents to complete during this time period too, such as to become autonomous and to develop intimacy with others. Finding one's sexual identity is an active process that involves repeated interactions with others, refining one's self-presentation and self-description, and homing in on a way of defining oneself (usually culminating in a category such as woman seeking man, woman seeking woman, man seeking man, or man seeking woman). While the majority of individuals in the United States identify as heterosexual, there are those that have different sexual identities, even at a young age. Some researchers refer to a sexual "minority" that includes gay, lesbian, and bisexual identities. In one study of middle schoolers in Los Angeles, 2.7% identified as bisexual, 1.4% as homosexual, and 1% as questioning their identity or unsure of it. If a youth finds herself or himself identifying with an identity that is not the norm, there may be barriers to developing relationships based on that identity. People part of a broader category of sexual identities, referred to collectively as "LGBTQ+" (lesbian, gay, bisexual, transgender, queer), might have trouble finding others like themselves; however, the Internet could form a partial solution as it is easy to find many other people online of a variety of types. In fact, one study found that LGBTQ+ individuals were 3.4 times more likely to have met a romantic partner online in the past 12 months than non-LGBTQ+ individuals.

The formation and presentation of one's identity are influenced by certain general characteristics of the Internet, as well specific uses of personal technology. The many processes involved in establishing one's identity—sometimes referred to as "identity construction" or "identity work"—were linked to adolescence by influential figures in psychology, such as Erik Erikson. Self-disclosure and risk-taking are important steps in identity formation, including a sexual identity. Sexual experimentation can be risky, but may be necessarily so. The Internet provides a few mechanisms that allow people to explore and shape their identities online or "behind the screen." Three of the general characteristics of the Internet that contribute to its influence on identity work are its around-the-clock availability, its anonymity, and its affordability. Collectively known as the Triple-A Engine, these characteristics drive many Internet behaviors, including self-disclosure. The ability to carefully craft one's online persona, to experiment anonymously online, and to interact with numerous others might also allow people to explore their identities in many ways, like trying out different personalities online. Early researchers who studied the world of the Internet, like Sherry Turkle at the Massachusetts Institute of Technology, famously touted the Internet as the "great liberator" for the disadvantaged (perhaps sexual minorities), but the scientific studies since then have not fully supported this grand vision. For example, at a major dating website in the United States, Match.com, people who are partly white (i.e., partly Caucasian) are less likely to date outside of their ethnic category than other people, consistent with a real-life racial system putting white people at the top of an order and other ethnic groups below them.

Specific technologies affect or influence the identity formation process. In the world of online dating, for instance, a person can manipulate the text and images in a dating profile as a "filtering" process for finding people with specific sexual identities or preferences. Sexting—another example—is seen by many as a safe space to express one's sexual identity or to experiment with new sexual identities. And online social networks can be used to find intimate partners, taking advantage of access to a great many potential dates. However, the great promise of exploring alternate sexualities has been shown to be hampered by the fact that the rigid social networks that exist offline are mostly the same ones that exist online.

ROMANCE

Most people worry about the impression they make on others. Interacting with other people requires putting together an outward image, or "self-presentation," part of which is deciding what personal information to disclose, and how much to disclose. Whether in person or online, impression management involves constant tinkering with one's outward impression by changing the words one uses, the physical appearance one takes, the ideas that one expresses, and the behaviors that one shows. Self-disclosure is the process and act of revealing information about oneself to others. When a person self-discloses, she usually has a reason or intent (e.g., to find a date) that guides decisions about how honest to be, how many interactions to have with any one person or group, and whether to share positive or negative information about herself.

The online world changes this process in particular ways, leading to interesting outcomes. When a person goes online, or is behind a screen, there are few physical cues to her identity compared to when she meets someone face-to-face. While physical cues can be very important in developing real-world relationships, the lack of physical cues in the online world makes other information—such as self-disclosure—more important. This leads to greater self-disclosure. This phenomenon is one of several that have driven scientists to give online communication unique names compared to offline communication: computer-mediated communication (CMC) or computer-mediated relating (CMR). Another difference between CMC and face-to-face communication is that trust is necessary for people to share private information about themselves in the real world but not so much in the online world. In the online world, people disclose more when there are not time constraints, for instance during a relationship that unfolds over days or months. For most people, the ultimate goal of self-presentation is to make a favorable impression upon others, but research shows that longer lasting friendships develop when there is authentic and honest self-disclosure between people. While self-disclosure is an important part of identity development and impression management, it also carries risks. For instance, youths who share personal sexual information online may be a greater risk than others of receiving disturbing sexual solicitations online, or they may be more likely to meet a stranger in the offline world.

One place where self-disclosure is critical to success is online dating. The perception of online dating used to be that it was limited to people who have had trouble finding romantic partners in real life. The fact is that approximately one-third of the new romantic relationships in the United States start online. In short, the Internet has become one of the places where romance seekers find partners, and has probably lessened the importance of family, school, the neighborhood, friends, and the workplace in finding them. However, it is true that some social groups benefit more from Internet dating that other groups. For instance, people seeking partners of the same sex gain more from online dating than others, possibly because it is harder to find others of the same sexual orientation in real life. Men are more likely to use online sites for meeting others than women, and they are also more likely than women to use the sites to find sexual partners. Women are more likely than men to use these sites to be social. Those daters looking to start online and then move offline with their relationships—the mixed-mode relationships—were found to share long-term offline goals that included long-term dating, establishing a committed relationship with one person, and finding a lifelong or marriage partner. Early research into Match.com users found that these long-term thinkers perceived themselves to be relatively successful online, perhaps because they self-disclosed more frequently and honestly, leading to early detection of "deal breakers" (information that would make you reject a potential date) before initiating an offline date. Finally, certain psychological factors also affect one's likelihood of using Internet dating. For example, some people are more sensitive to rejection than others, and a person's level of "rejection sensitivity" predicts the use of online dating sites, with those people high in rejection sensitivity being more likely than others.

If the goal in using a dating website is to secure a date or to find a partner, then there are certain tactics that have been found to be most successful. A wide body of research into online dating has been conducted and the results are relevant to getting a first date with a partner. One of the advantages of the online world, compared to the real world, when it comes to dating is that there is an opportunity in the online world for greater selectivity in how a person presents herself. This opportunity provided by the Internet is referred to as selective self-presentation. Using certain words in messages to potential dates is important. Strong emotional words make a positive impression on the potential date, and also increase the chances of being selected for a date. Research clearly shows that, for most online daters, selective self-presentation is balanced by guiding beliefs about how one should behave toward others. These beliefs, or ethos, limit what online daters are willing to say and do online when seeking partners. It is not uncommon for those seeking dates to embellish their written online profiles in an attempt to increase their success at dating; however, most embellishments are carefully written so as not to create the appearance of obvious deception. Another way to improve the odds of success at online dating relates to the selection of photos that are used in dating profiles. As with the words that are used in messages and profiles, a significant portion of online daters—about a third—use photos that are inaccurate in an attempt to increase their physical attractiveness. But as with words, the photos tend not to be so obviously enhanced that the user would be judged as deceptive. Another reason why online daters will not overly embellish their profiles is that they want to tell themselves that they are virtuous persons—not liars or cheaters. This idea has been called a self-concept perspective on how daters' behaviors are constrained: daters want the internal reward of being a good person, irrespective of what other people might think of them.

With the variety of online sites available for dating, it is easy for just about anyone to participate as a user. In fact, the proliferation of dating sites or dating applications has led to a large number of people meeting romantic partners online. In America, less than 1 percent of couples met each online prior to 1979; by 2007–2009, the percentage had grown to over 20%. Further, a number of these individuals are interested in long-term relationships. Among Match.com users, for example, the typical user finds long-term relationships to be an important reason for using the site. Although dating websites often claim that a person is more likely to achieve a positive romantic outcome using their websites than in the real world, scientists have found these claims to be offered without being backed up by credible evidence.

As a user, a person has access to very large numbers of other users' profiles, but the profiles cannot capture the true essence of a person. Also, although the sites claim to help users find compatible partners, not enough is known scientifically about what makes one couple more compatible than another couple to be of practical use in online dating. On the other hand, the communication tools that are built into dating websites and apps provide a potentially effective means of establishing a relationship that can lead to a real-world encounter.

The possibility of finding a happy, long-term relationship online has been disputed by some researchers who subscribe to the "liquid love concept." According to this concept, the virtual world has changed relationship formation in a way that focuses more on the superficial aspects of relationships, for example, one's profile picture, because of the shopping-like experience of using an online dating system. One paper succinctly defined liquid love this way: "relationship formation is constructed as individualistic activity based on rational choice—with love only a few mouse-clicks (and a small financial investment) away" (Barraket & Henry-Waring, 2008). It is argued that it is difficult to find a deep level of intimacy with a person under these conditions. Indeed, in-depth interviews with people who use online dating systems has revealed many problems that people experience due to this relatively shallow way of evaluating others. At the same time, online daters report that they have experiences of a deeper nature, called "pure" or "ideal" relationships by some researchers, when an online relationship becomes a face-to-face relationship. The reason this might happen is that online interaction with potential mates often speeds up the processing of meeting people and then reflecting upon one's dating experiences, possibly improving the chances of a successful long-term outcome. Many of the experiences of online daters appear to be universal, because the same themes emerge both in the United States and outside it, for example in studies done in Australia and Mauritius.

Some researchers have set out to use publicly available data to assess how well online dating leads to successful relationships. In one study in the United States, more than 19,000 people who were married between 2005 and 2012 were studied. The study found that couples that first met online had slightly more marital satisfaction than couples who did not meet online, and that the former couples also had slightly less chances of marital breakup. In another study based in the United States, data from more than 3,000 adults showed that meeting online did not significantly change the chances of breaking up after one year compared to meeting offline.

SEXTING

Sexting is linked to romance as well. There are many forms of sexting, with different meanings depending upon who is involved, adults or adolescents. While it is possible to give a very general definition of sexting, it is also helpful to think of sexting as a collection of different behaviors that are loosely related. A broad definition of sexting, provided by Dr. Michelle Drouin, the expert interviewed for this chapter, is that sexting is "the transmission of sexually explicit material via text or Internet messages." Sexting can include written messages, photos, or videos, and may include material that is sexually suggestive, seminude, or nude. These messages, called sexts, are self-produced and usually distributed by the persons that make them. The photos or videos usually are of intimate body parts, masturbation, and sexual intercourse. Also, when sexting is meant to shame or harm another person, then it is considered a form of cyberbullying. This type of sexting could include sending messages depicting someone without that person's consent or sending messages or images that portray a person in a negative light.

As more and more teenagers owned cell phones, sending and receiving sexts became more popular. At the same time, sexting among teenagers has sometimes been interpreted as illegal child pornography, and other times as simply dangerous (for example, when teens are sexting with adults). The legal system first started scrutinizing sexting by teenagers in 2007, when it was seen as overlapping with pornography. A well-known national survey of teenagers in the United States around the same time found that around 26% of teens had sent a sext (then defined as a nude or semi-nude pictures or videos of himself or herself). With respect to adolescents, sexting that involves an intent to harm another person, substantial recklessness, or an adult has been described as "aggravated," while sexting that involves part of normal adolescent development—for instance, sexual identity work—has been described as "experimental."

The behaviors that are considered to be sexting also depend upon how the behaviors are measured. In truth, there is no uniform definition of sexting, so the research that is done on the topic should be interpreted with respect to how sexting was measured in each study, a concept known as the operational definition of sexting. The most common way to measure sexting is to ask people to self-report, that is, to reflect upon their experiences and share them with the experimenters. Two example self-report questions are:

- Has anyone ever sent you naked or nearly naked photos or videos of themselves?
- Have you ever sent a sexually suggestive text or instant message, for example, sexting? (Davis, Powell, Gordon, & Kershaw, 2016)

Counting up how many people sext—known as the prevalence rate—is not an easy task, and it started with some simple research on what was then an emerging phenomenon. To be most informative, prevalence rates must be broken down into different groups by age (adolescents versus adults) and the particular acts or behaviors related to sexting. When looking at prevalence rates across wide age groups, researchers find a clear split between youths and adults. Because of growing concerns about what young people were doing online or behind a screen, early studies of sexting targeted preteens, teens, and young adults. These studies looked at large samples of Americans, meaning more than 1,000 participants in each sample. Intrigued by the topic of digital media use in young people (defined as 14 to 24 years old), the famous American television channel, Music Television (MTV), partnered with the worldwide news agency, Associated Press (AP), to assess what was going on. The results, published in 2009, were very interesting, showing the beginning patterns of sexting: 3 out of every 10 young people had been involved in some way with sexting, 1 in 10 had shared a sext of himself or herself, and females were more likely than males to have done so. Another early study, also published in 2009, used a nationally representative sample of American teenagers, which means that the researchers collected data from teens of all backgrounds. What the survey found was that receiving images was more popular than sending them (15% versus 4%) and that older teens were more likely than younger teens to have done both.

In a more recent review of sexting rates in youths, broken down by particular aspects of sexting, one set of authors inferred the following pattern:

- creating and sending sexts, 18%–28% prevalence rate in older youths (1.3–2.5% in all youths);
- receiving sexts, twice as high as rates for creating and sending texts;
- being asked to make and send a sext, 68% for girls, 42% for boys; and
- forwarding or sharing sexts, 21% for older girls, 27% for older boys.

For the most part, the rates tend to be higher among sexually active groups; thus, older adolescents and young adults show the highest prevalence rates of all of the age groups. In the United States, only 6% of teens have had sex by age 15, but by age 19, 71% of people have done so. When it comes to adults—defined as people who are 18 years old or older—the prevalence rates match what one would expect based on sexual activity: younger adults do more sexting than older adults. One study found that 13% of 18- to 29-year-olds had sent sexts, while only 5% of 30- to 49-year-olds had done so. Among young adults, most sexting is with people that they already know, but about 15% of young adults have sent intimate content to a stranger. However, research also shows that sexting is on the rise among adults on the whole. Over the short period of 2012–2014, there was a 6% increase in sending sexts and a 15% rise in the number of people who had received sexts.

The term "sexting" originally was used to describe *text messages* containing sexually suggestive or explicit content. But many researchers now use to the term to refer to the sending and receiving of such content on any form of social technology, even though text messaging still appears to be the preferred choice of medium. One recent study found that 79% of U.S. college students had sent a racy text and 50% had sent a sex-related picture or video via text messaging. The range of media used for sexting includes text messaging as well as social media platforms, instant messaging, and email. One recent example is Snapchat, a phone-based application that people use to send pictures and videos to each other. In Snapchat, the messages are not permanent; they disappear from the recipient's screen after a brief period of time. This makes Snapchat an ideal piece of software for sharing messages that the sender wishes not to share with anyone other than the recipient. Not surprisingly, Snapchat has become a prominent source for sexting.

There is sufficient evidence from research studies, including studies that look at adolescents' sexting behavior over time, to conclude that sexting and sexual behavior are linked. Tracking people over time helps to deal with the "correlation does not imply causation" problem in social science research. Consider a hypothetical research project in which a scientist asks 1,000 junior high school students to report how much they have sexted in the past 3 months, as well as what sexual behaviors they have engaged in during that time period. The scientist might find that those students who have done relatively more sexting are also the ones who have engaged in sex-related behaviors like intercourse. However, it would be wrong for the researcher to conclude that sexting leads to intercourse. It would be wrong because both behaviors occurred at the same time. This is known as cross-sectional research. It may well be, for instance, that having sexual intercourse leads to sexting. For example, sexting might be part of the natural, emotional, aftereffect of having sexual relations with a person. Another possible explanation for the link between sexting and sex could be that there is another factor influencing the results, like impulsiveness. Preteens who are impulsive may be more likely to both sext and to have intercourse. This other factor is known as the third variable. The longitudinal research design gives researchers a way to partially overcome these problems.

Researchers in Texas have tracked high school sexters over time—sometimes, as long as 6 years—to see whether sexting is a precursor to other sex-related behaviors. These longitudinal studies show that sexting is indeed linked to sex-related behaviors in adolescents. One study found that students who had sexted were more likely to also have already begun dating and to have had sex. In another of the studies, the high school students who had sexted were more likely to engage in sexual intercourse the following year, noting that it may be a normal pattern in relationships where "sexting may serve as a prelude or gateway behavior to actual sexual behaviors, or as a way to indicate one's readiness to take intimacy to the next level" (Temple & Choi, 2014).

A separate question is whether sexting is part of normal sexual development (the normalcy discourse) or whether it also represents teenagers who engage in risky sexual behaviors (the deviance discourse). Enough research on the topic has been done to warrant literature reviews—formal summaries of what's known about a scientific topic done by experts. In one recent literature review on sexting, the author noted that most of the published work on the topic connected sexting to risky sexual behavior, rather than being part of the normal sexual development of adolescents and young adults. The author framed the normalcy discourse as sexting being normal intimate communication for people who are "exploring and growing into adult relationships" (Döring, 2014). Another recent literature review noted that those who sext the most also happen to be the ones who are beginning to engage in sexual behavior: while only 6% of teens have had sex by age 15, 71% have had sex by age 19.

Unfortunately, there is also sufficient evidence to conclude that sexting is, in fact, connected to risky sexual behavior in adolescents. In teenagers, research has found that sexting is associated with anal sex, having four or more sex partners, not using contraception during the last intercourse, and being forced into sexual intercourse. Into young adulthood, a possible link between sexting and risky sexual behavior continues. Undergraduate students in the United States have been found to show connections between sexting and engaging in unprotected sex. In young adults, other studies have found links between sexting and having more casual sex partners, having more unprotected sex, and having sex while using illicit substances. However, in these slightly older young people, those aged 18 to 24, the link between sexting and risky behavior may be weaker than in adolescents. Even then, there is evidence that sexting is linked to such behaviors. In a national sample of more than 3,000 U.S. young adults, researchers compared people who did not sext (the "nonsexters") to people who only received sexts (the "receivers") and people who both send and received sexts (the "two-way sexters"). For nonsexters, the proportion of their sexual partners with whom they had unprotected vaginal sex was 0.24 (24%), a fairly high number. But for the receivers and two-way sexters, the numbers were higher: 0.25 and 0.30, respectively. For the other risky sexual behavior in that study—unprotected anal sex—the numbers were 0.04, 0.06, and 0.10, for the nonsexters, receives, and two-ways sexters. Despite not passing the scientists' tests for statistical significance (i.e., they might not be reliable figures), these results clearly show a pattern supporting an association between sexting and risky sexual behavior.

SEXUAL KNOWLEDGE AND INTERCOURSE

Sexting allows for people to share personal, private sexual information about each other, but many people also are looking for general sexually related materials. It has been known for a long time that people, and youths in particular, learn information about sex from TV and film that is biased in its positive portrayal of sexual events. Research in the late 1980s and early 1990s found that television and film had a high rate of references to sexual behavior with very few of those references containing information about the risks or consequences of sex. Estimates suggested that the typical adolescent in America was viewing nearly 14,000 sexual references per year with only 1–2% of those references containing information about risks and/or consequences. The positive nature of the sex-related material comes about because of the lack of discussion of the risks and/or consequences of the behaviors. This potential problem of the information presented in the media applies to other types of information that teens are learning about as well, including drugs and drug-related behavior, information on HIV/AIDS, violence, and relationships. This was very disconcerting to those who worry about adolescent health, especially given the fact that teenagers have been found to get more of their sex-related information from the media than from school.

Official recommendations about how to address the problem of sexual content on television and in film had been refined by the early 2000s. Pediatric researchers recognized that youths learned about sex and sexual behavior not only from TV shows and films, but also from advertisements (e.g., ads for contraceptives). To deal with potential harm to young people from what they learned in these forums, the American Academy of Pediatrics in 2001 said that pediatricians should:

- encourage discussion between patients and their families,
- help parents and adolescents identify inappropriate portrayals in media,
- encourage the television broadcast industry to produce programming with "responsible" sexual content,
- encourage the broadcast industry to use public service announcements (PSAs),

- encourage movie theaters and video store owners to enforce ratings systems,
- encourage schools to create media education programs, and
- support further research into the topic.

Not much has changed with the advent of home computing, personal gaming, and the Internet, except that even more sexual information is available, it is searchable, and there is more interactivity with the material. American media content has long been characterized as sexually suggestive and permissive, and these descriptions also apply to content in "new media" such as video games. Sexually suggestive content includes media content that only hints at sex or sex-related behaviors, and some researchers have suggested that American television and film have the most sexually suggestive content in the Western hemisphere. The permissive stance toward sex—meaning that sex-related behaviors are encouraged or presented as risk-free—has also been found to apply to the portrayal of violence in the media. The public and governmental agencies in the United States and Canada were so worried about the portrayal of content in computer and video games that the game producers developed the Entertainment Software Ratings Board (ESRB) to give ratings to games. Games with violent or sexual content, for example, are marked as such on the packaging and there is an easy-to-access website for parents to review video games before purchasing them for their children. In the United States, researchers have found that parents use active monitoring of their children's media habits in order to counteract any unwanted messages from the media content. One of the main forms of active monitoring is discussing topics such as teen pregnancy, drugs, alcohol, and suicide as they are encountered in the media, whether it be on television or on the Internet.

Not all views of sex-related material are negative. Awareness of the powerful educational aspect of the Internet also emerged at the start of the new millennium. The Internet allowed for people—not just youths—to find sexually related material for educational use. The Internet also provided a way for people to buy and sell sexually related goods for educational purposes. Youths can learn about sex-related topics quickly online, due to the vast amount of information available and to the ease of searching online materials.

Despite the possible misinformation about sex that appears on the Internet, there are good reasons why the online realm has become a "virtual practice world" for sexual behavior. Meeting people online to make contacts leading to real-world sex is referred to as offline sex. A significant number of people use the Internet to find partners for physical sexual activities, but many also engage in virtual sex, also known as cybersex, which can take different forms. Since the late 1990s, researchers have acknowledged cybersex as a major sexually related behavior online. When researchers first wrote about the Internet as a virtual practice world, they recognized that cybersex was allowing individuals to explore their sexual fantasies, to try out new behaviors in a safe way, and to investigate sexual feelings. Early observations of how people use the Internet for sex also found that people were lurking (i.e., watching or reading about other people engaging in sex).

An important factor in the study of romance and sex online is the influence of these on a person's risky sexual behaviors. Sex and sexual behavior are accepted as normal parts of an adult's everyday life. Therefore, Internet-based or computer-based activities that contribute to normal sexual behavior are not perceived by experts to be unhealthy for adults. For instance, having frequent sexual intercourse with committed partners is linked to improved mood, a feeling of well-being, pain reduction, improved cardiovascular function, decreased stress, decreased cancer risk, and longevity. There is also a period of time in a person's development during which sexuality is emerging, typically during adolescence and early adulthood. During this time, there is a gray area between behaviors that are developmentally appropriate and those that are not. For instance, it is during this time that sexual experimentation is seen by some researchers as an expected part of growing up. Some children and adolescents do engage in sex-related behaviors such as kissing, "petting," and intercourse during this time period. In the Los Angeles Unified School District (LAUSD), it was found that 11% of middle school students had had sex by any definition (vaginal, oral, or anal sex). Nationwide in the United States, about 47% of high schoolers report having had sexual intercourse. But the potential negative effects and outcomes of these behaviors, especially intercourse, lead many scientists to conclude that any sort of sexually related behavior is risky. In the LAUSD study, 61% of the middle schoolers having sex had not used a condom, and in the nationwide study, only 59% of the students used a condom in their last sexual encounter.

There are certain behaviors that carry emotional, physical, and health-related risks at any age. Having unprotected intercourse with a person who is not a regular relationship partner is an example of one of these behaviors, as this behavior increases the chances of both infection by a sexually transmitted disease and pregnancy. Having intercourse with multiple partners is also considered a risky sexual behavior. College students who have intercourse with multiple partners experience more psychological distress than students who have only one sexual partner. This might be because having one partner is the sign of a committed and intimate relationship that reduces stress. Further, even kissing, petting, and intercourse with a committed partner can be problematic, as in the case when the activities are consensual but unwanted by one of the partners. The rates of the latter are not insignificant; of nonvirgins, the percentages of people who have engaged in unwanted but consensual sex are 27% in Japan, 34% in Russia, and 47% in the United States.

Reducing the risks associated with real-life sexual activity and offline sex, cybersex can lead to a sense of sexual empowerment that benefits one's sexual life. Two of the significant risks associated with physical sex are unwanted pregnancy and sexually transmitted diseases; cybersex (e.g., via sexting) allows sexual activity without these risks. In addition to the lack of physical risk in online sex, researchers recognized that there were other features of the Internet that made cybersex popular: the fact that cybersex is legal, the privacy of the Internet, and the low cost of Internet access. Also, for some cybersex users, there was no guilt associated with having sex with other people online while simultaneously having a physical romantic or sexual relationship with another person.

Cybersex is known to provide some of the same gratifications and pleasures as physical sex, yet in a forum that is free of obstacles such as the fear of rejection due to uncommon sexual inclinations or preferences. Other important aspects of cybersex may include the ability to collect a range of new sexual experiences and the ability to become sexually involved with a diverse range of sexual partners. Consider the possibilities of online sex, as described in early research by one prominent researcher in the psychology of the Internet:

> If a woman is curious about what it would be like to make love with another woman, she can enter the Lesbian Sex Chat room. If a Black man is curious about what it would be like to have sex with a White woman, he can enter the Black Man for White Woman chat room. If a man has a foot fetish, he can enter the Foot Fetish room to find others who share his interest. If a woman wonders what it would be like to be with an older man, she can enter the Older Men for Younger Women chat room. (Young, 2008)

There are several potential outlets for practicing sexual behavior, including sexting, and these outlets benefit from the anonymity and interactivity of the Internet. The major information medium prior to the Internet—television—did not allow any interactivity at all, so there was only the opportunity for passive consumption of sex-related material. Despite being virtual and digital, the Internet provides the interactivity that allows people to heighten their sexual experiences. For example, a sexually active woman might be able to do all of these online: exchange sexually related emails, participate in sexual chat rooms, engage in live video with a partner, and communicate online while masturbating. In addition to the lack of physical risks, cybersex as a form of sexual practice is encouraged by the anonymity of the Internet. When people are behind a screen and anonymous, whether it be a laptop screen or a phone screen, they tend to engage in riskier behaviors than they would in face-to-face settings.

However, it is important to see if online risky behavior is connected to real-world risky sexual behavior. The rates of risky sexual behavior in teens in the United States—including early intercourse—are on the decline. Rates of intercourse and pregnancy in teenagers in the United States have been declining for decades, and despite the amount of unhealthy behavior portrayed in the media, not all teenagers are "drunk, chain-smoking, anorexic, fat, or pregnant gun-toters" (Brown & Witherspoon, 2002), as one research team pointed out. For at least two decades, teenagers have been waiting longer to have intercourse for the first time and have been more likely to use condoms when having sex than in the past. At least one prominent researcher has speculated that easy access to pornographic materials has contributed to this trend. But there still is concern that media content is influencing when adolescents first have intercourse, leaving many youths who may be at risk of being negatively influenced by what they see and hear in the media. This quote sums up the concerns over sexual media content nicely:

> Do the media teach our youth that violence is an appropriate way to resolve conflict, that sexual intercourse comes before love, that only thin girls can be popular, that smoking, drinking, and using other drugs are cool? (Brown & Witherspoon, p. 153)

Several psychological mechanisms have been proposed to explain how exposure to media content can affect sexual behavior, although not all of the studies have found this connection. Media content could influence behavior through changes in knowledge and attitudes gained from viewing sex-related content. Some studies have shown that what adolescents view on television impacts their sexual behaviors. A sex-heavy TV diet is associated with the initiation of intercourse. One possible explanation of this effect is through sexual scripting theory and social learning theory, mainly that the content might contain sexual "scripts" that are learned from viewing. According to sexual scripting theory, our behaviors for sex are shaped by memories of how sex should be performed. These scripts for sex tell us who to have sex with, how to have sex, in what situations to have sex, and when it is ok to become sexually aroused. An interesting study done in Croatia with young men aged 18 to 25 years elicited the internal scripts for real-life sex and for pornographic sex from the men. The results suggested that viewing pornography shaped men's scripts for real sex to be similar to the scripts for how sex is portrayed in pornography.

A study done in the United States with more than 1,700 adolescents found a link between consuming sexual content on television and then initiating sexual intercourse one year later. It made no difference if the material viewed showed actual sexual behavior or merely included discussion of sexual behavior between characters, suggesting that the adolescents were learning through other people's descriptions of a behavior—a hallmark of social learning theory. Social learning theory would apply not only to what is seen on TV, films, or visual media content online, but also to what is heard, for example, through popular music or music videos. (One music critic described music videos as a young adolescent male's sexual fantasy, implying that they do not realistically portray sex or sex-related behavior.)

Additionally, or alternatively—there is nothing to prevent multiple mechanisms from being in play—content might provide media personalities that influence adolescents. This account, called identity simulation, is rooted in the study of how video games affect behavior. Playing graphic, violent games is associated with many types of behavioral deviance (alcohol use, cigarette smoking, aggression, delinquency, risky sex) in U.S. adolescents, possibly because the game players identify with the characters in the games who have deviant personalities and are who would be likely to engage in these behaviors.

Overall Internet use might not be a factor influencing intercourse; rather, specific, technology-related behaviors may be important. One large study in China with more than 2,000 college freshmen did not find a link between heavy, overall Internet use and sexual intercourse. In another study done in Canada, when adolescent technology use was broken down into specific types—texting, browsing the Internet, video gaming, and television—only texting was linked to sexual outcomes, a link which is described earlier in the chapter. Also, the country in which people live will also influence this relationship between technology and sexual behavior. In Switzerland, where adolescents are believed to have advanced knowledge and experience with sexuality compared to the United States, no link between viewing pornography and sexual behavior has been found.

Significant effort has been put forth in the United States to deter adolescents from engaging in risky sex and subsequent pregnancy. Risky sex includes having sex at a young age (often defined as before 15 years old), not using a condom during intercourse, and having many sexual partners (e.g., four or more). Teens and young adults are exposed to sexual media content that includes discussions and depictions of sex and pregnancy. While television is probably still a significant source for learning about sex and pregnancy, new media content also is a factor. By the early 1990s it was clear that teenagers were learning specific sex-related knowledge from television, such as the meanings of homosexuality and prostitution. In the mid- to late 1990s, it was known that more than half of teens in the United States learn about birth control and pregnancy from watching television and movies. In the mid-1990s, researchers had analyzed the content of television shows in the United States with precision. Shows that started airing around dinner time—the so-called prime-time TV shows—showed scenes of sexual behavior that rarely included any planning for sexual activity, any discussion of "safe sex," identification of the negative consequences of sexual activity (for example, pregnancy), or portrayal of the realities of being pregnant.

In addition to watching online shows and videos that include sexual content, young people are getting exposed to this content in social media platforms and using the Internet to ask their own questions and get answers about sex and pregnancy. Young people are looking online for answers to their questions because it is a relatively safe place to do so: it is less intimidating than talking to a parent or older sibling about sex, and going online can be done anonymously. The National Campaign to Prevent Teen and Unplanned Pregnancy—a longstanding non-profit organization in the United States—co-commissioned a study in 2008 to look at how sex-related attitudes and behaviors were entwined with behavior in "cyberspace" among adolescents and young adults. The basic results of the "Sex and Tech" survey showed that sending or posting sexually suggestive images, videos, and messages was a fairly common part of sexual life among teens (20% sent or posted images or videos; 39% sent or posted messages) and young adults (33% sent or posted images or videos; 59% sent or posted messages).

The sexual content in the media may influence the sexual scripts that teens and young adults form in their minds. Those exposed to this content may acquire scripts that influence how they later behave in real-life settings, although not all people may be affected equally. There is a clear theoretical path of how sexual content in the media might affect youths' behaviors, but the link between media content and pregnancy is not completely mapped out. According to one theory of how sexual scripts are formed and used—the acquisition, activation, and application model ($_3$AM)—some scripts are newly acquired by exposure to sexual content (the "acquisition" of scripts), some scripts already exist in young people's minds and are activated by sexual content (the "activation" of scripts), while media encourage both types to be used in real life (the "application" of scripts). The younger one is, and thus the less sexual experience one has, may affect how much influence sexual content in the media will have. Teens and adolescents might not realize that the sexually explicit content of pornography, for example, does not represent sex as it occurs in real-life, and they may be more at risk for incorporating pornography scripts into their own mental life.

Whether there is a definitive and critical link between media exposure and the chances of pregnancy for most adolescents may depend on many factors. While some researchers have speculated that the decline in teen pregnancies over the years in the United States is partly due to the rise of online pornography, a link between sexual media content and teen behavior in other countries is not always apparent. As pointed out earlier, other factors are at play in determining the likelihood that media exposure to sex or sex-related talk will influence adolescents' risky sexual behaviors. The large study of Swiss adolescents is a case in point: in that study, the amount of exposure to SEM did not influence the chances that an adolescent had become pregnant or made another person pregnant.

Researchers have looked at how individuals use technology to specifically seek out casual sexual relationships, a phenomenon known as hooking up. Sexting has been seen in some cases as a gateway behavior—a precursor to actual sexual behavior. Among college students, about a third report that sexting makes hooking up more likely, and a frequent motivation for sexting is to initiate real sex. It also is true that some people are using online dating as a way to find sexual partners, although there are other reasons as well. Seeking out sexual activity via technology may have a gender component, where males behave differently than females. In evolutionary psychology, the branch of psychology that tries to understand behaviors as a result of human evolution, a commonly held point of view is that men try to increase their chances of passing their genes on to offspring by having intercourse with multiple partners. This may be why men, for example, are relatively more tolerant of lying in online dating than women. The gender differences in partner seeking may be impacting college campuses in the United States, too. More college campuses than before now have an imbalance in gender makeup with women outnumbering men. The scarcity of men in the dating population gives men the opportunity to control how relationships form and what types of relationships form, with objective observers noting that hooking up is becoming more common. As one sociologist has commented, "women do not want to get left out in the cold, so they are competing for men on men's terms" (K. A. Bogle, 2010; in Williams, 2010).

Many people looking for "hook-ups" use dating websites or applications to do so. One of the benefits of using the Internet to find romantic dates is that these systems allow people to greatly expand the number of potential dates one has access to. One popular dating website, PlentyOfFish.com, claims to have 145 million monthly visitors that users will gain access to. An additional benefit of seeking love on the Internet is that a user can instantly communicate with a potential date using built-in communication systems such as instant messaging or live video software. Skype and Facetime are two popular systems for doing live video. These benefits of using the Internet to find romance also make the platforms conducive to finding partners for casual sex. Within the realm of applications on mobile devices, Tinder is an example of a dating service that has a reputation for facilitating casual sex among users. Easy-to-use features, such as the famed right-swipe motion to search through user profiles, lend to its popularity. Because of the built-in communication features of the application, this social media platform also allows for users to sext each other. Scientific research into how people use low-cost, easy-to-navigate social media and dating programs and software reveals that a significant subset of users is seeking casual sex. In one study of young adults in Holland, 19% of the people in the research sample had experienced a one-night stand (having sex and then no more contact) following a match with another user on Tinder. One of the common reasons given for using the program is to find casual sex, although the motivation to find a romantic partner is more common than casual sex. Interestingly, men are more likely than women to report that they are motivated by casual sex, and men are more likely than women to experience a one-night stand. This result is in agreement with the evolutionary psychology approach to understanding sex differences in dating behavior.

The Internet benefits people who want to hook up and stay secretive about it. Websites that cater to these people—also known as "infidelity sites"—allow users to find partners for casual sex or to have extra-relationship affairs and often have descriptive names that give away their purpose. Examples are IllicitEncounters .com, OnlineBootyCall.com, and GetItOn.com. One website that originated in North America has a name that is derived from selecting two typical-sounding American girls' names, Ashley and Madison, and combining them. In 2013, AshleyMadison.com boasted more than 21 million users, and, by the time the organization was hacked in 2015, had records for at least 36 million users from over 46 countries. At that time, 1.2 million people from the United Kingdom were signed up for the service, equivalent to about 5% of the country's married population. The original slogan of the organization was, "Life is short. Have an affair." One study of AshleyMadison users found high rates of virtual sex through texting (29%) and high rates of sexting (51%), consistent with the link between sexting and actual sex behaviors described earlier. Further, AshleyMadison users were found to have high rates of cheating on their mates in real life (74%) in addition to high rates of cheating online (64%). The theme that men are more likely to have casual affairs than women also is supported by data from the AshleyMadison website: around 70% of the members are men.

Hooking up does not necessarily mean that two people cannot also find an intimate or longer-lasting relationship at the same time. Although having a one-night stand may be the only time two people meet each other on an intimate basis, there are variations in the hooking up phenomenon that can lead to a long-term relationship. One of these variations, the "booty call," has been characterized by researchers as involved repeated sexual encounters with the same person without a romantic expectation. Apparently, this type of relationship not only meets the sexual gratification needs of men, but also can satisfy the relationship stability needs of women. An even deeper type of relationship, the "friend with benefits," occurs when two close friends add sexual intimacy to the relationship. Scientists studying this type of relationship have noted that, even in this case, men are focused on the sexual aspect of the relationship while women are focused on the emotional aspect of the relationship. In all cases, the chances that the sexual encounters will develop into a romantic relationship are improved when the sexual encounters are voluntary and not forced, when there is communication about the meaning of the sexual encounters, when the encounters generate positive emotions in the partners, and when there is a social network that supports the relationship.

PORNOGRAPHY

There is no doubt that Americans and Western Europeans view pornography online. Researchers who study online pornography tend to agree that viewing online pornography is prevalent in the United States. By the time students get to college, most of them have used online pornography. Among male college students, 93% report having viewed online pornography before they turned 18 years old. Among female college students, 62% have viewed online pornography as minors. Regular pornography viewing by adults is higher among men than women, with women showing a somewhat consistent rate of viewing sexual material in the high teens over the decades of the 1970s, 1980s, and 2000s. European studies show significant rates of viewing pornography not unlike what happens in America. Researchers in Croatia, for example, have been able to pinpoint that certain types of online pornography are especially popular. "Amateur" pornography—defined as material showing unpaid models and nonprofessional productions—is the top type of pornography viewed by men, while "threesomes" pornography—sexual acts involving exactly three people—is the top type viewed by women. In Denmark, two-thirds of adult men and nearly one-fifth of women regularly view pornography (at least once per week).

Trends show that pornography use is on the rise, most likely due to the Internet becoming commonplace in people's lives. There are several reasons for linking the Internet to the high rates of pornography viewing. Rates of pornography viewing have gone up at the same time that the Internet has become accessible, SEM is readily available online, and usage patterns show that many people use the Internet for finding pornography. The Internet has provided an explosion of pornographic materials, making access to pornography very easy for anyone, even children. The trend began in the 1990s, when SEM became widely and easily available and, in many cases, free. In the 1970s, 28% of young adults aged 18 to 30 years old in the United States regularly used pornography, but the number went up over time, reaching 34% in the 2000s. This increase is attributed to the online presence of SEM that occurred in the 1990s. A sizeable amount of Internet traffic has been attributed to pornography use. One estimate put pornography use at 13% of total Internet traffic. Technological improvements in home computing and networking contribute to making pornography even more available and accessible to all. Broadband technologies—technologies such as cable modems that allow high-speed transmission of data—allow richer, more complex, and larger data files containing pornographic material to be delivered at home to regular people. These improvements bring SEM not only to adults and older teens, but also to children. Another marker of the rise in pornography viewing is a similar rise in how much research is being done on pornography addiction.

Sexual arousal, including that for pornography, has direct links to activity in the brain. A system in the brain commonly referred to as the reward system provides a positive experience to us when we have certain experiences or show certain behaviors. In the case of sex-related behaviors, researchers have linked sexual arousal—for instance, the pleasant experience of viewing pornography—with the brain areas linked to the reward system. The reward system is important because the experiences or behaviors that get a positive, pleasant reaction are made more likely to occur again in the future. Researchers consider sexual arousal and orgasm to be highly reinforcing. When a teenager goes online, navigates to a particular site, and finds a rewarding pornographic image, those behaviors will be more likely to occur again the future.

For some individuals, sexually related activity, such as pornography viewing and cybersex, rises to the level of a compulsion or an addiction. People who overuse pornography to the point that it interferes with their work, family, or relationship commitments might be experiencing an addiction similar, in ways, to drug addictions. For these people, specific brain networks have been sketched out by scientists as being responsible for these problems. In fact, scientists who study pornography argue that both types of addiction activate the brain's reward system so much that addicts find it hard to stay away from objects that are part of the addiction, in this case pornographic images. Further studies of addiction to pornography suggest that additional brain areas might be involved. The frontal lobe, where high-level "executive control" over our behaviors takes place, could possibly be responsible for keeping our sexual impulses in check, while "craving reactions" (part of the brain's emotional response system) could be driving those impulses. In people with pornography addiction, viewing pornographic images might make it harder to control their use of SEM by reducing the functioning of the executive control areas of the brain. It was shown in one study that addicts had an approach-avoidance pattern of processing pornographic images; that is, the addicts either overused the images (approach) or they neglected the images (avoidance) when compared to those who do not have addictive tendencies. Addicts appear to show positive emotional reactions to SEM, sometimes called cue reactivity, where the pornographic images are the cues. This influence of the brain's emotion system could explain why pornography addicts show higher levels of arousal to sexual images while also reporting more everyday life problems associated with cybersex.

Not all of the research supports a parallel between pornography addicts—sometimes referred to as compulsive pornography users—and drug and alcohol addictions. For example, experimenters who measure brain activity of pornography addicts while viewing SEM do not always find the same pattern of activity that is found in other addicts. The P300 is a pattern of electrical brain activity that is detected on the scalp when people are emotionally engaged with a stimulus, such as an interesting picture. In one study, compulsive pornography users showed no more engagement with pornographic images than they did with neutral, non-sexual images. Scientists argue that more studies are needed to fully find out if the brains of pornography addicts function similarly to the brains of drug addicts.

For some technology users, problems arise due to overuse or inappropriate use of the Internet or computer-based devices. This problematic Internet use (PIU) has repeatedly been linked to viewing online pornography. In fact, viewing Internet pornography is one of the two activities most often related to PIU, with the other being gaming. In many cases, researchers use the term Internet addiction instead of the term PIU, although there also are subtle arguments between researchers over which term is best. One definition of Internet addiction is that it is "the phenomenon of excessive, uncontrolled usage of specific online-applications (e.g. online-gaming, use of online-pornography or social networking sites)" (Müller, Dreier, Beutel, Duven, Giralt, & Wölfling, 2016). Scores on tests of Internet addiction are associated with the amount of use of Internet pornography websites. Also, people with Internet addiction are often addicted to online pornography. In one study done at the Center for Internet Addiction, 39% of male addicts and 25% of female addicts were addicted to online pornography. People whose PIU involves online pornography also spend more time online that a typical person does. Researchers have suggested that Internet pornography provides stimulation and sexual arousal that is gratifying to the users. One of the possible reasons that problematic Internet users might compulsively consume pornographic material is that they are unable to imagine the future negative consequences of overuse. Another possible reason is that viewing pornography might lessen bad feelings or moods that one is experiencing. For example, job burnout or money problems can be forgotten by entering a virtual world through the computer.

Not all Internet addicts experience their addictions in the same ways. Some addicts might be addicted to pornography, others might be addicted to gaming, others might be addicted to online financial trading. While the most frequent form of addiction for men is to online pornography, the most frequent addiction for women is to chat rooms, including sex chat rooms. In light of this, specific forms of addiction have been proposed; cybersexual addiction is a form of Internet addiction that is defined as "compulsive use of adult websites for cybersex and cyberporn" (Young, Pistner, O'Mara, & Buchanan, 1999, p. 457). One way that scientists measure cybersexual addiction is to use a questionnaire that asks a person what kinds of problems he or she experiences in daily life as a result of online sexual activity or Internet sex sites. A sample question is, "How often do you find that you stay on Internet sex sites longer than you intended?" Researchers have formalized the distinction between general forms of Internet addiction and specific forms by referring to the former as Generalized Internet Addiction (GIA) and referring to the latter as Specific Internet Addiction (SIA). The causes of the two types of addiction may be different. GIA might be related to a lack of social support and to someone being socially isolated or lonely, problems for which the ability to communicate with others online provide relief. On the other hand, SIA—which includes addiction to pornography—might be related to having a need specifically related to the content of the addiction. For pornography addiction, this means that the addict would seek pornographic material in any format, online or offline.

In all cases of PIU, afflicted individuals become dependent upon their technology. Without access, addicts may become agitated, sad, depressed, or hostile. People who become cybersexual addicts often experience changes in their real-life sexual behavior, in addition to their online activities. Some addicts use the Internet to meet all of their sexual needs, replacing sexual intimacy with real-life partners; in one investigation into cybersexual addicts, it was found that 75% of the addicts preferred online pornography over engaging in normal sexual activity with a mate. Further, addicts may incur financial problems with the costs of subscribing to sex-related websites. In order to overcome the dependency, addicts must learn new behaviors, new ways of thinking, and new ways to relate to others that take them out of their virtual environments and into more constructive ones. For addicts to pornographic sites, this is not easy, and makes addiction to pornography one of the most complicated forms of addiction. Through interviews with Internet addicts, including cybersexual addicts, it has been learned that the anonymity of the Internet is a key factor in PIU. First, the feeling that one is anonymous online encourages deviant, deceptive, and criminal acts that include viewing and downloading obscene and illegal images. Second, anonymity provides the context for shy or self-conscious people to interact in a seemingly safe environment. Third, anonymity facilitates easy interactivity with others online, a necessary component of having cyberaffairs or online extramarital relationships. Fourth, anonymity allows a person to develop alternative online personas that either give a person a way to successfully interact with strangers or to justify other online behaviors.

Another component of addiction to Internet pornography might be arousal. In a laboratory study, adult males were shown pornographic images typical of what would be found on the Internet. For each image, the study participants were required to indicate how arousing they found the image, using a scale of 1 (no sexual arousal) to 7 (high sexual arousal). A person's arousal levels were related to how many problems they experienced in daily life due to online sexual activity. Hence, a high level of reaction to the sexual stimuli—known as cue reactivity—might be important in how cybersexual addiction begins and is maintained. Control over one's behavior is a frequent problem with both GIA and SIA. Addicts might not be able to stop using the Internet when they want to. Luckily for those addicts whose addiction is related to online pornography or other sex-related websites, some of the tools used to control children's behaviors online can be applied to the addiction problem. For instance, addicts can install and use "filtering" software on their devices. This software blocks access to specified websites. A simple framework for understanding the formation of Internet addictions is that it is the result of the combination of the extreme accessibility of sex-related material or other people online, the loss of personal control over technology usage, and the positive feelings associated with Internet usage.

To understand the complete cycle of how a cybersexual addiction can take hold of a person, researchers have invoked an old concept from behavioral psychology that occurs when a person takes an action that provides some kind of satisfaction. The satisfaction that is received serves as the reinforcement and makes it more likely that the person will carry out the actions again in the future. Engaging in cybersexual activity online could provide reinforcement in at least two ways. For one, the sexual stimulation that the person gets when engaging in the activity could provide a positive reinforcement that makes engaging in the activity more likely in the future. For example, the person would be likely to seek out pornographic images online in the future because it was pleasurable to do so right now. The other way is that the activity could provide a distraction from real-life problems that the person is experiencing. The distraction reduces the bad feelings that a person is experiencing at the time in a phenomenon known as negative reinforcement.

Pornography use is of special interest to researchers interested in the plight of youths. For many people, the following events will sound familiar. A UK teenager being interviewed as part of a study on online security reported having had this experience: while doing an Internet search for information about a basketball team, the teen clicked on a promising link, only to be sent to a website containing unwanted pornographic images. Another teenager in the same study reported being sent unwanted pornographic images through email. The messages were frequent enough and disturbing enough that the email account was shut down.

Worldwide, it is generally accepted that spending more time online will increase the chances that a youth will encounter pornography, whether on purpose or by accident. Not only will SEM be encountered, but also violent material, material that promotes substance abuse, racist material, and material that encourages unhealthy eating habits. In Switzerland, 47% of male adolescents and 35% of female adolescents report being accidentally exposed to pornography online. In the United States, estimates of the number of adolescent Internet users who have accidentally come across pornography while online range from 25% to 70%. Accidentally being exposed to pornography comes with an immediate cost. It makes some youths feel very uncomfortable or very upset.

The chances of a young person having been exposed to SEM go up when those youths purposefully seeking out pornography are added into the mix. For example, in the Swiss study, 74% of boys had been exposed to SEM for any reason in the month prior to the study. Boys are more likely to seek out pornography than girls; only 36% of girls had been exposed to pornography in the month prior to the Swiss study. In the United Kingdom, 57% of 9- to 19-year-olds reported having seen pornography online. Other factors put certain youths in a group that will be more likely to encounter SEM than other youths: regularly downloading music or images posted online by other people, having been victimized offline, being older, and being in a state of depression. It has been suggested that being victimized offline is a sign that a youth is either impulsive or has compromised judgment, two factors that also could explain what that youth would also be more likely than other youths to accidentally encounter SEM online.

There are ways to control a youth's exposure to unwanted or sought-after pornography. Filtering software that restricts which websites can be visited has been shown to be effective, although it is not fool-proof. One systematic test of the filtering software typically used in libraries and schools found that the software was able to block out 87% to 91% of pornographic websites, depending on the settings of the software. It turns out that having adolescents attend an online safety seminar— for instance, one offered by the local police agency—also reduces the likelihood that those youths will later find SEM online. Finally, the style of parenting matters too. Having consistent and strict rules for Internet use, being more involved in the online activities of their children, and knowing more about the types of websites that their children visit all make parents more capable of reducing the amount of pornographic material that youths are exposed to.

Online pornography may not be bad for youths all of the time. Pornography is not created to educate; it is created as a specific form of entertainment. Here is one definition of pornography among scientists:

> Pornography is . . . "any kind of material aiming at creating or enhancing sexual feelings or thoughts in the recipient and, at the same time, containing explicit exposure and/or descriptions of the genitals and clear explicit sexual acts." (Hald & Malamuth, 2008)

But, perhaps surprisingly, the proliferation of pornographic material online might be contributing positively to people's knowledge of sex and sexual behaviors. Among researchers, there is little doubt that young people must acquire knowledge and attitudes toward sex and sexual behaviors in order to become healthy, sexually responsible individuals. In other words, people are not born with the knowledge about sex that is needed to function well as an adult. By the time adolescents become young adults, there is evidence that pornography has helped to educate the youths about sex-related words, behaviors, and practices. Studies have been done of college students and young adults in the United States and European countries in which people were asked to report the influence that pornography has had on them. Across the studies, scientists have found a positive link between viewing pornography and sexual knowledge. For example, in one study, 63% of college students said that they learned about new sexual techniques from pornography. In another study, 50% of the college students said pornography was a source of information about oral and anal sex, while 43% of students learned about foreplay through pornography.

At the same time, pornography might be contributing to risky sexual behaviors in youths. Early exposure to SEM is linked to double the risk of engaging in sexual intercourse at a young age, and pornographic websites were one of several types of websites found to be associated with increased chances of an adolescent meeting a stranger face-to-face after having first met the person online. (The other types of websites were sites depicting violent or gruesome pictures and sites containing hate-related material.)

Adolescents are sometimes copying what they see in pornography in their real-life sexual behavior. This might not be so disruptive when the pornographic content involves what is considered normal, one-on-one sexual intercourse, but could be extremely unhealthy when behaviors from so-called "extreme pornography" are copied. Examples of extreme pornography include public humiliation and incest, real or portrayed. Public humiliation was deftly described by a 17-year-old female in one American study,

> Which means they tie the girl up, say on the statue or pole or something. Then they strip them down naked and a guy or girl will embarrass them in public. But the person wants it, so they ask for it . . . so they're, like, forced to do things. . . . (Rothman, Kaczmarsky, Burke, Jansen, & Baughman, 2015)

Interviews with teenagers have also found that there is pressure in some dating relationships for individuals to make their own pornography—a highly risky behavior given the discussion on sexting. Violent sexual images might also be disruptive. In young men, there is some evidence suggesting that exposure to violent pornography is related to sexually aggressive behavior, including rape. However, there is no evidence to suggest that violent pornography has widespread effects on sexual behaviors throughout a society. Psychologically, some researchers have suggested that there are certain mechanisms through which even a short exposure to extreme pornography could influence the sexual behaviors of adolescents. When, for instance, an adolescent has pre-formed ideas or beliefs about unusual or extreme sexual behavior, seeing pornographic material that confirms those ideas and beliefs could cause that behavior to become more likely through reinforcement.

In the United States, it should be kept in mind that the rate of teen pregnancy has been declining for years, as established by official government research. That has led at least one researcher to suggest that online SEM could be contributing to the decline, rather than increasing the overall rate of risky behaviors among teenagers. Another potential factor influencing how SEM affects behaviors is the cultural setting that youths come from. A large-scale study of more than 6,000 adolescents in Switzerland found almost no links between online pornography and risky sexual behaviors. In Switzerland, youths are known to have high sexual literacy rates—that is, knowledge of sexual practices and behaviors. Thus, Internet pornography would have little effect on those youths' behaviors.

How does pornography affect what people learn about sex? When people experience repeated events in life, they form ideas or concepts that capture those events in mental form. The ideas and concepts tend to contain the core essence of a type of event without the details of specific exposures to an event. For example, repeated visits to the drive-through window at a fast food restaurant might cause the creation of a fast-food drive-through memory that looks something like this:

1. Pull car up to ordering station.
2. Review menu while waiting for employee to contact you through intercom system.
3. Give order to employee.
4. Pull car up to food station.
5. Give payment to employee at food station.
6. Wait for food to be passed to car.
7. Drive away.

This memory, called a schema or a script by scientists, maintains the overall structure of a visit to the fast food restaurant without keeping any of the particulars (for instance, there is no specific restaurant name or food item).

Likewise, people are presumed to form scripts for sexual behavior that guide them in their sexual experiences and encounters. Youths, lacking numerous sexual experiences, may be forming scripts based on events that are portrayed in movies, television, books, and Internet-based content, including pornography. In addition to informing and altering youths' scripts for sexual behavior, media can also be shaping sexual norms (i.e., what is considered normal and abnormal behavior) and sexual attitudes (i.e., the values placed on sex and sexual behavior)—both of which are presumed by many scientists to affect actual sexual behavior either at the time or later into adulthood. Unfortunately, when researchers have analyzed the content on pornographic websites, they have found that 55% of the sites are consistent with sexual scripts that are biased in some way, including espousing hypermasculinity—defined by one writer as "having a calloused attitude toward sex, a sensation-seeking tendency, and a tight control over emotions" (Scharrer, 2013; in Dill, 2013)—having a theme of male domination over women, and prioritizing the pleasure of men over the pleasure of women.

One way that exposure to pornography could alter sexual scripts, norms, and attitudes is through learning principles. Learning principles are processes that occur in the mind that lead to changes in thoughts and behaviors. One learning principle is reinforcement. In the case of sexual scripts, pleasure derived from exposure to pornographic images that are consistent with a budding sexual script could reinforce the sexual script and the behaviors that are associated with it. Two other aspects of learning principles are that the amount of reinforcement depends on how important or valuable the exposure to pornography is to a person, and that people learn scripts, norms, and attitudes by watching others—for example, in a pornographic video. These aspects are essential components of an approach to behavior called social cognitive theory.

These learning mechanisms in youths may be affecting how people behave later, as adults. While adults have been found to use pornography more than youths, the adults who use SEM tend to be the same individuals who used it during their youth. One piece of evidence that adults use pornography more than adolescents comes from a large-scale survey of adolescents and adults in Holland. In that study, there was no case where adolescents used SEM more than adults; whenever there was a difference between age groups, it was the case that adults used SEM more than the adolescents. There are two reasons to believe that pornography viewing habits are set in youth. One reason is that having viewed pornography as an adolescent makes a person more likely to view pornography as an adult. A Croatian study of more than 600 young men aged 18 to 25 years found that the amount of pornography viewed at 14 years of age was correlated with the amount of pornography viewed as a young adult. The other reason is that the factors that predict pornography viewing in adolescence are the same factors that predict pornography viewing in adulthood. These factors include being a male, being a "sensation seeker" (in other words, a thrill seeker), not being exclusively heterosexual, and having lower life satisfaction. One might expect youngsters to use pornography quite a bit because they are not legally allowed to use it—the forbidden-fruit effect; however, adults actually use more pornography than adolescents. The motivation to use pornography may partly be to escape from life's circumstances as suggested by how it's used by people with low life satisfaction.

Youth is a time of relatively little real sexual experience. In some cases, the lack of sexual experience might protect adolescents during exposure to the stereotypes present in SEM. For instance, the stereotype of women who put up "token" resistance to sexual advances (i.e., they say "no" when they mean "yes") is less likely to be absorbed from SEM by adolescents than by adults, perhaps because youths lack a real-life sexual reference point to process the stereotype. There is an impact of viewing pornography during this time period upon adult outcomes. Viewing paraphilic pornography—pornography that depicts sadism, masochism, fetishism, bestiality, and other infrequent types—in adulthood is more likely if a person viewed pornography as a youth. The link between early SEM viewing and paraphilic pornography has been tied back to the operation of sexual scripts. Youths who view more pornography are more likely to encounter deviant forms of pornography which, in turn, alters their views of what sex really is and what is should feel like.

This further affects intimacy in adulthood. Early viewers of pornography experience less intimacy in relationships as adults, but only in adults who view paraphilic pornography. But there does not seem to be any effect of early viewing upon sexual compulsivity (out-of-control sexual thoughts and behaviors) as an adult.

CONCLUSION

This chapter showed that the Internet has established itself as a place for meeting potential romantic partners, and thus somewhat has deemphasized traditional meeting conduits such as the family, school, the workplace, etc. But romance in the online world is different than romance in the offline world. Physical features in potential mates can become less important, and people can use software tools to carefully craft their dating profiles. In the course of building romantic and sexual relationships, sexting may become a factor. Sexting appears to be a form of normal intimate communication for people growing into adult sexual relationships, meaning sexting and sexual behavior are linked. Sexting prevalence rates tend to be higher in sexually active groups: adolescents and young adults show the highest rates. At the same time, sexting is linked to risky sexual behaviors in adolescents.

When young people go online, they are also looking for answers to their sex-related questions. Sexual information is now more prevalent, easier to access, and searchable, compared to before the Internet; however, much of the information—at least in the American media—may be permissive about risky sexual behaviors. At the same time, the Internet provides a safe place for people to explore their sexual fantasies and to investigate their sexual feelings. The interactivity of the Internet and online applications may heighten the level of engagement in online sexual behavior, or cybersex. Additionally, pornography use is on the rise, probably because of the Internet. Pornographic images provide a mental reward, or reinforcement, to those who are seeking out the images, and make the act of seeking pornography more likely to happen again. However, this can become a type of compulsion or addiction for some people. On the other hand, young people can learn about sex by viewing pornography; this may occur through the formation of sexual scripts based on media.

Interview with an Expert: Dr. Michelle Drouin

A developmental psychologist and professor at Indiana University-Purdue University Fort Wayne, Dr. Michelle Drouin has an extensive background in studying issues related to technology use by adolescents and young adults. Her research interests include sexting, social media, mobile phone addiction, literacy, language, and learning, and her work that has been published in scientific journals includes projects on sexting, texting and literacy, and online education, among others. She published very influential papers on how "text speak" may be influencing literacy and on how students in online classes develop a sense of community. She participated in the early debates about the effects of sexting, pointing out that sexting may have positive, in addition to negative, effects. For example, her research found that emotionally distant men might benefit from sexting as it could help to fulfill relationship needs. Dr. Drouin has called for changes to sex education in the United States, primarily to incorporate aspects of "digital sex" that involves sexting, for example. Teaching the responsible use of technology, she has argued, could lessen the problems created when people are coerced into sexting. Through her current research projects and her related professional activities, she is an active contributor to the state of knowledge in her field. She is sought by organizations as a topic expert and an expert witness. She is now collaborating on a project tracking couples over time to see how their relationships are influenced by technology. Dr. Drouin recently presented her work at the United States Marine Corps Social Media Misconduct Symposium that was convened in response to reports and accusations of gender discrimination and harassment on social media sites related to U.S. Marines.

Q: In general, what do we know about sexual behavior online?

A: In general, what we know is that as soon as we entered the online world, people started negotiating many of their social interactions online, and this includes their sexual interactions. And with the ubiquity of technology, the use of the online world for sexual interactions is ever increasing. As evidence of this, in 2012, I knew of two studies on sexting, and now I probably review ten manuscripts per year on the topic. With regard to their overall findings, most of the studies (and the media) portray online sexual behavior (e.g., sexting or cybersex) as a negative behavior, associated with risk factors and not many positive consequences. However, more recently, a number of researchers have attempted to explore the positive consequences (relational or individual) of online sexual behavior.

Q: What does research tell us about online dating?

A: More and more couples are meeting online. It has become mainstream, even among teens and young adults. In the past, online dating may have been perceived as a last-resort method for people who maybe weren't having much luck in a face-to-face environment, but now it's become so commonplace with apps like Tinder, Match.com, and Bumble that even young adults who are actively dating in the offline world are using these apps as a source of dating prospects. Additionally, a lot of relationships are started online, even with people who are known in offline contexts. Today, people can use a variety of popular social media platforms, like Facebook, to reach out to a potential dating partner and say "Hey, want to grab a drink?" This facilitates the relationship initiation phase, and many aspects of the ensuing relationship might be negotiated through online contexts, even its eventual dissolution. Thus, even though these relationships may not be considered "online dating" relationships in the traditional sense, they still may involve a lot of online dating behaviors.

Q: What do we know from research about sexting in terms of its prevalence, ensuing problems, and psychological ramifications.

A: Sexting is prevalent among both teens and young adults. As you go from the teenage years into young adulthood, it increases in prevalence, so you don't have a lot of 12-year-olds who are sexting but most 21-year-olds have at least sent sexual text messages, not necessarily videos or photographs, but most have sent sexual words. It's not as prevalent among married couples; only about 12% have ever sent a sexual picture to their partner in their lifetime. However, when you are looking at young adults you have, depending on relationship context, anywhere from 30% to 50% who have sent photos or videos to different types of romantic partners. In some of my past research, I found that young adults were more likely to send explicit images or videos to committed partners—there is more trust in committed relationships that the image won't be shared. Thus, not surprisingly, fewer people had sent explicit images to casual sexual relationship partners. That said, those statistics are a few years old now, so I would not be surprised if there were increases in the number of pictures that are being sent in these casual sexual relationships.

In one of my recent studies with Elizabeth Tobin, we found that on average, young adults had sent about 40–80 explicit sexual pictures or video messages to romantic partners in their lifetime. Men and women differed significantly in the lifetime prevalence of sending sexting pictures both in the number of partners to whom they sent pictures and the total number of pictures sent. In both cases, men sent significantly more sexual pictures than women. This may be because of a gender divide in the consequences of sexting and people's expectations of men and women's sexual behavior. Past research has shown that women may be subjected to more negative criticism when they send this type of material. There may also be more to be lost in terms of reputation when women are sending this type of material, and that has a lot to do with traditional gender roles. There is also an expectation that men will send pictures and men have to be sexual, so there are pressures on both men and women to conform to gender roles.

From a psychological perspective, the most recent research suggests that among teens, sexting seems to be a fairly common behavior. Sexting is correlated with sexual behavior, so teens that have more sex are also sexting more often, but teens who are sexting do not seem to be engaging in more risky sexual behaviors than teens who are not sexting. For example, they are not having sex with multiple partners or having sex without condoms at a higher rate than teens who do not sext. Among young adults, results are more conflicting. Some studies have shown links between sexting and risky sexual behavior, substance abuse, and psychological issues (e.g., attempted suicide or histrionic personality traits). However, there are other studies that show no differences between sexters and non-sexters on these variables.

All of this said, one of the psychological consequences of sexting that cannot be overlooked is the suicide, depression, and reputational damage that might arise from the unlawful distribution of these private images via sharing or forwarding. When these explicit photographs are used to bully or for revenge (called revenge porn), this can have severe psychological consequences for the victim, and it is also associated with stiff legal consequences for the perpetrator.

Q: Are there any groups who are more susceptible to the negative impacts of sexual content on the Internet?

A: Children are definitely susceptible to negative impacts of sexual content on the Internet. The average child or teen who is 8 to 18 spends approximately seven and a half hours interacting with media every day, and a lot of that time is likely unsupervised. Therefore, we have children who are potentially accessing pornographic material or other kinds of inappropriate sexual content. And when that's happening without a parent there to explain or contextualize the material, that's definitely something that can be potentially psychologically damaging. With regard to adults, I study Internet addiction, and in the case of Internet addicts, you often see a cluster of different types of addiction. In other words, Internet addiction can be comorbid with sexual addiction or other types of addictive behavior. In one of my recent studies with Dan Miller, Elli Hernandez, and Shaun Wehle, we found a link between Internet addiction, pornography use, and sex site visits. Moreover, when we looked at how these online behaviors related to risky sexual behaviors (i.e., intent to meet up with someone known only online for offline sexual behavior and sending sexually explicit photos of videos to those known only online), each of these online behaviors predicted engagement in risky sexual behaviors. However, pornography usage and sex site usage were serial mediators in that relationship, so it's not that Internet addiction alone is predicting these risky sexual behaviors, but when that progresses to excessive pornography use and then progresses to more active pursuit of sex online, then it leads to these other risky sexual behaviors. So, another group that I would say is more at risk or susceptible to the negative impacts of sexual content on the Internet are people who are addicted to the Internet and using pornography and sex chat sites to engage in risky sexual behavior.

Q: What practical advice would you give to an adolescent or young adult about sexual content and sexual behavior on the Internet?

A: My practical advice is to be very, very cautious. Obviously, adolescents and young adults have curiosity about their bodies and other people's bodies, and their sexuality in general. However, they must remember that whatever happens on the Internet is permanent. I have often used the phrase "digital billboard" to explain one's online presence, and I think that phrase captures both the positives and negatives of the medium pretty well. Everything you put into cyberspace has the potential to be broadcasted in a large and permanent way on your digital billboard. Forever. So, for example, as you are heading into college admissions and then afterwards wanting to start a career, you need to be very conscious of what you are putting on your digital billboard. This applies to not only the sexual content that you might be sending, but also to any behaviors that could be misinterpreted by others or that could affect your public image in a negative way.

I think many are misinformed about how often these sexual behaviors are happening between adolescents and adults. For example, research conducted by the National Center for Missing and Exploited children found that between 2000 and 2010, the rates of children reporting online sexual solicitations from strangers dropped from 19% to 9%. Moreover, many of these online solicitations of children are not from adults, but rather they are from strangers who are in their own age cohort. Thus, the Internet may be perceived as more dangerous than it really is in terms of online sexual solicitation.

Additionally, in my main area of study, sexting, I think people think that sexting is a really deviant behavior. However, the prevalence statistics suggest that it isn't, and in fact, it's quite commonplace.

My latest research with Manda Coupe and Jeff Temple examined the potential emotional benefits of sexting among young adults and found that when one was sexting within a casual sexual relationship the negative consequences were many and the positive emotional benefits were few. Moreover, even in a committed relationship, you didn't really see many positive benefits of sexting. Thus, you really need to weigh the costs and benefits of these types of computer-mediated sexual behavior. Many people have regrets about sexts they sent to romantic partners. They worry. When the relationship ends, they are afraid of what with happen to all of those extremely intimate pictures. I am still waiting for that definitive research that shows me that sexting has some benefit. So far, I'm not convinced. Overall, I am pretty solid in my stance that there is definitely more risk involved than there is benefit to be gained from sexting.

5

Information and Attention

Case Study: Texting in the Classroom

Current estimates identify text messaging as a prime culprit for causing classroom distractions. Most of the published studies have been done at the college level, and estimates of the number of college students texting during class show that the majority are doing it. Using a phone or laptop to access social media is typically the second culprit, with estimates hovering around a quarter of students reporting that they do some social networking in the classroom. A somewhat neglected aspect of research is the online class, yet the little research that has been done shows the same pattern, with texting and social networking representing the "one-two punch" against focused learning. In fact, distractions during online learning appear to be more prevalent than in the face-to-face classroom. One study found that while 50.6% of college students frequently texted in physical classrooms, 69.3% of them did so during online instruction. For social networking, the numbers were 24.7% in the face-to-face setting and 62.7% in the online setting.

As students have become more adept at personal technology use, the potential for losing engagement with learning has gone up. As shown in this chapter, attention is a precious commodity when it comes to learning; very little, if any, useful learning can take place without a student putting her focus of attention directly on the material to be learned. Thus, distraction and disengagement from learning during instruction place the quality of learning at risk. Physically being in a classroom appears to keep distractions in check, compared to taking an online class. It is too easy for a student to physically move away from the computer screen during online instruction and, say, cook dinner at the same time.

The amount of learning that is lost when distracted by personal technology has been estimated in several ways. A common approach is to survey students in a class about their in-class distractions, assess learning with a test or a final exam, and then correlate the level of distraction with the amount of learning. But, as researchers know well, this approach confuses cause and effect. When distraction is associated with learning, two interpretations are possible: distracting oneself with devices interferes with learning, or students who are poor learners are more distractible than other students. In science, the gold standard for untangling an effect is the experiment wherein students are randomly assigned to different levels of distraction and the impact on learning is measured. An illustrative example is a study done with American university students who were asked to watch and remember information from a video about theories in the field of communications. Having to simultaneously respond to simulated text messages at the rate of one every 60 seconds reduced the number of details remembered by roughly 20%; responding at the rate of one message every 30 seconds reduced memory of details by more than a third. Further, on a multiple-choice test of the material from the video, students who were distracted by messaging scored 1.5 letter grades lower than students having no distractions. Thus, texting caused a significant and meaningful decrement in learning.

Research consistently finds that distractions with technology are associated with decreased learning. One review of the scientific literature estimated that the typical effect of texting in the classroom is a 10–20% decrease in learning. Beyond immediate learning, texting in the classroom has been linked with other interesting outcomes. In American college students, the amount of texting in class—as well as the amount of Facebooking—is associated with grade-point average. Specifically, texting in the classroom is negatively linked with grade point average. Texting, Facebooking, and other device-related distractions in college have also been found to be associated with more alcohol use, more cigarette smoking, and more marijuana use.

By the early 2010s, teachers were harboring negative attitudes toward devices that could be used as distractions by students. Eighty-seven percent of teachers in the United States, at the kindergarten through twelfth grade levels, believed that personal technologies were shortening kids' attention spans. Also, 64% believed that the computer-based devices did more harm than good when it comes to academic learning. Faced with the challenge to their teaching effectiveness, teachers around the world have been wrestling with strategies to control their students' technology use in class. Teachers want to avoid the roughly letter-grade reductions in learning that occur when a student repeatedly texts during a lecture. Of course, teachers are worried about the same when it comes to laptop use. Using a laptop in class does not just interfere with the laptop user's learning; it is shown to interfere with the learning of students seated around the laptop user, too. Formal school policies on classroom technology use assist the teachers in controlling behavior, and also give the teachers authority to deal with violations in the classroom. For instance, some schools require that mobile phones be kept in lockers and not taken into the classroom during the day. However, it has been reported that the phones are vulnerable to being stolen when they are kept this way. An alternative policy is to allow students to keep their phones, but put them into their backpacks in the classroom. But teachers' accounts show that students routinely break the rule and are caught using the devices, sometimes surreptitiously, like putting their hands and phone under the desk. Complicating the situation is that teachers occasionally desire students to use their phones as part of a class exercise. This might happen, for example, when there are not enough computer workstations in a room, when students are asked to look up information online, or when students are working on group projects.

In the absence of a school policy, or when teachers want to set their own limits, what teachers do in the classroom runs the gamut from absolutely no limitations to extreme rules. No matter what rules are set—or not set—a common technique is to educate students about how cell phone use interferes with learning. The question is still out on what the best additional strategy for changing and maintaining appropriate student behavior is, but here are a few examples of teacher approaches to this issue:

- Set no rules, and count on the students' own desires to do well in class as a check against disruptive mobile phone usage.
- Require students to put their phones into paper bags, staple them shut, and keep them with them at their desks; if a student can't resist using the phone, the paper will crinkle, making an uncomfortable sound and alerting everyone.
- Implement a strict no-use policy, with partial or complete letter-grade reductions for violating the policy.

The problem in identifying the optimal in-class strategy to attack the problem may be that there are multiple factors at play. One is the intensely attractive nature of the mobile phone that provides access to games and one's friends. A second factor is the background of each individual student: some students—but not all—are motivated enough to learn how to manage their technology use during a class period. A third factor might be the nature of in-class learning itself. Namely, lectures can be boring and lend themselves to mind-wandering.

INTRODUCTION

The introduction of this book said that human attention may be a commodity over which hardware and software manufacturers fight to control. This may be true, but before the value of attention in information and communication technology (ICT) was seen as a phenomenon, many experts viewed information as the key item of value in the Internet era. ICT allows the capture, stockpiling, retrieval, analysis, distribution, display, and dissemination of information, leading one researcher to describe information as the ultimate currency. The net generation, also known as digital natives, are the first group of people in the world who had access to computer-based technologies from birth, so they have become the first group of people to deal extensively with information overload, a compulsion to multitask, and overwhelming access to multimedia materials.

THE INFORMATION AGE

The computer is one of the original information technologies of modern times, and it has been around long before the Internet existed. Computers allow for the collection and storage of vast amounts of data in convenient ways, a significant advance over earlier technologies for handling information. (In Chapter 3, it was pointed out that the collection of huge amounts of personal data by computers fueled fears by consumers that their information would be used in ways that would hurt them.) A computer processing chip, also known as a computer processing unit (CPU), is the integral part of a computer that manages the flow of information through the computer, allowing for the rapid and accurate processing of information. Thus, devices that contain processing chips are information technologies themselves. Connecting devices that have computer chips lets devices exchange information, and also lets users exchange messages using the devices. Early forms of remote communication devices thus enabled social platforms like newsgroups and bulletin boards, where a user could connect his or her computer via telephone line. In present times, mobile phones not only allow for information processing, they also allow for communication between individuals. As the computing power of CPUs has increased, and the storage capacity of computers has gotten bigger, the kinds of information that can be exchanged and processed have broadened to include images, videos, and long texts, among others. We take this ability to share photos and videos for granted now, but people were only able to communicate with each other via words in the not too distant past.

During the information age, information technologies have not only brought forth an amazing amount of information about the world, but they have provided new tools for people to communicate with each other. When the Internet became available outside of military and university settings, companies and other organizations began posting information to it. When tools were developed to allow regular people to create web content from home—known as the Web 2.0—the amount of information online skyrocketed. Without being able to quantify the amount of information online, social scientists are left to use words like "immense," "enormous," and "impossible to encompass." One researcher characterized the information available online as the "collective history of human knowledge" (Mills, 2016). No matter how the amount of information is described, it is certain that the world's population has access to more information now than they have had in the history of the human race.

The vast amount of online information, arriving through different channels that include our cell phones and computers, may lead to information overload. Information overload is fatigue connected to being exposed to a lot of external stimulation. For some people, the information that arrives is overwhelming and becomes a stressor. Also, information that is stored in the Internet may have changed the way we think and our experiences and expectations of where and how we can find knowledge. It may be true that the vast amount of information online is forcing people to change their way of processing and thinking about that information, causing some commentators to accuse the Internet of dumbing us down. It has not been definitely shown in experimental research, but there are reasons to believe that the Internet may cause permanent changes in how people handle information. Computer users are known to skim screenfuls of information, rather than read them thoroughly (described more in Chapter 7). Further, people who do a lot of multitasking with computer media (known as heavy media multitaskers) show an inability to focus on information that is central to a task. So in some ways, it appears that people's cognitive skills may be worse—that they appear to be dumber—when online than when offline. Additionally, knowing that information is available online may have led people to stop storing information in their own biological memories. Virtually all of school learning is about memorizing. Traditional studying is about committing new information to memory. The Google effect shows that the Internet affects students' learning. Students who know that they can later use the Internet to find information are less likely to commit new information to memory. Thinking more broadly, the Google effect may be changing millions of people's memory for information, not just students'. A similar effect occurs with opening and closing computer files. If people save a computer file before closing it, they remember less information from the file than if they close the file without saving it first.

The information age may also be creating an expectation of rapid access to information that generates a constant need for instant gratification. Earlier, it was discussed how ICT is causing increasing amounts of information to be available for all. Another aspect of this development is the speed of information access. In the early days of the Internet and the World Wide Web, nearly every session spent surfing the web involved waiting for information to be downloaded to one's computer. Wait times were frustrating for many. With the improvements in technology, the bandwidth—the amount of information transmitted in a short period of time—has increased dramatically. This increase has seemingly eliminated wait times in all but the rarest of circumstances.

AFFORDANCES

Computers and the Internet give people access to dizzying amounts of information; at the same time, computer- and Internet-based devices shape the thoughts and behaviors of users because of how these devices are designed. To use technology, we must interact with it physically through finger movements, grasping, holding, etc. Thus, the size, shape, and location of the physical features of technological devices impact our physical interactions with these devices. Similarly, the programs that run on the devices determine the kinds of actions that we can take. For example, we are restricted to the choices made available by the software when we use a pull-down menu. The physical actions and program-related actions that are allowed are called the affordances of the devices. Broadly speaking, an affordance is a physical or software feature of technology that puts constraints on how we use the technology. Affordances were first proposed as representing features in the environment. The human brain can pick up information directly from the environment that gives clues as to what is going on in the world around it. For example, as the eye gathers light from the world, the amount of light arriving from an object will be changed as the object moves closer to the eye. This affordance of the environment is a clue to the object's depth or distance from a person. When it comes to physical objects, a good definition of affordances is that they are "physical properties of objects that enable people perceiving or using those objects to function in particular ways" (Baron, 2008). A very basic example would be the example of a sheet of writing paper. Writing paper can be handled only in certain ways with the fingers and the hands, and it holds information—that is, words, numbers, and figures—only in a particular way, as they are put down with a pen or pencil. Also, no power source is needed to use paper to write, so this makes paper portable in ways different than the portability of electronic devices. Regarding the affordances of objects, scientists have learned that the objects themselves, upon sight, activate the motor parts of the brain associated with the correct physical properties of the object. This bottom-up activation effect occurs whether people see a real object, a picture of an object, an object on the computer screen, or retrieve an image of an object from memory. The image of a coffee cup activates motor networks, or motor programs, related to grabbing the coffee cup handle with one's hand.

As researchers began to study the impact of computer-based technology upon our lives, scientists applied affordances to the use of technology, pushing the concept to include not only affordances tied to the physical dimensions of technology, but also affordances that are mental in nature, such as changes in how people think about technology. Very abstractly, technological devices are tools that we use to carry out our intentions. Because each tool has a set of affordances that go with it, our ability to carry out our intentions is transformed by the tool and the actions—both physical and mental—that we can apply to the tool. In psychological parlance, executing our intentions is mediated by the tools that we use, creating a set of mediated actions. Further, as we learn how to use a tool, we also change our thoughts in a way that matches what we know about the tool—both its affordances and its restrictions—also referred to as the mediational means. Affordances not only affect the thoughts we have and the actions we take, they also can create friction with our ultimate intentions. At least four types of affordances can interfere with our cognitive control, that is, our effectiveness in maintaining focus on getting our goals accomplished. One, electronic devices provide immediate gratification. It's easy to get a physical or mental reward with a few taps or clicks on a device. Launching a social networking app on a cell phone quickly shows a series of posts or messages that intrigue and please us. Effective cognitive control often requires putting off a reward until a much longer and more complex series of actions are taken; this is known as delayed gratification. Two, technology encourages the buildup of habits. This is partly the result of immediate gratification; repeated short-term rewards for using technology shape our behavior and increase how much we use the technology in the same way again. Effective cognitive control involves novel, well-reasoned behaviors—not habitual responses. Third, due to the widespread availability of the Internet anywhere at any time, technology is encouraging us to use it all the time. Effective cognitive control may require getting away from technology during critical time periods in order to accomplish other tasks, like driving. Four, devices and software provide notifications, alerts, and messages that interfere and interrupt us.

There are too many affordances of the physical features of devices to list here, but some excellent examples come from tablet computers, video games, mobile phones, and virtual reality. The affordances of the physical features of tablet computers, like the iPad, are seen when comparing tablets to other devices that run similar functions. While desktop and laptop computers can run both a greater number and more sophisticated versions of software, such as word processors, tablets provide orientational flexibility: the user can rotate the tablet and the screen will adjust itself to match the eye level of the user. This provides tablet users with the flexibility to compute while, for example, lying on the couch, reading in a recliner, or resting in bed. Another physical feature of the tablet that is important to affordances is the large screen. Compared to a cell phone, the tablet provides more room for information to be presented on its screen. This enables software developers to provide more complex software and apps than what can be put onto a cell phone. Regarding video games, when a person plays a video or computer game for the first time, there are a set of basic hand and finger movements that must be learned in order to control the action of the game. These movements are determined both by the physical dimensions of the game controller or keyboard, and by the software that runs the game. In the gaming world, getting better at manipulating the gaming environment—known as mastery of controls—leads to even more affordances, this time within the game environment itself. After gaining mastery of controls, a player will be able to take actions that were not available before, such as exploring a virtual world, solving in-game puzzles, and effectively winning combat scenarios (and amassing victories). For mobile phones, aside from the physical dimensions and the software affordances of them, the small size and high levels of functionality provide another important feature: portability. The portability of cell phones has created a world where people can move about in the physical environment and not lose access to the many desired functions of the phone. In other words, the portability affordance of cell phones has increased the variety of physical spaces in which telephones can be used. Finally, for virtual reality, a growing trend for gamers involves the use of virtual reality to enhance the gaming experience. Virtual reality is usually achieved by supplementing the gaming devices with additional devices. One such device might be a virtual reality headset or goggles. Another might be a peripheral device that allows for new input into the gaming system, such as a joystick that controls movement within the game. These additional devices allow for several important features to emerge, that is, new affordances. Peripheral devices can often provide physical feedback to the player. For example, in a flight simulation game, the joystick can be made to shake when there is turbulence in the gaming simulation. Interactivity with the game involving feedback can be said to be an affordance of virtual reality systems.

Relationship management and multitasking are two broad areas where the affordances of devices and programs have had significant impacts on our higher-order behaviors. Many affordances related to relationship management behaviors come about through the particular design features of social networking sites, including how we find and build new relationships, how we maintain existing relationships, and how we terminate relationships. Social networking sites (SNSs) make searching for new relationship partners easy. For example, at dating sites, thousands of profiles of other users can be searched in a few seconds and, in many cases, for free. Lowering the time-related and financial cost of finding a new partner contributes to break-ups; getting a new partner is significantly easier now than it was in the past, before the Internet was used to manage relationships. The ease of making and manipulating relationships on SNSs has been a factor in cheating within romantic relationships. Snapchat, the social networking application, made headlines because it has a mechanism in it whereby messages disappear after a short period of time. This has made flirting a phenomenon in the program. There is no long-term evidence of flirtatious messages being sent, so users feel comfortable sending messages to other users that they might not otherwise send. Another importance affordance of SNSs is the semi-public nature of the information that is posted. Although users can communicate with each other privately if they choose to do so, they can also air their private communication publicly by posting their messages to each other in a public part of the SNS. This gives users the opportunity to manipulate relationships. One way to do so is to publicly post fights between romantic couples, a move that lets other users get involved in the fight. The fact that relationship connections are often public in SNSs gives rise to another affordance of social networking with the Internet; since other people can see who a user's relationships are, the user can influence those other people by making relationship connections. For example, whether it is intended or not, a romantic partner can make connections with relatively weak friends (e.g., an old flame who hasn't been physically seen in years) that will spark jealousy in the current romantic partner. The ugly specter of jealousy and cheating on Facebook and other SNSs has led to concerns among researchers that SNSs are harming relationship quality.

There are related affordances from other properties of Internet communication and electronic devices more generally. These other affordances also affect the different parts of the relationship management process. Creating a user profile is an important step in the relationship management process because the profile paints the picture of a user that will be shared with other user in the system. Ongoing management of the profile affects how other users react, and is also important in developing and maintaining relationships. While people must also craft their public personas in real life, the Internet gives affordances that are different than real life. The limited cues available online mean that a user's self-presentation completely manipulates what other users know and feel about her. In addition, most communication in SNSs relies on asynchronous communication—messages that have relatively long intervals between them—that is very different from real-life conversations. The gaps in communication in the online world allow for fine-tuning and crafting of one's profile, as well as one's messages. Before the widespread use of cell phones, people relied on their home telephone to take calls. When people received a call on their home telephone—the so-called landline—the telephone would ring, and they had no information about who was calling. Most people's phones did not show the name of the caller when a phone call was received. Caller ID was an extra feature—and extra cost—to home telephone plans. In contrast, the software on most smartphones—the phone app—has caller ID built in because it the phone's software can compare the incoming telephone number to the list of contacts stored in the phone. The caller ID feature gives people additional information about the caller, allowing for better decision-making as to how to handle a call. If a person is avoiding discussions with another person, then they can let the call go to voicemail. Even when there is no stored information about the caller, the lack of information can be used to the receiver's advantage. A number that is not listed in the receiver's contacts list may signal an undesirable phone call, say from a marketer.

HUMAN INFORMATION PROCESSING AND ATTENTION

The human brain is tasked with handling large amounts of information in the context of the affordances of electronic devices. More than one million years of evolution have transformed the brain so that it can perform complex tasks and solve detailed and intricate problems. Yet the human brain cannot do everything at once, despite the apparently unlimited amount of biological tissue available. The capacity of the brain to process information is limited, requiring it to focus on a small set of incoming information and ignore distracting information when a task or set of tasks put a high load on the system. Information processing is the set of mental procedures that people carry out in order to make sense of the world, to perform cognitive tasks, and to remember information, including information from online sources. The information processing system is comprised of many pieces. Perception is the set of processes that give meaning to information that our body collects from the environment. When a sound, say the chirp of a bird, reaches our ears, our brain processes the information and decides that it is a bird sound. When multiple pieces of environmental information are available to be processed at once, like when watching the busy television screen of a cable television news channel, the brain must ignore some of the information and focus on the other information.

Working memory is a mental structure that lets people hold a small amount of information for the execution of complex tasks; working memory holds information temporarily while we engage in an activity. Typing a term paper may require typing words while keeping in mind what was typed in earlier sentences, in order to make the whole set of sentences coherent, for example. Or many have experienced problems with working memory while shopping at the grocery store. A shopping list provides a tally of all of the items that must be purchased, but shoppers often glance at the list and commit to memory a few items at a time as they are shopping. However, there is a limit on how many items can be committed to memory while shopping; this is the working memory capacity. Working memory is important for taking notes in class, comprehending lectures, and doing homework. When taking notes, the note taker must temporarily hold in mind information from the lecturer that will be written down on paper. When comprehending lectures, the listener must hold in mind information from one part of the speech until later, in order to make sense of the presentation. When doing homework, many homework problems require that the student hold information temporarily in their memory in order to solve the problem (e.g., math problems). Long-term memory contains all of our memories that last more than say, 30 seconds to 1 minute. As we perform complex tasks, it is important to call up information from long-term memory. but it is also important to ignore irrelevant information that is activated in long-term memory.

Attention is the mental act of selecting a subset of information in the world to process. Attention is part of the human information processing system. Two kinds of attention exist; one related to organizing and carrying out daily tasks and one related to how we view the world. The outer layer of the brain is known as the cortex, and the main place where organizing and attending to tasks occurs in the brain is in the frontal cortex, or more specifically, in the prefrontal cortex (PFC). Scientists know that the frontal cortex is important for attention because of at least two key reasons. For one, people with damage to their frontal cortex have problems when performing attention tasks. Secondly, brain imaging studies show that the frontal cortex is active when people use their attention to perform a task. The different parts of the PFC work together to help us perform complex tasks successfully. The PFC is also connected to other parts of the brain that are active when we behave, such as motor regions—areas that control our movements—and emotion regions. The parts of the PFC control how much these other parts of the brain affect our thoughts and behaviors. One of the functions of the PFC is to be an attentional gateway. Decisions must be made in the PFC about how much attention to give to events or items in the environment compared to thoughts in our heads. For instance, serious writers—as I consider myself right now—must alternate between focusing on their internal ideas for what to write and competing events in the surrounding environment such as someone in the room who is asking a question. Many other situations require the attentional gateway. For example, there is the situation when doing a main task—like writing—and the mind starts to wander to irrelevant ideas, such as needing to make a bank deposit. This is called mind wandering. Attentional control must be exerted to keep the main task on track. Another situation—faced frequently by high school and college students—is when trying to complete an inherently boring task, like comprehending and recording notes during an in-class lecture. Attentional control must be exerted to keep the brain processing the relevant material, the lecture, and not switching to something else. A particular part of the PFC, the rostral prefrontal cortex, has been linked to the attentional gateway.

The PFC is not fully matured until late into adolescence, or even into young adulthood. This means that high school students and traditionally-aged college students have brains that are still maturing. Some neuroscientists warn that the developing brain is vulnerable because technology use may put pressures on functions that are not functioning at full capacity. Neuroplasticity means that the brain changes in response to what it does. In other words, using a part of the brain to perform a task in a particular way can leave temporary or permanent changes in that part of the brain. Even the prefrontal cortex can show neuroplasticity. Not surprisingly, getting old affects a complicated system like this one. The information processing system, especially with respect to the basic aspects of attention, is complex and is sensitive to aging. As people get older, they tend to lose their ability to ignore irrelevant information. This is a key ability, as it provides the basis for focused attention and dealing with the capacity constraints of the information processing system. In fact, getting worse at ignoring information impacts a range of other aspects of cognitive control.

Under normal circumstances, the brain must allocate its capacity—in other words, its attention—judiciously, in order to get the most important tasks done. When faced with competing demands, the brain enables processes that focus attention onto the high-priority information and tasks. Some high-priority tasks for students are studying for an exam, completing an assignment by the deadline, and comprehending what the instructor says during class time. The processes that monitor and command our focus are routinely collectively referred to by scientists as cognitive control processes. Attention is guided by our goals and, in the best of circumstances, is under cognitive control. Maintaining focus is hard to do, but it is essential for performing at high levels in many realms of life. Since the typical high school or college lecture is at least an hour in length, maintaining focus—also known as attention span—is necessary for learning the material that is presented. Educational tasks at home are not much different. Reading a chapter in a textbook is an exercise in sustained attention and can easily be ruined by getting interrupted multiple times or losing focus. Blocking out distractions, through the manipulation of our attention, is an important part of cognitive control. People with weak cognitive control are easily distracted, and people who do not have long attention spans are said to be easily bored. While some scientists have argued that our mental resources can be split across multiple tasks at the same time, others have argued that, in most cases, we must mentally switch between tasks as we attempt to multitask. Regardless of the truth, it is well known in the research literature that switching back and forth between tasks requires cognitive control, and actually requires additional cognitive effort, called a switch cost.

How does our brain organize all of the processes that are required in order to carry out very complex tasks, like researching a topic online and taking notes about it, at the same time? To prevent the brain from executing processes in a frenzied, free-for-all fashion, an executive process must oversee what is going on and make sure that all of the activity is organized and fruitful. The different processes involved in the complex task—picking out parts of the screen to attend to, comprehending the words on the screen, mentally converting the information from the words into notes, turning the ideas for notes into actual words in a word processor, etc.—need to come out in a concerted manner in order to achieve our goal. The different processes, also called resources, are managed by the cognitive control functions, and are part of a set of processes known collectively as executive functions. Each complex task is performed by using one or more of the executive functions, basic mental processes that are used to reign in behavior so that it is efficient, organized, and purposeful. One of the results of exercising our executive functions is that our behaviors and thoughts keep us from being extreme; that is, we maintain self-regulation. Let's say that you want to plan a party for your friend's birthday. As you sit and construct a list of invitees, you must keep in mind names, phone numbers, addresses, relationships, and other information for the potential guests. Juggling all of this information in your mind requires your working memory. Every once in a while, you will spontaneously remember some other smaller task that needs to be done for the party to go well, something like ordering a cake. Taking a bit of time to jot down some notes about ordering a cake and then returning to your guest list task requires task-switching. If your phone suddenly buzzes and beeps with an incoming text message, then you will have to decide how to handle the interruption. Do you stop what you are doing and grab the phone to check the message? Or do you wait until later to check the message because you are in the middle of an important task that has a deadline? Either way, you are engaging in decision-making. And, if you decide to withhold your response to the phone for now, then you are performing inhibition (of the phone alert). Finally, if you realize that your memory of people's names, numbers, addresses, and relationships is pretty poor, and you are not making much progress, then you will have to switch to another strategy to complete your list. Perhaps you will have to start emailing people to gather the necessary information. Switching strategies requires cognitive flexibility. Often, the three core executive functions are listed as working memory, cognitive flexibility—also known as shifting—and inhibition. Hopefully, you can see how important executive functions are to being in control of one's behavior, one's thoughts, and even one's mood.

DEVICES THAT AFFORD MULTITASKING

Many devices and software afford multitasking—working on more than one task at a time—or task-switching—the rapid switching of attention from one task to another—as exemplified in web browsers, electronic texts, and instant messaging. The main way that devices provide the affordance of multitasking is through their operating systems—the software programs that run the device's main features and allow other programs or applications to be launched and executed. Members from older generations of computer users experienced devices and operating systems that let users run only one program at a time. Contemporary operating systems—on phones, tablets, laptops, etc.—permit the user to open several different programs at once. It is clear that operating systems technically allow multitasking because it is possible to work on more than one task at a time; what is not immediately obvious is that operating systems may even encourage multitasking. That is, they may lead to you multitask in situations where you might not normally. A similar affordance lies within web browsers. They let users open multiple tabs at once, setting up situations where users are simultaneously working across multiple tasks. Another pretty basic feature of devices that encourages multitasking is a large screen. The larger the screen, the more windows a user can have open at the same time. Each window might represent a different task.

The web browser has another affordance that relates to multitasking. Most web pages contain hypertext—text embedded with clickable links—that permits users to move freely among many different web pages. Clicking on links creates a non-linear browsing style that is different from what happens when a person reads a printed page. A user might not even finish reading a web page before moving on to another web page. It's not uncommon, for instance, for difficult-to-read words to be set as links that, when clicked on, take the reader to the definition of the word in an online dictionary. Checking definitions of words and other tangents created by hypertext create an environment of multitasking; multitasking is known to distract people, causing learning and comprehension to suffer. Surprisingly, experienced computer users are more prone to this type of distraction than inexperienced users; they have built up a habit of non-linear browsing with past web surfing. Digital stories read on electronic devices by children are also examples of hypertext. Researchers have argued that children are subject to the same encouragement to multitask when they read the digital stories. The links, images, video clips, and other hypermedia available to the child discourage focused attention on comprehending a story and instead promote poor comprehension of the material. The downtime waiting for computer processes to complete—for example, a web page to download—also encourages multitasking. This downtime—called slack—is when the user is waiting for the computer to complete a process. Theoretically, a computer- or device-user can do whatever she wants during the slack, even nothing. But scientists have found that most technology users prefer to use the slack to do another task, often on the same device. Take the situation when a person is going online to check the status of a package that they have sent to another address using a delivery company. After entering the tracking number of the package into the online system, there often is a noticeable delay of five to ten seconds while the computer system checks the package routing. This delay opens up the possibility for many simultaneous activities like checking text messages, opening up an email application, or sending a quick instant message (IM) to a friend. IM applications, as other programs, provide another feature that affords multitasking. They often open a pop-up window, sound an alert, or flash a window on the device's screen to indicate that a message has been received. This sets in motion psychological processes that create an urgency to respond, thus facilitating interruption of the current task and performance of another task, that is, task-switching. These affordances of IMs, as with many of the affordances of technology, battle with our cognitive control in that they compel us to behave in ways that are not effective for achieving our long-term goals, like focused studying. Since all of these affordances are found in laptop computers, the laptop has been identified as the prime seat of multitasking. A large, national study of American youths found that the device most associated with multitasking in daily activities was the computer. This is not surprising given all of the affordances for multitasking discussed above. That the study was with youths should not be interpreted to mean that the same result would not hold for adults who own a computer; adults use most of the same programs and applications on a computer—often while using a cell phone at the same time—as youths do.

COGNITIVE LOAD AND ALLOCATION OF ATTENTION

People have their own reasons for multitasking. Scientists have tried to understand the reasons why people are compelled to multitask with their technologies. The most obvious answer to the question would be that people multitask in order to get more work done than if they did not multitask. But it turns out that the proclivity to multitask, at least in college students in the United States, is associated with negative mental health symptoms that include depression and social anxiety—worry about interacting with other people. This raises the possibility that people multitask for emotional reasons, not for cognitive ones. In this case, multitasking—going off-task while engaged in a main task—may provide relief to socially anxious or depressed people who are experiencing negative emotions or mood. If a college student is depressed, she may suffer from negative thoughts while she engages in prolonged homework sessions. In an effort to eliminate the negative thoughts, she may distract herself with pleasing activities like watching videos from a video streaming site interspersed with the homework. Unfortunately, the high levels of multitasking might also be linked to negative emotional and mental health outcomes. For college students in the United States at least, having a high level of multitasking is linked to being depressed and to having signs of social anxiety (discomfort being around other people). It's well-known in psychological research that depressed individuals tend to dwell on negative thoughts. Healthy, non-depressed, individuals are able to exert cognitive control in order to suppress those thoughts and maintain a balanced emotional state. Therefore, it has been suggested that engaging in a lot of media multitasking might disrupt a person's attentional control, leading to the inability to inhibit negative thoughts and ideas, thus laying the groundwork for depression.

Multitasking with technology is affected by the limited capacity of the human brain. It is well established that using one's cell phone during class or during homework interferes with learning. This is most likely due to the fact that the brain is limited in how many different psychological processes can be carried out at once. Another term that is used to represent this limited capacity of the brain is cognitive load. Cognitive load theory says that each task that is performed requires a certain amount of mental workload. Because there is only a fixed amount of workload available, due to the natural wiring of the brain, there is a limit on how many different tasks can be performed at once. In terms of the classroom, students who use their cell phones may be putting excess load on the brain, causing a reduction in workload available for learning. The capacity limits of the brain are not solely psychological constraints. As one group of researchers have put it, an attentional capacity limit can be thought of as ". . . a biological constraint that limits the amount of systematic neural activity that can be distributed across parts of the cortex" (Just, Keller, & Cynkar, 2008).

Sending and receiving text messages would appear to be a simple task that places little burden on our brains. After all, the messages are short and require few key-strokes, skilled texters can type messages quickly, and the conversational topics in text message threads are typically neither advanced nor abstract. Despite this impression, research has repeatedly shown how text messaging places demands on the information processing system that can interfere with other ongoing types of information processing. Using a smartphone to send and receive text messages dur-ing class time is a great example, because multiple research studies (described in Chapter 8) have found that doing so causes interference with learning from the teacher. In other words, text messaging places a significant cognitive load on human information processing. Trickier situations involving more complex tasks are sure to place a heavy cognitive load on the information processing system, resulting in a decline in performance. Trying to read articles for a course while simultaneously watching video clips online would be one of these trickier situations. Through experi-ence, most of us have learned that certain technologies are conducive to multitask-ing. In contrast, a few technologies put so much cognitive load upon the information processing system that multitasking is unlikely to occur. One example of a technol-ogy task that might not be conducive to multitasking is video gaming. Video gaming typically requires the use of both hands, severely restricting how much multitasking can physically be done. And video gaming seems to put a high cognitive load on the player, meaning that there does not appear to be enough attentional capacity for play-ers to play a video game and do another task at the same time.

Distractions are another factor that can lead to multitasking. Distractions can come from anywhere. The most obvious distractions are ones that come from the environment, known as external distractions. Consider a student writing a term paper in his bedroom. As he focuses on the task of writing, he will be distracted by sounds coming from outside of the house. A dog will bark, a car will honk its horn, or a group of people engaged in conversation will walk by. There will be other external distractions that cannot be ignored easily. A parent will ask the student a question, an IM will pop up on the computer screen, or a reminder alert will sound from his smartwatch. All of these distractions put demands on the brain's infor-mation processing system, with some distractions putting greater demands on the system than others. Another source of distractions is the student's own mind. The student will have a thought that writing is boring, remember that he has a club meet-ing tomorrow during lunch period, or notice that he is fatigued. Known as internal distractions, these types of distractions are not as well studied as external distrac-tions, though it is certain that internal distractions can create internal interfer-ence with focused attention the way that external distractions can create external interference. Sometimes, the phenomenon of losing focus due to an internal distraction is referred to as an attentional lapse.

Personal technology may be having several different effects on our behaviors like multitasking, and on our thoughts, such as on our processing style. Watching television while studying would be a good example. The goal of watching television is to comprehend the meaning of the message in the TV content; the goal of studying is to fix new material or new skills in one's memory. As mentioned earlier, technology affords multitasking, so it is natural for people to switch between tasks fairly frequently when using technology. Naturalistic experiments show the high rates of task-switching with technology, prompted not only by the affordances of technology but also by the emotional aspects of wanting to get things done and by internal triggers that are distracting. In one study with U.S. college students, it was found that students naturally switched between watching a television and using a computer at a rate of 4 switches per minute—that's one switch every 15 seconds—even when they didn't have to. In another study of middle school, high school, and college students in the United States, switching between doing homework and doing something else, like checking Facebook, occurred every 5 to 6 minutes. Over the course of a 15-minute study period, the students averaged only 10 minutes on task. In another study with U.S. college students, the students were allowed to switch between six different tasks in the laboratory. After observing how often students switched, the researchers asked the students to explain their switches. It was found that many of the switches were caused when students began to have negative feelings about the task they were doing; the negative feelings prompted the students to switch to a new task. Thus, there are internal triggers of task-switching called self-interruptions. Research into the motivations for multitasking with multiple forms of media shows two main reasons. One motivation for media multitasking is cognitive: people think that multitasking will help them get more work done. The other is emotional: multitasking can lift a person's mood. For instance, turning on the television while studying turns studying into a fun activity. Unfortunately, the cognitive motivation for multitasking is not fulfilled; people do not find that multitasking gets more work done.

OTHER TECHNOLOGY EFFECTS ON ATTENTION

Many researchers who study multitasking with technology feel that the largest impact of multitasking is upon younger individuals, the group that multitasks the most. Students have many opportunities to multitask because they spend time "at work"—that is, doing their schoolwork—unsupervised, usually at home or in a library. Analyses of the kinds of multitasking that students do suggest some common patterns. For one, reading and studying on a computer often are combined with IMing. IMing frequently occurs at the same time as surfing the web for schoolwork and as using email. Additionally, when students browse the news online or when they use the web for leisure, they also tend to IM or email at the same time. There is evidence that the biggest multitaskers have shallow and distributed attention spans, rather than a propensity to focus on one incoming stream of information at a time. At the end of the 2000s, a paper from Stanford University was published that set off a series of studies looking at how young people multitask with technology and digital media. In the study, college students were asked to report how often they combine different tasks at the same time, including many technology-based tasks and tasks in which they are consuming digital media. All of the students who were in the study were also given a set of tasks to do that were designed to measure some of their basic cognitive abilities related to attention. For example, one task required that the students pay attention to visual information in the center of a computer screen while ignoring information that appeared around the edges of the screen. The results showed that heavy media multitaskers (HMMs) had more difficulty ignoring the distracting information than light media multi-taskers (LMMs). The research team speculated that, among other possibilities, the HMMs may have developed a style of information processing in which all information from the environment is scanned. Often referred to as a breadth-biased pro-cessing strategy, this approach to handling multiple sources of information would maximize the chances that an important sign or signal would be detected in the environment, but would reduce the amount of elaborate, meaningful processing that any one piece of information would receive. In contrast, LMMs may have retained the traditional information processing strategy of focusing their attention on one aspect of the environment and ignoring the rest. Evidence of a link between HMMs and poor attention abilities comes from studies outside the United States, as well. In Holland, for instance, it was found that adolescent HMMs did worse than adolescent LMMs on measures of staying focused and switching between tasks. Although it is tempting to conclude that media multitasking is the cause of poor attention abilities, as many commentators have done, it should be pointed out that there is an alternative explanation. It is possible that young people who start out with poor attention abilities are attracted to multitasking because it is a natural fit for their scattered attentional strategy. Although the results of the Stanford study are highly cited among researchers, the final conclusion about how being an HMM affects cognition is up in the air, as several follow-up studies have not found the same result as the original study. Being an HMM has also been found to affect relationships with others, possibly because HMMs may have strong urges to use their electronic devices while they are talking with someone face-to-face, an act that is perceived by many people to be offensive. When young girls in the United States (8- to 12-year-olds) were assessed for their technology habits, it was found that the HMMs among them were more likely to have difficulty making and keep-ing friends than the LMMs. HMMs also were less likely to talk to other people face-to-face.

A recent review of the scientific literature confirms a link between media and Internet use and having a breadth-biased form of attention. Breadth-biased atten-tion means that people are more interested in shifting their attention across mul-tiple sources than they are in focusing on one source, or a small number of sources, for in-depth analysis. The reasons for the connection between media use and breadth-biased attention are not clear. It could be that the Internet is shaping our attention; it could be that people with poor attention skills are drawn to the Inter-net. The breadth-biased approach to handling information is related to the possibility of a shorter attention span. If a person is more interested in processing multiple streams of information than just one, then that person will also have a shorter attention span, because they are shifting their attention frequently. That person might also constantly be on alert for new information—such as the next incoming text message—leading to mistakes and false alarms in processing information. This could explain why many people have phantom vibration syndrome, the repeated experience of feeling your cell phone vibrate even when it did not. Even vague bodily sensations coming from the area near a phone may trigger the feeling that a message has been received. Not all of the research supports a connection between ICT use and attention problems. College students report that their IM use interferes with their ability to self-regulate. When a pop-up window indicates that a new message has arrived, students say that the pop-window grabs their attention and prevents them from focusing. They say that the same happens when there are auditory alerts and flashing windows from the IM program or application. Not only do students claim the affordances of the technology create this problem, but also their own self-interruptions and the psychological pressure of feeling the need to respond to friends' messages, known as social norms. However, when students assess their own attention spans using a psychological measure (a questionnaire on which, one item, for example, asks the respondent to rate the sentence, "I am distracted when things are going on around me"), no relationship between social media usage and attention span is found.

You might have heard that the Internet is shaping our attention spans as well. Writers in popular culture speculate that the Internet is permanently changing people's attentional processing, and it's a commonly reported experience that people find it difficult to stay focused and pay attention to what they intend to do when using the Internet, a laptop, or when they have a cell phone nearby. There are hints of support for this assertion from among the research findings by scientists. When it comes to cell phones, there are immediate effects of the device upon our focus and attention. A cell phone that signals an alert or notification grabs the attention of a person when the person is attempting to focus on another task. Even a silent cell phone can impair attention; a silent cell phone in view can impair our ability to focus. Some researchers suggest that just seeing our cell phone is sufficient to activate a whole range of memories and emotions related to the social network that the cell phone represents. These internal triggers can lead to self-interruptions. However, when scientists measure the executive functions that are affected by the presence—or absence—of a cell phone, it is working memory that is affected by having the phone nearby, not sustained attention. This result suggests that actively inhibiting thoughts and ideas generating by a close-by cell phone takes its toll on other cognitive functions—in this case, working memory—in a phenomenon called brain drain.

In the realm of social interactions, technology has mostly been found to have a negative relationship with attention. The device most connected to social interactions is the smartphone. As one author has said, the smartphone provides access to the ". . . broad social and informational network . . . that one is not part of at the moment" (Thornton, Faires, Robbins, & Rollins, 2014). The reader would probably not be surprised to learn that talking on a cell phone or hearing another person talk on a cell phone can affect the ability to pay attention to a task for long periods of time. However, it is more surprising that merely having a cell phone present, without the cell phone making any sounds at all, can interfere with sustained attention. Imagine a wife who is very attached to using her cell phone. If she talks on the cell phone frequently or if she checks the cell phone often (say, to look up information), then she is likely doing this in the presence of her spouse or partner. The limited capacity of our information processing system will most likely prevent her from being able to use her phone and simultaneously pay attention to her spouse, listen to her spouse, and have a meaningful conversation with him. In fact, this interference with social interactions, what has been called technoference, can lead to relationship problems and conflict. Finally, college students who do a lot of online social networking also are reporting problems with their attention. Students who find themselves frequently checking their social networks during homework or at work are also spending more time socializing online in total.

THE REWARD SYSTEM

Our brains are hardwired to seek out cases of novelty and new items in the environment. Thus, our attention can be directed by what is inherently rewarding or pleasing to us. One way that the brain achieves this is by providing a rewarding feeling when new and novel events are noticed. Not only will novel events that occur on the Internet grab our attention, but also any events whose content is emotional or surprising. The reward that is received by these events may involve a heightened sense of arousal. Using the computer mouse to click on an item in a game that then reveals a prize activates the reward system. Activating the reward system might also increase the chances that we will reproduce the actions that led to the reward at a future point. This process of reinforcement may mean that we will look for opportunities to play this game in the future. A similar chain of events could occur for finger swipes on a screen, like when using the dating app Tinder, or for using a keyword search function on a website like YouTube. In other words, the reward system can drive our attention, which might also change our behaviors. The parts of the brain that are involved in the reward system include the amygdala (processing of emotions), the hippocampus (processing memories), and the frontal cortex (coordinating brain processes to produce behaviors).

The brain's reward system works to direct our attention toward pleasing events and activities, while our executive functions work together to keep us focused and on task. The main functions within the executive functions are inhibition, task-switching, planning, monitoring, and working memory. Inhibition is a process that suppresses irrelevant information. An example is when a student is studying in front of the television. It's easy for the student to move her eyes away from the TV and toward the material to be studied, but it's harder to ignore the sounds and speech from the television. The latter requires inhibition. Task-switching is an important part of multitasking. When trying to do two tasks at once, a person must repeatedly shift from focusing on one task and then focusing on the other task. Most of the processing involved in executive functions takes place in the prefrontal cortex, a brain area beneath the forehead. While the executive functions provide very basic modules that support more complex behaviors, they also allow an even higher level of thoughts and behaviors that are known as metacognition. Metacognition, taken literally, means thinking about thinking. Metacognition includes our knowledge of our own knowledge (e.g., you can instantly say whether you know the names of all U.S. states in alphabetical order), our estimates of our own abilities (e.g., how good of a learner you are), and our strategies for learning and processing information (e.g., your preferred method for learning a long list of names). While metacognition is important for academic and intellectual tasks, another psychological concept relates to broader control over our thoughts and behaviors. This is the construct of self-regulation, which includes our ability to self-reflect and to make adjustments to our future thoughts and behaviors. Self-regulation keeps our activities—both mental and physical—in synch with our current and future goals. Metacognition and self-regulation are both associated with activity in the prefrontal cortex.

VISUAL ATTENTION AND PROCESSING

As the brain is limited in how much mental processing it can do at once, so is our visual processing; these limits on vision are referred to as visual attention. As people move about in the real world, they must take in information from the environment, process that information, and then act on that information. Taking information in from the environment occurs primarily through our five senses, with vision being the most important sense for humans. If you look in any given direction, then there is an array of information presented to our eyes. There are colors, edges, shapes, depths, and brightness, all of which are gathered by our eyes, retinas, and visual processing system. The gathered information is used by the brain, mostly in the brain's occipital lobe—lying at the back of the head—to identify objects in the world. Unfortunately, the brain's limited capacity prevents it from simultaneously processing all of the visual information that is out there in the world. The brain must make decisions about which information is to be processed and which information is to be ignored. These decisions constitute the process of visual attention. Visual attention occurs in a different part of the brain than the general attention mechanism described earlier, and has been linked to very specific technology use, namely, action video game playing. The areas of the cortex at the back of the brain, called the occipital lobe, process visual information. In conjunction with the parietal cortex—located in the middle top of the brain—attention is allocated to objects and events in the visual world and in particular locations within the visual world, known as spatial information.

Scientists dissect every process and experience that goes on in the real world, and many times they do so by first simulating the real-world processes and experiences in laboratory settings. The visual attention process has frequently been studied by using the visual search scenario to simulate the choice of selecting certain information from the environment and ignoring other information. In the visual search scenario, participants sit in front of a computer screen and see an array of visual items on the screen. They are searching for particular targets (e.g., "F") and ignoring others (e.g., "T"). By analyzing the speed of reaction of the participants, researchers have come to learn that there are two broadly-defined phases of visual attention. In the pre-attentive phase, all visual information is processed simulta-neously before a decision has to be made about which piece of information should receive focus. In the selective attention phase, the brain has to make a decision about which piece of information should receive focused attention for further processing. Our current goals influence visual attention. We attend to visual information that is relevant to our task. And, by extension, we ignore information that is irrelevant, if possible. In the brain, the cognitive control center in the PFC, right behind the forehead, is responsible for keeping the other parts of the brain on task. (Cognitive control is described in more detail in Chapter 6.) In fact, the prefrontal cortex is connected to the visual cortex in the occipital lobe; this connection provides the PFC with a pathway for modulating activity in the visual processing areas. Hence, the PFC influences visual attention.

Heads-up displays are images that are projected onto glass in front of a person while the person is engaged in another task. The projected image provides addi-tional visual information for the person in order to complete the task. A few auto-mobile manufacturers have incorporated heads-up displays into their car models for several years now. In the case of BMW, for instance, certain car models come with a heads-up display that shows the current speed of the vehicle on the glass in front of the driver, but below the main field of view. Google Glass is another exam-ple of technology that incorporates a heads-up display. In the case of Google Glass, the user wears a goggles-like device that projects visual information onto the lens of the goggles. This allows the user to see the real world while seeing the additional visual information at the same time. In laboratory experiments with Google Glass, using the device interfered with a visual search task that appeared on a com-puter screen. In other words, using Google Glass disrupted visual attention toward the real world.

The most studied technology with respect to visual attention is video gaming, especially action video gaming. Action video games have several important fea-tures that include the presentation of large amounts of information on the screen, suddenly and rapidly appearing visual information, multiple moving objects on the screen, and the requirement to react quickly to events that occur in the game. Exam-ples of commercially-available games that have been used in studies are the 007 series of spy games, *Counter-Strike* (about terrorists and counter-terrorists), and *Halo* (military science fiction). Action video game players (AVGPs) appear to ben-efit from game playing in several ways, including increased attentional resources and visual attention, and improved sensitivity to visual information. One of the first steps in processing visual information from the world—or a computer screen—is to create a copy of the information inside one's mind so that the information can be processed even more. The copy of the information, such as the memory of the visual material in the world, appears to be of better quality in AVGPs than in non-AVGPs. AVGPs may have better working memory than non-AVGPs as well. And the link between action video game playing and attention seems to apply to young people; children ages 7 and older who play these types of games show an increased spread of attention compared to other children. That is, AVGPs monitor more of the visual information in the environment than the non-AVGPs. The people who multitask a lot, the HMMs, tend to have a split type of visual attention; that is, they pay attention to more information in the visual environment than LMMs. There is also another possible way for visual attention to be altered by technology use. For people who are addicted to gaming, there appear to be decrements in visual attention. This is different than the pattern for AVGPs. In Internet gaming addicts (see Chapter 10 for a longer discussion of Internet Gaming Disorder), brain studies show that it takes more effort than normal to carry out visual attention. One suggestion from scientists is that repeatedly using one's visual attention processes at maximum capacity—known as long-term hyperactivity of visual attention—results in declines in brain processing efficiency.

CONCLUSION

The next step in the evolution of the Internet may alter the way that people find information online. As of today, the information that is online comes in a dizzying array of forms and formats. For instance, each website has a unique layout that often makes it hard to find what one is looking for. Many researchers are working on creating the Web 3.0, or the Semantic Web. In the Semantic Web, information presentation will be standardized. This will make it possible for companies and organizations to create tools that accumulate and consolidate information across many sites. If this happens, the researchers predict that people will be able to use the web in a natural way that makes it easy to get information. For example, if a person types a query asking about the different strains of tomatoes and what they taste like, then the Semantic Web will return a complete answer compiled from many different sources. The promise of the Semantic Web goes beyond simple factual information. It may be possible to ask deep, conceptual questions. For instance, if a person enters a query about the reasons that the United States entered a war on Iraq, then the Internet search tool will return the logical argument presented by the United States for doing so, based on collecting information from many different web sources.

Yet the human brain still will be required to carry out information processing to make sense of all of this information, and to take responsible actions. The amount of information online is so great that people have access to more information that ever in the course of human history. The information age has put increasing demands on a human information processing system that was already limited in how much information could be handled at once. In particular, the prefrontal cortex helps direct attention so that our thoughts and behaviors stay on task. Multitasking with technology is nearly impossible, due to the brain's limited capacity. Meanwhile, in a few cases involving visual attention, which guides the processing of visual information, video gaming technology may be improving our attention.

This chapter presented the basic machinery of information processing that provides the foundational elements for people to perform complex feats, like learning to play a piano and completing a semester-long school course. Chapter 6 presents advanced mental processes known as higher-order processes and reviews how the higher-order processes are affected by technology use.

Interview with an Expert: Dr. Larry D. Rosen

Dr. Larry D. Rosen, an experimental psychologist, is currently professor emeritus and past chair of the Department of Psychology at California State University, Dominguez Hills. Dr. Rosen has accomplished a wide range of research related to the psychological impact of technology, including how technology use affects course performance, generational differences in technology use, how technology affects health and sleep, changes in language due to technology use, and how people use the Internet to get advice. He and his colleagues have collected data from more than 30,000 individuals in 24 countries in a little over 25 years, and Dr. Rosen has turned his many research projects into books about the psychology of technology. Author, co-author, or co-editor of six books in the field, Dr. Rosen's latest works are *The Distracted Mind: Ancient Brains in a High-Tech World* with Dr. Adam Gazzaley and *The Wiley Handbook of Psychology, Technology, and Society*, co-edited with Doctors Nancy Cheever and Mark Carrier. Dr. Rosen has also applied his findings and knowledge in many school and work settings as a consultant. He teaches college students what he has learned in a class that he developed called "The Global Impact of Technology."

Q: What is it about technology—about the devices themselves—that makes us want to use them?

A: Technology has continued to advance, and one of the ways it has done so is to make it easier and easier for people to use it . . . and to feel that they want to (or have to) use it. Tech companies have become what I refer to as "attention merchants" where their goal is to keep you on their website, phone, whatever by making it difficult to disconnect. This unleashed a set of chemicals in our brains that keep us at a constant state of wanting to check in with our various social media sites, plus other ways we communicate in the virtual world (texts, emails, etc.) by continuing to flood our brains with chemicals that signal anxious bodily feelings. These chemicals are those associated with anxiety, and when we feel too anxious, we have to stop what we are doing and check in. The only way our brain can get rid of those chemicals is to check in with whatever sites we are ruminating about and then the chemicals abate . . . for a while. Social media is one of the most common activities that we do with our smartphones. It accounts for most of our interruptions, either through alerts and notifications, as well as through internal distractions of thinking about who might have posted and what we might be missing out on. Some call it FOMO—fear of missing out—but it really is an anxiety about missing out and that drives our attention to switch from whatever we are doing to check in with our many social media sites. Most teens and young adults have five to six active social media accounts that they check at least once a day, if not more often, and this means there is a lot to catch up on each time you check in. We know that young adults check in with their smartphones 50 times a day for 262 minutes, and half the time they check they have not received an external alert or notification.

Q: When someone is driven to use technology, what is happening in his or her brain biochemically?

A: Most likely their brains have sent an internal notification in the form of an anxious feeling that we might be missing out on something if we don't check in quickly. Another brain chemistry issue is when we are addicted to something technological, such as gaming. In this case, as we start to think about playing a game, chemicals such as dopamine and serotonin start to be released and give us a pleasurable sensation. This drives us to play the game to get more of this pleasure, and over time we need more playing time to feel the same level of pleasure. The omnipresent smartphone plays a major role in our brain functioning, in that we always have it with us, we check it very often, and we need to switch our attention from what we are doing at the time to what we find in our phone. This redirects blood flow that carries oxygen and glucose to those neurons involved in doing whatever we need to do from our virtual connection, and takes time to redirect it back when we are done. What we know is that the prefrontal cortex is the last part of the body to complete the process of myelination, where neurons are wrapped with fatty cells that speed the connections between them. The prefrontal cortex is your body's controller, and if it is not complete until you reach your mid-to-late twenties, then this means that you are not making good decisions and not able to attend well. Technology may play a role in this in that it is constantly available to distract this brain area and redirect our attention elsewhere.

Q: Can people really multitask? If they are not multitasking, what are they doing?

A: People can only multitask if one task is automatic and well learned. We can walk and chew gum and even read a text message because walking and chewing gum are automatic and require little mental effort. We can't read our chemistry book and check a text message because both require mental effort. If we watch the brains of people trying to multitask, what we see is the flow of blood carrying oxygen molecules going to parts of the brain to deal with one task, and then starting to leave those brain areas and move to new areas to work on the second task. This is called task-switching and it is really what we are doing when we think we are multitasking. If, after switching, we then return to the first task it will take extra time to reactivate the neurons being nourished by the oxygen and glucose, and that means that it takes longer to complete two tasks when switching from one to the other than it does to complete one task and then the second task by focusing on each separately. The research on task-switching shows that we may perform worse on both tasks than if we did them separately, it takes us longer and it creates more stress. If you think you can multitask, turn on the TV to CNN and first listen carefully to the host speaking, but look at the scroll at the bottom. You will not be able to get much information at all from the scrolling information (unless you cheat and switch your brain from the host to the scroll). Now try it the other way. Look at the scroll and read along with it and then see if you heard anything the host said.

Q: What are the consequences of multitasking for learning during class and studying at home?

A: Nearly all the research has found that multitasking during class leads to worse grades because you are simply not paying attention to the teacher just like you could not attend to the host when reading the scroll. Even just glancing at a text message means that you are missing material then, as well as after, as you ponder the message you just read. When we interrupted students during a lecture with text messages; those who responded immediately to our text got a significantly worse grade on a test on that lecture than those who responded at a later time, when they felt the material in the lecture would not be on the test. We have also watched middle school, high school, and college students study and found that even when they were studying very important material, they paid attention only about 10 minutes out of every 15 minutes of studying, constantly switching from studying to something else, usually technological communication. And remember, switching back means that it takes extra time to ramp up the material that you were studying, and that means that it will take you longer to study. There is no evidence to show that teens and young adults are better at multitasking because they have grown up with technology. In fact, some evidence shows that the younger generations are actually more susceptible to interference and distraction.

6

Higher-Order Processes

Case Study: When Self-Regulation Fails: Cell Phones and Driving

Driver statistics show that people use their cell phones while driving, and accident data links the cell phone to accidents as well. Surveys of drivers over the years since cell phones became popular show high rates of cell phone use while driving. By the late 2000s, more than a quarter of all American teenagers were using their cell phones to send or receive text messages while driving, and almost half of them had ridden in cars where the driver had sent or received text messages behind the wheel. By 2015, even though there had been massive media coverage of the dangers of driving with a phone, about one-half of older adult drivers were still using a cell phone behind the wheel. By 2010, the percentage of all deaths due to accidents that could be attributed to texting was approaching 20%. By the mid-2010s, it was shown that more than one-half of the crashes involving new drivers were related to being distracted just before the accidents.

Research done in the laboratory and out in the field makes a clear case that handheld and hands-free cell phones interfere with driving, sometimes with disastrous results. Using the meta-analysis technique, scientists have shown across many studies that using cell phones is distracting for drivers, impeding drivers' reaction times to events on the road, sometimes as much as drinking alcohol does. Plus, hands-free devices are no less distracting than handheld phones, and are more distracting than talking to a live passenger, showing that our cognitive control ability of attention is impaired while driving with devices, not just our ability to move our hands while operating the car. As a result, there is a consensus among researchers that drivers should avoid using these devices as much as possible. According to scientists, anyone who uses a cell phone while driving is engaging in a problematic behavior, because most people now know that it is dangerous to do so. New drivers (i.e., teens) and older drivers are most vulnerable to the negative impact of driving with a cell phone. It has been known since at least the mid-1990s that American teens have twice the death rate of the general population in auto accidents. To change people's behaviors, researchers have come up with several recommendations that include cell phone applications that automatically disable themselves in moving vehicles, mass education of drivers, and simulated experiences that change new drivers' attitudes toward cell phone use.

Scientific knowledge and driver data instigated the movement to place restrictions on cell phone use while driving. U.S. states are slowly developing state-level driver restrictions, but 95% of the cell phone industry was represented by the Cellular Telecommunications Industry Association, which put up stiff resistance to regulation on cell phones while driving. By the beginning of the 2000s, the Association was lobbying state governments to support driver education efforts instead of enacting regulations on driving while using the devices. While the cell phone industry calls for changing drivers' behaviors using means other than legal restrictions, states have gradually fallen in line with the scientific and consumer perspectives. Although 11 municipalities in the United States had put laws into place to control cell phone use while driving, no states had done so by early 2001. Over the 2000s, states began seriously considering legislation affecting drivers. In 2001, legislators in 35 states had submitted bills to control cell phone use while driving. Family members of accident victims—organized into a group called Advocates for Cell Phone Safety—rallied on behalf of the bills. The first state passed such a law in 2001; New York was the first U.S. state to pass legislation, banning driving with handheld cell phones on June 28, 2001. Nearing the end of 2001, the number of states considering driving legislation grew to 43, and the District of Columbia, as well as the U.S. territory of Puerto Rico, were also considering legislation. By 2007, there were 34 states with distracted driving laws. Slowly, nearly every state passed serious distracted driver laws. The exceptions are Arizona, which bans school bus drivers only, and Montana. A further wrinkle is that many states ban only the act of texting—not overall use of the cell phone. States' legal restrictions still fall short of placing restrictions on hands-free devices; a glaring hole in all of the states' laws is that they do not address distractions from these devices, leaving drivers free to engage in a very attention-demanding—and potentially interfering—behavior.

By the time that New York had enacted distracted driver legislation in 2001, at least 24 countries had already legally addressed the problem with nationwide laws. The types of laws varied, with countries like Israel and Japan banning all phone use while driving, some banning handheld phones, for example, Australia and Chile, and others having variations on these. Japan enacted its ban of all phone use while driving—including hands-free phones—in 1996. Yet a ban at the United States national level seems unobtainable. Around 2000, when research was clearly showing the problems with distracted driving, the push for states to enact legislation was not well organized and had not yet gained momentum. Further, analysis of the costs of implementing distracted driver laws at the national level were disappointing, revealing that it would be very expensive for the national government to implement and enforce such laws compared to the gains made. In one mathematical calculation of the cost of enacting national distracted driver legislation in the United States, it was determined that it would cost anywhere between $50,000 to $700,000 for each year of lives saved. Given that other driver safety measures costed much less than that—$24,000 each for air bag requirements and seat belt laws—the analysts involved in the calculations could not support the feasibility of such a law. The analysts also found that lowering the costs of making telephone calls, while good for consumers in general, was very bad for drivers, as it would increase the number of accidents due to cell phone use. Some expert commentators, exasperated with the state of affairs, said that the burden of dealing with the problem must fall on the drivers themselves. Harkening back to the era of the inventor of the telephone—Alexander Graham Bell—in 1876, one writer somewhat jokingly called for drivers to follow this commandment: "Thou shalt not make frivolous calls on thy cell phone whilst operating thy horseless carriage." Although many nations have banned or restricted cell phone use at the national level, the legal structure of the United States and the potentially high cost of implementation appear to be preventing a similar ban in the United States.

INTRODUCTION

Basic mental processes, known as low-level processes, collect information from the environment and do some initial processing of that information. Low-level processes include sensory processing (the information from the environment is converted into electrical impulses in the brain) and motor processing (taking our intentions and translating them into commands to move our muscles). Low-level processes feed into high-level processes, also known as higher-order processes, that turn that information into complex concepts; combine the information with memories, thoughts, and experiences; and produce elaborate responses. The processes that convert stimuli in the environment—for example, sounds—into representations in the brain (letter sounds) are considered low-level processes. Taking those representations and combining them into a complete understanding (a sentence) is a high-level process. Think of high-level processes as being separated or removed from information in the environment by layers of analysis by the brain; in addition, high-level processes may be removed from our movements and actions by several layers of analysis. Any task that we perform that requires understanding, analysis, synthesis, evaluation, or application to new settings would be a higher-order task. So tasks like reading comprehension, writing an essay, teaching yourself to cook, learning, reasoning, and intelligence would all be considered to be of a higher order. Memory is a classic higher-order process; information extracted from the world goes through several processing steps before it becomes stored in our brains, and memories need to be processed and shaped before they can be turned into actions. Language, composing and making music, and creative activities like drawing and poetry are even more complex and refined higher-order tasks. The ultimate high-level process is the mind as a whole, our self-awareness—the totality of our experience and existence—that has been referred to as "the emergent higher-order function of that biological machine, the very core of our identity and consciousness" (Gazzaley & Rosen, 2016).

The theory of how the brain works to achieve higher-order functions is that low-level processors provide information to complex brain networks, out of which higher-order thoughts and behaviors arise. When researchers have examined, investigated, analyzed, and reduced the brain into its essential elements, they have found it difficult to identify one particular area, or even a few areas, that are responsible for high-level processes. Rather, they have come to learn that high-level processes are the result of many areas and networks of areas operating simultaneously in the brain. Higher-order thoughts and behaviors are said to be emergent, in that they are the end product of these other processes and networks being engaged. Some of the essential properties of the brain that provide this emergent behavior are that information is distributed—not localized into one spot—throughout the outer layer of the brain (the cortex [Latin word for bark]), that there are specific modules for sensory and motor processes, and that multiple networks of neurons overlap and are superimposed on top of each other.

The human brain is a complex, dense package of billions of neurons—cells that transmit bioelectrical signals. The neurons are grouped together in bundles that connect one part of the brain to another in order for those parts to communicate with each other. The brain, divided into large sections called lobes, works to keep every-thing on track as we work in the world, guided at the highest level—top-down—by the frontal and parietal lobes. Achieving our goals is made possible by the mental processes of cognitive control. Without cognitive control, none of the higher-order processes would be achievable. A central, controlling brain region keeps all of the processing on track to help us achieve our short-term and long-term goals: this area is the prefrontal cortex (PFC), part of the frontal lobe, located right behind our foreheads, introduced in Chapter 5. The PFC stores goals and intentions, and it directs the activity in other brain regions in order to help us achieve those goals; this is top-down processing. For example, visual attention is a process that our brains use to select certain parts of the visual world for further processing; this causes other parts to be ignored. We do not process complex scenes—for example, a view of the countryside out of your window—all at once. Cognitive control allows the brain to make sure that the parts of the scene most relevant to your current goals are attended; scientists call this selective attention. Cognitive control has a unifying effect on our thoughts and behaviors. As succinctly stated by scientists in a recent text, "You can think of all aspects of cognitive control as the higher-order actions of the prefrontal cortex that mediate our goal-directed control over how we both perceive and act in the world around us" (Gazzaley & Rosen, 2016).

You could not function effectively if it weren't for high-level processes like self-regulation and metacognition. Self-regulation is when you know that what you are currently doing or thinking is not helpful, so you adjust your actions or thoughts or both. Metacognition is when you reflect upon your own thinking processes in order to improve them. Both of these processes affect how well we perform many different tasks. In the world of technology use, impairments in fundamental higher-order pro-cesses like self-regulation are associated with painful results, such as technology addictions. Meta-attention is part of metacognition. Like other aspects of metacogni-tion, highly functioning individuals are aware of the status of their mental processes—in this case, their attention—and those individuals are capable of utilizing strategies to direct and refine their attention as needed. When you are driving your car, for instance, people with good meta-attention skills know not to use their phones while they drive, and they may even use strategies like putting their phones out of sight into a purse or backpack before driving the car. Learning is a complicated task that involves metacognition in many ways. Aside from using meta-attention, learning involves knowing how to learn, which learning strategies work best under different conditions, and how to use feedback to improve learning. Sometimes self-regulation and metacognition are referred to as executive functions, fundamental processes that work together to help us achieve cognitive control.

THE HIGHER-ORDER PROCESS OF CRITICAL THINKING

Imagine that a student does an Internet search on a topic for a school paper, and that the search generates a list of thousands of websites and web pages that contain material. The student is now faced with a decision: which websites and web pages provide the most useful material? The most useful websites will be those that pro-vide accurate information, otherwise the student might get a low grade on the assignment, and that provide relevant information, otherwise the student will waste time accessing the website. The results list itself does not assess the accuracy or the relevancy of information, despite what claims the search engine provider may make. So, the student must use her cognitive faculties to do the assessment. In other words, she must think. In this case, the best kind of thinking will be thinking that is slow, methodical, and goal-focused. Also, the thinking should be done without common thinking errors known as fallacies. This kind of thinking is known as critical thinking. Critical thinking has been defined in many ways. Two excellent definitions are that critical thinking is "disciplined, self-directed thinking which exemplifies the perfections of thinking appropriate to a particular mode or domain of thinking" (Paul, 1995) and that critical thinking is the "ability to actively use formal logical procedures to understand the world beyond its literal or surface-level meaning" (Ryder & Graves, 1994).

It is not humans' natural tendency to evaluate information analytically. Our natural tendency is to seek out information that confirms our pre-existing beliefs. This confirmation bias pushes us, for instance, toward websites that show material that supports our beliefs and away from websites that contain material that conflicts with our beliefs. Confirmation bias may come into play and affect our actions when we are conducting an Internet search using a search engine. If so, then the bias may interfere with optimal critical thinking at this important point in the steps involved in finding useful online information. At the highest level, critical thinking is about finding the truth, usually described as a summary of a topic based on accurate and credible sources and arguments. Finding the truth, from a critical thinking perspective, means actively preventing one's personal biases from affecting one's thoughts and behaviors. As two critical thinking experts once stated,

> . . . critical thinking varies according to the motivation underlying it. When grounded in selfish motives, it is often manifested in the skillful manipulation of ideas in service of one's own, or one's groups', vested interest. As such it is typically intellectually flawed, however pragmatically successful it might be. When grounded in fairmindedness and intellectual integrity, it is typically of a higher order intellectually . . . (Scriven & Paul, 1987)

Experts agree that critical thinking is necessary if people want to use the Internet effectively. The Internet has been transformed since it started in the early 1970s as a national computer network set up by the U.S. Department of Defense. When the public accessed the early form of the Internet, there was not much content compared to today; there were not many websites, and very few images and videos. Also, many of the first websites were corporate websites that were credible representations of their products and services. The Web 2.0 allows anyone from anywhere to post online any information they want to; thus, there is a burden on consumers of online information—including students—to distinguish between low- and high-quality information. Today, the wide range of quality and credibility of online information places strong demands on critical thinking. If all of the material online were credible, then a student could take a sponge approach to learning; a student could find ideas and information online and use them directly, without contemplation. The Internet would effectively function as an encyclopedia of validated knowledge. But online material varies in usefulness, quality, and reliability, and this creates a challenge for students. As one researcher has pointed out,

> . . . given the ease with which anyone can submit arguments to the Internet, the resulting sponge approach to learning is even more problematic than it is for print media. Consequently, the most foundational step in preparing learners for using critical thinking on the Internet is convincing them that such an approach to understanding and belief formation is dangerous and confused. (Browne, Freeman, & Williamson 2000)

From a broader perspective, critical thinking is key to effective learning, whether that learning involves the Internet or not. Deep learning strategies go beyond mere memorization and recitation of school material. These surface learning strategies may result in the acquisition of information by students, but they do not allow for the formation of advanced beliefs, the analysis of the quality of information, the integration of newly learned material with prior knowledge, or the generation of new ideas based on old ones. The latter activities require intense mental processing by the student; that is, they require critical thinking. (Critical thinking is not the only essential feature of deep learning; deep learning also requires excellent self-management and self-regulation skills.) However, students are not naturally good at critical thinking in general when using the Internet or being behind a screen. People born after 1979 are often referred to as the net generation, with "net" being short for Internet. When these people entered the school system, computers were fairly common at school and at people's homes. Many of them also experienced access to the Internet as children. The net generation was heralded as a new wave of individuals with advanced computer skills and complex information processing skills that let them perform feats like multitasking without performance decrements. It was widely assumed that net gen-ers would also grow up with sophisticated critical thinking skills because they had spent their childhoods online, navigating ever-increasing amounts of information and materials. Yet, by the mid-2000s, researchers began doubting the existence of a group of young people with amazing technical and cognitive abilities. and teachers and other professionals who interact with students started reporting that net gen-ers did not seem to have these special qualities. In fact, teachers were reporting declines in student's cognitive skills, rather than improvements. About one-half of the teachers surveyed in the early 2010s believed that contemporary technology was hurting—not helping—the critical thinking skills of students. They felt the same about the ability to do homework. Even more teachers perceived that students' writing and face-to-face communication skills were growing worse than they were before the Internet era. In the classroom, teachers were reporting differences in how they interacted with students in order to achieve learning goals. Students appeared to be more bored now than ever before. This necessitated that teachers work harder—using more interaction and in-class activities—to capture students' attention and to hold it during the unfolding of a lecture.

Also at the beginning of the 2010s, most teachers in the United States—about three-fourths of them—were convinced that the ease of generating search results on the Internet was causing students to give up too quickly when locating information online. Surveys revealed that students commonly accessed the first, and only the first, source that appeared on search results. The first item on the search results list routinely was a listing on Wikipedia, the online encyclopedia written by anonymous individuals. Rarely did students look at more than one page of search results, even though the order of results was, and still is, largely determined by an algorithm that knows nothing about the quality and credibility of information on websites. As a result, teachers felt that online information and search engines were curtailing students' use of critical thinking skills. This cycle of events, in which students are trained by the Internet to stop short when looking for useful information, is called the Wikipedia problem. Multitasking may be another problem. Information and communication technology (ICT) use and multitasking affect critical thinking and, in turn, affect learning. Critical thinking takes time. Mental processes that compare, contrast, reflect, and analyze material are slow, and thus slow down a task, like doing an Internet search. Applying critical thinking skills to the search results lengthens the duration of the information search process and places great demands upon our mental machinery. Critical thinking has a high cognitive load. The high cognitive load ties up mental processes through the act of evaluating the search results, preventing the psyche from working on other tasks. Yet people can choose to do another task while conducting an Internet search, if they want. This might happen when people are bored. (Remember from earlier that students typically find homework and other schoolwork done at home to be unpleasant.) If people choose to carry out another task—for example, if they choose to check Facebook—then the critical thinking processes will have to stop. In other words, multitasking will prevent critical thinking and self-reflection that would otherwise improve a person's performance in the information search task. If this choice becomes habitual, then it leads to a pattern of superficial processing of online information called continuous partial attention, which is similar to the concept of skimming. According to experts, multitasking not only prevents critical thinking from happening, but it also prevents imagination. Imagination is an important component of creative thinking, and may be crucial for innovative and scientific thinking. Because humans are not born with superior critical thinking skills, students need training on how to process material in a critical fashion, and they need opportunities to practice critical thinking.

One unexpected example of poor online critical thinking comes from the phenomenon of Internet pornography. Online pornographic materials are biased: they tend not to depict sexual acts as they occur in real life. Rather, they contain stylized representations of sexual encounters that contain distortions from reality. (Chapter 4 contains a lengthy discussion of online pornography.) One of the most common biases is that online pornography shows people engaged in casual sex—sex between strangers or people who do not know each other well. The scientific data show that teenagers are fooled by this bias. Teens that are exposed to relatively large amounts of online pornography show signs that they have incorporated this bias into their belief system. For one, these teens are more likely than other teens to engage in casual sex. Another sign is that these teens have different beliefs about sex than other teens, beliefs that are skewed toward the biases represented in online pornography. Experts say that teenagers who exercise critical thinking skills will be able to differentiate between the presentation of sexual behaviors in pornography and the reality of sexual behaviors in regular life. And it's not only teenagers who are susceptible to this bias; adults who view pornography are influenced by it, too.

The idea of a well-skilled young computer user does have some research support. In some cases, young people may be at an advantage for critical thinking over older individuals. Critical reading is the process of applying critical thinking while reading. People who are good critical readers are, among other things, able to extract the meanings of passages and compare what they read with information that they already know, leading to a nuanced understanding of the reading material. Online reading materials function differently than printed reading materials because they can let the reader move around in the text by clicking on links. (Chapter 7 elaborates on the differences between online and printed materials.) The potentially confusing, non-linear approach to reading online materials is often criticized by educators. As expected, net gen-ers who are college students show better critical reading when they read print materials than when they read digital materials. In contrast, there is a surprising advantage for the next youngest generation, the iGeneration. The iGeneration is the group of people born after 1989. The "i" in iGeneration is said to refer to the individualized or personalized nature of technology, and is based on the iPod, Apple Computer's revolutionary digital music player. This group was exposed to contemporary personal technology as children, including the Internet. Presumably, the iGeneration grew up in an Internet-immersed environment that included exposure to many digitized texts. With iGen-ers, at least one study has found that critical reading occurs more naturally in digital texts than printed texts.

Further lending to the overall pattern of a lack of critical thinking online is that people are not aware of the factors that influence how they process information online. One factor is the loss of information when materials are digitized and put online. Print materials contain information that is not part of the content itself. A printed book contains a front cover, frequently with an image and design, and a back cover that may contain an image as well as extra details about the book or the author. When books are digitized for the Internet, often these parts of the book are not placed into the computer file. Even more extreme situations can arise when considering historical documents. A historical document, such as a centuries-old treaty or declaration, may have handwriting, a certain typeface, particular layout, and paper qualities that influence how the document should be interpreted. These non-content elements are called contextual information. Entering the text of the document into a computer file for display on a web page causes the loss of the contextual information, and thus may alter the interpretation of the document. Another factor in critical thinking online is a person's self-assessment of how well they use the Internet. It's clear that the Internet era has improved many people's computer-related skills, but people's actions are not based on skill levels alone. They are affected by their perceptions of their own skill levels. When people perceive that they have relatively poor computer skills, then they will avoid doing computer tasks that they could probably do successfully, based on their actual skill levels. One entire segment of society may perceive themselves to have worse computer and Internet skills than others—women. In a laboratory setting, female Internet users in the United States proved that they are as good as male Internet users in finding information online. An example task was to look up the U.S. President's views on abortion. But when asked to rate their skill level at finding online information, the average female rated herself at a lower level of skill than the average male user.

DECISION-MAKING

When functioning well, our brains provide the mental processing that leads to good decision-making. Inhibition, for one—one of the key executive functions—is critical to decision-making. Inhibition allows us to suppress impulsive thoughts and ideas that might lead to poor decisions. Sometimes, it is important for us to suppress short-term desires over long-term plans that are healthier for us. For instance, when deciding whether to stay up late and play games on a school night, inhibition keeps us from going for the fun alternative of gaming and helps us focus on the long-term gains of getting a good night's sleep. According to the known architecture of human cognition, decision-making is a key function that is so attention-demanding that it limits our ability to multitask: only one decision can be made at a time, according to the wiring of our brains. Psychologists learned decades ago that people could not perform two simple tasks simultaneously without one of those tasks being delayed or postponed. Through laboratory experimentation, scientists proposed the existence of a processing bottleneck in our psyches. The bottleneck prevents two decisions or selections of an action to be made at the same time. (Other limitations exist in mental processing that prevent, for example, paying attention to many objects at the same time.) Therefore, when people try to multitask in real life, as when driving a car and checking text messages, there are consequences such that they might not be aware of everything going on around them, they might have low quality decision-making, and their responses may be delayed. Because access to our brain's decision-making mechanisms is limited to one decision at a time, the cognitive control processes that operate using our executive functions must work to optimize what decisions get made. Think of decision-making, like working memory, as so precious to our thinking and behaving that our brain must control access to them and allocate them in a way that is best for our thoughts and behavior. In other words, the brain has processes that act as executives in charge of our psyche's limited resources; hence, we have executive functions. If one thinks of the entire history of the human race, then it makes sense that cognitive control would evolve in the brain in order to manage these limited resources. This would promote survival in a harsh world. This is a good example that researchers have given that shows how important it is to suppress impulsive thoughts before they influence our decisions: Let's say that you are driving your car and you have your smartphone in your pocket. If a text message is received, your phone may buzz through the vibrate function on the phone. If you don't immediately suppress the thought of checking your phone, then your brain will begin to evaluate the message. For instance, you might begin to wonder who is sending the message and what the message might be about. This evaluation process has a good chance of leading to you actually checking the message while you are driving, a highly dangerous decision and action. This tension between needing to immediately suppress a distracting interruption and wondering about the details of the inter-rupting message is called the interference dance. Also, online, losing a sense of individual identity, known as deindividuation, leads to a loss of self-regulation (maintaining proper control of one's thoughts and behaviors facilitated by cognitive control processes) and an increase in impulsive behavior. The frontal lobe, especially the prefrontal cortex, plays a critical role in our ability to make beneficial decisions, as with other high-level processes. Researchers speculate that different sub-regions of the frontal lobe play different roles in decision-making. For example, the inferior frontal cortex—located on the outside, lower part of the frontal lobe—is believed to give us feelings of risk that are useful in decision-making. Another sub-region of the frontal lobe, the orbitofrontal cortex that is located within the prefrontal cortex, is involved in evaluating how rewarding an object or action might be, and thus in making decisions.

Research shows that, under the right conditions and with the right games, gaming can improve decision-making (as well as attention and self-control) in children and teenagers. However, adolescents and young adults—those who game a lot—can fall prey to negative effects of the Internet in general and gaming in particular upon decision-making. One of the negative effects of gaming is involved in playing violent video games. It is known from laboratory studies that playing a violent video game can lead adolescents and young adults to behave aggressively right after playing. When confronted with an ambiguous situation in which another person's actions are not clear (for example, a person rushing by you in the hallway and bumping you), you must interpret the action and decide how to respond. Playing the violent video game increases the chances that the other person's action will be interpreted as hostile, and that a decision will be made to react accordingly. And as to the Internet in general, several different factors about how the Internet works might be interacting with the qualities of adolescents, giving them a heightened vulnerability to poor decision-making in the online world. For one, the Internet provides a sense of anonymity because of the lack of visual cues to people's identities. When people go online, they tend to exist as a username in text form rather than an image of a real person. In gaming worlds, players probably exist as an avatar—a fictionalized, graphical version of themselves—rather than a real photo. This anonymity leads to a sense of security, because it is perceived that users cannot really know who other users are. At the same time, a need to explore their identities exerts a strong force on adolescents to try out new behaviors, expressions, and thought processes. The normal factors that prevent people from making impulsive or rash actions—the possibility of being known, fear of reactions, etc.—are lessened in their influence online, allowing more risk taking than in real life. This explanation has been used to understand, for instance, why teenage girls make poor decisions like responding to predatory messages from strangers. Another way to conceptualize the situation for adolescent decision-making is to think of decisions as the process of comparing the benefits of taking an action against the risks associated with that action. When situations or contexts are more familiar, actions taken in those settings will be more familiar and perhaps seem less risky. Adolescents, who spend by far more time online than adults according to most published statistics, see the online world as familiar and thus, less risky. This may bias them toward taking actions that adults perceive as risky.

Numerous studies show a connection between technology addictions like Internet Gaming Disorder and reduced decision-making. Additionally, researchers are beginning to learn which parts of the brain are involved in these relatively poor decision-making processes. For those with technology addictions, one of the most important decisions they make each day is whether they should get online. If they are aware of their bad habit, then it is most advantageous for them to be online as little as possible, in order to avoid the long-term negative consequences of these types of addictions (discussed in more detail in Chapter 10). To ensure their best health, they should choose to avoid being online and suppress the urge to fulfill their immediate needs. By definition, technology addicts cannot do this well; the addicts have been described as having a "myopia for the future." In fact, some scientists consider impaired decision-making a critical feature of having a technology addiction. One proposed definition of Internet addiction, for example, has three general patterns that a person must meet to be considered an addict, one of which includes poor decision-making along with poor self-control. It may even be the case that repeated poor decision-making about when to go online or to use electronic devices is the causal factor in developing a technology addiction. However, for now this is only speculation, as scientists have not determined which comes first, the poor decision-making or the addiction. It has become apparent that people with Internet addiction are strongly driven by the possibility of immediate rewards, even when scientists adjust those immediate rewards to be unlikely to happen. One technique used to determine how well a person's frontal lobe was operating was to ask people to perform task that placed mental demands upon this part of the brain. For instance, the dice task is a task that involves making decisions. Players are given money to place bets on the outcomes of dice rolls. People can place risky bets—ones with a low likelihood of succeeding—or safe bets, those with higher chances of being fulfilled. How well a person does on this task has been found to be linked to how much damage they have in his or her prefrontal cortex. In artificial game environments within laboratory computer tasks, scientists can manipulate how rewarding a person's decisions will be. One well-cited study is an experiment done with Internet addicts in Germany. The study involved gamers who played massively multiplayer online role-playing games (MMORPGs) like *World of Warcraft*. The gamers played the dice task. All of the gamers were excessive players who qualified as addicts based on a set of screening questions. Compared to a group of people who don't play games, the gaming addicts made riskier and less advantageous decisions in the task, leading to poor (fictitious) financial rewards. Whereas the control group was able to earn themselves 1,032 euros on average, the addicts lost money overall, with an average loss of 637 euros. Internet addicts also show relatively poor decision-making in the cups task, a task similar to the dice task. Another task that is done in the laboratory and involves decision-making is the Iowa gambling task. The Iowa gambling task is a laboratory-based decision-making task where people must make choices without knowing the likelihood that their choices will pay off. Over time, they learn which choices are more advantageous than others. However, Internet addicts perform more poorly than non-addicts in this task. Internet addicts have been observed to make poor, impulsive decisions. Not only do Internet addicts make poorer decisions in laboratory tasks than control groups do, addicts also take longer to make those decisions—a sign that they are struggling to make the decisions. As is the case with most research subjects in psychology and neuroscience, not all studies have found the same result that Internet and gaming addicts perform poorly on laboratory-based decision-making tasks. But, people with Internet Gaming Disorder do show abnormal brain activation in areas related to decision-making that include the anterior cingulate cortex (ACC), an area in the interior of the frontal lobe; the posterior cingulate cortex, lying right behind the ACC; and the middle temporal gyrus, located in the temporal lobe.

REASONING

Another important high-level processing is reasoning. Reasoning is a complex process that has several different facets. For hundreds of years, deduction—the mental act of determining if a conclusion follows logically or plausibly from a set of evidence—has been considered the bedrock element of formal reasoning. The most basic aspect of deduction is figuring out if one statement supports another statement. For example, given the fact that more boys than girls play video games, can one conclude that video games are designed for boys? The answer is no. Although it may be true that most video games are designed for boys, that conclusion is not warranted solely on the information that boys play more games than girls. Another name for the classic form of reasoning is abstract reasoning, reasoning that allows a person to apply generalized rules to any sort of information. This is the kind of reasoning drilled into the members of older generations—the book generation to some—in school. Nonverbal reasoning is solving problems without using language. Different measures of nonverbal reasoning exist. One way to measure nonverbal reasoning is to have people perform a task that involves blocks. In the Wechsler Adult Intelligence Scale—a famous test for measuring intelligence— test takers see a picture of an arrangement of blocks and must use real blocks to recreate the arrangement. No words are required to perform this task and the task measures a person's ability to think and plan how to make the proper block arrangement. Another often-used test of nonverbal reasoning is the Raven's Standard Progressive Matrices (RSPM) test. Despite the complicated title, the task involved in the test is very straightforward. The test-taker is shown three images that make a sequence. None of the images involve words. Then, the test-taker must predict what the next image in the sequence would be. Like other nonverbal reasoning tests, this test requires the test taker to solve a problem by applying mental processes that lead to the correct solution. Nonverbal reasoning is considered by scientists to be part of a specific type of intelligence called fluid intelligence, notated by the letters Gf. Gf is the set of mental processes that allow people to solve new problems. Gf is contrasted with crystallized intelligence, the set of processes that relate to our current knowledge, and to our skills in performing well-learned mental tasks. Deduction and other types of reasoning, such as nonverbal reasoning, depend upon the basic executive functions such as working memory. Thus, the primary location in the brain that is important for reasoning is the prefrontal cortex. The prefrontal cortex develops slowly; it is not fully matured until a person reaches her late twenties. The neurons in the brain—the central elements of information transmission—require a form of biological insulation called myelin in order to function properly. Myelin develops slowly and is not complete until around 30 years of age. This has raised concerns that mental processes relying on the PFC, such as reasoning, can be altered somewhat easily by extensive technology usage.

There is ample evidence to suggest that the Internet and the computer programs that we use are affecting our reasoning, although the pattern of results is complicated and nuanced. On the positive side, there are activities done online that now are known to improve a person's deductive abilities. One of these activities is using the Internet to find information that is relevant to a topic. This activity, when performed in the context of school—known as a WebQuest—has been shown to improve deduction in teenagers. Some of the activities that we do online are similar to the tasks that we do offline, such as searching for information on the Internet, and activate similar parts of the brain that involve reasoning. The more that an online activity is similar to an online reasoning activity, for example during gaming or social media use, the more the online version is expected to help or to improve reasoning. This is called "near" or "proximal" transfer of skills. Using the Internet to look for information—for example, with Google searches—activates the same parts of the brain that are involved in reasoning tasks. However, this only occurs in people with relatively high levels of computer experience, suggesting that people need to learn how to search effectively with online tools before they fully engage the reasoning areas of the brain. Puzzle games are a category of games in which players must match objects, perform logic, use deductive reasoning, or other high-level mental feats. Playing puzzle games would be expected to improve or provide practice for reasoning skills. On the other hand, other types of games would probably not help reasoning skills. A study done in Holland with young adults found that players of first-person shooter games—for example, *Call of Duty*—do not have better nonverbal reasoning that nonplayers. However, players of first-person shooter games do show signs of improved task-switching over nonplayers. As with many studies like this, though, it's not clear if the gamers started out with superior task-switching skills or whether those skills developed as a result of playing the games. In other cases of being online, like reading, there might be vast differences between how people perform the online and offline versions of tasks, leading to the possibility that technology use could alter reasoning and create a new type of reasoning. Reading print material makes a reader use many different high-level processes that include comprehension, reasoning, evaluation, and cognitive flexibility. When people read online, they self-report that they are using these same basic psychological processes, but other research shows that the affordances of the online world can make reading very different. The highly clickable interface of a computer or touchable interface of an electronic reader or tablet computer provides many ways that a reader can exit one screen of text and switch to another. These switches can interrupt the dynamics of normal reading processes, such as drawing inferences from the text and extrapolating a global meaning for an entire passage—in other words, reasoning. It has not been firmly established with scientific data, but a new type of reasoning, a direct result of spending time online, has been described. This type of reasoning involves somewhat randomly poking around on the Internet to solve problems; it is not deductive reasoning. Formally known as trial-and-error learning, some researchers have referred to it as bricolage. Searching for information online is an interesting case. Because the Internet allows access to a huge amount of information contained in a large social network, information is available to an individual that would not have otherwise been, if he was working on his own. Scientists have shown that doing reasoning tasks is improved when people have access to the Internet to help them do these tasks. But there is a downside; the same research shows that using the knowledge stored in this gigantic information network has a cost. After using the Internet to do reasoning, people are less likely to use their own reasoning processes in subsequent cases.

Personal characteristics of Internet users, such as their ages, are important in determining how reasoning relates to technology use. Because children's brains are still developing, they may be more at risk for negative influences of technology use when it comes to reasoning skills. Young kids have not yet developed the ability to perform abstract reasoning, the skill of taking details that are presented and drawing high-level conclusions from them. Because of this, young kids are more likely to accept fictional information, such as the content of television shows or the storylines within computer games, as real. In other words, they have difficulty separating fantasy from reality. At the same time, there is evidence that the brains of older individuals are adaptable enough to learn enhanced reasoning and other skills through technology. Despite the fact that the frontal lobe declines with age, particularly affecting executive functions, the right kind of video games may be able to improve executive function skills, including reasoning. Computer and video games have become more complicated over time. Early games, the so-called first generation video games, were relatively basic and straightforward. These games included, for instance, *Tetris*, *Pac-Man*, and *Donkey Kong*. Playing these games increases speed of reacting in older adults, but not high-level skills. Newer games require a mix of basic, low-level processes and high-level thinking. For example, the computer game *Rise of Nations* is a strategy game that involves quick responses, as well as complex tasks like building and monitoring cities and making plans for expansion of one's borders. When older adults are trained to play *Rise of Nations* for four to five weeks, they improve in their task switching and reasoning skills, as measured with the RSPM test. There is not improvement in most low-level skills and attention-related skills.

Finally, a person's background is important, too. If a person has a lot of experience multitasking with technology, then that person's reasoning may be affected by these experiences. There is an association between being a heavy media multitasker (HMM) and having relatively poor nonverbal reasoning. In college students, it was found that students who do the most multitasking with technology in their everyday lives also do worse on the RSPM task. However, because the research is correlational, it's not clear whether multitasking causes poor reasoning, people with poor reasoning are attracted to multitasking, or there is some other relationship. Two unrelated traits of people—need for cognition and thinking style—may also affect how technology shapes their reasoning. Need for cognition is a personality trait related to people who like to think. That is, people with a high need for cognition enjoy thinking and seek out experiences that challenge their mental processes. Not surprisingly, people who have a high need for cognition use technologies that require them to use their high-level mental processes, including reasoning. Another case is that of concrete versus abstract reasoners. Concrete reasoners focus on the details of an argument or situation, while abstract reasoners are able to draw inferences from information in order to make larger statements about the argument or situation. In college students, being a particular kind of reasoner affects how much personal technology is used and for what reasons. In a study of Chinese college students, it was found that concrete thinkers use electronic devices for entertainment and communication for more hours per day than abstract reasoners. Further, there is a connection between how a student uses her devices and her grades. The Chinese study estimated that every hour of using devices for education increases a student's GPA by .04 (on a four-point scale), while one hour of non-educational usage decreases GPA by .02. Thus, abstract reasoners have an advantage over concrete reasoners when it comes to grades. A similar effect happens with prior computer experience. People with relatively high reasoning abilities are more likely to use computers and have significant computer experience. It has been suggested by researchers that these reasoning abilities allow a person to acquire new skills (such as using technology) better than those without these abilities.

COMPUTER LITERACY

One last type of high-level skill that is relevant to technology use is computer literacy. Computer skills and knowledge are important for being successful as an employee, a citizen, and a family member in contemporary society. In the 21st century, information and communication technologies have become so woven into the fabric of society that many jobs require knowing how to use the computer and software, or computer literacy. Life as a citizen demands computer literacy, as well. One must know, for instance, how to use the web to gather information and purchase goods and services. Therefore, it is advantageous for all people to become computer literate. There are different kinds of skills and knowledge that are wrapped into the concept of computer literacy. Various cases have been made for which kinds of computer literacy are the most important for the general public to learn. Three kinds of computer literacy are computer programming, computational thinking, and gaining the knowledge of when computer-like thinking is most beneficial. Computer programming involves knowing how to write computer code that solves a problem, provides a service, or performs another task. Python, for example, is a widely used computer programming language in the world of ICT. There is a certain way of thinking associated with computers, and scientists believe that members of the public can benefit from learning to think this way. Thinking like a computer is referred to as computational thinking. To think like a computer, one must be able to break a problem down into parts, with each part being clearly defined, and then convert the conceptual information about the sub-problems into actual steps to take to solve the sub-problems. Experts say that this kind of thinking can be applied to many different situations with success. At the same time, other experts argue that not everyone needs to learn how to program a computer, but everyone does need to learn what computers are good at and what they are not good at. This knowledge helps a person decide when to use the computer or Internet as a tool to solve a problem and when not to use them. Not all problems require computational thinking, so it is important that people learn to recognize when this kind of thinking is appropriate and when it is not. Because the software that runs computers and devices has become much more user-friendly over the last few decades, knowing how to program a computer may be less important nowadays for being a productive person than it was in the past. It may be important to be able to have general skills that don't rely on particular technologies, such as multitasking and communication. Due to the rapid change of technology, people will always need to learn new skills. But some experts highlight the importance of knowing how to be smart online; that is, how to interact online and conduct business online while maintaining a high level of intellect—in other words, executive functions.

Computer literacy can help people deal with the headaches and hassles of life online. One example of dealing with the negative aspects of the virtual world comes from the phenomenon of cyberbullying. Researchers expect that most young people will have the technological skills to react to advances from a cyberbully. For instance, cyberbullies can be blocked using blocking tools provided by social media platforms. But older individuals might not have the same level of computer skills necessary to deal with such problems. In this case, parents and teachers might need to acquire some of these skills in order to monitor online activities and keep children safe. Another example of an Internet-related problem is how not to be a victim online. This is particularly problematic for adolescents, especially girls, who are targeted online by predators. One of the riskiest actions a youth can take online is to make friends with strangers and later meet that person in the offline world. The stranger may be a sexual or other type of predator, and the meeting can lead to kidnapping, manipulation, or worse outcomes. By becoming familiar with the technical aspects of using social media and other types of programs for communication, an adolescent will have the electronic tools available for dealing with such predators.

The biggest potentially positive impact of becoming computer literate will come for young people. As young people growing up in a world filled with computers and the Internet, these individuals will naturally acquire skills and knowledge related to computer literacy. In the late 1970s and early 1980s, more and more homes in America started to get computer-based video games. As the 1980s progressed, home computers became popular. Trying to assess the impact of these technological changes on young people, researchers developed several phrases for people born after 1980. Three such phrases are digital natives, the net generation, and millennials. Researchers assume that digital natives grew up learning some basic skills with computers that include keyboarding, running programs, and so on. Later, when the World Wide Web (the graphical version of the Internet) came into being, digital natives learned how to use web browsers and to find information online. Even younger people will have grown up with different skills. People who were born in the late 1990s and 2000s—sometimes referred to as the iGeneration—grew up with a completely different set of devices and programming technologies than the earlier generation. Gaming, for example, moved from being based in video arcades, on home computers, and on simplistic gaming devices to highly sophisticated at-home video game platforms. Despite a tremendous amount of computer know-how, though, training might still be necessary to get the right kind of computer literacy for doing well in school, at jobs, avoiding Internet-related problems, and being maximally productive. The computer skills and knowledge that kids learn from growing up and living their everyday lives might not be what is best to know for school learning. As discussed earlier, effective learning requires focus, paying attention for long periods of time, and handling abstract and difficult information. In contrast, much of what young people do online is sporadic and concrete, partially due to the affordances of the technology. One particular fear that parents have is that, in the future, the routine tasks done by human employees will be done by robots instead. This parental fear is driving some of the computer literacy training for young people. If the fear becomes a reality, then it will be pointless for children to learn how to do those routine tasks now. Rather, it will be critical that children learn to program the robots, if they want to have jobs. Hence, there has been a rise in computer programming training for children, even preschoolers, where the kids learn, for example, how to program a simple robot to dance.

There are myriad interesting effects associated with the Internet revolution that started in the 1980s and 1990s. On the one hand, as more and more people began using computers at home and at work, positive benefits have certainly accrued to society. Evidence that getting computers at home boosted computer literacy came from studies of high school students in the 1980s and 1990s. Students who used educational software at home showed higher levels of computer literacy than other students. Learning computer skills in coursework, at all levels, also boosts computer literacy. The aftereffects of doing so can be unpredictable but positive. For example, in the case of a class in the early 2000s for college seniors that required non-computer majors to learn how to build a website, it was reported that one of the students got a paid position building a website as a result of the class experience. Another student, who had no prior knowledge of computers, purchased and set up a computer at home, incorporating the computer into his everyday life. One prominent scientist has gone so far as to attribute part of the Flynn effect—the international rise in IQ scores during the 20th and 21st centuries—to the computer revolution.

On the other hand, computer training or experience has its downside as well. For some individuals getting involved in computer literacy, there can be an aversive reaction to computers. Known among researchers as computer anxiety, the aversive reaction is both physical and psychological. Physically, people with computer anxiety become negatively aroused when they use or even think of using a computer. Psychologically, people experience fear and concern. Unfortunately, this anxiety may reduce people's belief that they can effectively use computers or computer technology. Some research suggests that the solution is computer literacy: as people become more computer literate, their negative reactions to computers lessen, and they become more confident in their abilities. And issues around gender and socio-economic status are still present. A long-lasting gender gap in computer literacy exists that may have been exacerbated by other gender differences, such as those in game playing. Playing computer games is a good way to gain computer literacy skills, but boys are documented to play games significantly more often than girls. This may be putting girls at a disadvantage for computer literacy. In the 1980s, camps for young people wanting to learn to code computers became popular. For a fee, parents sent their children to learn computer-related skills that included computer programming. Yet most of the children who received the training were boys. One study in the United States estimated that computer camps and classes in the United States had a ratio of three boys to every girl. The precise cause of the gender gap in computer training is not known, but several possibilities have been offered. One is that boys are more interested in computers because they are more interested in math than girls are. Another is that there are stereotypes that favor men becoming computer programmers. Science fiction movies that were blockbusters in the 1960s and 1970s in the United States tended to show computers being controlled by men. Examples are *2001: A Space Odyssey* in 1968 and *Star Wars* in 1977. Further, computer and video games are more likely to have male-oriented themes than female-oriented themes. Finally, one possibility is that parents encourage boys, more than girls, to learn about computers. Any or all of these forces might be operating to reinforce the gender gap. By the early 2000s, the gender gap in computer usage had diminished. However, despite the ubiquity of computer training opportunities available now to almost anyone, girls still report feeling underrepresented in the world of computer science. One way around the gap might be to provide girl-focused computer training. Computer skills training for girls can include computer camps and boot camps that are designed for them, as well as other forms of outreach. For instance, fictional books that feature female characters who solve problems through coding are being marketed in an attempt to change the stereotyped views of coders. Also, poor people may not get access to the same computer literacy-building experiences as other groups of individuals. The digital divide refers to the difference between people who have access to the Internet and those who do not. In the United States and many other countries, access to the Internet is not free, so people who do not have very much money might not have Internet access. This could mean that children from poor families will not gain computer literacy at the same rate as other children.

Luckily, there are numerous opportunities for anyone to become computer savvy; trends in computer training, not only in the United States, but worldwide, give people of all ages opportunities to build computer literacy. Some opportunities are online, while some are in-person classes and workshops. Coding opportunities start at a young age, run through college, and exist for seniors as well. In the last ten years, massive open online courses (MOOCs) have been run where anyone in the world can learn a new skill in any domain or gain some new knowledge on any topic. Courses have been known to have tens of thousands of students enrolled them at any one time. It turns out that the most popular MOOCs are computer programming classes and computer-related technical skills courses. There is an impressive variety of ways to build one's computer literacy. There are paid academies, free online lessons, free online video instructions, web-based courses, courses on location at colleges and universities, boot camps, and many others. The experiences reach far and wide; one large training organization claims to have 45 million users, with one million of those being seniors aged 55 years old or older. Not surprisingly, the push to get more young people trained in vital computer skills is supported by the technology companies located in the famed Silicon Valley in California.

THE FLOW STATE

Working online can be a pleasurable experience that causes people to lose track of time. In unusual circumstances, people's attention can become so focused that the situation results in alterations and distortions of experience. The flow state occurs when a person becomes so involved in what they are doing online that they stop paying attention to their surroundings and cannot compute the passage of time correctly. Research shows that web browsing, social media, and general online interactions with other people can induce flow states in users. When people go online or play video games, their mental and physical processes may become highly dedicated to just one task—say browsing products at an online retailer. In a flow state, computer and technology users report that they lose awareness of aspects of the environment other than what they currently are doing. The people might not respond to other information in the environment, like another person calling their name. Online shopping is just one of several situations that might induce a flow state. Other situations include playing a video or computer game, surfing the web, interacting on social media, and watching streaming videos. Researchers investigating flow states in computer-related settings have found several factors that contribute to the flow state, aside from ignoring irrelevant information in the environment. In a flow state, users feel a level of challenge that is neither too easy nor too hard, get the feeling that they are part of the computer-based environment— known as telepresence—and have access to hardware and software controls that do not impede performance, such as an effective user interface. This extreme form of involvement in a computer-based task also might include time distortion: users frequently report losing track of time or spending more time on a task than they originally had anticipated.

RESTORATION AND REJUVENATION OF COGNITIVE FUNCTIONS

Psychological processes like executive functions, as well as our physical processes, benefit from taking breaks from technology for many reasons, including avoiding addictions, avoiding physical injuries, and easing one's anxieties. Breaks can also help people get through boring tasks. Boredom may develop when using computers to complete tasks that last a long time; that have repeated, simplistic elements; or that require intense focus. Writing an essay using a word processor is a good example; doing online research is another. A significant portion of people naturally give themselves breaks from technology. If you are an American adult and you use a cell phone, then you are most likely using a smartphone, spend a significant amount of time texting, and frequently share photos or videos with your phone. Additionally, there is about a one-third chance that you impose cell phone breaks upon yourself; one nationally representative survey found that 29% of American cell phone owners took breaks regularly by turning their cell phone off for a while. Younger adults, ages 18 to 20 years, are more likely to take breaks than older adults, ages 65 years and older. But people often take breaks by switching to some other technology-based activity, like checking one's social media page. Experts recommend taking breaks that do not involve technology or computers. These might include staring away from the computer for a brief period of time, letting oneself daydream for a while, and taking a cat nap. Here are some of the other forms of breaks that experts have recommended: turning off notifications and alerts, forcing yourself to talk with someone in person, read a book—a printed one—or a newspaper, listen to music (and do nothing else at the same time), or laugh. Going into nature is a commonly recommended treatment for the anxiety related to the Fear of Missing Out. And there is scientific evidence for the benefit of nature breaks, through Attention Restoration Theory (ART). ART argues that we need breaks during which we stop using our top-down cognitive control processes and instead let the environmental input into our brains guide us—bottom-up processing. By doing so, we rejuvenate the top-down control processes so that they work more effectively after the break. Longer breaks, where people go without using any technology for a day or more, show interesting effects. In one study—the world Unplugged study—students from universities around the world went 24 hours without any technology, including music and radio, and kept diaries of their experiences. Despite reporting difficulties like being fidgety and feeling anxiety, students started engaging in healthy activities that they don't normally do, like going for walks and listening to the sounds of nature.

Researchers have also examined the psychological and neural impact of taking extended breaks from gaming, and they are also concerned with the physical injuries that might come with long bouts of game playing. Gaming has a powerful effect on some individuals, possibly leading to a gaming addiction. Experts recommend that parents encourage their children to take regular breaks when gaming in order to avoid physical injuries. Another way to reduce physical injury is to position the computer, gaming equipment, and one's body in a way that is comfortable and safe. This ergonomic approach can be achieved by studying the instructions and warnings that are bundled with the equipment. A study of Australian gaming addicts was conducted in order to figure out the withdrawal effects of not playing games for one weekend. Significant withdrawal symptoms were expected, given that people with other types of addictions go through painful and emotionally wrenching phases when abstaining from their addictive substance or behavior. Surprisingly, the gaming addicts in this study suffered only very mild symptoms that included boredom and a need for mental stimulation. Further, addicts made changes to their behavior that could only be construed as positive: they started socializing with real people (not online), were intimate with their partners in real life, and resumed their other hobbies, among other behaviors. As with many pleasing and fun activities, game players can get into a flow state when gaming. While a flow state may be optimal for game enjoyment, it can also wreak havoc on a player's ability to control her gaming habit. She may be unaware of real time, thinking that very little time has elapsed when, in fact, a lot of time has gone by. She may be unable to stop playing because of the intensely rewarding nature of the flow state. Therefore, parental monitoring software—programs installed by parents to limit or reduce their children's online activities—can be used to monitor and disrupt gaming on the computer. Adult gamers can use these programs on themselves. Other programs can be installed that provide reminders to take breaks. These micro-pause programs are helpful, not only for avoiding the psychological issues associated with extended gameplay, but also for the potential for physical injury due to the repetitive motions involved in playing games. The abstention might be worth it, as changes in the brain take place that may relate to improved neural functioning. Adolescent gaming addicts who reduce their gaming for a one-month period show a shift in brain activity from areas not under much cognitive control to areas involved in cognitive control. An area of the PFC known as the right dorsolateral prefrontal cortex becomes more active after the four-week period.

Unfortunately, people are not very good at estimating how much time that they spend on their technological devices, which could pose a problem for deciding if you need to take a break. People inaccurately self-assess how much their use their devices; there tends to be a difference between people's self-estimated technology usage and their actual usage. This has been determined by using tracking software or technology company statistics—the gold standard for measuring device and Internet usage—to compare to people's self-reports. Concerning smartphone usage, young adults are not good at self-reporting how much they use their favorite apps, or in determining which of their apps are most used. Tracking software on phones has found, for example, that college students in Asia play games on their phones about one and a half times more than they report. The same holds for the use of social networking sites. Some people underestimate their device usage while other people overestimate their device usage, probably for several different reasons. Underestimating how much time one spends with technology can be problematic when trying to work efficiently on an important task. For instance, a student might believe that checking his text messages in the middle of studying will take only a short amount of time. But if he has underestimated how much time he tends to spend on texting, the break from studying will last longer than expected and undermine the work that needs to be done. And many studies find that people overestimate their usage of technology and the Internet. This has been found with how long people talk during a cell phone conversation and also with how much a person uses Facebook. When looking across several studies, a pattern of underestimation and overestimation emerges. This pattern—called regression to the mean—shows that light users of the Internet or computer technology tend to overestimate their usage, while heavy users tend to underestimate their usage. Regression to the mean had been shown with TV viewing in the past.

Even if people are not 100% accurate in how well they self-estimate their phone, computer, Internet, or other technology use, it might be possible that people are at least fairly good at it. Scientists determine how close people come to estimating their true technology usage by calculating the correlation between self-report data and actual tracking data. When using personal computers and tablet computers at home, adults' self-reports only modestly track real usage. In a study in Holland, for instance, people were asked to report how much they used these devices the day before the questionnaire was taken; the results showed that the correlation between self-report and actual usage was .29, a rather low value indicating that less than 10% of the actual usage was predicted by the self-reported usage. (Scientists use the squared value of the correlation to determine the percentage of actual usage account for.) The same value was found for the correlation between self-reporting a typical day's technology usage and actually recorded data from the devices. When people self-report at-home web browser usage, only about one-third of them are accurate. Further, the correlations between self-report and tracking data are modest, showing that people's self-reports are only partially related to actual usage. With more than 3,000 participants installing tracker systems into their home web browsers, a study in Germany found that all of the correlations between self-report and tracking data were less than .40, meaning that self-reports predicted less than 16% of the actual usage data. There were several kinds of inaccuracies made in self-reports. In the case of general Internet use, tracking data showed that 15% of the participants were heavy Internet users, using the Internet more than once a day. However, self-report data showed that 54% of the participants thought that they were using the Internet this much. In Norway, using telephone network data, researchers were able to confirm low associations between self-report and actual usage of cell phones in adults. In this case, the correlation was .23. However, people were a bit better with reporting their text messaging activities, revealing a correlation of .58. When looking at how well people self-report the use of specific apps on the cell phone, people tend to do well with browsing apps, social networking apps, and productivity apps. But again, many of the correlations are low, signaling problems for people's self-report in many cases. For the number of calls made on a cell phone, the correlation is .47, and for the duration of cell phone calls, the correlation is .32. Another study of the number of calls and the duration of calls for correlations of about .30 and about .10, respectively. The very low correlation between self-report and actual call duration indicates that people were essentially guessing how long their calls had lasted. Sometimes, fairly high correlations are found, like the .62 correlation between self-report and actual calls in one study, but many are much lower. Even in the same study, the correlation values can vary widely. In another study done in Belgium with college students, their friends, and their family members, investigators looked at texting behaviors. There again was a wide range of correlations, from .42 to .81, and it became apparent that the precise wording of questions to participants influences how well they remember their texting patterns.

Two of the main reasons that people are not good at estimating their own technology usage are social desirability and the weakness of estimation strategies. Social desirability means that "respondents would over-report behavior that is perceived to be positive by their social group, and under-report behavior perceived to be negative" (Araujo, Wonneberger, Neijens, & de Vreese, 2017). A good example comes from a study on video gaming: relatively wealthy people tended to under-report their video game usage compared to less wealthy people. Another study showed that people tend to overestimate their usage of map-related, news-related, and music-related apps on a cell phone, possibly because of the appearance of being intelligent through map- and news-related apps. However, another factor in the inaccuracy of reporting may be difficulties in remembering. When we are asked to assess how much time we've spent using our cell phones, for instance, we may have already forgotten many of the instances or the details of when we used the device. When it is hard to remember the details of past technology usage, then people must use some sort of strategy to reconstruct what they did in the past. This opens the door for all sorts of errors in self-estimates, because these strategies tend to have bias, a consistent pattern of mistakes in one direction or the other. For instance, if people use enumeration strategies to self-report—counting their memories of using their devices—then their counts may be limited to only those events that they can remember at the moment. Other times that they used their devices may have been forgotten and will not be counted. This particular bias related to memory—called availability—means that only the most memorable uses of devices will be recalled and counted.

Another issue is that people often take a break from technology by using technology. Much of what is known about why people use technology to take breaks comes from a population that is repeatedly asked to engage in long, attention-demanding tasks: students. Proper studying may require hours of focus upon a topic assigned by an instructor. If reading is part of the studying requirements, then this adds an even greater need to concentrate, as reading is well-known among scientists as an attention-demanding task. High school and college students are well-known for either not taking breaks from technology or using technology to take breaks. Students use technology to take breaks from studying, from schoolwork, and from lectures; additionally, some students use technology breaks to control their attention spans. Students may need to take breaks from such focused work, either because their brain's mental processes become fatigued or because they come to a point where they find nothing interesting about what they are studying; in other words, they become bored. In either case, the mind may generate internal interruptions to the main task of studying and these interruptions may lead students to switch away from their main purpose of studying and toward some pleasing technology that is nearby. Studies of students tell of how, for example, they use Facebook as such a break. Facebook is accessible on almost any device and is easily available to a student whether they are studying at home, in a library, or at a coffee house. Completing schoolwork has properties similar to studying. It is lengthy, highly demanding, and involves high-level mental processes. For these reasons, students take many breaks while doing schoolwork and those breaks often involve technology. Again, social media, especially Facebook, are popular choices. During class time, students are required to pay close attention to the teacher, taking notes appropriately, for 45 minutes or longer without breaks. Not surprisingly, all of the research shows that students' attention spans waver during lectures, and the students look for ways to deal with this problem. When asked, studies find that students use technology to take a break due to boredom or exhaustion, as they do with studying and with schoolwork. Social media may figure prominently, both Facebook and other sites, such as Twitter. When studying, schoolwork, and class lectures do not provide much pleasure for students, the students may become susceptible to the rewarding, reinforcing effects of other tasks or stimuli. In other words, they may be using these other tasks as an escape from their main task. Because taking a break using technology in the classroom or while studying leads to students becoming temporarily disengaged with the to-be-learned material, there is the strong possibility that learning will be affected. Several experimental studies have shown how text messaging during a lecture, for instance, leads to decreases in learning by as much as 10%, a whole letter grade. This caused a few scientists to refer to the cell phone in the classroom as the disrupter. However, a subgroup of students seems to believe that taking breaks with technology can actually improve their attention so that they can refocus on the lecture. Students with high levels of metacognition—knowledge and skills related to managing one's school environment—report that they use technology not only to take a break, but also to serve as a reward for not taking breaks. They have claimed that by doing so, they are able to maintain focus for longer periods of time before taking breaks. Some researchers also have endorsed these tech breaks as a way for students to increase their ability to stay focused on school-related tasks; however, tech breaks have yet to be evaluated scientifically.

There are potential problems with these technology usage strategies, including effects on health and sleep. The strategy of not taking breaks can be especially harmful, with studies showing that continuous gaming or general computer use is linked to unhealthy outcomes. The time of day that one spends using technology without breaks may be important. For example, gaming late at night, before bedtime, has several negative effects upon sleep. Prolonged or excessive gaming (60 minutes or more) before sleep caused preteens and teenagers to need 22 extra minutes to fall asleep according to one research report. Over longer periods of time, there also may be effects of not taking breaks upon sleep. A study of Swedish adults found that men were more likely than women to avoid taking breaks on the computer (38% compared to 12%), but that the impact on women was worse than for men. Using a computer without taking at least a 10-minute break every 2 hours was linked to sleep problems, symptoms of depression, stress, and reduced performance at work or school for women one year into the study. Based on analyses of people's overall technology use, scientists have tried putting all of the information together to find general patterns and sequences of events that explain how and when people take breaks—or fail to take breaks—with technology. If you have ever been under time pressure to accomplish a task, then you have probably experienced feeling the need to skip normal activities in order to stay on task. These might include not eating when hungry, not sleeping, and not going to the bathroom. Another normal activity that is important in staying on task is to take breaks. So students, who may feel that they are perpetually under time pressure, may be less likely to take the breaks they need to clear their minds. But anyone who uses the computer to get work done may feel time pressure if they have spent too much time doing tangential activities with technology when they should have been focused on getting their work done. In either case, not taking breaks may take a long-term toll due to the failure to rest one's mental processes. Additionally, people under time pressure might also be more likely than others to have poor posture and to not set up their computer workstation in an ergonomic fashion. In some ways, multitasking and taking short breaks while working are indistinguishable from each other. If your breaks using technology involve an ongoing tech-based task, such as carrying on an IM conversation with a friend while you are doing homework, then you are essentially multitasking—doing two tasks more or less simultaneously. For instance, one poll of Americans found that 38% of cell phone owners use the cell phone during the commercial breaks during television shows. However, it has been learned that the type of break taken is affected by the motivation for taking a break. Researchers have found that college students are more likely to use social media (including texting) than other technologies or applications to escape, and that they use music when motivated to relax.

CONCLUSION

Any project that is worth doing, like writing a 20-page research report for a class, forces people to use their most advanced cognitive skills, also known as high-level processes. The key high-level processes are those that perform cognitive control; that is, they manage the brain's processing to make sure that we achieve our goals. In this regard, successful people rely on their executive functions—high-level processes that include attention, working memory, and mental flexibility—to manage complex and important tasks. Juggling the multiple components of a task or handling multiple tasks at once are common features of a big project. As people become more experienced with computers and personal electronic devices, they may find themselves trying to do more than one task at a time—multitasking—due to the affordances provided by technology. But the research shows that people who multitask are not more efficient than other people. In fact, frequent and persistent use of technology may create feelings of stress and anxiety. Therefore, taking breaks from technology use is generally helpful to people, especially if the break involves spending time in nature. One benefit of spending time with computers and devices is the development of computer-related skills or computer literacy. Computer literacy can take different forms and all forms may be important to learn. There are other key high-level processes that were not discussed in this chapter. Reading and writing are sophisticated skills that take years for people to learn. The rise of the Internet and the availability of personal electronic devices may have impacted these two skills; the research is described in the next chapter (Chapter 7). Learning for school is a complex task that involves many of the executive functions when done well. This high-level process is discussed in Chapter 8.

Interview with an Expert: Dr. Nancy A. Cheever

Pursuing a career in the media, Dr. Nancy A. Cheever gained extensive experience as a journalist and editor with newspapers and magazines. In her 20-year career, she had been a magazine editor, an entertainment editor, a dining reviewer, a features writer, a reporter, and a designer. Now, she takes on the responsibilities of being professor of communications at California State University, Dominguez Hills. Dr. Cheever is chairperson of the department and her research specialty is in the area of media psychology. She draws on her knowledge, skills, and experiences in the journalism field to shape and inform her scientific research agenda. She has made numerous scholarly contributions to her field. Dr. Cheever is a founding mentor in the George Marsh Applied Cognition Laboratory and has co-authored or co-edited three books. She co-authored *Rewired: Understanding the iGeneration and the Way They Learn* (2010), co-authored *iDisorder: Understanding our Obsession with Technology and Overcoming its Hold on Us* (2012), and co-edited the *Wiley Handbook of Psychology, Technology, and Society* (2015). Dr. Cheever also teaches courses related to her expertise in journalism and the psychology of the media. Dr. Cheever's courses fall into four general categories: media writing, theories and methods of research, media psychology, and reporting/information gathering.

On top of her duties at the university, Dr. Cheever consults with organizations, sharing her research knowledge and skills. As a consultant, she provides workshops, makes presentations, and gives trainings to parents, teachers, and organizations about new technologies and psychology. As busy as she sounds, she knows the value of self-regulation. To balance her work life, Dr. Cheever practices what she preaches about lessening the potentially harmful effects of excessive technology use at work and in personal life. She plays classical piano (since the age of 6) and she enjoys the outdoors. The homepage of her professional website prominently features a photo of the outdoors. The photo shows trees, forests, and mountains that stretch for miles, reaching out to snow-covered peaks in the far-off distance. Dr. Cheever notes: "Although my work involves sitting in front of a computer most of the time, I gain a great sense of peace and inspiration from being in the natural world and away from technology!"

Q: How do smartphones change thinking and behavior? What kinds of complex tasks are disrupted by smartphones?

A: Smartphones are powerful devices that we rely on for almost all communication. Since they have the ability to allow us to communicate and access information, these little computers change our thinking and behavior in profound ways. First, they have changed the way people communicate. Before the introduction of smartphones, people had to speak to one either in person or on the phone. Now, the number one communication method, regardless of age, is text messaging. So we are not speaking to each other as much, and not listening to one another as much, both because of texting and also because of how frequently we use the devices—at the dinner table, on romantic dates, in the classroom, out with friends. Smartphones have also changed our thinking, in that we have become so dependent on them the device itself becomes an object of obsession that we constantly think about.

It is extremely important that people self-regulate their personal device use and use metacognition to understand the effects of their smartphone use. Besides the obvious issue of the smartphone being a huge time-sucker (i.e., you plan to check your social media or email for a few minutes, which turns into a few hours), people form opinions, shape their values, and make important decisions about their personal finances, education, child rearing, etc. based on the information they seek through their devices. Understanding and processing how we use the devices is the first step to becoming media and information literate, and mitigating the ill effects of overuse. Based on what we know about the negative psychological effects of using too much technology—including sleep deprivation, anxiety, depression and the relationship to a host of other associated psychiatric disorders—it is important that people take breaks from their devices. I recommend at the very least turning the phone off at night and resisting the urge to check it constantly throughout the day. The positive effects of this will vary depending on the person, but in general people should feel more calm, less anxious about, and less dependent on their devices.

Q: What demands do our personal technologies place on our critical thinking skills?

A: Once people engage in self-regulation and metacognition about their devices, attempting to navigate through the enormous amount of spurious information that can be accessed through the devices places high demand on our critical thinking skills. Sometimes called information overload, this also places a heavy load on our cognition, or cognitive load. Also, the ease of access to information makes it difficult for the average person to understand what information is reliable and what is not. It is extremely important that people use critical thinking skills when accessing information online so they can make informed decisions about their lives and the lives of the people around them.

People are curious, and therefore generally interested in information. However, we are not naturally adept at locating the best information online. We know from research that most people only click on the first four or five links in a Google search, when the best information may be located on the second or third page of links. Advertisements, search engine optimization, and prioritization based on paid placements make it very difficult for people to understand where the best information is located. Also, people want instant gratification, and most are unwilling to take the time to locate the best information, instead opting to go with the first source that appears to be credible. All information affects our decision-making, but the Internet is the most widely used source of information and therefore impacts our decisions the most. For instance, more than two-thirds of adults use their smartphones to look up information about their health, and in some cases, they make decisions about how to treat their condition rather than see a medical doctor.

Q: Is Wikipedia a valid information source?

A: Wikipedia is essentially a free information source that usually pops up first in a Google search. It has source credibility because of its pleasing layout and the depth of information on a given entry. Because it is so widely used, people assume the information is reliable and valid. Wikipedia can be very handy for people who are casually interested in a topic and want information for their personal edification. However, it should not be used as a research tool as the information on the site is not reliable. Anyone can edit or alter the information, and unbiased experts are not the people most likely to do this. The site is unable to keep up with edits to every page, and on any given day the content varies from completely unreliable to 100% accurate. That's why Wikipedia is not a valid information source.

Q: What research is missing on these topics and where do you see the field headed?

A: Because the technology is still fairly new, no longitudinal studies exist that look at the long-term effects of using smartphones. We will see these studies emerge in the next five to ten years. Also, because the American Psychiatric Association has not yet recognized problematic smartphone use as a psychiatric disorder or even a sub-category of an existing disorder, yet it has some of the same withdrawal symptoms and characteristics of a disorder, more research in this area is needed. Researchers in Asian countries see the relationship as an addiction that needs clinical intervention. Studies on the information and news literacy show we have a long way to go in teaching people how to identify, understand, process, filter and use online information.

7

Reading and Writing

Case Study: Text Messaging with Ferocious Velocity

"The razor-toothed piranhas of the genera Serrasalmus and Pygocentrus are the most ferocious freshwater fish in the world. In reality they seldom attack a human."

Who is the world's faster texter? This sentence, selected by Guinness World Records, challenges the competitors. The company requires that the phone used be one that is commercially available. And to beat the standing record, the typist must be able to finish the challenge without mistakes. One of the earliest world record holders for fastest texter was James Trusler from England. Called "amazing thumbs" by one commentator, Trusler became the world's fastest texter in September of 2002, when smartphones were rare and when mobile phones used the number-pad layout borrowed from old telephone keypads. These were the days prior to the insertion of a full keyboard layout on mobile phones. The old layout organized letters into clumps associated with one of a small number of keys on the keypad. For instance, the letters a, b, and c might have been mapped onto the 2 key. This layout requires that the user frequently make multiple keypresses to enter the letter of choice. In this case, to make a letter c, the user has to press the 2 key once, then press the down arrow key twice in order to complete the typing. Like all of the world record holders, Trusler is an avid text messager. He texts with two hands without looking. In one interview he said, "If I wasn't texting my life would be totally different—using my mobile phone is how I got my job, met and communicated with my fiancée—it's everything to me" (Collyns, 2004). Trusler's world record speed was 67 seconds. According to Trusler, using older technology, the difficult parts of the standard message are the upper-case characters, the hyphen, and the periods, all of which require additional keypresses on an older phone keypad. The rare words are also a challenge.

The world record holder has been located in different parts of the world over the years. Craig Crosbie from England took the world record in 2005, tapping out the standard message in 48 seconds. In 2008, the record holder was Kimberly Yale from Singapore. Rapidly-changing technology keeps helping challengers break records. As phone technology improved, the record times got faster. Early mobile phones had small screens that did not use touchscreen technology. With touchscreens, the ability to enter letters into a message became physically faster. The significant change in technology led to the increased specification of the world record criteria by Guinness. The new world record category was the fastest text message using a touchscreen. This record was first held by an American, Franklin

Page, who typed the standard Guinness text message in 35.54 seconds in March of 2010—nearly twice as fast as Trusler's record with an old-style phone. As the mobile phone industry became increasingly competitive, third-party companies began creating even more efficient keyboards that could be downloaded and installed onto a phone by users. Additionally, useful features like predictive texting—the phone guesses your next word—and autocorrect were injected into text messaging software, although these features are not allowed by Guinness during a world record attempt. By 2014, there was a quantum jump in typing times. Marcel Fernandes Filho, a teenager from Brazil, broke the world record, keying in the Guinness standard text message in 18.19 seconds, less than a second faster than the 18.44-second record that he beat. Filho's phone was a smartphone—a Samsung Galaxy S4—enhanced with the Fleksy keyboard application to make typing more efficient. Filho superseded his own world record; switching to an iPhone 6 Plus—but still using the Fleksy keyboard—he achieved another record a short while later, texting the standard Guinness prompt in 17 seconds.

Other formal competitions surround the activity of text messaging, including texting while blindfolded; the current world record for blindfolded texting is 45.09 seconds to type the standard Guinness prompt. Some competitions pit teams from different countries against each other. For example, the Mobile World Cup invited teams from around the world to compete in a speeded competition where texters had to copy phrases moving across a monitor as quickly as possible without errors. The messages were presented in the native languages of the teams, carefully crafted so that each team had to type the same number of characters. In 2010, the winning team, from South Korea, included Yeong-ho Bae, who was able to type at the rate of six characters per second. This contributed to his team's winning of the grand prize of $50,000. Bae and his team mate, Mok-min Ha, had both received mobile phones as children and felt comfortable with texting on the phones. Ha said, "I text while walking, eating, watching TV." Texting poetry competitions challenge creative writers to work in short messages that typify the "text-speak" language that has evolved around text messaging applications. For example, Graham Francis won the prize for best creative use of SMS in 2002 for this poem:

GLSTNBRY FSTVL

seasnd w msts n fruitlss mellwnss
n pungent smlls f grss ovr hay
we flp nto ponchos fr a mnts rest
n try nt t pln t rst f t day

While achieving world-record speed is not the goal of most people using a text messaging application, there are aspects of texting that compel ordinary people to go quickly when sending messages and replying to messages. One aspect is the fact that text messaging often occurs as a naturally flowing conversation between two people in real time. Another aspect is that typing seems to many people to be a very slow method of communicating, and is perceived to necessitate speed in movement. Speed in responding is also facilitated by the nature of text-speak itself, since it contains shortenings and abbreviations that save on the number of characters in a message.

INTRODUCTION

Reading comes in two forms now. One form is the traditional print form, as exemplified by printed books, magazines, and newspapers. The other is the digital form. Digital forms include websites, handheld electronic readers (e-readers), and text messaging threads. Reading on electronic devices, while still involving English—or whatever language you are used to—is different than print reading in several ways. Researchers are investigating whether these differences are changing people's reading style and reading skills. Another interesting question is how the Internet era is affecting reading in general. Is the rise of digital reading affecting how much time spend in print reading? Are electronic devices and pastimes, such as gaming, having the effect of reducing how much time people spend reading? Reading also has been affected by new styles of writing. For instance, Internet-enabled digital devices have spawned NetSpeak, text-speak, and Webspeak, to give a few of the many names for this new style. Along with the new style of writing, various innovative products of writing have arisen, such as Wikis and blogs. Scientists are looking into how writing with electronic devices and platforms may be altering people's language skills.

PRINT VERSUS DIGITAL READING

People might not realize how much reading they do on their devices and computers. Reading is necessary for processing information in social media like Facebook; comprehending texts presented on computer, tablets, and mobile phones; reading and replying to emails; checking the news; and gathering information from websites. Reading also occurs in many activities on a cell phone, such as replying to text messages, reading the news, finding information on websites, looking for addresses, using social media, and sharing pictures. Even more examples of reading with technology include reading and commenting on blogs, reading and editing cloud-based documents, and managing one's appointment book. Sometimes we read material online even when we didn't intend to do so. For instance, on Facebook, we are exposed to many messages that scroll by on our screens that we did not set out to read. This is known as passive reading of messages. It's been a long road for the development of electronic texts, and of specially-designed hardware to support them. The first electronic text was the United States Declaration of Independence, typed up and posted online from the University of Illinois in 1971. From that initial act came a movement to make free, electronic versions of important texts known as Project Gutenberg. More than 28,000 titles have been made available. Commercial versions of texts became noticeable only more recently. In 2010, these texts, known as e-books, accounting for only 5% of all book sales in the United States. Since then, advances in software have led to enhanced e-books that contain extra information beyond mere text, such as embedded pictures, videos, and links to other content. The Kindle and the Nook are two devices specifically designed for reading. They were introduced in 2007 and are available for both the general public and student use. Since electronic texts are less expensive than purchasing hardcopies of texts, e-readers allowed people to acquire texts at a lower cost than in the past. However, dedicated reading devices come with their own problems due to the hardware, one of which is the difficulty in reading letters on a screen in a wide variety of changing light conditions. Although e-readers made inroads into the reading habits of the general public, devices that existed solely for the act of reading gave way to multifunction devices that allowed for reading, plus a variety of other commonly-performed Internet-based activities, like playing games. Finally, the coexistence of tablet computers like the iPad led to the introduction of applications for tablets that brought the e-reading experience to those device owners.

Along with these developments came side effects associated with reading from an electronic screen. The blue light emitted by e-readers has been criticized by scientists as producing sleep-altering effects. Normal light, the light reflected when reading from a printed page, contains a variety of wavelengths—the physical properties of the light); however, e-readers and other small screens, such as phones, tend to emit light that is centered around a wavelength that humans perceive as blue. Most readers can sense the change in light when they look at their small screens, but it is not possible to sense the effects that the blue light might be having on one's physiology and brain. Not all small screens are the same, however; in at least one study of the properties of small screens, the Kindle e-reader was found not to emit any light except for the room light that was bounced off of the Kindle screen. Especially when e-readers are used in the hour before going to bed, blue light can make people unnecessarily alert, suppress melatonin—the body's natural chemical signal to go to sleep—and alter the normal sleep cycle—a phenomenon known as phase-shift. Another potential impact of reading on an electronic device prior to going to bed is not feeling alert after waking the next morning. In one study, reading an e-book, compared to reading a printed book, caused a delay of 10 minutes to fall asleep, reduced the amount of healthy Rapid Eye Movement (REM) sleep, and reduced how alert people felt the next morning. The negative effects of the e-book may have been through the operation of melatonin, an important chemical related to our daily sleep/wake cycle. Melatonin signals the body to be sleepy, thus encouraging sleep. However, with reading e-books, the release of melatonin was delayed by one and one-half hours, and the amount of melatonin was reduced by over 50%. Another one of the problems with reading on a screen is visual fatigue, often associated with how often a person blinks while reading. In a seemingly backward move, e-readers morphed into devices with black-and-white screens that are designed to mimic paper. New screen technology, for example the Kindle Paperwhite e-ink, has been invented to improve reading and reduce visual fatigue. Over long periods of reading—one study looked at reading sessions spaced out over 10 days—the new screen technology may reduce fatigue.

THE MENTAL CHALLENGE OF READING

Various psychological processes are needed to carry out reading of printed materials, with some of them taking years to develop. The fact that reading is a psychologically complex process is reflected in how reading activates the brain. When adults are reading, multiple areas of the brain are working. These areas include language regions, words and letter-shape regions, memory, and vision regions. Although reading is mentally demanding, it is not physically demanding. Scientists placed reading on the list of sedentary activities that may contribute to poor health; other sedentary activities include eating and talking. Because of the complexity of reading, it is hard to do another task while reading. In one study, it was found that reading—as well as playing video games—was a task that was all-consuming, in the sense that people found it hard to multitask with other tasks. Before children are reading, they are developing narrative skills—the skills of listening to stories and creating stories. Reading processes start with early skills, known as early literacy, and advance to more complex skills, later literacy, during one's childhood. In the preschool years, kids should learn how to identify and manipulate speech sounds—the skill of phonological sensitivity—and also learn about the alphabet, basic vocabulary, and even some rules about word order, or syntax. Speaking, reading, and writing are intertwined; many of the basic literacy skills touch upon all three complex tasks. When a child is two to three years old, he or she must continue to grow a word vocabulary; when a child is in the range of three to six years old, he or she must increase the vocabulary more, plus acquire harder words and improve his or her ability to articulate. From six to eight years old, a child must further develop an understanding of language sounds, or phonology, and of sounds that differentiate words—also known as phonemes (e.g., the "p" sound in tap as opposed to the "b" sound in tab).

Eventually, people learn to perform reading comprehension and writing. The ability to focus one's attention becomes very important when the complex literacy tasks like reading comprehension or writing essays are performed. Working memory—the ability to hold small amounts of information in memory while doing a task—is critical to reading. To read effectively, a person must be able to hold onto information from one part of a passage until a later part of the passage is reached. Then, the multiple pieces of information are processed together in order to make sense of the passage. The same occurs within a sentence or across a whole page of text. Not only will people with limited working memory have trouble with reading comprehension, but they may also find that reading is less pleasurable because they are unable to read effectively. Years of basic research into working memory and reading have established their connection, and it has shown that people with better working memory are also better at reading comprehension. Scientists can measure working memory as it contributes to reading by using the reading span task. In the reading span task, participants in an experiment view a series of sentences and then, after all sentences are viewed, are prompted to recall the final words of each sentence. The more words recalled correctly, the higher the reading span, and thus the better the working memory. Working memory is strongly affected by age: from one's 20s to one's 80s, there is a consistent reduction in performance.

Even at the skill level of reading comprehension, reading processes require different levels of effort, depending upon what is learned from reading. After a person's reading skills have fully matured, he is capable of extracting more than just superficial information—facts—from texts. He is able to draw conclusions from what is read (inferential reasoning), to bring information from memory to bear upon the argument laid out in the text (critical analysis), and to wonder how the material applies to his own life (reflection). These deep reading skills take many years to develop. To pull out the factual information from a passage, a reader might need only one or two passes through the passage. To extract subtle meanings from a passage or to understand complicated information, a reader might need multiple readings of the passage. The latter would apply to reading a textbook for class, reading a poem, or reading the privacy information on a website. Another way to say this is that reading creates increasing mental demands as the goal of reading gets more complex. Researchers have identified multiple types of reading, with the easiest being pulling out information that is overtly stated in a text. This is Level 1 of the Question-Answer Relationship Framework, a template for understanding the complexity of different types of reading. The next level of difficulty, Level 2, is drawing conclusions—also known as inferences—by connecting information that is located in different parts of the text. Level 3 involves combining information from memory—the background information—with the material contained in the text. Level 4, the hardest level of reading, requires that the reader not only perform the mental acts from the lower levels, but also perform critical thinking, such as reflection, to draw even more conclusions from the material. It's also the case that different people use different strategies when reading. The strategy can be picked in order to achieve a particular goal, such as a quick scan of the reading to look for relevance to one's goals. Some strategies may change the amount of mental effort required to finish reading. For instance, if one's goal is to learn what's contained in a reading passage, then one would apply a study strategy, such as taking occasional pauses to test oneself on what has been read so far. This strategy would increase the mental demands of the reading task.

And reading never really gets easy. It takes years to acquire reading skills, and then even skilled readers need focused attention for reading comprehension. Reading may be one of the most mentally demanding tasks that a person performs in his or her everyday life. When people do pleasure reading, for example, they report that they can't do other tasks at the same time. In other words, reading does not allow for much multitasking. Interruptions during reading might actually come from within a person's mind. It's not uncommon for a reader to think of other topics or events while trying to read. It's not just reading a text that requires focused attention. Other tasks that involve some reading also need a person to remain very focused on the task. A task like doing homework, for example, which often involves reading, involves shifting one's attention to doing the homework and keeping one's attention there for long periods of time. And students who take standardized tests must still retain their ability to read carefully and remain focused without distractions for long periods of time, despite how reading unfolds in everyday settings online. Aside from the standardized testing instituted within each American state, there are national-level tests that allow students to move on from secondary school to college—the SAT, for example—and to move on from college to graduate school—for example, the GRE. In all of these cases, students are tested in quiet environments where all of the distractions are removed, including cell phones. Another important part of reading is the background knowledge that a reader brings to bear upon the text. In order to understand what is being read, a reader must apply knowledge about vocabulary, general knowledge about the world, and specific knowledge about the topic of the text. The amount of background knowledge needed to understand a passage affects the difficulty of reading the passage. When very little background knowledge is necessary, or when the reader already knows quite a bit about the topic, then reading is relatively easy. In other cases, reading can be very hard.

Reflecting on the changes made to the printed text, it is clear that texts have been transformed through computer technology. Texts that contained mostly letters now contain images, video clips, and other types of materials. The new style of reading can improve reading comprehension for some readers. In the case of people with poor reading skills, the extra materials that can be embedded into a passage through hyperlinks can improve understanding. Plus, texts are rewritten and altered as they pass through various authors online. Finally, texts are becoming shorter. Reading text on a device is very different than reading traditional, printed texts because the hardware and software on a device give readers new physical and mental actions that they can take when reading. When people read from a computer or device screen, some of the reading processes may be altered or function differently than when reading printed materials. While the act of reading from a screen has not changed some of the key processes involved in reading, other processes seem to be affected by reading electronically. When people read electronic texts, they do not appear to employ some of the activities that are associated with reading printed texts. Readers of e-texts are less likely to highlight passages, use bookmarks, and annotate text than readers of printed texts. Further, just because reading material is presented electronically, it does not mean that reading is any easier for people. For instance, the working memory demands of reading electronically are no different than reading in print. Actually, reading the kind of language that is often present in electronic messages—known as text-speak—has been found to be harder than reading regular language. Text-speak contains shortenings, abbreviations, and other tricks for reducing the number of characters in messages, as well as for adding emotional content to a medium that allows only characters to be shown. Scientists have demonstrated that text-speak is harder to read than regular language by asking people in a laboratory to perform a mundane task while simultaneously reading text-speak or correctly spelled language. It turns out that the text-speak causes more interference with the mundane task than does the correctly spelled language. This result shows that reading text-speak puts greater demands on our mental faculties, a phenomenon known as cognitive load. Another study showed that reading text-speak activates the brain in ways that are similar to reading words in one's second language. Part of the alterations of reading by the advent of the Internet has to do with phasing out old skills. Technology gurus and pundits claim to observe some skills that are dying out. It will no longer be necessary to know how to read printed materials or to read an analog clock.

The basic message from research is that reading electronically does not negatively affect a person's ability to comprehend a written passage, but the time needed to read may be extended. A further factor is that it is much more tempting to multitask when reading electronically than when reading print, thus introducing potential distractions to the reading process. When students read and study on the computer, they tend to also multitask. This occurs for high school students and college students. Instant Messaging (IMing) while reading is a popular way to multitask, as is surfing the web and using email. Whether reading from a printed text, a laptop screen, or a tablet computer screen, skilled readers are able to extract the information necessary to comprehend the text. When multitasking while reading, reading times are longer but comprehension is unaffected. One research team referred to this slowdown of reading as a "loss of efficiency." Let's say that a college teacher assigns a book chapter—available electronically—for reading at home. Different students will take different strategies for reading the chapter. Some will use strategies to focus their attention on the text as they read it, such as closing all other open applications on their computers. It is likely that another subset of students will not take any precautions to safeguard their reading, leaving open various applications that could interrupt reading comprehension. For instance, they may leave open an IM or chat program that alerts them to incoming messages from their friends. The students who respond to these messages will take significantly longer to read the chapter. In a well-known study conducted with college students in Connecticut, this exact scenario was simulated in a laboratory. Students who read the text without interruptions took 37 minutes, on average, to do so; students who responded to occasional instant messages took 46 minutes, on average. This represents a 24% loss of efficiency. And this loss in efficiency was not just due to the time it took to respond to the IMs; the reading times had already been adjusted for IM activity. Thankfully, the slowed reading times do not translate into worse reading performance, as both groups performed at the same levels on a subsequent test of the material contained in the text. Another situation that people, especially students and employees, often find themselves in is reading from Microsoft PowerPoint slides. It turns out that the same general pattern of results applies to reading in that situation, as well. As long as there is unlimited time available to read the slides, then simultaneously responding to unrelated messages does not interfere with reading comprehension; however, it does slow down the reading process. The effects of reading on computers upon reading time extend to other electronic screens, like tablet computers. As has been shown with printed reading materials, multitasking while reading impairs comprehension when there is limited time for reading.

The Internet and our digital devices have changed our relationship with reading material. Instead of reading dry, boring written materials, digital technology and the Internet provide access to an unlimited number of emotionally gratifying messages to read through social media. Much of the reading that occurs with technology is satisfying and interesting, a fact that people find out very quickly when they join a new social medium. The material has an allure to it that competes for our attention. The impact on reading is noticeable. Reading for school or work, compared to other reading on the Internet, is often described by experts as boring, uninteresting, and lacking emotion. This creates a conflict between the pull of interesting material on our devices and the rational desire to stay focused on the boring but important reading material. The conflict puts demands on our cognitive control mechanisms, whose job it is to keep our attention focused on tasks that help us achieve our long-term goals (as described in Chapter 6). One way to think about the competition between reading and other, more interesting tasks is to think of boredom profiles. Boredom profiles are the ways that certain tasks do or do not grab our attention. Tasks that provide frequent rewards tend to have stimulating profiles; tasks that have rewards that do not come about for long periods of time tend to have less stimulating profiles. For example, reading websites as part of research for writing a paper may be inherently less stimulating than playing computer games. Doing tasks with uninteresting boredom profiles, like reading academic websites, might be made more exciting by multitasking with a different task. IMing, for instance, while doing online research might alter the boredom profile of the academic reading task to make it more interesting. Multitasking during tasks that have relatively uninteresting boredom profiles, like reading, doing homework, and listening to lectures, has been well documented in young people—those who are born in 1980 or later and often referred to as digital natives. (It is said that digital natives are more at ease "reading" multimodal texts [i.e., those with images and videos] than traditional texts, but there is not much research to support this assertion.) It has been documented that students all around the world are prone to multitasking while doing schoolwork, including reading and studying.

The Internet has given people access to a staggering amount of written material. Before the Internet was widely available, there were few situations where someone looking for reading material would be faced with an overwhelming number of possible reading sources. Perhaps the library was the only such place that would have available a large number of texts on a single topic. Standing at the book shelves, a person would have to pull books off of the shelf, review them one at a time, then decide which books represented the best reading sources for the person's goals. This time spent perusing the shelves represented an additional load of work that had to be done when faced with multiple reading sources. Nowadays, the problem is multiplied greatly, as even seemingly simple searches in an Internet search engine generate thousands of listings. Looking for information about health can yield not just thousands, and not just tens of thousands, but millions of listings. One published research paper investigating health information online found that a search for "HIV status" produced more than 7.5 million listings. While many—if not most—of the listings will be irrelevant, there will be a very large number of relevant listings that require time to process. So what do people do when faced with an overwhelming number of web-based reading sources? There are really not many options available except for the strategy of skimming, defined as a "rapid, selective reading strategy such as omitting words, paragraphs, or pages" (Duggan & Payne, 2009). Many factors influence our reading, and our reading strategies, when online. When faced with a mountain of information to process, as might happen when we do an Internet search on a topic, we have to make choices about what to read and how much time to spend reading it. When time is limited, people tend to choose easier texts to read. When our goals are lofty, such as researching a term paper, we tend to choose harder texts. Because valuable time can be spent just deciding which texts to read, people are known to switch to a strategy called satisficing. Satisficing involves choosing the first, satisfactory alternative that comes along instead of looking through all options to find the best one. Regarding textual information returned from an Internet search, satisficing would comprise the strategy of reading the first text that meets our minimal informational needs. How do we know when a document will meet our needs? We perform a rapid judgment of the document that perhaps includes the skim approach.

The merging of text and other media within the same document is embodied in electronic storybooks for children. Children having language or reading difficulties may benefit most from electronic storybooks, as the additional information provided by the multimodal format helps them comprehend the material. Animations added to stories can help children learn the stories. On the downside, the interactive features of storybooks that include hyperlinks to additional information can be distracting and impair understanding and learning of a story. Having to juggle understanding the text at the same time as gathering additional information from the hyperlinks creates additional cognitive load for the child readers—cognitive overload—that interferes with effective reading comprehension. This distraction effect occurs even with older children. Eighth graders have been found to be adversely affected by hyperlinks, with their comprehension of material compromised when compared to traditional texts. The problem of distracted reading is compounded for children because their executive functions—key psychological processes that guide our behaviors to be in line with our goals—are not mature yet.

At the same time that reading is becoming electronic, much of the reading material requires high levels of reading skills, putting significant demands on readers' mental faculties when they read. Researchers can apply mathematical formulas to texts in order to calculate how difficult the texts are to read. Some word processing programs have reading level formulas built into their systems. A widely available formula is the Flesch-Kincaid scale that is accessible through, among others, the Microsoft Word program. The resulting value, often called the reading level of the text, is an indicator of what grade level of education a person would need to have to be able to understand the text. Much of the important reading material online is written at a reading level higher than many Americans have. Millions of Americans not only have weak reading skills, but also a significant chunk of U.S. citizens is functionally illiterate, meaning that they do not have reading skills sufficient for succeeding in contemporary society. A good level for general understanding is 10.5 on the Flesch-Kincaid scale. In contrast, one report on privacy policies at popular Websites found an average reading level of 12.3. Another published analysis found that documents posted at the U.S. National Cancer Institute's website had an average reading level of twelfth grade. This level is higher than many Americans' education levels.

EFFECTS ON READING SKILLS

Two ways that reading skills are affected are by intentionally using computers to improve reading abilities, and by the effect of using computer-based writing styles on reading abilities. Teachers and educators may intentionally try to train people, especially kids, to become better readers. Putting material online for children to learn can improve their educational outcomes. Third graders, for instance, improve their reading skills more when they are taught using the Internet than they are when taught with traditional instruction. Even non-educational exposure to the Internet is associated with better reading. Children who have more Internet exposure than other children also have better reading scores on standardized tests. One study showed that "brain training" can be used to improve reading skills in children. Brain training means that learners perform tasks on the computer that are designed to improve basic mental skills like focused attention, withholding impulsive responses, and being mentally flexible. In second graders, doing short brain training exercises prior to doing reading-related exercises raised scores on the exercises. Additionally, giving extended brain training to the second graders improved their scores on a reading achievement test. Similar results were found for math skills. The short-term effects may be the result of cognitive priming that occurs when memories related to reading, for example, how certain letters make certain sounds, are activated during brain training and then help in the subsequent reading exercises. In other cases, there were no changes in reading skills after children were given computer training. Computer programs used for third through sixth graders in one study and first through fourth graders in another study did not improve reading skills. It might be possible to explain why training only works sometimes. The time displacement hypothesis says that computer training will only be effective if it replaces activities that do not involve training for reading. If a computer training program is used at school, then it might only be displacing an already rich array of learning activities, so there will be no overall improvement in reading. If a computer training program is used at home, then it could displace non-educational activities, like social media use, and lead to better reading. One special population of readers is students who are trying to learn a second language. The Internet can be useful in improving these second language learners' reading skills. For example, it has been shown that using the Internet to carry out research tasks—known as WebQuests—for school leads to improvements in vocabulary, reading skills, and reading comprehension.

Earlier it was established that attention is an integral part of reading, so computer training that improves attention might also be able to improve a person's reading skills. One such type of training is visual crowding training. Visual crowding occurs when a person has to pick out information from a screen that is obscured by other close-by objects. However, this type of training does not improve reading skills. Another type of training is playing action video games. These types of games ask the players to, among other things, track multiple moving objects, find target objects within a crowded visual field, and monitor the whole screen for objects that might appear. All of these mini-tasks within the game use the player's attentional skills. Indeed, researchers have shown that action video game players do have better attention skills than non-players in several different ways. Further, action video game playing can improve reading skills, although not for all players. The people who have been found to benefit are children with limited reading performance, such as dyslexic children.

Although not exactly the same concept as computer training, there is a very interesting relationship between habitually using text-speak in one's messaging behavior and a person's reading skills. Quite a few studies have been published on this topic, and general patterns have emerged. The patterns depend upon a person's age level. For children, one might be tempted to think—based on negative media coverage of text-speak—that reading a lot of text-speak would lead to a decline in reading skills. However, the opposite is true. Generally speaking, children who write a relatively high amount of text-speak—including using textisms like contractions and abbreviations—tend to have better, not worse, reading skills than other children. But in adults, the relationship between using text-speak and reading skills seems to be non-existent. That is, adults who use a lot of text-speak tend to have no better and no worse reading skills than adults who don't use much text-speak. One explanation is that children, who are in the learning stage of reading skills, benefit from text-speak because it frequently requires analyzing sets of letters into the corresponding sounds—a skill known as phonological decoding. On the other hand, adults have already acquired the phonological decoding skills that are necessary to be a skilled reader.

DISPLACEMENT EFFECTS

Although people may not be sitting down to read printed books as much now as in the past, people are still reading; it's just that the reading may be on a screen. A typical net gen-er (another name for digital natives) has been found to spend a little over one hour per day doing pleasure reading on a typical day. Reading might take place with printed books and magazines, or with online materials. And pleasure reading gradually increases over a student's career. In middle school in the United States, one study found that the average student did pleasure reading for about half an hour per day. By the time students make it to college, the average student was reading for nearly an hour per day. In fact, despite the diversions provided by the Internet, and by social media during the 2000s, more people were reading than in the past. By 2009, although only about one-half of Americans were considered readers, there was an upward trend in how much Americans were reading literature. The largest gain was in young adults (18 to 24 years old). On the other hand, for many people, focused reading seems to be taking a backseat to other computer-based activities. This is a phenomenon known as displacement. Net gen-ers spend significantly more time on technology-related activities such as texting (more than 4 hours) than they do on reading, raising the possibility that technology use displaces reading and other important activities (studying, housework, etc.). For children, parents are authority figures at home, and therefore exert control over their behaviors. One of the ways that they can exert this control is by setting rules regarding the use of electronic devices. These rules, often called parental limits, require that parents monitor what their kids are up to, including what they are viewing on screens and how much time is spent in front of screens. Setting parental limits has repeatedly been shown in research to be effective in reducing kids' screen time. Further, these changes are associated with increases in how much children spend reading. College students must exercise self-control if they want to avoid the distracting effects of technology upon reading. One of the biggest influences on reading time in college students is IMing. In fact, college students who admit to being highly distractible while reading—as measured through a questionnaire—also use IM more than other college students. Further, students who IM more than others also do less reading than other students. The latter finding suggests that IMing displaces reading. Displacement can work in multiple directions. While technology use like video gaming might displace reading, reading might displace other activities. For example, reading by oneself at home has been suggested to displace behaviors that help in child development, such as socializing with other children or playing outside.

WRITING

When psychologists think of writing, often they think of the means of writing as a tool for communication. In the past, with paper and pencil, penmanship—the ability and quality of writing out letters and characters—was an important skill for children to learn as a communication tool. It was practiced incessantly in the early school years. Virtually all people from older generations (prior to the net generation) in the United States will have experienced this. Old-fashioned writing with a pen and paper has certain affordances due to how the tool works. The pen or pencil itself affords grasping with the hand and various motions that can be made with the fingers and hand. Widespread use of computers by children, in the classroom and at home, emerged during the 2000s in the United States. Activities on the computer included writing. Perhaps the most significant trends in computer-based writing in recent decades occurred with the rise in cell phone use during the 2000s that ignited an explosion in text messaging. Cell phone use impacted a wide range of age groups; some studies found that very young children were getting cell phones, sometimes as young as 6 years old. The real boom in text messaging started in the late 2000s and continued into the early 2010s. As with other behaviors, digital technologies have created new affordances related to writing. With increasing trends in information and communication technology (ICT) use, the affordances of devices led to changes in language and new kinds of written products.

One affordance of a writing tool is the speed of writing. Pen and paper, in comparison with typing on a keyboard, might be seen as affording a slow writing speed. As with reading, a new affordance of digital technology for writing is multitasking. Switching between writing on a keyboard and doing another task is easier than in the past because electronic writing provides access to other activities and programs that are on the screen simultaneously, in the case of a laptop or computer screen, as well as some tablets. Even when writing with pen and paper morphed into writing on a typewriter in the not-too-far-away past, keyboarding with a typewriter did not afford multitasking. In surveys, high school and college students report frequent multitasking while writing on a computer. A commonly mentioned task that is combined with writing is IMing. That the Internet—with access to online chat, attention-grabbing news, and friends on social media—is a key driver for multitasking while writing was shown in a smart study in a research laboratory. Student participants were asked to write an essay on paper, write a report on a computer connected to the Internet, or write a report on a computer not connected to the Internet. Rather than helping students write a better product, the Internet-enabled computer produced lower quality reports than the computer without Internet. The hardware and software components of a phone affect the nature of the language used to write on the phone. For example, predictive texting allows people to use longer words in messages than they would normally write. This is because the predictive texting software inserts an entire word into the message with only a few keypresses by the writer. Therefore, it would be expected that a rise in predictive texting use would coincide with a reduction in the use of certain kinds of textisms that are used to save keypresses. Contractions, for example, are used by texters to conserve keypresses. In fact, a four-year Australian study in college students found that a rise in predictive texting was correlated with a reduction in contractions. Full keyboards on mobile phones speed up the writing process, making it easier for people to send text messages. Touch screens allow for software that facilitates extra features like the use of emoticons. Offering phone plans that include unlimited text messaging encourages text message creation. Going forward in time, with the changes in school education related to technology, experts say that penmanship will become unimportant as a skill to have. The constellation of skills that will be required to be an efficient communicator in the Internet era—known as Internet literacy—will not include penmanship; instead, a new set of skills, like keyboarding, are necessary.

CHANGES IN LANGUAGE

There is a wide variety of situations where an informal language makes sense for communication purposes. Language online and through computers has a more informal structure in many ways than other forms of written language, partially because much of the writing through ICT devices is part of a dialogue between individuals. Scientists have noticed that some forms of communication involve fast, immediate responses between people, while other forms of communication do not. An example of the former is text messaging. (When the software and hardware first appeared for use, it was known as the Short Message Service [SMS].) An example of the latter is email. Communication forms that require quick responses are known as synchronous forms of communication; other forms of communication are known as asynchronous. Synchronous forms of communication afford rapid writing. The social pressure to produce a response to a message in a short period of time will encourage writers to use writing tricks, such as word shortenings and abbreviations. In text messages and in IM, for instance, writers may leave out punctuation and they may replace whole phrases connoting emotions with single graphical representations of emotions—emoticons. Emoticons (shorthand for emotion icons) capture emotional information that is difficult to express in words. In some cases, they may serve as a shorter substitute for words when expressing emotion. Some commonly used emoticons by college students are the smiley face (:)), the sad face (:(), and the happy face (:D). As ubiquitous as emoticons appear to be, their actual use is rather limited, compared to textisms. In American college students, emoticons are used in only 4% of text messages. One possible reason for their absence in most text messages may have to do with the text messaging as medium for communication. When it was invented, it created a means of simple communication between two people. As such, there might not be a need in most cases to enrich messages with complex, emotional information. Asynchronous forms of communication afford slow writing; there is no rush to compose and send a message. Despite the fact that online discussion forums and email are asynchronous and afford carefully crafted messages with formal language, much of the content in those venues is informally written. Another factor has been identified by scientists as influencing the kind of language used in ICT. The audience—those to whom a message is directed—affects the style of language, and whether it is formal or informal. For example, weblogs (now known simply as blogs) often are aimed at casual audiences and contain high levels of informal writing. An additional venue where informal audiences are addressed is posts on social media like Facebook.

A large body of research has focused on one particular type of language, that of text-speak, a communication form that is increasingly supplemented with another invention of the Internet era, emoticons. Text-speak is a generic label that applies to many different forms of writing within text messages and other synchronous communication systems. Text-speak contains textisms, a set of always-changing shortenings and variations of language that reduce the lengths of messages and add liveliness to the messages. Using textisms is a rampant behavior, as readers already will know through experience. Statistics from England show that elementary school students have a textism density of 28%, defined by researchers as the number of textisms per word in messages. This translates roughly into one textism every four words. College students have a textism density of 20% (one textism per five words). The highest rate of textism use is 40%, for high school students, a value that has been interpreted to show the importance of wordplay in high school students' social lives. Wordplay might be indicative of a period of life when youths are exploring their own identities by crafting and shaping messages to others, and looking to see how others react to those messages. Text messages collected from college students' phones show a textism density of 19% in Australia and 16% in Canada. Differences in rates across countries have been attributed to different levels of technological innovations reaching those countries. For instance, the higher rate of textisms in Australia might be due to the fact that the software on phones at the time placed greater constraints on text message length. Popular types of textisms among college students are "accent stylization" ("gonna" for "going to") and "omitted capitals" (e.g., "i" for "I").

Surveys of college students repeatedly reveal high rates of text messaging. Some students have reported such high rates of text messaging that researchers estimate they spend 15% of their waking hours engaged in the behavior! By the mid-2000s, the news media were sounding an alarm about text messaging. One content analysis of more than 100 international news reports about texting found that most of the reports put a negative bias on text messaging. Concerns in the research literature are that text-speak is infiltrating everyday language, that it is corrupting people's reading and writing skills, and that it has negative effects on children's language development. Close examination of the types of textisms that people use in messages reveals how there would be concern that the English language is deteriorating. Scientists who study the topic have grouped textisms into categories that represent different kinds of language alterations. The category of single homophone, for example, includes textisms that shorten a word into a single character or a small set of characters based on the sounds associated with the word. Good examples of single homophones are "u" for "you" and "2" for "to." The category of "contractions" includes textisms that shrink words into smaller units. For instance, the word "message" is frequently shortened to "msg" in text-speak. Not surprisingly, in the spirit of wordplay, multiple textisms can be present in the same word. "Lolllll" is one such case; it contains an initialism (representing a phrase using the first letters of the words in the phrase, Laughing Out Loud) and extra letters (used for emphasis).

For children, textisms do not appear to be creeping into regular language. In Australia, for example, children writing messages in conventional English showed only a small number of intrusions of textisms; the intrusion rates were only 2% to 4%. It is interesting that despite the intention to use text-speak to speed up the writing process, it doesn't, at least in children. Australian children are no faster at writing with text-speak than in conventional English. However, new software technologies can alter this pattern. Predictive texting—when a device picks your words for you based on a few characters of input—actually speeds up writing in children. Textisms do not appear to be infiltrating the formal or creative writing of college students much. Business letters are one example of formal writing. One study in the United States gave students this instruction: "Pretend that you want to complain to a company from which you bought a product. Write a letter to the company manager complaining about the quality of service that you received or the product itself and what you want them to do about it." Only 27% of the students used textisms in their letters. In the same study, students were asked to provide an essay of a more personal and expressive nature: "Please describe in detail what it feels like to be unhappy. What should a person do to become happy again? What have you done in the past when you were unhappy?" In this case, only 25% of the participants used textisms. And college students writing real assignments for school have extremely low rates of using textisms. In papers written for final exams in Australia, the most common category of textism used was contractions, but it occurred only 39 times across 533,500 written words collected from 153 undergraduate students. The next most common type of textism, omitted apostrophes (e.g., "havent" instead of "haven't") occurred only 26 times. In Irish college students, one-quarter of the words in the text messages use textisms. One might imagine that the worst kind of textism would be one that is not decipherable. In other words, the message recipient would not be able to make sense of the textism and decode its meaning. However, these cases of semantically unrecoverable textisms are rare in college students' text messages. In the Irish sample of 139 college students, semantically unrecoverable textisms occurred less than .2% of the time. Although the rates of textisms in college students' messages are significant, they show that most of the text messaging by English-speaking college students is written using standard or conventional English. Text-speak is, however, leaking into other forms of online communication that are relatively informal. Rates of textisms in Facebook postings are about the same as in text messages for college students when the messages are for friends. The textism densities in this case are about 23% for Australian college students. Textism use in emails is lower.

Scientists who study text messaging behavior find that texters are aware of their audiences; they adjust the language used in a message so that is appropriate for the message recipient. Less formal text messages are used with friends, while more formal text messages are used with acquaintances and authority figures. College students in Australia report that they are aware that using textisms for formal interactions with people is not appropriate. While the least appropriate occasion for using textisms was perceived to be school assignments, other occasions were also perceived as unfavorable for textisms. These included emails to strangers, emails to teachers, online chat with strangers, and text messages with strangers. Further, there is more evidence that students, at the college level, adjust their use of textisms to meet the needs of the audience. When naturalistic text messages are collected from college students' phones, messages sent to friends have the highest textism density, followed by messages sent to peers, followed by messages sent to authority figures.

Students who text have not lost their ability to identify ungrammatical messages. Research in England found that there were high rates of ungrammatical messages in students' text messages: about 50% of all word use in elementary and high school students' messages was ungrammatical, and about 25% was ungrammatical in college students' messages. At the same time, when given tests of formal grammar, students performed at a significantly better level. The error rates were cut in half. Again, even at the level of college students, text messaging does not appear to be damaging people's language skills. In the United States, college students who send the most text messages tend to have the highest scores on spelling and reading tests. Rather than having negative effects on children's language skills, using textisms is probably having a positive effect on skills in elementary-school-aged children. Experts in the field find that textism use is positively associated with spelling skills, reading skills, and phonological awareness—knowledge of the sounds that letters and words make. Of course, it is important to remember the adage that correlation does not imply causation; one cannot definitively conclude from this association that texting causes better language skills. For grammar skills, the results are not so obvious. Some studies support a positive link, others do not. When children are in high school, the relationship changes. There is evidence that texting is negatively associated with language skills. Adults do not show a consistent pattern across studies. The seemingly bigger benefits for elementary school children have been attributed to the practice with language that texting provides during a period of language development. For children, experts argue that text-speak can benefit language development because it is a playful style of writing that encourages analysis of words and their spellings. The characteristic of playfulness in text-speak has been noted in other forms of computer-mediated communication, as well. In order to make sense of the actual pattern of textism use among phone users, some scientists have advocated a low-road/high-road theory. The low road occurs when textisms might find their way into a person's writing even when writing in settings other than a text messaging program. It says that two writing tasks that share features—for instance, texting and another synchronous form of communication like online chatting—will allow for the transfer of textisms from one setting to the other. This is purported to happen unconsciously, in the sense that writers are not consciously intending to do so. The high road occurs when writers realize that they are writing for a formal audience, such as their teachers, and consciously avoid using textisms.

NEW KINDS OF WRITTEN PRODUCTS

The information age spawned new forms of written work, each taking advantage of the features of the computer and the Internet. The storage capacity of the desktop computer and the ability to program reading software allowed for the creation of hypertext. Hypertext is a form of writing that mixes together text and clickable links to other content, known as hyperlinks. Many people take hypertext for granted; it is so common today because it is the way virtually every web page is written. Yet, as a form of writing, hypertext was revolutionary in the sixties when it was being developed and named. A key difference between traditional text and hypertext is that hypertext is read in a non-sequential way. Readers do not start at the top of a page and work their way to the bottom; rather, they interrupt themselves as they read down the page, clicking on various links that take them to other pages in a document. When the reader is ready, she can find links that allow her to move back to the original page, or she may never come back to the original page. Desktop computers let many additional pieces of information be stored and linked to a hypertext document. The Internet took this action a step further, allowing for access to an essentially unlimited amount of information.

In the initial stages of the Internet, most of the websites were commercial, military, educational, or governmental. When regular people were given the tools to add their own content to the Internet—the phenomenon known as Web 2.0—the amount of written material online skyrocketed. The Web 2.0 allows anyone to publish a website. The availability of massive amounts of information and personal interconnectivity facilitates remixes and wikis. At least two important forces came together to create a remix culture online starting in the 2000s. One force was the Web 2.0, with millions of individuals posting written and non-written products that they created, along with the presence of many commercially-developed products, sometimes posted legally, sometimes not. Another force was the development of digital tools for downloading content, editing content, creating content, and posting content online. Materials found online are downloaded by people and dissected into parts such as text, audio, and video. The parts from different source materials are recombined in new ways and then uploaded to the Internet. Blogs are an excellent example. Blog writers contribute their own text to a written product, but also borrow other people's text, images, graphics, etc. and use a hypertext style to represent the material online. People who remix material want to include a lot of hyperlinks because hyperlinks drive other people to view the material. The hyperlinks are picked up by search engine bots that roam the Internet for information to include in search engine results.

Wikis also are inventions of the computer age. It's a funny name, but the concept takes advantage of the fact that thousands of individuals can have access to a single hypertext document. Each person contributes as an author to the document, providing original content, editing existing content, adding and altering hyperlinks, and uploading supplemental content such as images and video clips. From the wiki emerges a collective writing style, since multiple individuals contribute to the writing. Perhaps the most famous wiki is Wikipedia.com. Wikipedia has its own rules for content creation, author collaboration, and editing. These restrictions also serve to frame the style of voice that exists on the website. The advent of the Web 2.0, when combined with hypertext, has led to wild and unpredictable content being posted online. One researcher refers to this as "feral hypertext." Consider the difference between two websites, both of which aim to capture the true knowledge of the world: Encyclopedia Britannica and Wikipedia. The former, commercially-driven, has predictable content created by authors hired by the company behind the website. The latter, a wiki, contains content that varies tremendously in completeness, coverage, and credibility of information.

ISSUES AROUND LITERACY DEVELOPMENT

All of the skills related to language use and communication are often lumped together into the concept of literacy; literacy skills, defined broadly in this way, refer to reading, writing, and speaking. Gaining literacy skills is a long process that begins with emergent skills and then early literacy skills. Emergent literacy skills begin by preschool age and include recognizing shapes, recognizing sounds, and becoming familiar with concepts related to language, for example, "pages" and "books." Another emergent literacy skill is using the hand and fingers in movements that precede real writing. In order to be literate, one of the first types of learning that must take place is orthographic learning. Orthographic learning is memorizing the relationships between letters in the alphabet and the sounds that the letters make. These memories are referred to as orthographic representations. Research has examined the impact of computer-based technology on these beginning literacy skills. Computers, with digital tools that allow for writing, have been noted as helpful for emergent literacy. Young children who do not know how to write yet can find opportunities for learning on full-sized and tablet computers. In the 2010s, when tablet computers started being mass marketed, very young children—two to three years old—were found to be enamored with the devices. Using their fingers to make shapes and marks in drawing apps, these young children were doing pre-writing, getting practice with the physical movements required in writing. One way to acquire orthographic representations is to learn to spell. To study the optimal method for orthographic learning in this fashion, research has compared printing letters to typing letters, or keyboarding. In second graders, both types of training produce the same amount of orthographic learning. However, kids who learned by typing did better when they also had prior keyboard experience. For several of the skills in emergent literacy, there is an advantage for children who use tablet computers at home. As demonstrated in an Australian study, writing with tablets at home is associated with higher scores in print awareness (recognizing concepts like a paragraph), print knowledge (knowledge of letters and numbers), and sound knowledge (the sounds that letters make). Even simple apps on a tablet computer may provide practice with early literacy skills. Four- and five-year-olds have been observed using doodling apps to make letters and words, and to form messages. Kids have been observed doing the same behavior in apps where "magnetic" letters are used to make signs. As children get a little older—when they are five to six years old—tablet computers provide a venue for creating messages through writing, writing out their names, and typing messages to others. This is not to say that young children should use tablets for gaining their early literacy skills; at-home writing activities that do not involve technology also correlate with emergent literacy.

On the down side, letter recognition may be affected negatively by learning to type. Three- and four-year-olds who learn letters by typing on a keyboard do less well on letter recognition than kids of the same age who learn letters by handwriting them. (For two-year-olds, the method of learning does not matter.) Handwriting letters requires that children move their hands and fingers in ways that match the visual shapes of the letters. For example, writing out the letter "C" requires a continuous curve that is created through a hand and fingers motion. Finding letters on a keyboard requires only a quick keypress. This difference in movement might underlie the benefit of handwriting for later letter recognition.

Keyboarding is at the early end of the writing process; full-blown composition, in adults, writing is a complex psychological process. Writing involves many separate component tasks; each of these tasks requires focused attention to carry out, placing heavy demands on our mental systems in order to make high-quality written products. One of the component tasks is planning. Effective writers plan ahead. They think about many different factors that will influence their later essays and written words. For example, writers must consider the basic factor of length. In a school assignment, students are given a minimum essay length, and must estimate how much material they will need to write in order to achieve the minimum length. Even in informal writing, length is a relevant factor. When the maximum text message length was 140 characters, a skilled writer had to think ahead—even if only briefly—about how he could squeeze his message into that limited writing space. Another component task is reflection. A skilled writer will review what has been written before submitting an essay or sending a text message. Often, the review will reveal changes to the writing that need to be made. A common type of error found in this step of proofreading is grammatical errors. For instance, the text message writer might notice a mismatch between the subject of a sentence ("Johnny") and the possessive article ("her"). After review, a critical component task is revision. Skilled writers edit the written material in order to fix the problems noticed during review. All of these component tasks require mental focus, which means that other tasks should not be performed at the same time, or else the quality of writing suffers. Psychologists say that writing has a high cognitive load.

Using a keyboard to write, as opposed to other tools for writing, may impact those processes. Keyboarding may be impacting how cognitive load is distributed in the brain, how adults learn new writing knowledge, and which skills are important for people to gain. One way that cognitive load might be affected is by writing speed. In children, keyboarding takes more time to write than handwriting. When second graders, fourth graders, and sixth graders in England were asked to write different messages (e.g., "the five boxing wizards jump quickly"), typing on a computer produced slower times than writing with a pen. This suggests that writing with a keyboard at a young age puts a greater cognitive load on our psyches than handwriting does. Researchers have raised concerns that the additional cognitive load from keyboarding may take away mental resources from doing other important component tasks of writing. This may possibly result in less creative written products. As discussed earlier, children may be suffering when they type on a keyboard because orthographic learning may not be as effective. Apparently, the same might be true of adults. Although adults have already learned all of the letters of the alphabet well, there might be limits on how well they can learn new characters when using a keyboard. The parts of the brain that become active when learning new characters through handwriting overlap with the parts of the brain that are active when recognizing familiar letters. However, this is not the case when learning new characters through typing. Handwriting activates parts of the brain that are involved in hand and finger movements—known as motor knowledge—that relates to the shapes of the new characters. Typing does not; it involves pointing movements that occur when typing. Learning new characters through typing is also less effective than learning through handwriting.

Additionally, the software tools for writing have been studied for their impact upon the quality of writing. If one thinks of a writing medium as a tool, then one can ask which medium is most effective for writing. While there are clear differences in the behaviors associated with different writing tools, the final written products may not differ very much. For tenth graders, using a computer and word processor to write essays produces longer and neater papers than writing with a paper and pencil. There is no difference in the number of errors, but there is a more formal nature to the essays from the computer. One subgroup of tenth graders does benefit from paper and pencil; those who have relatively little experience with word processors do better with paper and pencil, possibly because they are not distracted from the extra effort required to use a tool that they are unfamiliar with. College students report that there are pros and cons of writing with pen and paper that are different than the pros and cons of writing with a computer. For instance, writing with paper affords immediacy (the written product is done as you write), personality (use of handwriting to inject style), and portability (can be done anywhere). In fact, pen and paper afford more positive aspects than negative ones, according to these students. At the same time, college students perceive writing with computers to be quicker than with pen and pencil; the computer fulfills a growing need in students to write more quickly and instantly without losing time. Interestingly, computers make note-taking easier for students, but do not produce better notes. The ease of taking notes on a computer was revealed in a study of college students in Finland where the students reported that they could take class notes without looking at the keyboard. However, they agreed that it is not possible to do the same thing with pen and paper. Experimental comparisons between note taking on computers and note taking with pen and paper show a disadvantage for computers. When students take notes using laptop computers, they tend to take verbatim notes, simply copying down words and phrases from the presented material. This style of note taking encourages learning about facts, but not a deeper, conceptual understanding of the material. Discouraging students from taking verbatim notes on a computer does not seem to help the problem. As the experimenters noted in their report on this subject, ". . . despite their growing popularity, laptops may be doing more harm in classrooms than good" (Mueller & Oppenheimer, 2014).

ADDITIONAL ISSUES RELATED TO WRITING

Some non-English-speaking countries worry that English is infiltrating their cultures. The Internet and computer-based communication are seen as contributing to the problem. English is the top language online: more websites are written in English than in any other language. Further, much of the technical jargon related to computers and the Internet is based on the English words and phrases for those concepts. "Email," for example, is a word known virtually everywhere around the globe despite the fact that it is a shortened form of the English phrase, "electronic mail." Studies done in some of these countries have tried to determine how much their own languages are being overtaken by English. One such study, done in Sweden, analyzed the discussions had by Swedish citizens in Internet chat rooms. The researchers looked at 4,116 postings in the chat rooms, counting how many times English words appeared in the postings. Not only was there a very low number of English words found (123 words, or 2.9%), but the English words were also often part of song lyrics being shared by the chatters. The words were not replacing Swedish words. From these results, it was concluded that, at least in this case, English was complementing, rather than replacing, a native language.

Another issue is Internet plagiarism. The Internet provides an abundance of seemingly free materials for people, especially students, to borrow for use in their own writings. Plagiarism—borrowing other people's work without given them credit—is common among college students. Research shows that many students think of the Internet as a free zone for written material that does not need to be credited to the original authors. After all, some students seem to think, doesn't online material represent general human knowledge? In one study, 62% of undergraduate students and 59% of graduate students admitting plagiarizing. Cut and paste plagiarism is a term used to describe the current state of affairs with respect to the Internet and writing. However, there are significant legal and academic restrictions on how this borrowing must take place. In many Western countries, the existing laws and rules regarding plagiarism, even those policies set for students in educational settings, are based on very old concepts related to printed texts. These old concepts come from the idea that a printed text is the work of a single author and that, because the text is printed, it is unchangeable. Because of the Internet, digital writing tools, collaborative settings like wikis, and the remix culture, the old concepts are difficult to apply to many of the new written works. As one writer on the subject noted, "the world of digital work production is very different from the world of the eighteenth century print text production, and the laws that arose to protect print works" (Sutherland-Smith, 2015). At the same time that the Internet has made plagiarism easier, it also has made it harder. Teachers regularly use software tools to detect plagiarism in their students' papers. One such tool is TurnItIn. TurnItIn compares a student's paper to a large number of other sources and reports on any overlap that is detected. Not only is software detection of plagiarism becoming routine in educational settings, but also it is increasingly being used in scientific settings. Scientists who submit plagiarized work to academic journals may be detected if the editors of the journals apply plagiarism detection software. Just like the massive publicity and concern around student plagiarism in the educational world, there has been the sounding of an alarm in the academic world due to plagiarism.

One approach to handling the discrepancy between what is available online and what people write in their essays is the reader-writer contract. The contract, which is not a physical contract but a mental contract that the writer makes with her future readers, says that writers should assume that their readers will come to the text with a certain mindset. That mindset includes an understanding that the text was written by the listed authors (originality), that the figures, references, etc. are accurate (accuracy), and that the text has never before been published (novelty). If there are any deviations from this mindset, then the writer must make an explicit statement to that effect. For example, if a portion of a paragraph—even if paraphrased—comes from another author, then that other author should be cited or acknowledged in the work.

CONCLUSION

The Internet and communication technologies have led to the formation of new types of reading and writing. Text-speak—the shortened form of language used mainly in text messaging—is one of the most prevalent new types of writing. In contrast with the dire predictions of many in the media, text-speak has not taken over formal language: it does not appear very often in writers' formal documents and it does not lead to big losses in language skills. In fact, children who text, and who are knowledgeable about text-speak, perform better on tests of early literacy skills than other children. ICT also has changed the way that people read and write. For instance, note taking on a computer may be easier than using old-fashioned pen and paper, but computer-based note taking leads to superficial notes. In another example, reading online material probably involves more skimming—skipping sections of text—than reading print material. Further, many of our devices, as well as the software that comes with them, encourage multitasking, so people tend to read and write while they carry out other tasks. Reading while multitasking causes reading times to get longer, but does not appear to have large effects on comprehension. Writing while multitasking may influence the quality of the written product.

It's clear that digital technologies are altering our reading and writing habits and processes. The biggest impact of these changes might be in classrooms, where reading and writing are core skills upon which higher-level skills, like learning and reasoning, are based. The effects of technology upon school learning will be discussed in the next chapter (Chapter 8).

Interview with an Expert: Dr. Beverly A. Plester

Dr. Beverly A. Plester is a professor of psychology from the University of Plymouth (UK) and an expert in the study of literacy skills and technology. Despite universal fears that text messaging is harming children's language skills, Dr. Plester and her colleagues contributed key evidence to the research literature that text messaging is positively related to children's language skills. Putting an optimistic spin on the results, Dr. Plester has stated, "We are interested in discovering whether texting could be used positively to increase phonetic awareness in less able children, and perhaps increase their language skills, in a fun yet educational way" (Smith, 2006). In 2013, Dr. Plester co-authored *Text Messaging and Literacy— The Evidence*, a scholarly book that reviewed the scientific evidence on the effects of text messaging on children.

Q: How is the act of reading the same or different using a print source or an electronic source?

A: Reading is the same in that we are looking to derive meaning from written words, but the process seems to be quite different. Reading from a digital source is widely found to be more superficial, lending itself to less rereading, to more browsing, looking for key information containing words. The aim seems, from widespread research, to be collecting information rather than depth of understanding. "Power browsing" is Naomi Baron's phrase in her excellent book *Words Onscreen*. I recommend her book, and *The Shallows* by Nicholas Carr as follow-ups to this discussion. Students report that they remember less from digital sources than from print sources, perhaps because of the more shallow approach to reading online.

Q: How might reading and writing on a digital device affect the development of literacy skills?

A: Our research is currently comparing reading comprehension in pre-teens, across digital and paper formats. Reading teachers need to be aware of the distractibility element in online reading, when there is widespread belief that one can multitask with impunity. See the previous chapter here, and Gazzaley and Rosen's *The Distracted Mind*. We also need to be sure that we, as a culture, still value depth of thinking as well as collection of bites of information. Children need to be taught how to read for understanding, not just how to decode written words.

Cursive handwriting practice helps develop small motor skills, and there is some research that indicates that children who use smartphones a lot are less able to hold and control a pencil. There need not be one "correct" handwriting style, but the small motor coordination can contribute to other useful skills. When texting was new, critics claimed that text abbreviations were going to ruin children's language skills, if not the language itself. Our research has repeatedly shown that the use of text abbreviations is associated with good literacy skills in pre-teens, being so often based on phonological awareness. Frequency of texting itself is not as clearly associated with literacy skills, but more with distractibility, which interrupts deep reading attention. But the question is still open about the use of emoji as nonverbal shortcuts. If textisms are any indicator, I would predict no negative effect, but I would also ask teachers to encourage wider descriptive vocabulary. Emoji are generally seen as an indicator of an informal tone in the writing, and children need to be taught about registers of language and when the more formal register is appropriate. Cogent essays require depth of understanding and rationale, and children need to be shown how to construct good arguments using evidence.

Q: How is writing on a smartphone or computer different than with a pen and paper?

A: For people who touch type, writing on computer is much faster than pen and paper, but for those who don't, and those using the tiny keyboard of a phone, it may be slower than pen and paper, but it does have the advantage of spelling and grammar checking, and rapid access to alternative wordings. But it is also easier to lose your work if you forget to save it regularly.

Q: What do you see as the unanswered questions on the impact of screens on reading and writing?

A: The most important, I think, is determining how important depth of thinking, depth of reading, understanding rather than mere accumulation of knowledge is in the racing speed western culture of today and tomorrow. Do we really care? How important is it to us that other writers' words are not simply purloined because they're appropriate to a question? Preference for computer marked assessments need not altogether avoid depth of understanding, but it takes care in the construction of questions and acceptable answers. First returns from a study of preferences in pre-teens in the UK suggest that, as university students have said elsewhere, if the reader really wants to "get into" a piece of reading, paper is the preferred mode of reading. But as Japanese young people have been more widely using smartphones for longer, their preference for paper is less powerful than US and European young people's, but even they prefer paper for depth of involvement. (See Baron [2015] as above.) Further research with younger readers, played against their ownership and use of screens, may show a decreasing preference for paper. I would like to see research looking at ways of teaching depth of thinking using screen based reading. That we tend to power browse onscreen doesn't mean that it is the only way one can use digital reading materials. But as with other emerging technology, we need to learn an array of ways of using it to our own advantage.

8

School Learning

Case Study: Khan Academy—Putting Math Information Online

Sal Khan has college degrees from the Massachusetts Institute of Technology, as well as an MBA from Harvard University. He applied his advanced mathematical and financial knowledge in his career as a financial analyst. With impressive credentials, Khan was a great choice for tutoring his family members in math. But Khan grew frustrated with the amount of time it was taking to tutor his family. His challenge was to make learning efficient and to deliver the learning remotely. He got the idea to record videos and make them available to his family member students. How to deliver the videos was a bit of a puzzle at the time. YouTube.com—the video sharing service—was not known for educational content. Khan has described the state of YouTube back then this way: "I thought YouTube was for dogs on skateboards" (Khan, 2012; in de Bertodano, 2012) and "YouTube was for cats playing the piano" (Khan, 2013; in Adams, 2013). YouTube had a 10-minute time limit on the lengths of video clips. So Khan created his training videos to fit within this short timeframe. Thus, Khan Academy started by accident.

At the Khan Academy online learning system, students watch short videos and track their progress. The videos themselves are not complicated. Each one gives examples of the math concept being taught, and a narrator—who is not shown—provides instruction. Viewers can see the actions of the instructor on screen. There are several reasons for the success of Khan Academy, not the least of which is Khan's effective presentation style. Khan narrates many of the videos that are available at the website. Observers give Khan's presentation style as a key ingredient for the website's effectiveness. In addition to characterizing his narration as friendly, cordial, and simple, they say that it's avuncular and mellifluous. The whole process of using Khan Academy is simple, a key component of the system's success. Almost anyone can sign up, begin viewing videos, take the tests, and track his or her progress. It turns out that the videos available at Khan Academy are a form of example-based learning, a style of education known to researchers as being effective. Khan dedicated himself to running Khan Academy full-time in 2009.

The short videos provide the raw elements for the ingenuity of the Khan Academy. The system can be used from home or in the classroom. Khan Academy can be used as part of a flipped classroom—courses in which the lectures are absorbed outside of class time and the skill-building takes place when students meet. This allows for a serious and thoughtful discussion of problem solving skills during class periods, rather than rote math exercises.

An alternative to flipping a classroom is to use Khan Academy as a tracking system that lets teachers know when they must intervene to help particular students. In a real classroom, students can each use the system from their seats, and the teachers can monitor progress for each student from their own computers. The software lets teachers know when a student is not advancing at an optimal rate through the learning system. This prompts teachers to assist those individual students.

Based on a personal interest in education, Khan developed the grander plan for Khan Academy that is touched on in a book that he wrote: *The One World Schoolhouse: Education Reimagined*, published in 2012. Like millions of students and former students around the globe, Khan says that the traditional structure of education—the repeating pattern of "lecture, homework, lecture, homework" (Khan, 2013; in Adams, 2013)—is unpleasing and not particularly effective. He always envisioned a lively and interactive educational system that inspired students to achieve high levels of success—in his own words, "a small Hogwarts kind of school . . . where I could be surrounded by really neat kids and other faculty members and just play: build robots, do whatever" (Khan, 2012; in de Bertodano, 2012). Khan's ambitions apply not just to the students, but to the parents of the students, as well. He argues that parents could become highly successful tutors for their children if the parents also used Khan Academy to learn about the topics being studied by their kids. He estimates that an hour per day of learning online would do the trick. This would magnify the learning for the students. Khan sees a world where every child can perform at very high levels academically. From his roots on the West Coast of the United States, he offers acceptance into Stanford University as an example of very high academic achievement levels. The problem is, children must start mastering math at a young age. His claim is,

> If your child is not placed in the fast track for math in sixth grade, his chances of going to Stanford are close to zero. His chances of becoming a doctor or an engineer are probably zero. And it's decided when he's 11 years old. (Khan, 2012; in de Bertodano, 2012)

Many people perceive Khan Academy to be for kids because the videos break down learning into small units and because the narration is straightforward. However, adults use it too. It has become even more appealing to adults as the organization has expanded its educational materials collection beyond just basic math to include topics such as computer programming. The learning system has millions of regular users each month, and millions more who view the videos that are posted there. The project is recognized for its effectiveness; in the United States, Khan was honored by being named one of the top 100 most influential people in the world (number four on the list, in fact) on *Time Magazine*'s well-respected list. But Khan is not interested in developing it as a business venture. Khan desires to keep the Khan Academy as a non-profit organization.

Khan's experiences and philosophy came along at just the right time in the history of education and the Internet. The digital revolution provides people around the world with informational content that was relatively hard to access in the days prior to the Internet. It also makes it easy and very convenient to find the information. Older readers will remember when many people did not have access to the Internet at home. For those who did, the process of connecting to the Internet was slow and cumbersome, and restricted to the location of the desktop computer, because the wireless Internet connection did not exist in homes. Now that Wi-Fi is common in homes, and mobile devices have access to the Internet, through the Wi-Fi or data service from a cell phone company, learning can take place anywhere in the home. Khan Academy is one of many forms of massively open online courses (MOOCs) that are heralded as opening the door to mass education. MOOCs—other examples include Coursera and EdX—take advantage of the wide reach of the Internet to offer free or near-free educational content to unlimited numbers of students. The vast amount of information online is another important aspect of the digital revolution. Much of the information found online is of questionable quality, but the material on Khan Academy is held in high regard by scientific researchers and educators. TED talks—the famous series of lectures by leading thinkers on a variety of topics—is another example of high-quality information made accessible to millions of individuals via the Internet.

INTRODUCTION

There have been concerns about the effect of technology on education and learning for many decades; television worried educators more than 50 years ago. If students did their homework while watching TV, wouldn't comprehension and learning be damaged? The TV generation of students has given way to the Internet generation of students. The more recent generation of students who were born after 1979 goes by many names, including millennials, Generation Y, and the net generation. Internet-based technologies were being introduced into school settings while this generation grew up, and these students had access to the Internet at home. Computer-based technologies became smaller, portable, and personalized. By the time they went to college, American net gen-ers had high ownership rates of smartphones (89%), computers (84%), tablet computers (54%), and music players (51%). The level of penetration of personal technology is even higher for the next round of students in the educational system—the iGeneration. The iGeneration is the set of students born in 1990 or later. For these two generations, information and communication technology (ICT) has significantly changed how education is delivered and how learning, studying, and homework take place.

IMPACT ON MODALITIES OF INSTRUCTION

Surveys of teachers in the early 2010s showed that there was strong enthusiasm for and budding use of portable devices like tablet computers in classrooms. Portable devices provide important affordances and are often used to give students access to digitized content. The portability of portable devices is one of their affordances. Their relatively small size is another one. Because they are small, they allow a person to hold them in their hands—sometimes just one hand. Being able to do so lets a person assume a variety of postures while looking at the screen. A student can sit at a desk, sit in a chair without a desk, and even lie down on a sofa and use the device. Software affords certain activities and behaviors, too. For example, social networking software like Facebook affords socializing and interaction between students. This is an important point, because learning has a social component that can be reproduced online with social networking sites.

Devices that are portable and have Internet access have the potential for improving the efficiency of education. For one, their portability solves some problems that have existed in classrooms for many years. With printed copies of textbooks, students must lug around heavy copies of texts within the classroom, as well as between home and school and vice-versa. With electronic copies of learning materials, no strenuous book carrying is necessary. Also, when texts are updated by the authors or by publishing companies, expensive printed copies of the new versions do not need to be purchased; rather, low-cost versions available in electronic form make the near-instantaneous replacement of the old versions with the new ones possible. In addition, e-readers make it possible for students to make notations on their electronic texts, save these notations for use in the future, and access from anywhere there is an Internet connection. Further, an Internet-enabled device gives students the possibility of accessing other information online that could be useful to understanding a text. These other types of information could include word definitions, encyclopedia entries, and educational video clips.

One prominent 2011 survey of American teachers, pre-kindergarten through twelfth grade, revealed that the laptop computer was viewed as having the greatest potential, endorsed by 81% of respondents. Tablet computers and e-readers were endorsed by 53% of the teachers. By the early 2010s in the United States, there was significant use of portable devices in schools. Middle and high school teachers in a survey published in 2013 reported that 45% of their students were using e-readers and 43% were using tablet computers to finish assignments or to do work in class. (These rates of usage were already exceeded by the cell phone—73% usage—but the educational promise of the cell phone is greatly tempered by its association with distraction, as described later.) Some school districts spent large sums of money to give students these devices, as exemplified by the action taken by the Los Angeles Unified School District. In 2013, spirits were high for the school district. It had the ambitious plan to put an Apple iPad into the hands of each and every student in the district. This plan made perfect sense from the perspective that portable devices were the wave of the future in education. If accomplished, this plan would also even out the disparity between poor students and wealthy students, where previously only the wealthy could afford the educational perk of owning a tablet computer. On June 19 of that year, Apple Computer company issued a press release touting the arrangement between the two organizations. The school district committed itself to an initial $30 million investment in purchasing iPads. In the press release, one of Apple's senior vice presidents proudly beamed, "Schools around the world have embraced the engaging and interactive quality of iPad with nearly 10 million iPads already in schools today" (Schiller, 2013; in Apple, Inc., 2013). But the high spirits did not last. As students received iPads, a few significant problems arose. One problem was that students were able to bypass the security systems embedded into the systems. Another problem was that the educational content was incomplete. The vendor responsible for providing that content gave only a partial set of materials. Also, teachers were not prepared to incorporate the iPads into their curricula. By 2015, after more than 40,000 iPads had been purchased by the school district, the relationship between Apple and the Los Angeles school district soured. The school district terminated its dealings with the company and other firms involved. Eventually, Apple agreed to provide a settlement to the school district that enabled the district to purchase computer equipment for schools that were lagging behind in their technological capabilities. In the end, portable device usage tended to promote content delivery over other important aspects of learning. The problem with the portable devices may be that they encourage a weak approach to education. Namely, they function as a viewing device for digitized educational content. As will be explained, effective learning requires many parts, only one of which is the content itself.

The Internet as a whole affords certain activities. Blended learning and flipped classes are two examples of harnessing the affordances of the Internet. In its most basic form, the Internet contains a huge collection of informational sources that can be used for educational purposes. A web browser with a built-in search function affords looking for and accessing information on a topic. Educators take advantage of this by moving some of the in-class lecture and discussion to online sources. This is how blended learning courses work; a portion of the traditional classroom learning is moved online. Doing so frees up in-class time for other activities on which the teacher wants to focus. In flipped classes, the lectures are moved from the classroom to online and outside of class time. Flipped classes take advantage of several features of the Internet. First, contemporary Internet technology easily allows for the posting and sharing of large computer files, such as high-fidelity recordings of instructors giving lectures. Second, the Internet serves as an archive of information—in this case, the recorded lectures—that can be accessed by anyone at any time. Third, almost all students now have access to the Internet at home. The lectures are often recorded using digital video technology and posted onto a website or into a learning management system. Students use their time outside of the class periods to view the recorded lectures, take notes, and learn the lecture content. This approach frees up class periods for working on skill building. A common strategy is to flip the courses that have a significant homework component, for example, math courses. The class period is used for direct instruction on how to solve problems, rather than to deliver the rote content of mathematics. This is a key aspect of flipped classrooms, because learning how to solve problems or to carry out other skills benefits greatly from having the instructor interacting face-to-face with the students. Research has found that flipped classrooms boost student engagement. Engagement is a core construct in the psychology of education; it means that students have positive attitudes toward learning, have positive attitudes toward the course, participate in the activities prescribed by the instructor, and intend to be active in the course until it ends. The most widely accepted models of learning in school include engagement as an important factor for maximizing learning in the classroom.

Starting in the 2000s, more and more whole courses were put online. Online courses benefit students because they give access to otherwise hard-to-get courses. Small school districts may not have the resources to offer classes that will have low student enrollment. Advanced classes are a good example. Small districts, such as rural school districts, might only have a limited number of students who qualify to take an advanced class. Further, rural school districts in remote locations may be too far away from other school districts that offer the class. Therefore, putting the advanced class online allows for the extension of the enrollment of a course into a remote, small school district. Online courses give more students a chance to take a course. There is no apparent limit on the size of an online class. In theory, a single teacher could reach hundreds or even thousands of students. From a resource perspective, this reduces the number of teachers that must be hired to provide education to students. Reducing the number of teachers also lowers the cost of providing education.

Some online courses test the upper limit on the size of a course. Ten years ago, in 2008, the name massive open online courses (MOOCs) was given to these types of classes. These courses tend to be free to use, open to anyone, and accessible from around the world. Coursera, EdX, and PSPU are examples of non-profit organizations that offer MOOCs for free. While many institutions in higher education—college level or higher—provide online courses, those courses can be expensive for students to take. The philosophy behind MOOCs is to offer courses for free or at low cost, in order to give access to as many people as possible. For many, MOOCs represent the latest and greatest use of technology for educational purposes. As with other types of online learning, MOOCs make learning convenient because it can be done from home, from one's neighborhood, and even from a cell phone. According to those organizations that offer MOOCs, learning is also improved because the learning environment is comfortable; that is, it can be done at home, in one's favorite location in the house, and at one's own pace. One of the most famous MOOCs in the United States is Khan Academy, described in the case study. Udacity is another main provider of MOOCs. Like the other organizations that provide MOOCs, these groups find that programming and technical skills are the most popular topics for students. On EdX, the most popular course is Introduction to Computer Science. MOOCs are also special because of the high quality of the material contained in them. The courses are frequently taught by a leading educator or scientist in the field of study. MOOCs can be used to deliver course content at all educational levels. In the United States, many MOOCs offer topics that come from college curricula. The ease of access to MOOCs has caused millions of people to sign up to use them. MOOCs took off as a phenomenon in the United States. EdX is run by Harvard University and the Massachusetts Institute of Technology, and passed 9 million registered users in 2016, offering more than 900 online courses. Coursera passed 20 million students in 2016. Although they are relatively new, MOOCs have made an impression upon educators and other observers. *The New York Times* declared 2012 to be the year of the MOOC. And MOOCs are emerging in other countries. For example, Oxford University in the United Kingdom offered its first MOOC in 2017. The topic of the course was "From Poverty to Prosperity: Understanding Economic Development."

The effectiveness of a MOOC may depend upon how it is implemented. It is relatively straightforward for course designers to move the content of a traditional, face-to-face course online by digitizing the lectures and other materials. However, this approach to an online course does not take into account the important social component of learning. In a face-to-face classroom, students interact with the instructor and with other students in rich, meaningful ways that involve verbal and nonverbal communication. Nonverbal communication includes aspects of interactions that do not have to do specifically with the words that are said. Facial expressions are one aspect of nonverbal communication that contribute to the effectiveness of communication. Verbal and nonverbal communication are used to have discussions that facilitate learning of the lecture material and they are also used when students interact with each other to study, work on projects, and ask questions of each other. Thus, there is a critical formal network of social interaction between the instructor and students, as well as an informal network of interaction that takes place among the students. Course designers can put online tools for social interaction into a MOOC to provide the opportunities for formal and informal social interaction. These kinds of MOOCs are called connectivist MOOCS (cMOOCs). MOOCs that are modeled on the old-fashioned learning approach of providing video presentations followed by tests are known as xMOOCs. In other words, xMOOCs concentrate on content delivery of the course material. cMOOCs encourage students to collaborate and to communicate with each other. The classes may ask students to be creative through project assignments, and they may nudge students toward independent thinking instead of learning cookie cutter solutions to problems. cMOOCs have advantages over xMOOCs in several ways. cMOOCs promote diversity of opinions, independence of students, and freedom to express ideas. But research shows that these advantages do not come automatically. The instructor or course designers must manage a course while it is being run in order to achieve the full benefit of a cMOOC. When instructors and course designers do this, then students feel enabled to learn the material and they feel a sense of connectedness to the other students.

The increasing sophistication of online educational software has allowed whole curricula to be put online. In many places in the United States, high school students can complete their entire degree online. A key feature of online high schools is the flexibility in scheduling that they give to students who are busy with other activities. Online high schools let students have jobs while earning their degrees. Other types of students may also benefit, such as students who are professional athletes. Further, the majority of colleges and universities in the United States have one or more entirely online certificate programs, college minors, college majors, or master's degree programs.

TAKING INTO ACCOUNT HOW LEARNING WORKS

The dominant theories of learning point out that good education is a lot more than just content delivery. Unfortunately, the affordances of the Internet, web browsers, and electronic devices make it natural for educators to use these tools for content delivery only. Psychosocial development, interpersonal skills, critical thinking, peer to peer learning, and lifelong learning skills are other critical factors for effective education. Psychosocial development includes a range of mental and emotional skills that support learning. For instance, self-regulation is helpful for staying on track and staying focused for the duration of a course. Students who are successful at self-regulation are able to monitor their learning progress, compare their progress to their goals, and adjust their actions when their progress is not sufficient for meeting their goals. Interpersonal skills mostly relate to communication between students and communication between a student and the instructor. As described earlier, there is a strong social aspect to learning. Students who have mastered interpersonal skills have a better chance than other students of doing well in a course. Critical thinking is fine-tuning one's thought processes in order to become more efficient and more effective as a learner. Critical thinking has many facets, one of which is to be able to process a complex message so that the core idea (i.e., the thesis) can be determined. This particular skill is beneficial when reading materials, listening to lectures, and participating in discussions. Peer to peer learning is the sharing of information among students. It might involve asking questions of other students and the formation of study groups. Finally, lifelong learning skills are the set of general skills that aid a person in mastering newly encountered information. A good example of lifelong learning skills is learning the mechanics of how a particular type of class works. Laboratory-based classes, for example, tend to involve a series of lab-based activities that each require a written report. Students who take a laboratory class will do better than other students if they have previously taken a lab course and performed well in it.

Learning is more effective when the students in a course become a community of learners. Students who form a learning community have a shared purpose—to learn and master the course material—that improves learning for all of the community members. Feeling that one is part of a community also improves communication with other community members. Additionally, learning communities tend to adopt unstated rules about how members treat each other. The rules touch on fairness, justice, respect and caring. The creation of a learning community solves a problem created by online courses. Students, especially those who are physically distant from each other, can develop a feeling of social isolation in online courses that focus mostly on content delivery. Community building is a technique that the course designer or instructor can use to create a learning community. One way to build a community is to ensure that software tools are used that let students interact with each other easily. Researchers argue that community building improves students' sense of belonging—the feeling that the student is an important part of a group or project. A sense of belonging, in turn, contributes to a shared set of ideas and values among the community members. Most high school and college students are already social network site users; thus, they are members of at least one online community. A successful path to building a learning community can therefore involve using the existing social network as part of a class. The advantage to this path with students, according to one review of the literature, is that it lets teachers work with them where they are. The students are part of a prior online community in which the students are highly engaged. Using the existing social network appears to help to transfer that engagement to the class activities.

Proficiency is an important part of being an effective student. Proficiency is multifaceted, but it includes basic reading, writing, and math skills; self-regulation and metacognition (knowledge of one's knowledge); organizational skills; and general administrative skills. Research shows that proficiency levels do not matter in blended courses—those courses that use the Internet as a source of supplementary material on a topic. There are other times when less proficient students will not do as well as more proficient students in online courses. At the high school level in the United States, less proficient students might have reduced performance when taking online classes. One research project looked at students who failed algebra and were placed into follow-up courses, known as recovery courses. These students, presumably already less proficient than the students who passed the algebra class, did worse when randomly assigned to an online recovery course than when assigned to a face-to-face course. Having a relatively low high school grade point average (GPA) is one sign of lack of proficiency in college students. Students with low high school GPAs did worse than other college students in one study of hundreds of thousands of students in online courses at a large, for-profit university in the United States.

There are potential pitfalls of online learning, including MOOCs. Web browsers encourage users to click on links representing tangential information. Doing so may shorten the amount of time spent processing information that is presented on a screen, for instance a passage that needs to be read and understood. As touched on in Chapters 5 and 7, some people may have developed a style of information processing online that encourages skimming rather than doing deep elaboration of content material. Further, the potential for distraction by irrelevant information—as well as other programs and apps running on the computer screen—can interfere with a person's ability to stay focused on a learning goal. In other words, educating people through online systems can challenge a students' cognitive control, those mental processes that allow us to stay on track in complex tasks. By the mid-2000s, researchers had established that learning behind a screen had disadvantages for students who had a lot of prior experience using computers. These students appeared to be using the shallow, superficial strategy of skimming online material rather than learning the material in depth.

Although many educators are skeptical of MOOCs, a small body of research has demonstrated that they can be effective in some ways and under certain conditions. Several of the strengths and weaknesses of cMOOCs were revealed in case studies of a MOOC named Personal Learning Environments, Networks, and Knowledge 2010. This cMOOC gave students a chance to interact with each other, showed that students use the built-in tools to gather information relevant to the course, and encouraged the sharing of information between students. However, the creative aspect of the cMOOC was used by only a small number of the students: only a minority of students created and distributed content to the other students. In fact, there were students known as lurkers who silently collected information and shared it with others without participating in the creation of materials. Being a good manager of one's time, setting useful and appropriate class-related goals, and investing time into the course all improved participation in the course. Also, students who had taken other MOOCs had higher levels of engagement than students who had not, with the latter acting more like lurkers than content creators. Students who created and distributed materials were confident in their ability to use MOOCs.

The potential pitfalls necessitate integrating online coursework with learning theories by taking into consideration several factors that include the social dimension of learning and levels of student proficiency; these considerations will guide how technology is used during the educational process. Recent scholarly reviews of the research into online learning conclude that there is a need for more studies. Several factors that affect the success of online learning have been identified, but many of the studies done have used a correlational design, a relatively weak research method. The correlational design shows that two factors are associated with each other—for example, creation of content and prior online learning experiences—but it does not prove that one factor is the cause of the other. To support the existence of a causal link between factors, more powerful experimental designs need to be employed by researchers.

TECHNOLOGY DISTRACTIONS IN THE CLASSROOM

Long before the Internet existed, students have been distracting themselves in school classrooms when they should have been paying attention to the teacher. (The present author sheepishly recalls reading the newspaper during college lectures whenever it was possible to hide in the back row of a large lecture hall.) Widespread access to the Internet via small, portable devices—read: smartphones—has given students new ways to disengage from learning within classroom settings. Teachers began to notice what their students were up to in the 2000s, and by the mid- to late 2000s, researchers started documenting student activities in the classroom, as well as the implications and repercussions. Some of the distractions identified by scientists were not new ones. Students still eat and drink during class and work on material from other courses, for example, just like they have been doing for decades. However, due to laptop computers, mobile phones, and earbuds, new distractions include social networking—primarily Facebook—and sending and receiving SMS messages, as well as instant messaging and listening to music. In some cases, activities that seem incongruent with the classroom environment are taking place. For instance, students have reported talking on the phone and videoconferencing in the middle of a class lecture. Many instructors—and researchers—have noted that contemporary students do not hide their technology use in the classroom; actually, students have been described as asserting or demanding their right to do so.

Students don't need scientists to tell them that using technology in the classroom is distracting and detrimental to learning. Students' own experiences with using technology in the classroom have given them a firm understanding of the consequences. Generally speaking, students have a negative attitude toward texting in the classroom; further, they are aware that classroom distractions will affect how much they learn during lectures. One nationwide study of college students in the United States asked the students to guess how damaging it would be to send and receive text messages during a lecture. Ninety-nine percent of the students owned cell phones at the time of the survey, in 2009; thus, the students had sufficient experience with phones to base their guesses on real events from their lives. The students had to estimate how many of 10 questions from a lecture they would correctly answer if they were texting and if they were not texting. As a group, the students estimated that they would get about one-third fewer answers right when texting than not. In the second part of the study, college students were actually tested in a simulated lecture environment. Performance on the test confirmed the estimates made by the students in the first part of the experiment. When texting, students remembered 27% less material than when not texting. And in the classroom, a significant portion of students are affected when other students use their phones for text messaging. In fact, approximately 23% of American college students report that they are affected by cell phone use around them during lectures.

Yet students continue to do it. Texting in the classroom is widespread. Students admit to texting in the classroom. The percentages of students who do it range from about one-quarter of students to over one-half of students. Other studies have found much higher rates, sometimes 90% or higher. Students know that texting is bad for their learning, but they do it anyways, because classroom lectures are universally perceived as boring, making it difficult to stay focused for the entire duration of a presentation. In the days before the Internet era, students who got bored in class would resort to doodling or even napping, both of which are also counterproductive to learning. Students also report that class duration and boredom cause them to use their phones during lectures. Class durations in college push the limits of students' attention spans. While high school classes tend to last around 50 minutes, college classes often last for 75 minutes or longer. Instructors who are not skilled at motivating or engaging their audiences contribute to the problem, causing students to become disengaged and possibly distracted by other thoughts and activities. Students know when it is appropriate to use technology during class-time and when it is not. College students in the United States report that using technology for learning—such as looking up information on the web—is acceptable, as is using technology—cell phones—for emergencies. When asked what should be done about disruptive cell phone use in the class, most students actually endorse banning their use.

In many rigorous investigations, researchers have demonstrated the interfering effects of classroom distractions related to technology. There are different ways that students jeopardize in-class learning using technology, including using laptops in the classroom, checking their social media during class time, and text messaging. Students who use laptop computers in class get lower scores on quizzes and assignments than students who do not use the devices. The best evidence about technology distractions comes from experiments that simulate the classroom learning environment. Rather than hearing and seeing live lectures, experimenters frequently use previously-recorded lectures to simulate the instructor's presentation. This method allows the researcher to duplicate the simulated lecture many times for different sets of students. It also allows the researcher to precisely control the messages in the lecture, rather than relying on a live instructor who may be unpredictable or make mistakes while lecturing. When college students receive and reply to text messages during a simulated lecture, there is about a 10% reduction in the amount of material learned. In other words, their scores on a test of the lecture material drop by about one grade level. Surprisingly, the same sized drop in performance happens when students put their phones in silent mode by turning off the ringer before viewing the lecture material, possibly because of the anxiety of not having one's phone. The best performance comes when students give up their phones completely before watching a lecture. This result suggests that instructors should use a strict no-phone policy in classrooms if they want their students to learn the most during lectures. Other experiments show the spreading effect of in-class technology use. If a student fails to silence her phone, and if the phone rings during class time, then the students around her are negatively affected. In fact, decrements to the innocent bystanders can range from 25% to 40% of learning. Even instructors are impacted by students using distracting technology. The teachers report that cell phone use interferes with their ability to concentrate and stay focused. Further, the negative effect of technology distractions extends to the people seated around the student who is using the technology.

Much of the research into in-class texting has been done with college students. This is because college students are easily accessible by college professors, the professionals who do most of the research into the topic. However, the effects occur at all levels of the educational spectrum, including elementary school, junior high school, and high school. Not only are tests of the lecture material impacted by cell phone use in class, but so are course grades more generally. In fact, there is sufficient research to conclude that personal technology as a whole has a negative impact upon classroom performance, broadly defined to include test scores, course grades, semester grades, and overall GPA. Studies of social media use often focus on Facebook use, because Facebook is wildly popular with college students. The studies tend to find that students who spend the most time accessing Facebook in class or at home while doing schoolwork have the lowest GPAs compared to other students. In some cases, social scientists ask students to fill out questionnaires in which the students report their cell phone and texting habits. When the scientists correlate these habits with overall GPAs, the results often reveal that GPAs are negatively correlated with cell phone use. Not only are learning and academic performance impaired, but there may be other negative associations as well. The causes of texting in the classroom could go beyond the somewhat superficial dimensions of boredom and class length. One study showed that college students who texted often during class also experienced more anxiety and had lower life satisfaction than other college students.

Students' habits and impulses regarding their personal technologies tend to make them distracted. Habits regarding cell phone use in the classroom could have developed over many class meetings and many academic terms, making them hard to break. Even getting the students more engaged in classroom activities does not seem to break the cell phone habit. For instance, when teachers make a concerted effort to make eye contact with students during lectures, and to grab their attention by calling their names, students become more motivated to learn than otherwise. But texting in the classroom doesn't stop; in fact, it remains unchanged. One bright spot in all of this is that there are other ways to lessen the negative outcomes. When you are in a state of not knowing how to deal with technology distractions, then you have low metacognition, which is, "knowledge of one's knowledge, processes, and cognitive and affective states; and the ability to consciously and deliberately monitor and regulate one's knowledge, processes and cognitive and affective states" (Hacker, Dunlosky, & Graesser, 1998). One of the benefits of having metacognition related to technology use is that it could allow students to deal with interruptions, like an incoming text message, during class time. An example of how metacognition helps students deal with distractions in class is when they receive an incoming instant message from a friend while studying on the computer. Students with high metacognition—including having the skills to deal with disruptions to learning—will not respond to the message right away. They will wait until later to check the message. Students with low metacognition will respond to the message immediately, potentially disrupting the learning process.

You might also have a lot of distractions going on both inside and outside of your head, contributing to mind-wandering. Mind-wandering is the name of the state of affairs when a person is not thinking about the task at hand. For instance, a student working on her laptop screen to write a paper might actually be thinking of her friends and unrelated issues, although her face is pointed at the laptop screen. As most students and former students know, mind-wandering is common in school classrooms; one estimate is that each student in a classroom mind-wanders for about one-third of the class period. Students might be able to move from a state of not knowing how to deal with distractions and not noticing when they are being distracted to a state of making smart choices about their technology use in the classroom. Mindfulness is the practice of noticing what one is thinking about. A critical part of mindfulness is not becoming bogged down in any one train of thought. This aspect of mindfulness has been described as ". . . tending to daily experiences without keen judgment" (Lee, Kim, McDonough, Mendoza, & Kim, 2017). It may be possible to use mindfulness to keep one's thoughts relevant to the task at hand—in this case, learning—but it alone might not be enough to deal with the types of distractions that students encounter. Mindfulness and metacognition are closely related to self-regulation, the process by which people manage their thoughts, emotions, and behaviors. Self-regulation involves purposeful and beneficial behaviors, such as knowing when to turn off and stow one's cell phone in order to make learning effective. Self-regulation seems to improve sustained attention—the ability to stay focused on a single task for a long period of time. When self-regulation has been measured in students, it has been learned that having the ability to self-regulate one's actions improves learning in the classroom, partly by reducing the chances that a cell phone will be used for text messaging.

A common recommendation from researchers is that teachers use tech breaks in the classroom to help focus students' attention. Tech breaks, short for technology breaks, are proposed as a way to improve students' attention in class; they are a chance for students to get out and use their phones, laptops, and tablets for irrelevant purposes as a reward for paying attention to the lecture or presentation. In other words, tech breaks might allow instructors to manage their students' attention and technology usage. The process of tech breaks involves several steps. Tech breaks are presumed to work when teachers first notify the students that the breaks will be used during the class period. The idea is that students will be able to maintain their attention on the lecture if they know that there will soon be a chance to use their technologies for irrelevant tasks. In a typical class period, as admitted by students in many studies, students multitask with their cell phones, driven by external and internal distractions—such as the Fear of Missing Out (FOMO)—leading to inattention and losses in learning, as demonstrated in research studies. To control the distracting, off-task multitasking, teachers might consider implementing the tech breaks about every 15 minutes. While no scientific studies of tech breaks have been published, researchers report anecdotally that tech breaks that last 1 to 2 minutes improve student alertness and focus.

The best approach is to turn off and stow one's phone. Experimental research shows that sometimes putting one's phone on silent mode just before watching a lecture is not enough to stop the phone from interfering with learning. How can a silenced phone interfere with learning? The answer is that there may be anxiety that students experience when they cannot monitor their phone, unless the phone is completely powered down. Anxiety over not having access to one's phone is called nomophobia. There is much evidence from laboratory studies and studies in classroom settings to assert that turning off one's cell phone will improve classroom learning. However, it is clear that some students are more motivated than others to do so. When given a chance by the teacher to give up their cell phones before the start of class, students who do so earn higher scores on class tests than students who do not. At the same time, students who started out with higher class averages than other students are more likely to give up their phones in the first place than the other students. So while removing one's cell phone will improve learning, students who start out as better performers know better than others that they should turn in their phones to improve learning.

STUDYING AND LEARNING OUTSIDE OF CLASS

It's normal for students to multitask while working on schoolwork outside of class. Scientists have documented significant media multitasking and task-switching by students when they are studying and doing homework. By the beginning of the 2010s, two-thirds of American college students routinely multitasked while in class, while studying, or while doing homework. For younger students aged 8 to 18 years, two-thirds of the time spent using entertainment media like listening to music was also spent doing another task like homework. Some common combinations of tasks are listening to music while working, browsing the web while working, and checking social media sites while working. Middle school, high school, and college students are switching between tasks as they do their schoolwork outside of class. Observations of students show that the students spend less than six minutes on schoolwork before switching to another task like stretching, walking, and using their personal technologies. Keeping multiple windows open on the computer is linked to spending less time on task, as is texting on a cell phone. Surprisingly, using a web browser is associated with more time on schoolwork, possibly because students use the browser to access school-related information. Further, multitasking while doing homework is not just an American phenomenon; it happens worldwide. One international project compared college students in Kuwait, Russia, and the United States. While Russian college students tend to multitask less than American or Kuwaiti students, the most commonly multitasked activities with homework across these nations are watching television, listening to music, using the phone, and browsing the Internet. Interestingly, gaming is not a task that students multitask. This might be because gaming places intense demands on a player's cognitive and other mental and physical processes. In the parlance of Chapter 5, gaming has a high cognitive load. The high cognitive load may prevent people from doing another task at the same time.

It's clear from the research literature that multitasking during these tasks negatively impacts students. Scientific reports and reviews of the research literature repeatedly find negative impacts of multitasking while doing schoolwork. The impact comes in the form of reduced learning and less time on task. The net long-term impact may be upon GPA, as described later. Multitasking can be caused by external factors like alerts from a phone and it can be caused by internal factors like thoughts about friends and family. In some cases, students appear to believe either that they are successful at multitasking or that multitasking actually helps them. In studies where U.S. college students are asked about their multitasking habits, the students often report that multitasking does not interfere with school-related tasks like reading. As multitasking became more common due to technology use in the mid to late 2000s, researchers were trying to uncover the reasons why students multitask when they ought to be focused on schoolwork. It was learned that a subset of students believed that multitasking was beneficial. The students said that their concentration improved when they let themselves briefly switch to another task, often one more interesting than doing schoolwork.

One way that ICT could affect academic tasks outside of class is through displacement. Imagine that a student, returning home from a day at school, decides to spend a little time playing video games instead of reading his textbooks. The time that is usually taken to read is replaced with time taken to play games. Another way to describe this situation is that video gaming displaced academic reading. Due to the introduction of many new activities that people have access to in the Internet age, displacement of beneficial activities like reading and studying is a distinct possibility. (Some examples of displacement have been discussed in other chapters.) Academic reading is a task that many students find to be boring or unpleasant; effective reading certainly is a task that places heavy demands upon our mental processes, generating fatigue. Therefore, one might expect reading to be displaced by technology-based tasks. Yet research indicates that for one academic task—reading—there is no displacement. At least with college students, the time spent reading has remained high even as personal technologies have become a part of everyday life. Students average almost 8 hours per week of pleasure reading and more than 15 hours per week of academic reading. This fact shows that personal technology use is not displacing academic tasks like reading. Another way to examine the possibility of displacement is to look at the numerical relationship between the number of hours spent reading and the number of hours spent on personal technology use. One should find that reading hours decline as personal technology use increases if displacement is in effect. However, researchers have found that there is a positive correlation between reading hours and Internet use hours: as the time spent using the Internet increases, so does the time spent reading.

The findings present a mystery. How can the number of hours spent on academic tasks not be affected if students are spending time on entirely new tasks like gaming, social networking, and browsing the Internet? The solution to the mystery is multitasking. The tasks overlap with each other in time. For example, students are using their social network sites at the same time that they are doing homework, reading, studying, and learning. Most likely, students are not doing two tasks exactly at the same time, but interleaving tasks, a phenomenon known as task-switching among psychology researchers. Media multitasking is the practice of interleaving a media-related task, such as watching a YouTube video, with another task like doing homework. Regarding academic reading, multitasking is common. Studies show that U.S. college students read while talking on the phone, and while sending and receiving text messages. Thus, another way that ICT could impact academic tasks outside of class is through media multitasking.

Multitasking does not always involve two entirely unrelated activities. There are many cases when a student would want to task switch between two tasks that are both aimed at achieving the same goal. When writing an essay, a student might want to write sentences as she does research using an Internet search engine. These cases are known as productive multitasking. Taking notes while studying is another example of productive multitasking. In contrast, many cases of multitasking involve two tasks that do not share goals. When writing an essay, a student might be tempted to be checking her social networking site. These are cases of distractive multitasking. A possible problem with distractive multitasking is that the unrelated task—checking the social networking site—might use mental processes that would otherwise be used in the academic task, writing. Broadly speaking, the unrelated task might deplete the pool of available cognitive resources, resulting in decrements in performance in the academic task. Chapter 5 explained how the human brain is incapable of processing unlimited sources of information all at the same time. It also described how the mechanisms of attention select subsets of these sources of information for processing. This way, the human information processing system is not overwhelmed with processing demands. But it means that our mental apparatus can handle only a relatively small set of stimuli or tasks at a time.

In short, multitasking or task-switching is not likely to be helpful to learning and studying, except for the cases of productive multitasking. Therefore, it behooves students to implement measures to reduce the need for multitasking and to decrease the chances that they will multitask. A straightforward action is to reduce or eliminate distractions while studying or doing homework. Turning off a cell phone is one way to eliminate distractions, such as alerts and notifications that come from the phone. Silencing the phone also will reduce distractions, although distractions can still arise from phones that are left in vibrate mode. The impact of distractions from music can be lessened by lowering the music volume or turning off the music altogether. Several types of distractions can be handled by closing windows on the computer. Closing the windows shuts down the programs and applications associated with the windows, thus preventing alerts and notifications from the programs, taking away the visual cues that remind a user to access the programs, and removing the temptation to use the programs. Many other strategies exist; students who are highly motivated to improve their learning will find the strategies that work best for them.

SMARTPHONES AND SNSs: TWO CULPRITS

The smartphone is a destructive force when it comes to academic activities outside of class—and, of course, it is a destructive force in class, as described earlier. Reports show that students frequently use their phones while studying, reading, or doing homework. It is well documented that college students have their phones with them and use the phones while outside of class doing schoolwork. The immediate effects of using the smartphone while doing schoolwork at home are to create distractions, increase multitasking, and impair a student's ability to achieve her schoolwork goals. Research examining cell phone use while doing schoolwork has been done in laboratories with college students. The students bring their homework to the laboratory and are allowed to use ICT as they would do at home on their own. In this setting, college students multitask with their personal technologies about 14% of the time. In addition, most students listen to music while they do their schoolwork. Cell phone use is the most frequently multitasked activity. Over a three-hour period, the average student uses his cell phone between 8 and 9 times to engage in distractive multitasking. The cell phone is primarily used to read and send text messages and to access the Internet. Unfortunately, it is possible that the data underestimate the true amount of multitasking done at home because students are in an artificial environment and are aware that they were being observed.

The laboratory setting lets scientists make measurements that aren't normally acquired in a home setting. For example, researchers asked students to write down their goals for a homework session, those being specific achievements that they wanted to make during the session. At the end of the homework session, the students indicated which goals had been achieved. When experimenters took away the phones of one-half of the students for the duration of the homework session, the number of goals achieved increased by 12%. Interestingly, the phone-restricted students did not feel that the quality of their homework session was any better than the students who were allowed to keep their phones. The scientists offered this explanation: taking away the phones stopped an unconscious or barely conscious urge to procrastinate using technology. In their own words, removing the phone "subtly manipulated the mindset of the participants" (Cutino & Nees, 2016). The long-term effect of using a cell phone while doing schoolwork outside of class is upon GPA. A study with Nigerian college students found evidence that phone habits affect GPA. The researcher measured the amount of time that students spend studying, the amount of time talking on the phone, and other aspects of phone use. The amount of time spent studying was the most important factor affecting GPAs, but the time spent talking on the phone also was a significant predictor of GPA. The more that a student talked on the phone, the lower his GPA became. In this African sample of students, males admitted always playing games and always doing social networking on their devices during lectures and schoolwork outside of classes. Females admitted playing games and social networking most of the time. Distraction and multitasking with the phone were shown to be factors in the relationship between phone habits and GPA. In many situations, the impact of the phone may be due to one of the most widely used applications by young people of student age: social networking sites. It is known that there is a negative correlation between communication activities—like text messaging and social network use—and GPAs. Researchers have mostly studied college students with respect to how ICT use affects GPAs, because college students are easy to access for researchers—most researchers are college professors—and college students are the top consumers of social networking sites. The relationship shows that GPAs go down when text messaging activity goes up. The same holds true for the relationship between GPAs and Facebook use. Further, research in the early 2010s found that college students who engaged in online social networking have lower GPAs than students who don't.

Media multitasking seems to play a role in this relationship between ICT and grades. Most studies—but not all—find that media multitasking while doing school-work, including in-class meetings, relates to GPA. There is variation in how much students multitask, but the students who report the most multitasking while doing schoolwork outside of class also have the lowest GPAs. The most likely possibility is that multitasking while doing schoolwork affects the quality of learning and studying. The vast majority of individuals cannot multitask effectively, as research on multitasking and attention has revealed. (There are a few individuals known as supertaskers who can multitask without decrements in performance on the tasks, but supertaskers make up about only 2% of the population.) One well-known study of this topic analyzed data from more than 1,700 college students at a university in the northeastern United States. In a web-based questionnaire, students reported how often they do several different activities while doing their schoolwork outside of class. The questionnaire asked about Internet searches not related to schoolwork, Facebook use, using email, using instant messaging, talking on their phones, and text messaging. The scientists pulled school records for each student to determine the student's college GPA and they statistically removed the influence of the students' high school GPAs in order to control for general academic ability. Among the different types of multitasking, only multitasking with Facebook and multi-tasking through text messaging had a significant impact on GPA. Both of these activities were associated with declines in GPA, but Facebook had a larger nega-tive impact than text messaging. The link between media multitasking with social networking sites and GPA may have a cultural component. When Ameri-can and European college students are compared, the American students who multitask are more susceptible to the negative effects upon GPA. The same is not true for European students. The explanation for the difference may lie in how the two groups of students control their use of technology, that is, how they self-regulate. European students may be more likely to self-regulate their social networking site use than American students. In fact, comments from American students suggest that they are more open to multitasking than their European counterparts. An example comment from an American is, "I usually do some work, take a Facebook break, then go back to school work." In comparison, an example comment from a European is, "If I am doing my work for school, I do not check my SNS."

Facebocrastination—a portmanteau word coined by blending Facebook and procrastination—is the act of using a social networking site to avoid working on an important task. Facebocrastination is irrational: logically speaking, a student should choose to spend time doing homework due the next day over checking Facebook for the latest news on friends and family. College students engage in Facebocras-tination frequently. A research survey in Germany found that the percentage of stu-dents who had not used Facebook to procrastinate was only 9%. The biggest risk factor for Facebocrastination is having low self-control, or the inability to inhibit the impulse to check a social networking site. Also, students who frequently check Facebook and students who enjoy using Facebook are at risk. Most importantly, students who frequently Facebocrastinate tend to have lower grades than other students.

MOTIVATION AND AFFECT

Students need to take breaks from their homework and studying, possibly because they find doing these tasks to be unpleasant. When American college students are asked why they need to take breaks while studying or doing homework, their reasons fall into general categories that include the need to escape from the academic task and the need to relax. Often, they use personal technologies to escape or to relax; 81% report communicating with other people through text messaging or instant message, 79% of students report using Facebook, and 72% report listening to music. The strongest motive for taking breaks with Facebook is to escape. College students who are asked to do their homework in a research laboratory, under careful observation and with no personal technologies available, show a pattern of negative affect—negative temporary emotions—that does not change over the course of the homework session. In other words, students find it unpleasant to do their homework. The pattern is different when the students are allowed to keep their personal devices with them and to use the devices as they wish. In a one-hour homework session, students spend a little over 10% of their homework session off-task due to using their devices, but their emotional state is better than when their device usage is restricted. When their devices are available, their negative affect declines throughout the homework session. Thus, the unpleasantness of academic tasks is likely one of the causes of multitasking when doing schoolwork outside of class.

In longer homework sessions there might be different dynamics. In a three-hour homework period, students become increasingly tired and their positive affect—positive temporary emotions—decreases over the time period. At the same time, when their negative affect becomes high during the homework session, the amount of time they spend multitasking increases. One possible explanation is that students multitask when the task of doing homework becomes irritating. But an alternative explanation is that distractive multitasking generates negative emotions under these conditions. Rather than feeling a need to escape from homework, there are some students who are intensely focused on getting their homework done. These students, who are said to have a high motivation to do homework, multitask less often than other students. These students also spend less time multitasking when they do switch to another, unrelated task. So students who are highly motivated to do homework are able to reduce their multitasking and improve performance.

IMPROVING MATH AND SCIENCE KNOWLEDGE AND SKILLS

Teachers and educators use the Internet and personal technologies to educate students on particular topics. There is a long history of using the Internet and other computer-related technologies for math and science education. Math educators have tackled gamification over the last 10 to 15 years as a way to improve educational outcomes. Gamification is the transformation of a traditionally uninteresting learning task into a game. Turning learning into a game is an old trick used by educators over many decades; it makes learning fun and increases the engagement of students in the learning task. Gamification capitalizes upon digital technologies by building games as websites or apps on mobile devices. The computer has also been used to run simulations as a way to improve math learning. Computer simulations provide many advantages in the math learning process. They can help students visualize mathematical concepts by depicting the concepts on a computer screen as numbers, graphs, or other interesting visual representations; they can be interactive, letting students change values in a simulated mathematical system, and then quickly observe the results of the changed values; they also give students an easy way to save the results of computations. Science educators also take advantage of computers for education. There are many ways that computer-based technology can support science learning. First, students can use the Internet as database, using it to search for and retrieve information on science topics. Second, students can use the Internet as a means of sharing information with other students as they work on science projects or as they engage in the social aspects of learning. Third, computers—with or without the Internet—can be attached to scientific devices like probes to collect data during science experiments. Fourth, computers and other devices have software that let students make graphs of scientific data. Fifth, computers can be used to create multimedia presentations that accurately summarize a student's knowledge about a scientific topic.

Some of the recent efforts at math and science education take advantage of the affordances of mobile devices and employ a theoretical approach in order to produce positive outcomes. Mobile learning allows students to access information in multiple venues and removes the temporal and environmental constraints of classroom learning. One venue is the classroom, where students are receiving information from the teacher or engaging in learning exercises during class time. Another venue is the mobile device, where students are accessing stored materials, and also engaging in learning exercises. Learning can take place at times other than the normal class period. Students can use mobile devices outside of class time while at school, or they can use the mobile devices at home to work on learning material. Mobile devices also extend the reach of social interactions. Social interactions can take place within the classroom in a face-to-face format; they can take place through social media software on devices during class time and at the school (i.e., mediated communication); and, they can take place outside of the school at home through the mobile device. One researcher in the field has defined mobile learning this way: "learning across multiple contexts, through social and content interactions, using personal electronic devices" (Crompton, 2013). A further advantage of using mobile devices for learning is that learning can be personalized. A student can advance at his or her own pace through a learning curriculum and the software can keep track of the progress made at each point in the curriculum.

Using mobile devices for science learning has evolved from the early days when the devices were employed as content delivery mechanisms. In middle schools and high schools in the United States, mobile learning in science and math education had originally been used in a transmissive fashion, with apps that merely presented new material for students to study and learn. By the mid-2010s, the software had improved. Contemporary mobile learning (m-learning) efforts add the other key characteristics of effective learning. Collaboration was added; the software tools encouraged students to work together to solve problems or to share their work with their peers. Inquiry-based learning was added. In inquiry-based learning, the learning process starts with an interesting question to answer. The learning proceeds by making attempts to answer the question. These attempts motivate students to look for information, evaluate information, design research studies, analyze data, and compare data to the hypotheses. In short, inquiry-based learning compels students to conduct science. The portability of mobile devices allows for authentic learning—also known as situated learning—studying and learning that takes place in a field setting or in a laboratory where science is typically carried out. Additionally, m-learning harnesses the power of the computer to improve science education. M-learning apps can provide highly detailed graphic visualizations of scientific concepts, allow for the representation of scientific constructs that are not visible to the naked eye, and give students an immersive experience through high-fidelity graphics, video content, and 3D-like effects. The results of studies on m-learning for math and science education have been favorable. One comprehensive review of the literature on math education with m-learning found that 27 out of 36 studies produced positive results; m-learning improved math learning. A detailed analysis of the published literature on science learning with mobile devices found that elementary school students formed the largest segment of participants in the research. All of the 49 published studies found positive results.

However, general ICT use at school does not always have positive benefits for students when it comes to math and science education. Researchers in Europe looked at how in-school and at-home use of Internet and communication devices affects students' math and science learning. The measures of learning came from the Programme for International Student Assessment (PISA), a test that 15-year-old students from many different countries take. The researchers collected a subset of data from two countries (Turkey and Finland) and compared test scores to how much time students say they spend using ICT at school and at home. In both countries, using ICT at school was a problem for learning. The more a student used ICT at school, the less well the student did on the math and science tests. However, the details of how students used ICT at school are not clear. It is conceivable that much of the reported usage did not reflect well-crafted educational interventions by the teachers exemplified by the scientific studies of m-learning.

There are three potential problems with interpreting the positive effects of m-learning. One of the potential problems is the researchers' bias. The researchers' bias occurs because many of the published studies on using m-learning for math education evaluate the effectiveness of the authors' own apps. Math educators frequently develop their own software for math education through m-learning, rather than use commercially available software. As such, the desire to positively evaluate the software could result in conscious or unconscious actions that shape the results, or the interpretation of the results. A very superficial example of this bias might be highlighting the beneficial aspects of a math education app while over-looking the negative aspects of the app. Another potential problem is the lack of replication. Replication is the process by which scientists redo experiments in order to validate earlier findings. Successful replication increases confidence in a finding—for example, that a particular app improves learning—and can be used to extend findings to new settings (e.g., applying an app made for fourth graders to advanced third graders). A third problem with the scientific body of knowledge on this topic is the possibility of publication bias. Publication bias is the systematic tendency for scientific journals to accept papers with positive or significant results. This could occur either because the reviewers for the publication have a bias toward positive results or because researchers themselves choose not to send papers with negative or non-significant results to the journals.

IMPROVING CRITICAL THINKING SKILLS

According to experts who study critical thinking, critical thinking is necessary for effective education. To many, therefore, education is not just about content delivery, where teachers provide knowledge and skills to students. It is also about teaching critical thinking skills. Critical thinking skills support deep learning, and it appears that critical thinking can be improved through intentionally designed interventions. Certain cases when teachers intentionally use technology to improve critical thinking skills have produced positive results. One type of activity that can improve critical thinking skills is the WebQuest. The WebQuest, developed in the late 1990s, involves the Internet as a supplemental information source for students. Teachers instruct their students to go online so that the students can find information that will help to answer a question or summarize a topic. WebQuests can be short, lasting one day or less, or they can be long, lasting up to three days. The WebQuest makes use of higher-order critical thinking, though the first impression of the WebQuest is that it is a content delivery method for education—one of the early, passive, and relatively ineffective approaches to Internet-based education. Well-formulated WebQuests require that students integrate newly acquired information with old information that they already have in their memories. Theoretically speaking, WebQuests meet several requirements of a critical thinking exercise. One piece of deep learning is to connect newly acquired information to information that is stored in memory. This process requires significant effort on the student's part, but pays off in improving long-term memory for the new material. WebQuests also put pressure on students to construct new knowledge, that is, to take information that is found online and process it in order to generate additional information. This mental act of making inferences from material is a significant aspect of critical thinking. One definition of critical thinking in the context of school learning has six main parts and WebQuests have been found to satisfy all of them. One, students practice critical thinking and their endeavors are compared to educational standards. Two, a critical audience—in this case, teachers—evaluates the results of the students' critical thinking efforts. Three, thinking is not routine, meaning it does not follow a simplistic pattern. Four, there are explicit definitions of critical thinking and instructions for doing it. Five, critical thinking involves monitoring one's own thought processes and correcting them when necessary. Six, the procedures used to do critical thinking vary with the setting, for example, students learn specific critical thinking techniques for judging Internet search engine results.

In practice, published research shows that WebQuests can indeed improve students' critical thinking skills. In the Philippines, WebQuests were tested in high school physics. The researchers assessed students' critical thinking skills prior to implementing the WebQuests. After five months of using WebQuests, students critical thinking skills were reassessed. Not surprisingly, the exercises helped students learn the course material. Also, all types of critical thinking showed improvement, but only one was statistically significant. Deductive reasoning increased from the beginning to the end of the research project. Deductive reasoning is the ability to apply the rules of logic to data, and therefore reach sound conclusions. On top of the gains in knowledge and critical thinking, the students enjoyed the WebQuests. Enjoyment, then, was perhaps a contributing factor to the benefits of using the web-based exercises. In China, WebQuests were tested in a high school chemistry class. Over the period of the course, the results showed that students improved in their critical thinking skills, especially in the ability to analyze and evaluate information.

Another example is critical reading, the case of critical thinking during reading. Critical reading benefits students because it raises comprehension and it promotes independent thinking. A straightforward way to improve critical reading with print materials is to write on the text, making notes (often in the margins), as well as highlighting sentences and underlining sections. These written acts are the product of applying mental processes to the text, and so they reflect critical thinking. Software for viewing digital texts can be coded with tools that let students mark up the digital text as if it were a printed text. An example is HyLighter, a browser-based piece of code that adds highlighting and commenting to digital texts, as well as document sharing. An evaluation of the effect of the code on students showed increases in critical thinking after using the tool. However, the increases were not statistically significant.

Even when software is not specifically designed to teach critical thinking skills to students, parents can be effective agents in the development and deployment of critical thinking skills when students go online. Online activities can be used as a launch pad for generating critical thoughts. Consider the phenomenon of violent video games. These have produced much debate and discussion in the American popular media (see Chapter 2 for more discussion). Many parents are tempted to place strict rules on the amount of time that their children can play these types of games. Such rule-setting, along with monitoring that the rules are being followed, represents a passive approach to parental mediation of media consumption. An active mediation approach is different. After playing a violent video game, a parent may want to have a discussion with her child about the nature of violence and when it is appropriate and inappropriate. The discussion promotes analysis and evaluation and gives the child important practice in critical thinking skills. Finally, certain kinds of computer-based games are expected to promote critical thinking skills. These kinds of games are often complex, requiring that players solve problems that have many different parts. An example is the game, *Rise of Nations*. In *Rise of Nations*, players must build new cities, improve city infrastructure, and expand one's borders. Researchers assert that this and similar games like massively multiplayer online role-playing games (MMORPGs) depend on logical thinking, memory processes, problem solving, visualization, and critical thinking. Consequently, critical thinking could improve as a side effect of playing games like MMORPGs.

CONCLUSION

Initial steps toward new modalities of instruction started with digitization of educational content and simple use of the Internet. The blended course is a simple-minded, although effective, approach to technology use. Teachers can ask students to find information online, using basic Internet searches or advanced online databases, as a supplement to learning that takes place in a classroom. These initial steps led to putting whole courses online. At the far end of the spectrum is the MOOC. MOOCs put the entire structure of a traditional course into an online format for access by thousands of students. It turns out that the match between the educational technology and theories of effective learning determines when students benefit from the new modalities of instruction. While new modalities of instruction were being created, electronic devices became portable and highly distractive. Students often believe that they can media multitask while studying or doing homework, and they do engage in a lot of multitasking; however, multitasking impacts learning and performance in cognitive tasks. The main culprits are smartphones and social networking sites, and students are motivated to multitask—or not to multitask—for emotional and other reasons. In the end, careful planning and construction of online activities can be used by educators to improve very important student skills, such as critical thinking, math, and science.

Save for becoming bored during lectures and homework, academics is a relatively unemotional activity. The next chapter (Chapter 9) delves into situations where more extreme emotions like depression may occur online.

Interview with an Expert: Dr. Laura L. Bowman

Dr. Laura L. Bowman is a professor of psychological science at Central Connecticut State University. Her research interests include memory, attention, and media use. Dr. Bowman and her colleagues have published some of the most highly cited studies in the study of how technology affects classroom performance. While she has completed the bulk of her research in the United States, Dr. Bowman has also investigated this question internationally. As she and her colleagues have written, "As the use of electronic media continues to grow, further research will tease out how media multitasking impacts young people's way of thinking and functioning in the world and what the long-term outcomes will be in many different societies" (Bowman, Waite, & Levine, 2014).

Q: From your work in this area would you allow high school students to use their personal technology in the classroom? How about college students?

A: Allowing students to use personal technology in the classroom *is* controversial, and there are different perspectives about what teachers/professors should tolerate, allow, or encourage. It's complicated not only by the age/maturity level of the students, but the goals of the course or task, the frequency of use, and the temptation to use technology for off-task activities (e.g., gaming). Some parents want their kids to have a cell phone for emergencies or to keep tabs on their location. Personally, I encourage and reward students who use their personal devices appropriately—there is a time and a place to use technology for personal use (e.g., lunch time), regardless of students' age.

Research indicates tablets/laptops can be useful tools in the classroom. For example, if students are involved in a group project in which they need to consult multiple internet or library sources simultaneously for a specific task, then having a device for each student can facilitate learning. However, the temptation to use these devices for off-task endeavors (checking social media) is overwhelming. If the instructor can manage/monitor the students' activities and the students themselves are mature enough to control their own behaviors, then the positives can outweigh the [negatives]. Distractions in the classroom from technology have a negative impact on learning and memory. Research consistently shows that activities like checking social media, texting, checking emails, etc., in class impair the ability to acquire and remember information. Anecdotally, the students who are not doing as well in my courses are generally the ones who text frequently in class. Research suggests that when students attempt to multitask, areas of the temporal lobe (striatum) of the brain that are associated with superficial learning are activated. That implies that if students constantly check and send text messages while in class or while studying, the material they are supposed to be learning at a deep level, will not be.

It's better to write notes by hand than on a laptop. Students produce higher quality notes and do better on tests of the material when they take notes by hand. Why? Students tend to take more verbatim notes when they use a laptop leading to superficial processing of the material. Handwritten notes tend to be more elaborative, leading to more permanent recall. Plus, students using laptops are more likely to shop online and check social media sites, thereby distracting themselves (and others). There are occasions in which a laptop might be acceptable—for example, if a student has a disability that makes taking notes by hand difficult. I know of no circumstance in which using a smartphone to take notes is preferable.

Q: What about studying and learning, in general?

A: Switching attention while studying is not always detrimental to learning. For example, if one has been studying or working on a task for a long time and becomes fatigued or stuck, then taking a break to do something else can be beneficial. However, if one is trying to learn something new and/or difficult and is constantly switching attention to watch TV or answer text messages, focus can be lost. The loss of focus might require starting over each time resulting in fatigue/boredom/increased learning time (and therefore have a negative impact on learning). Switching could lead to shallow processing.

Students can definitely profit from using technology appropriately. Some tasks are so much faster and more convenient/efficient with technology. For example, searching for sources on library-supported internet databases allows students to quickly access a wealth of resources. However, if students develop a pattern of voluntary distraction, not only will learning and memory suffer, but job opportunities, social relationships, and work-related activities could suffer.

Q: What research are you working on now and what questions still need to be answered to help educators make smart decisions about classroom technology use?

A: My colleagues and I are investigating the relationships among media use, multi-tasking, impulsiveness and reading comprehension skills, academic performance, and creativity. We also plan to examine whether or not students re-read material they missed when responding to text messages while reading academic material. There are so many questions that still have to be addressed regarding classroom technology. What are the best practices for use of technology in the classroom? Does this vary as a function of age? How can we promote responsible use of technology in the classroom? How can we convince students not to engage in distracting behaviors while studying/learning?

9

Emotions

Case Study: Elation and Dejection during the Big Election

Common wisdom in the United States tells us not to talk about religion or politics in polite company. Most people have deep-running beliefs and views on these two topics, and their emotions can run high when encountering people with opposing viewpoints. Few recent events in politics in the United States revealed the inherent truth behind this wisdom than the unexpected victory of Donald J. Trump in the 2016 general election for U.S. president. Americans concerned over issues of immigration, attitudes toward Muslims, and treatment of marginalized groups (for example, members of the LGBTQ+ community) experienced deep worry and, in many cases, outrage over the results of the election. While the traditional news media—television news, newspapers, and magazines—covered much of this emotional outbreak, Internet-based social media were a primary platform for individual expression of feelings toward the outcome of the election.

Prior to the election, several organizations had documented growing trends in how people obtain their information about politics and political issues. More people were using social media to learn about the news than ever before. Political groups—including presidential campaign organizations—were focusing on using social media to influence people's views toward their candidates, thus taking advantage of how regular people were using social media to learn about the world. In 2016, one research organization found that 79% of Americans who go online used Facebook, and that most Americans received their news from social media. Most observers of the 2016 campaign for U.S. president had noted the high level of emotional involvement by Americans in the issues; the emotions were amplified by the extremely polarized positions of the candidates. Average Americans and celebrities alike made public their views on the election via social media. Tweets (i.e., posts on Twitter) by celebrities made quite a bit of impact, as the fans of the celebrities would retweet (i.e., share the original post on their Twitter feeds) the messages to others, causing the original message to be seen by hundreds of thousands of people in some cases.

It was no surprise, then, that on November 8, the day of the election, a record was set for the number of people engaging in political discussion, with tens of millions of people sharing their views on Twitter and Facebook. For example, one celebrity, Seth MacFarlane—a writer, actor, and producer—posted this message on election day: "Some didn't like bush. Some didn't like Obama. But this is different. Forget dislike. Many are genuinely fearful now. This is new." (Nov. 8, 2016, 10:37 pm). The tweet was retweeted by 159,219 people and "liked" by 262,854. Kunal Nayyar—an actor in a popular television show and an Indian immigrant into the United States—tweeted, "Never in 15 years of living in this country have I ever felt afraid to look like I do" (Nov. 8, 2016, 7:35 p.m.). The tweet was retweeted by 5,099 people and liked by 10,403. In the evening, when the traditional news media, one by one, declared their predictions that Trump had won the election, social media channels revealed a massive outpouring of highly charged emotions, both positive and negative, almost immediately. More than 75 million tweets had been sent by the middle of the night, the time that Trump formally claimed victory. And there were more than 716 million likes, posts, comments, and shares on Facebook related to the election. Only about 31 million tweets had been sent on Election Day in 2012, the year of the prior presidential election. Observers of the activities in social media noted several different behaviors related to emotions and emotional expression: expressions of worry over the results of the election caused others to express comfort, expressions of concern linked like-minded people with each other, and marches and protests were organized and advertised using social media platforms.

In the 2008 and 2012 presidential elections, news media had highlighted how President Barack Obama had taken advantage of social media to reach out to young people during his campaigns. This strategy was seen as bold and cutting-edge. But the 2016 presidential campaign reached a new height of social media strategizing for political gain. Candidate Trump, an avid social media user prior to the election campaign, made use of social media, especially Twitter, to broadcast his message—and his personal feelings—to large groups of people. In one of many cases, in February of 2016, nine months prior to Election Day, Trump reacted to a news report that 1,400 American workers were going to lose their jobs when their factory would be relocated to another country: "I am the only one who can fix this. Very sad. Will not happen under my watch!" (Feb. 13, 2016, 7:01 a.m.). This tweet was retweeted by 2,621 people and liked by 5,616. Even after the election, and after being officially sworn in as the U.S. president, Trump continued to use Twitter to show his personal feelings about important topics. Here are two tweets made by Trump shortly after one of his first executive orders was halted by a U.S. federal judge:

- "What is our country coming to when a judge can halt a Homeland Security travel ban and anyone, even with bad intentions, can come into U.S.?" (Feb. 4, 2017, 3:44 p.m.)

- "Because the ban was lifted by a judge, many very bad and dangerous people may be pouring into our country. A terrible decision" (Feb. 4, 2017, 4:44 p.m.)

It is clear that social media during the 2016 U.S. presidential election campaign served several purposes and provides examples of concepts related to emotional expression online. Despite the lack of nonverbal cues in online communications and the pressure to keep written messages short, millions of people were able to express their emotions and to read and feel the emotions of others (i.e., empathy). Further, emotions experienced by one person almost certainly spread to others via emotional contagion.

INTRODUCTION

Emotions, sometimes called moods, are states of arousal that are either in the positive or the negative direction. The direction of the mood is referred to as the valence of the emotion by some researchers. While there is controversy over the exact set of emotions that humans experience, eight basic emotions are usually discussed: joy, trust, fear, surprise, sadness, disgust, anger, and anticipation. Despite the fact that we are not in front of a real human when we are using our computer or smartphone, the information from those devices is processed by our brains to infer emotions from others and to create emotions within ourselves. Driven by the public's concerns over the potentially damaging outcomes of using technology, much of the research on emotions online has focused on the negative emotions, as will be seen in the chapter.

BASIC EMOTIONS AND THE BRAIN

Cheerful, sad, active, angry at self, disgusted, calm, guilty, enthusiastic. What if you were asked right now to rate each of these emotions on to what extent you have felt these in the past few weeks? In fact, you are able to do so. This simple exercise shows that it is possible for scientists to measure a person's emotions in an easy and reliable way. This particular measurement system for emotions is a simplified version of the Positive and Negative Affect Schedule (PANAS), a commonly used tool to investigate how emotions operate in the online world and behind the screen. Because emotions—also known as moods—change over time, emotion is often considered a psychological state. That is, it is a psychological concept that is not fixed and is subject to moment-by-moment fluctuations. In contrast, some psychological concepts are traits—relatively permanent and hard to change. For example, the personality trait of impulsivity has been investigated frequently in the realm of Internet addiction. The core components of emotions are arousal and valence. Arousal is the intensity of the emotion. For example, joy can be rather mild in intensity on some occasions and very strong in intensity on other occasions (gleeful). Valence is the direction of the emotion, positive or negative. There are physiological, in addition to psychological, aspects of emotions. High levels of arousal affect our nervous systems in several ways. Scientists are able to use this fact to measure arousal levels by the use of physical sensors, such as a wrist band that contains a sensor sensitive to electrical activity in the skin.

Emotions are not random experiences that occur without causes and have little meaning in how we conduct ourselves in our lives. Rather, emotions are important indicators of how we respond to events and they give each of us information about ourselves. Emotions also help to prepare our psyches and our bodies for actions that will allow us to deal with certain events.

Joy, the first of the positive emotions, is for some people associated with pursuing activities that are exciting and, for others, it is associated with pleasant activities like having a meal with friends and family, learning to use new technologies, playing video games, or listening to music and songs. For some individuals, there might be joy in avoiding the use of computer technologies and getting away from the hassles associated with them, as captured in the phenomenon of the Joy of Missing Out (JOMO). It is shown in Chapter 10 that joy can be linked to negative outcomes of technology use, as when Internet addicts are joyful while on the computer but feel empty and joyless when not using the Internet. Trust, another positive emotion, means acceptance, mostly of others. The development of trust requires several stages when, for example, you work to establish trust with a person that you just met. Interestingly, the establishment of trust early on is fickle, as research has shown how the mere presence of a mobile phone in the room can interrupt the establishment of trust in a stranger. Surprise, characterized as a positive emotion, might occur when we are given an unexpected gift. However, surprise also might occur as a negative emotion when, for instance, an organization uses our private information in a way that we would not endorse. Finally, anticipation, the last positive emotion, occurs when people look forward to an upcoming event or activity, such as going online to see what their friends are up to on social media. Unfortunately, anticipation is part of being an Internet addict, as addicts feel anticipation and are preoccupied with thinking about going online. Facial expressions for trust and anticipation are subtle and not easily detected. In the online world, anticipation is hard to detect in emails, although people are able to express anticipation in social media posts.

Fear, one of the negative emotions, is associated with words like "afraid," "frightened," "shaky," "nervous," "jittery," and "scared." Fear appropriately helps us to avoid certain situations in life, and thus is part of a primitive defense and survival psychological system. With respect to technology, one commonly occurring fear is the Fear of Missing Out (FOMO). FOMO occurs with respect to social media and mobile phones. When one fears being away from her mobile phone, she is said to experience nomophobia, and is part of a measurably large group of individuals in society. Some estimates of the prevalence of nomophobia go as high as 90% of mobile phone users in the United States and two-thirds of users in England. Sadness, an intense negative emotion, is easily expressed online—for example, in social media posts—but needs to be suppressed when people want to stay upbeat. Sadness is part of a larger group of symptoms that form depression, and is also linked to problematic behaviors such as self-injury and escapism. A third negative emotion, disgust, occurs when people experience reactions to certain stimuli, such as elements of horror movies. Lastly, anger is an intense state of unpleasantness, such as the sudden termination of an enjoyable activity. Internet addicts may experience anger as part of their withdrawal when the Internet is not available.

Of course, other emotions exist aside from the basic ones. Empathy is the ability to detect and experience the emotions of others and has been considered an emotion itself. Although it had been speculated that empathy would not occur in online settings, much research has shown that members of online communities are able to express and presumably experience empathy. Online health forums, where individuals seek out information about health conditions and share their experiences with others, are particularly noteworthy for the level of empathy. Disappointment has been considered another emotion by some researchers.

While most people are able to maintain a mood that is neither too positive nor too negative, emotions become unpredictable and volatile for a few. The lack of emotional stability is referred to as neuroticism. Because neuroticism can become a pattern of moods and behaviors changing frequently over time, it is considered a personality trait, or a repeating and predictable cycle. As with the emotions, the trait of neuroticism can be measured using questions that ask individuals to rate themselves on various dimensions. Neurotics rate themselves highly on questionnaire items like "I am someone who gets nervous easily" or "I have frequent mood swings." Although not directly an emotion itself, neuroticism is linked to some of the same negative outcomes that poor emotions are linked to. Neurotics are more likely than others to have problematic use of the Internet, thus risking damage to their employability or harm to their personal relationships. Neurotics may also use the Internet in ways that are different than other people. The Internet allows a user to carefully craft messages before posting them and to rescind or erase messages that already have been posted. So neurotics could be more likely than others to become addicted to online activities compared to real-life, face-to-face versions of the same activities. Neuroticism has been linked to texting addiction, instant messaging addiction, and using online dating sites to craft an identity.

All of our thoughts, behaviors, and emotions emanate from processes that occur in the brain. Parts of the brain can be grouped together into neural systems that are responsible for specific types of thinking, behavior, or emotion. Two key systems of the brain are relevant to emotional experiences and the processing of emotions. The first is the limbic system, which is chiefly associated with emotion processing. Positive and negative emotional facial expressions activate this system that involves brain regions such as the amygdala, named after its shape (the ancient Greek word for almond). The second is a system that aids in conscious, reasoned thinking, sometimes referred to as a conscious control or executive control system. Many scientists consider these two systems to work against each other, with the emotion system pushing us into one set of thoughts and behaviors at the same time that the conscious thinking system is pulling us into another set of thoughts and behaviors. However, these two systems are not entirely independent of each other; a region called the prefrontal cortex—located approximately where your forehead is—gives rise to much of our conscious, logical thinking, but also has a connection to parts of the limbic system. This allows our conscious thinking to have a role in emotion processing and this is critical for humans to have goal-directed, meaningful patterns of behavior and thoughts. However, weakening of the role of the conscious thinking system has been put forward as a consequence of the disinhibition that occurs when people go online and the inherent reward of some online activities, leading to negative outcomes such as excessive multitasking and Internet addiction.

EXPRESSING, PROCESSING, AND SPREADING EMOTIONS ONLINE

Our ability to succeed in life's ventures requires that we can sense and interpret emotions in others, and that we can effectively express our own emotions. Real life provides a wide array of clues as to how we should feel in certain situations, some of which are not available in online worlds. For example, the ability to smell may lead to disgust when triggered by the odor of rotting meat. Even photographs can give enough information for a viewer to feel an emotion, as when emotional pain is inferred from seeing a photo of a serious car accident. When interacting with others face-to-face, their facial expressions offer much information about how they are feeling; there is also information provided by their body language and their use of language.

The rise of social networking sites (SNSs), as well as text messaging and instant messaging, has changed the expression of emotions. Behind a screen, words are key; the specific words that are used can be emotionally charged, in the sense that they convey the mood of the user. The words "like," "love," and "fond" all give a positive impression in the reader. Specific research techniques, such as Linguistic Inquiry and Word Count (LIWC), have let scientists analyze emotions by looking at the words used online, often putting the words into emotion categories like anger, anxiety, and sadness. Additionally, the relative anonymity of the Internet and the lack of direct face-to-face contact have both contributed to an increased likelihood that Internet users will share their personal feelings. For example, Asian cultures tend to be bound by a collectivistic viewpoint that deemphasizes the individual and stresses the family instead. As a result, individualism—including the expression of one's personal emotions—tends to be suppressed. However, cultural bounds are bypassed online, leading to a greater expression of personal emotions.

There is no doubt that the symbols and images that appear on a computer or smartphone screen can elicit a great range of emotions. For a long time, scientists believed that the limited communication abilities of technological devices would hamper effective communication between individuals. After all, in face-to-face communication, there are many clues available other than the words that are being used by the people engaging in a conversation. All five senses are engaged during face-to-face conversation (even smell!), whereas computer-mediated communication (CMC) might be based on just a limited set of senses. For example, short message service (SMS), another term for texting, relies mostly on vision and words, although one can add pictures and videos in modern versions of SMS. In some cases, such as email, some researchers still argue that the ability to interpret emotions is ineffective due to the reduced number of cues available to the users.

How do users get around the seemingly limited abilities of technology to communicate emotions? Aside from using words that state or describe an emotion, many techniques have either been invented by users themselves or built into communication systems by the computer programmers (the "coders"). The main problem for users is how to incorporate nonverbal cues into the conversation. Nonverbal cues are aspects of regular communication that are not contained in the words themselves. However, the nonverbal cues allow a person to express his or her emotions and they allow the receiver of a message to interpret those emotions. Here are some examples of nonverbal cues in real-life conversations:

- a speaker uses her tone of voice to convey emotion in a message, as in "I already told you three times" (yelled loudly to imply irritation)
- a speaker rolls his eyes when listening to someone else speak, conveying a negative emotion related to the other speaker's comment
- a speaker gives a "thumbs-up" while telling someone "You did a good job," giving an extra emphasis to the positive message

Over the last decade, scientists have studied a great many techniques that users have generated or used to overcome the originally conceived barrier to emotional communication on devices. In some of these techniques, users translate nonverbal cues into verbal ones, allowing the cues to be embedded into a word-based message, such as a text message. Consider the first example above. In the case of CMC, the user simply can change the case of the text to be all caps (i.e., all capital letters) and then this implies yelling: "I ALREADY TOLD YOU THREE TIMES." Contemporary texters may rely heavily on emoticons (a merging of the words "emotion" and "icons") to convey emotion in messages, as common text messaging applications now allow for their use. In the texting app, the message might come out this way: "You did a good job.👍" Users have overcome the inherent technical limitations of our devices and computer programs. Scientists have come to learn that, when it comes to communication via technology, users create, borrow, and alter whatever techniques are available in order to express themselves effectively. These techniques work well when they give the message sender a way to express his or her internal feelings, and when the message receiver accurately interprets the feelings based on the technique used.

Because of the tools available in CMC, emotional communication is believed to be fully alive online. The ability to express emotions and the ability to accurately interpret emotions gives people the opportunity to reveal and share their emotions in computer-based settings. Disclosing one's emotions is part of the development of emotional intimacy, a state that scientists believe is achievable online and behind a screen. Because people can be emotionally intimate with each other when communicating with symbols and images, a series of emotional exchanges can take place that form the basis of a short- or long-term online or screen-based relationship. Such a relationship might even become a romantic relationship—the subject of Chapter 4—showing that even complex feelings like love can be experienced via computer-based technology.

In addition to the development of emotion-based relationships online, the abilities to express and interpret emotions with computer tools has led to people gaining emotional support online and via CMC. Perhaps the best example of such emotional support is that of online health communities, where hundreds—if not thousands—of strangers go to investigate, discuss, and learn about particular health conditions that they and their loved ones are experiencing. In these contexts, researchers have found that the disclosure of information, for example, feelings about being afflicted with a medical condition, is followed by expressions of support from others in the online community. This might be called virtual empathy. Virtual empathy has been measured by scientists, and, while it does not appear to be as strong as face-to-face empathy—it's about one-sixth as strong—it is correlated with face-to-face empathy.

The idea that people could develop emotional relationships online seems natural now, but it was not obvious at the point in time when the Internet was first becoming popular. Internet critics created a dystopian view of the Internet as a place where all sorts of negative consequences were expected when people went online. For example, the Internet was described as a place that invites emotional swindles. Because emotions could be experienced online, it was noted that devious people could take advantage of those emotions. A striking emotional swindle took place in 2000, in the online gaming world of *EverQuest*, when a player, "Sheyla," with whom other players had developed emotional bonds, committed suicide. Later it was revealed that Sheyla was, in fact, a second identity created by one of the players and that no suicide had ever taken place.

In the 1990s, scientists made several attempts to capture the short- and long-term impacts of the Internet in American society. There was a relatively low rate of Internet use in the United States, coupled with the serious concerns about being online that were raised by Internet critics. One significant effort was the Syntopia Project, led by researchers at Rutgers University in New Jersey. Beginning in 1995, researchers carried out several nationwide telephone surveys, randomly sampling from the American population. By asking questions from a wide range of Americans, the research team wanted to find out about access to the Internet, community and group involvement, and social interaction and expression. In the realm of social interaction and expression, the multi-year study, combined with data from other research projects, showed that interaction online was, in the minds of many Internet users, equal to, if not better than, face-to-face interaction, and that emotions and other aspects of Internet relationships could be experienced to be as real as they were over other media or in real life.

Emotions play an important role in the development of relationships, and the online world is no different in this regard. For instance, in the context of online dating, word choice is an important factor for establishing emotional impact during the initial stages of contact between two people. Psychologists have studied the connection between word choice and emotional impact by using fake email exchanges between potential online daters. The email exchanges were reviewed by regular people and then the people were asked to make judgments about the email senders and the choices that the daters will have to make. Compare these two statements (excerpts) from men who were supposedly reacting to an email invitation from a potential female date named Jenny:

1. JimJ789: "I love my job and find that the time goes quickly."
2. FrankXYZ: "I would say that I am satisfied with my job."

Based on the reviewers' reactions, it is clear that the strong feelings conveyed by Jim (he "loves" is job) are more impactful than the moderate to mild feelings conveyed by Frank (he is "satisfied" with his job). Despite the similar amounts of information contained in the men's reactions to the female pursuer, about three-fourths of the reviewers (including both traditional and online daters) chose Jim as the man that Jenny should pursue, showing the power of the emotionality of the words that were selected by the men to describe themselves. Reviewers also ascribed more emotional states to Jim than to Frank, even though the information provided by the two men was equivalent in the amount of detail. In other words, the positive impression that Jim made by using strongly emotional words spread to other dimensions of his personality.

Effective expression of emotions in the computer world can help to spread those emotions to others. The idea behind emotional contagion is that emotions can be transferred from one person to another online, even though there is no face-to-face contact between the two, and online messages tend to be text-based and devoid of nonverbal cues. Emotional contagion was famously demonstrated in an experiment that induced negative moods in people by showing an emotionally distressing clip from a movie. Right afterward, the people had to communicate with others (the partners) via instant messaging about a topic unrelated to the movie. By measuring the emotional state of the partners, it was shown that the negative mood induced by the movie moved from the movie viewers to the partners—hence, contagion.

Indeed, emotional contagion has been found to operate in other online venues, as well. While using Facebook and other social media, users come into contact with many expressions of emotion. The emotions expressed by the message posters, and identified by other users, can be transferred to the other users. For instance, though reading a happy post from a social media friend can lead to a feeling of envy, it also can lead to happiness in the reader. Friends with whom we are most intimate and familiar with—and thus higher in tie strength—are more likely to facilitate emotional contagion than other friends. For example, on Facebook, it was shown that a rainy day in a major U.S. city caused residents to make fewer positive posts and more negative posts, and that these changes caused friends outside of the rainy area to post fewer positive posts and more negative ones as well.

SADNESS, DEPRESSION, AND SELF-HARM

One of the negative emotions, sadness—when intense—has been linked to problematic behaviors including binge drinking and compulsive buying. People try to reduce the influence of sadness in their lives by taking mental or physical actions that reduce the intensity of the emotion. One way that people mentally try to reduce their sadness is by suppressing it and redirecting their attentional spotlight in the direction of other, more pleasurable, stimuli. Another way that people try to reduce sadness is to escape from it through other activities, such as using the Internet. Kimberly S. Young, a pioneer in the research area of Internet addiction, once recommended that therapists ask Internet addicts, "Have you ever used the Internet to escape from feelings of depression, anxiety, guilt, loneliness, or sadness?" in order to assess their addictions.

It was pointed out earlier that sadness, as one of the "basic" human emotions, is linked to a distinctive set of facial expressions that is considered by many researchers to be universal, meaning they are the same across all cultures. Even though much of our CMC occurs without being able to see the faces of those with whom we communicate, we still are able to express sadness in our messages and identify sadness in other people's messages. On SNSs, for instance, the words that are used to craft messages can convey sadness effectively and get reactions from others online. Reactions might be expressions of sympathy, empathy from others, or experiencing new feelings in response to the originally posted feelings. In 2012, at Sandy Hook Elementary School in Newtown, Connecticut, a single gunman killed 26 people, mostly children. After this significant mass shooting, Tweets on the social networking application Twitter tended to express sadness in the region near the massacre while Tweets in other regions tended to express anxiety. In email messages, sadness—compared to happiness—is conveyed by using fewer words, more negative emotion words (not necessarily the words "sad" or "sadness"), more disagreeable language, and fewer exclamation points.

Sadness, along with hopelessness, unhappiness, and self-hatred are part of a depressive mood. Depression includes a persistent change in mood, along with other characteristics. According to the National Institute of Mental Health, signs and symptoms of depression include:

- Persistent sad, anxious, or "empty" mood
- Feelings of hopelessness, or pessimism
- Irritability
- Feelings of guilt, worthlessness, or helplessness
- Loss of interest or pleasure in hobbies and activities
- Decreased energy or fatigue
- Moving or talking more slowly
- Feeling restless or having trouble sitting still
- Difficulty concentrating, remembering, or making decisions
- Difficulty sleeping, early-morning awakening, or oversleeping
- Appetite and/or weight changes
- Thoughts of death or suicide, or suicide attempts
- Aches or pains, headaches, cramps, or digestive problems without a clear physical cause and/or that do not ease even with treatment

There are multiple forms of depression. For example, depression can take the form of a serious psychiatric disorder such as major depression or dysthymia (mild depression). Both of these forms must be diagnosed by a licensed therapist. When depression is investigated by researchers in the area of the psychology of technology, it is rarely studied in these forms. Rather, measures of depressive symptoms are used that are based on a person's self-report of their personal experiences. The Beck Depression Inventory—one of the most widely used measures in the field—contains a small number of questions that ask a person about his or her mood over the last two weeks. One question on the Inventory, for instance, asks a person whether she feels disappointed, feels disgusted, or hates herself (or none of these). Higher scores on these measures indicates more self-reported symptoms of depression, or, in other words, greater severity of depression.

Facebook depression refers to the perceived negative emotional effects of using social media. The sheer number of hours spent using social media has been linked to depression or depression-like symptoms. Also, studies that have looked at the kinds of messages posted on Facebook and other social media sites have found significant percentages of users who post messages indicative of a state of depression, with 25% to 33% of American college students having posted a comment indicating depression. The concerns over such negative effects of using social media for excessive amounts of time led the American Academy of Pediatrics Council on Communications and Media to issue a warning about it in 2011. Worries over

Facebook depression are especially relevant to adolescents, since the teenage years are rife with social comparisons, and thus there is great potential for envy and envy-related negative emotions.

However, research shows that the specific activities a person carries out on social media are important. Rather than using social media to pass the time, some of the behaviors on social media that have been found to either reduce depression-like symptoms or to increase happiness are:

- having a relatively high number of social media friends
- supplementing social media with talking on the phone
- projecting a positive self-presentation online
- supplementing social media with face-to-face social support
- using social media for interpersonal communication
- having positive interactions with others on social media

The additional social support gained from using social media appears to be a buffer against negative emotional symptoms.

Suicide is a serious worldwide problem that is associated with depression. In the United States, suicide is one of the leading causes of death in youths. In 2009, 6.2% of teenagers reported suicide attempts and 1.9% reported attempts that were serious enough to require medical care. India has 16% of the world's population, but one-third of the world's suicides, leading one writer to describe mental health in India as a "quiet crisis." A suicide attempt is the end-point of a series of suicide-related thoughts and behaviors. The Youth Risk Behavior Survey (YRBS) that involves a nationally representative sample of American teenagers asks teens these questions:

- During the past 12 months, did you ever seriously consider attempting suicide? (suicidal ideation)
- During the past 12 months, did you make a plan about how you would attempt suicide? (suicide planning)
- During the past 12 months, how many times did you actually attempt suicide? (suicide attempt)
- During the past 12 months, did any attempt result in an injury, poisoning, or overdose that had to be treated by a doctor or nurse? (attempts requiring medical care)

In the YRBS study, suicidal ideation, suicide planning, and suicide attempts were associated with five or more hours of daily video gaming and Internet use, with, for example, intense gamers and users being 1.7 times more likely than non-gamers and non-users to report suicidal ideation. However, the link between suicide and the Internet is multifaceted, with several possible relationships between the two. Because serious depression is sometimes associated with suicide-related thoughts and behaviors, people with pre-existing mental health problems who use the Internet might naturally have an increased risk of suicide-related thoughts and behaviors. Thoughts of suicide or plans to commit suicide are known to show up in posts on social media, leading social media companies such as Facebook to provide users with special procedures for reporting people at risk for suicide.

It was described earlier how there are situations in the online world that could lead to sadness and depression. This might also cause people to have suicide-related thoughts and behaviors, or to make them worse. There are online communities where individuals are known to discuss suicide, and exposure to these types of websites is known to be related to a higher chance of attempted suicide. Also, victims of cyberbullying are at an increased risk for depression and suicide-related thoughts compared to non-victims. One form of cyberbullying is shaming of an individual through public attempts to highlight the failings of that person. An example is publicly posting a homemade sex video in an attempt to damage the reputation of one of the people who appears in the video.

JEALOUSY AND ENVY

One of the most studied emotions online in recent research has been jealousy. You might experience jealousy when you see that another person has attained something valuable and you fear losing that thing for yourself. The most common fear is that of losing a romantic partner. An Internet user might feel jealousy when he or she sees pictures of a romantic partner together with another person on an SNS or reads posts on the "wall" of a romantic partner made by a peer. Jealousy is often confused with envy, because they are similar. However, envy arises when you see that someone is better off than you, regardless of whether you fear any loss. Jealousy and envy are both based on a process of social comparison, in which one person mentally compares the characteristics of another person to herself with an eye toward determining who is better off or who is of a higher social stature. As an emotion, jealousy is linked to one's social system because without social connections, emotions such as jealousy will not exist.

Most researchers believe that jealousy is a routine online experience for many people. Feelings of jealousy can lead to the Internet user engaging in monitoring and controlling behavior of their romantic partner by, for example, cyberbullying him or her. Jealousy occurs in other contexts using technology, as well. For example, even turning off one's mobile phone can lead to jealousy in a romantic partner, as described in this scenario by a university student in Tanzania, explaining why she leaves her phone on during class lectures:

> . . . I always use my smartphone to chart [sic] with my boyfriend who is doing business at Dar es Salaam and he is very jealousy [sic] in the extent that if my phone is switched off he reacts badly to me guessing that I'm with someone dating. So due to this I can't afford to switch off my phone even if I'm in the class getting lectures I have to put my phone in vibration mode to wait if any message comes on my way from him, I have to respond quickly . . .

To accurately measure jealousy in the context of SNSs, some researchers have used the Facebook Jealousy scale. The scale asks participants questions like, "How likely are you to become jealous after your partner has added an unknown member of the opposite sex?" and "How likely are you to monitor your partner's activities on Facebook?" It turns out that jealousy measured this way, in the context of Facebook, is linked to spending too much time on the profiles of romantic partners. The relationship between jealousy and Facebook use is bidirectional, due to a feedback loop; this means that jealousy leads to increased Facebook use (e.g., for the purpose of investigating ambiguous information found on a profile) and, at the same time, increased Facebook use leads to jealousy (e.g., as one uncovers more ambiguous online information about a partner). It also is true that being a generally jealous person contributes to Facebook jealousy, as does uncertainty about one's relationship.

Interviews with SNS users have revealed several themes around the stress that can be experienced while using the sites. Although not all of the stresses revolve around jealousy, it has been revealed that, for adults, social comparison occurs as one reviews the profiles of individuals who are potential mates of one's romantic interest or interests, or even as one reviews the profiles of individuals who are former mates. This might trigger jealousy and stress. Interestingly, social comparison with potential or former mates of a romantic interest occurs even after one is no longer in a relationship with the romantic interest, such as due to a breakup, especially for women. Users who have experienced this behavior report that they feel better when they see that the potential or former mates of the former romantic interest are worse off in some way than the users are. This is referred to as downward social comparison.

As noted earlier, the emotion of envy is experienced when you lack another person's characteristics, achievements, or objects of ownership and you wish that either you had those items or that the other person did not have them. The process of social comparison is necessary in order for envy to occur. There must be an upward social comparison, where you feel that another person is better off than you because of their characteristics, achievements, or objects. Further, envy is triggered when the result of the social comparison is that there is a threat to how you view yourself. In other words, simply seeing that another person is better off than you is not sufficient for envy to happen; you must also feel threatened in some way.

A further factor in the experience of envy is whether you find the other person to be similar to you. And the object of envy needs to be in an area of life that is important to you. Because it takes time to develop and shape one's priorities in life, the domains that a person finds important in life might not be fully defined until young adulthood, a time period that has been found to be rife with envy. Envy can produce various reactions in the person who experiences it, including inwardly or outwardly highlighting his or her own strengths in order to reduce a sense of inferiority. It is called benign envy when you are motivated to obtain or gain what the other person has; it is called malicious envy when you are motivated to have the other person lose what he or she has.

The research that is done on the topic of envy in the online world focuses almost exclusively on SNSs, as several features of these sites lend themselves to the development of envy. One feature is the ability to see the details of other people's lives so easily. Many people take it for granted that SNS users can upload their own photos, facts about their lives, family videos, etc. In the early days of the World Wide Web—the so-called Web 1.0—individual users and average citizens could not do so. Websites and the material on the websites were primarily constructed by companies, educational institutions, and governmental organizations. Only with the advent of user-generated content—the Web 2.0—could anyone with Internet access create customized content online, including user profiles, photo albums, and postings. Thus, the technology now allows for fast and rampant sharing of personal information. Another important feature of SNSs with respect to envy is the simple way that a user can grow his or her own social network through contacts and friendships. In many social networking applications, the system provides a list of potential friends from which the user can pick and choose. Adding contacts to one's social network this way often requires confirmation from the potential friend, but not always. Further, it is often possible to view a public version of a person's social networking profile without having a formal online relationship with that person. Therefore, the number of people to which a user has access is effectively unlimited. A third important feature is the availability of the Internet, day and night, 24 hours a day, on many different devices. Since users can view profiles and navigate their social networks online from just about anywhere, anytime, there is no upper bound on the amount of time that a person can spend accessing personal information about others.

For these reasons, viewing information on SNSs can lead to envy. Facebook envy refers specifically to the feelings of envy that people experience when using Facebook. One question on a scale measuring Facebook envy asks the respondent to rate his or her agreement with this sentence: "It is somewhat annoying to see on Facebook how successful some of my Facebook friends are." Envy is not the only emotion that is experienced, but it can be common. When reporting their overall feelings after a recent usage of Facebook, 43.8% of users reported at least one positive emotion, but 36.8% reported at least one negative emotion, including feeling envious. Adult users of Facebook have been found to experience social comparison that can lead to envy in different ways. Facebook users who started as adolescent users were caught up in a popularity contest over how many Facebook friends could be accumulated. As adults, users found themselves comparing their own lives to the many other lives they viewed on Facebook.

Facebook envy is higher when a user has a larger social network, as the number of Facebook friends creates more opportunities for upward social comparison. The types of friends make a difference, too. Earlier it was stated that experiencing envy requires that you see yourself as similar to the other person for which you experience envy. Online friends can be measured by the degree of closeness that one feels toward them in an emotional sense—in other words, having an emotional tie. This tie strength would be high in relationships with close friends or family members and would be low in acquaintances. As expected from what is known about envy, tie strength in SNSs is associated with envy. Yet the association occurs only with one type of envy—benign envy.

With envy, a phenomenon similar to the feedback loop of jealousy can occur. In this case, participating in an SNS can lead to feelings of envy and these feelings then lead to coping mechanisms that help to reduce the threat that one feels. A simple coping mechanism is self-enhancement, which is playing up one's own characteristics, achievements, and objects of ownership in order to feel better about oneself. The software of SNSs enables users to selectively edit their profiles and their walls—publicly displayed pages—in order to maximize self-enhancement. As a result, even more highly-edited, self-enhancing, information is posted in the SNS, ironically causing envy in others. The outcomes of this self-enhancement envy spiral are that more users will be engaging in self-enhancement, fueling the spiral, and that there are increased chances of other, more dangerous, coping mechanisms, such as hurting or degrading the person who is the target of the envy. Studies of the content of user profiles in SNSs often describe the content as narcissistic, meaning that the material is arrogant and shows a need for admiration. It makes sense that a narcissistic environment could be the result of spiraling envy.

Envy could have other negative consequences, too. Many researchers suspect that people who experience envy might frequently have a compromised well-being. It has been shown in college students that experiencing Facebook envy was related to having lower life satisfaction. Additionally, the material that leads to envy online is linked to other negative emotions, such as resentment and loneliness. Repeated experiences of envy in online settings could lead to depression. Because envy is associated with feelings of inferiority, repeated experiences of envy might, for some, lead to a chronic feeling of inferiority. Several of the signs and symptoms of depression listed earlier in the chapter would also be experienced as part of the feeling of inferiority.

THE IMPORTANCE OF EMOTION REGULATION

Self-regulation is a broad set of abilities that allow people to maintain mental and emotional well-being. Emotion regulation is one of these abilities, and it involves the attempt to change the frequency, intensity, or duration of mostly negative emotional experiences. Although there are many emotion regulation strategies that people use, the strategies can be placed into two broad categories. Adaptive strategies, when used in appropriate settings, maintain or improve well-being, while maladaptive strategies are those that can cause an increase in negative mood or lead to stress. Adaptive strategies include reappraisal—changing how we think about an emotional situation—and task coping—trying to resolve the situation at hand). Maladaptive strategies include escapism—avoiding an unpleasant situation by attending to a more pleasant situation—and rumination—becoming mentally fixated on the problem. Imagine an astronaut in space who realizes that an asteroid is rapidly approaching her spacecraft. It would not be wise for her to reduce her negative emotions by engaging in escapism by, for example, staring at a picture of her loved ones back on Earth while the asteroid is about to strike.

People's skill at emotion regulation is linked to their experiences while online. A person is more likely to have negative interactions on SNSs and more likely to be a victim of cyberbullying if they also have poor emotion regulation. People with poor emotion regulation are also more likely to have symptoms of Internet addiction (covered in Chapter 10) and to experience problematic use of SNSs. It may be that compulsively using digital media is a way to escape from negative emotions that can become maladaptive for some people. Internet use might interfere with the normal development of emotion regulation ability in adolescents. Emotion regulation initially emerges in older infants and toddlers but continues to develop during adolescence. Before popular access to the Internet existed, adolescents would spend significant amounts of "alone time" during which they would have to rely on their own psyches to sift through their thoughts and mentally prepare for the future. Now, they can seek support and feedback from friends online—a behavior that might be depriving them of the time needed to improve their emotion regulation. Because emotion regulation is an important factor in well-being, some people may benefit from trying to improve their emotion regulation ability. One suggested method for getter better at emotion regulation is mindfulness, a learned mental technique for monitoring and managing one's thoughts.

Certain emotions, such as shame and anger, are intertwined with emotion regulation. In real life, there is no doubt that shame is a negative emotion that most people want to hide or avoid. Shame is generally a social emotion—without interactions with others, there would be no reason to feel ashamed by our actions or statements. Some triggers for shame that have been studied include infidelity, being victimized by a bully, lying or deceiving others, having an addiction or other mental health problem, and having one's private information become public. One author has described contemporary society as "a source of embarrassment and shame." As one part of an emotion regulation system, shame serves to alter our behaviors and change how we express ourselves to and interact with others.

Because it is possible to maintain anonymity in the online world, some people may find the Internet to be a place to behave without shame. Sex addicts can frequent the Internet as a place for sex-related activities that might include having an online affair. People who would not normally reveal private information about themselves in face-to-face interactions with strangers are also more likely to do so online. For some people engaged in online deception, going online and deceiving others is not associated with negative feelings, but rather with positive emotions like enjoyment. On the other hand, the Internet is not devoid of shame. Researchers found that almost 10% of users experienced shame while engaging in social networking activities. Some known causes of shame online include being a cyber-victim, lying to others, procrastinating, online sex-related behaviors, having private information made public, and sexts becoming public.

The negative emotion of anger works both to spur us into action and to communicate our internal emotional states to others (for example, "I am annoyed with you"). In face-to-face interactions with others, anger is expressed through facial expressions, the content of our speech, and the style of speech (such as raising our voice). Because so much of online interactions are text-based, the use of specific words in online environments gives other people the information that they need to determine that we are angry. "Hate," "kill," "annoyed," and "mad" are common anger words used by people when they are behind a screen, but they represent only a tiny subset of the 184 anger words identified by linguistic researchers. When anger is used to communicate, there is often the expectation that our expression of anger will produce a response in others. This is called the instrumental function of emotions. In online social networks, anger expression is frequently used to elicit positive responses from others through likes. Showing anger also might be used, for instance, to intimidate others and stop them from an action that they were planning to take. Finally, it is not always wise to express our anger in all situations. Suppressing our anger in vulnerable interpersonal relationships might be preferred over sharing feelings that could damage the relationships. Consider a student who is online friends with her teacher in a social networking platform; it would be very risky and potentially damaging to the teacher-student relationship for her to express her anger online about a test grade that she received from the teacher. The decision as to when it is best to express or to hide our emotions is part of a human emotion regulation system that, when functioning properly, enhances our successes in life and protects us from harm.

In the real world, high levels of anger in individuals or chronic anger—sometimes called trait anger—have been associated with several different negative outcomes. These outcomes include binge drinking, binge eating, self-injury, and compulsive buying. In addition, high levels of anger can impact our executive functioning, the set of mental processes what we use to make decisions, reason about issues, inhibit risky behaviors, and plan for future events. In the computer-based world—behind the screen—anger has been linked to symptoms of Internet addiction as well as to aggression linked to violent video game playing.

In the online world, expressions of anger and hate proliferate. In the United States, free speech is protected by law, and there are relatively few laws and regulations that affect peoples' behavior on the Internet. In almost all types of online forums, groups that share values of hatred or racism create organizations that promote the groups' views. In the United States, such online organizations—often referred to as hate sites—center around themes that denigrate Hispanics, Muslims, and non-heterosexuals, for a few examples. In other countries, similar themes emerge. In India, there are online hate communities that focus on anti-Pakistan themes, for instance. Hateful or racist messages are often oversimplified so that they are easily digestible by the general population, which is believed to have very short attention spans due to the influence of information and technology overload. Unfortunately, the rise of hate sites is operating in parallel with an increase in racist activities and hate crimes in the United States, along with a global increase in ethnic conflicts.

Intuition tells us that expressing one's anger is a good way to relieve the tension or pent-up feelings of hostility. As long ago as ancient times, Aristotle argued that watching Greek tragedies was a way that people could purge themselves of their unhealthy emotions. The idea that engaging in real or imagined aggression in order to shed negative emotions and become calm is referred to as the catharsis hypothesis. There are several ways in which catharsis could be thought to occur in modern media outlets: violent video gaming, violent TV viewing, listening to violent or hateful music, and expressing anger or hatred online. However, researchers now know that these types of activities do not lead to catharsis. In fact, they have the opposite effect of enhancing and promoting anger and hostility. Expression of hatred online can be linked to online disinhibition, which is when people self-disclose or act out more frequently online that they would in person. Benign disinhibition, for example, exploring one's feelings, can serve as a cathartic process under certain circumstances, but disinhibition that does not promote personal growth and well-being—as happens at hate sites—can be considered a form of toxic disinhibition.

Concern over hate sites is strong in groups that are concerned with parenting and children. The U.S. National Commission on Libraries and Information Science (1998), using an older phrase for the Internet, referred to racists and hate-mongers online as one of several "dark and dangerous off-ramps of the [Information] SuperHighway." It is commonly accepted among researchers that teens online may regularly encounter hate speech, and that there are some children and teens who are participating in the hate rants, as well. Techniques used by hate sites to promote interest and participation among youth include making versions of websites that are specifically geared toward children, rewording and rephrasing ideas to make them understandable to young people, and providing messages to youths that are written by other youths.

CONCLUSION

The research reviewed in this chapter showed that jealousy, envy, and anger occur while people are behind a screen, and these emotions can sometimes lead to other types of reactions. Various forms of sadness can occur online, including depression, especially while using social networking platforms. Emotions in the online world and through computer-mediated communication take place in several ways. Most Internet- or phone-based communications are based on using words to transmit messages. The importance of individual words in conveying and invoking emotions is shown when researchers measure the emotional reactions of average people to experimentally manipulated words, as in the study on online dating that showed how the words in email messages are used to interpret the emotions of others. People have learned how to manipulate words and to use other tricks to convey their emotions (e.g., emoticons) when on the Internet. When people do successfully express their emotions electronically, those feelings can be spread to other people through emotional contagion. Computer- and phone-based applications provide another tool for people when it comes to emotions: they allow for people to regulate their emotions by interacting with others, or by using emotion-laden apps or services. People with emotion regulation problems can suffer from other complications online, such as Internet addiction, one of the topics of the next chapter.

Interview with an Expert: Dr. Megan A. Moreno

Dr. Megan A. Moreno, a professor at the University of Wisconsin School of Medicine and Public Health, has published research on a wide variety of issues that affect youths and young adults, for example, cyberbullying. With respect to young children, adolescents, and college students, Dr. Moreno's research interests cover the social, emotional, physical, and cognitive impacts and correlates of technology use. Dr. Moreno served on the Council on Communications and Media at the American Academy of Pediatrics that issued new policies for media and very young children in 2016. The policies aim to address problems of obesity, sleep deprivation, and socio-emotional and other delays in children that are related to technology use. When it comes to adolescents, Dr. Moreno's research takes advantage of how youths go online and use social media, looking at indicators of health risks through what adolescents post online. Dr. Moreno characterizes adolescents' plight as follows: ". . . each day they are faced with decisions on how to balance relationships, influences and experiences in both online and offline worlds." One of Dr. Moreno's original insights into youths is that they may hide their real-life behaviors in face-to-face interactions but at the same time make online displays of behavior (e.g., posts) that are linked to the real-world behaviors. With respect to young adults, namely, college students, Dr. Moreno has investigated the link between the Internet and mental health, including addiction to technology and depression. She was part of a study using cutting-edge research methods that failed to confirm a link between social media and depression in college students—the so-called Facebook depression. Finally, her investigations into cyberbullying have looked at how cyberbullying may be different than traditional bullying.

Q: What does research say about the impact of technology on positive and negative emotions?

A: A lot of technologies can take where you are and magnify it, so if you are using technology and you are in a pretty good confident place that could help magnify that and I think it also can provide social support for adolescents when they need it. If you use technology when you are in a bad place, I think that you may be comparing yourself to other people, feeling like other people are doing better than you. I think if you bring that in when you use technology, you are going to find that negative impact.

Q: Are there any groups that are particularly susceptible to those negative emotions in terms of age, gender, or cultural background?

A: I think adolescents as a whole spend a lot of their time comparing themselves to other people, so for them, negative emotions would be magnified, and they are not always in a place of stable identities, so they are probably also influenced by what they see. People of any age are probably more at risk for finding more negativity if they come in with a lens that is shrouded by depression, or if they filter life through a negative cognitive bias. The literature suggests that girls and women are more likely to use technology, and particularly social media, to connect to others and build social capital, and I think they can probably end up with outcomes that are both positive and negative.; whereas I think in general, lot of studies suggest that males are better at going in and using technology as a tool.

Q: Do you feel that you can adequately experience those kinds of emotions through a word-based system or are you experiencing a different version of an "emotion"?

A: One of the hallmarks of depression is that you withdraw from day-to-day, face-to-face social systems. So, I think young people are often looking for ways to connect that are not face-to-face, so that might be through other types of technology that are going to filter out some of those cues. For example, if you talk to someone on a telephone, you are filtering down to the audio feed, and if you are using communication tools that allow emojis and photos to represent feelings, I feel they really help kids who are able to use these new ways to find and express themselves. You have this place where you have text, but there is also this "art" side to it, where you can try to express yourself using color, or shade, or humor, or borrowing other people's images, or using your own.

Q: How do you feel about using the online world to deal with negative emotions to feel better about yourself, such as maybe when you are angry or depressed, but actually going online to try to feel better?

A: What we have seen in our research, and what I hear from patients, is that there are these incredible benefits; so you can go online and find a community of people who are feeling similar to you and then you can express yourself, you can feel really supported, you can make it anonymous if you need it to be anonymous, and it can really provide this boost, especially if you are in a place where you feel really alone. I think that the double-edged sword is if you find that you like this community and you get really wrapped up in this community, but you are ready to move on from that negativity, it can be hard to separate yourself from the negativity without feeling like you are losing a community. And I think that's similar to other issues like self-harm or eating disorders, where it can be so therapeutic to find a community that understands you but then it can hinder your ability to move away from the negative experience.

Q: What do you think is important for the public and for consumers of the Internet?

A: I think that the public has an incomplete vision of cyberbullying and I think this is, in part, because the media has represented it using words like epidemic and high-lighting the worst case scenarios. We had a kid in one of our studies and when we asked him if he had been cyberbullied he said, "You know I haven't killed myself, so I guess I haven't been cyberbullied" reinforcing the idea that if you are not ready to kill yourself, then it really does not count. Also, this idea that everybody is being cyberbullied, that it's an epidemic and is happening to everyone leads to a lot of misconceptions.

A lot of what I talk about with patients and families is that when adolescents are navigating online there is a lot of risk, but there is also a lot of benefit, and the way that they are going to be able to optimize those benefits is from learning, interacting with adults and peers, and feeling confident that if they make mistakes they have places they can go, which is essentially the offline world. There are lots of bad things to do out there and lots of good things and you need to have a good support system around you to help you figure it out. One thing that I think is intriguing to me is the line between personality and emotion. How much of your experience online do you bring with you as a personality trait and how much does the experience you have online alter your personality. We know our personalities are always shifting, especially among adolescents, so how much of that personality shifting growth happens through cues online?

10

Health

Case Study: Where Will the Pokémon Lead You?

Pokémon Go is an augmented reality game in which the player views the real world through the phone camera, and then the software adds virtual information to the live view. Created by gaming company Niantic, the game lets users find and catch species of imaginary creatures called Pokémon as the players move about in their own world. Discovering Pokémon is easy, as the game employs the vibration feature on the phone to notify the player that a Pokémon is near. To catch a Pokémon, the player (virtually) throws a Poké Ball at the creature. The word "Gotcha" appears on the screen to indicate a successful catch. Every interaction between the imaginary game elements and the real world is captured in the display on the phone screen because the two worlds are superimposed. Although it had a short run, the game was so popular that it broke the record for app downloads in Apple Inc.'s App Store in the first week of its release. There were at least 40 million active players in the United States in 2016. Masses of people were out and about, finding Pokémon. Numerous reports in the news showed how workers skipped their normal, sedentary lunches and went on the hunt for Pokémon instead. Large groups of hundreds of people walked together in San Francisco during an organized *Pokémon Go* event soon after the game was released.

A questionnaire study of mostly U.S. game players conducted in the first month after the game was released showed that the game was successful in getting people to move outside and into areas around their own neighborhoods. Further, almost one-half of the players at that time planned to make special trips—day trips or overnight trips—just to play the game. People who said they really enjoyed the game were more likely to travel around. At the same time, several sets of researchers attempted to quantify the impact of playing the game upon people's physical activity levels. For instance, researchers at Microsoft Corporation used data from their wearable sensor technology, Microsoft Band, combined with data from Internet searches on Microsoft's search engine. Based on searches related to *Pokémon Go*, the researchers were able to identify intensive gamers and less intensive gamers. It was shown that intensive players significantly increased their physical activity. For example, players who made 10 Internet searches related to *Pokémon Go* within the first two months of the games release increased their daily steps by 1,479 steps. A separate study used data from players own phones to track their physical activity. The researchers obtained screenshots of iPhone players' screens from the game and from their Health app that automatically tracks daily steps. The number of daily steps increased by 955 on average for game players in the first week of playing. However, tracking the data over time, the scientists also found that the effect was gone by the end of six weeks of playing. The game is noteworthy for its effect on social relations, as well. While players were prevented from contacting each other within the game itself, many people played the game in groups. Even playing as an individual was sure to lead to social interaction because they were built-in geographical locations—the PokéStops and Pokémon gyms—where users would congregate in real life. Online, there were droves of people getting together to talk about the game on social networking sites like Facebook and Reddit. Users reported that playing the game made them feel like they were part of a social community.

Because the game asks players to move about in the world in order to achieve goals, the game has the dual distinction of making people healthier by walking and by making them less safe by having them pay only partial attention to their surroundings. The game is well-known for mishaps like people inadvertently wandering into the street while playing. The police in England believed that inattention to their surroundings contributed to three teenagers being robbed at gunpoint in a local park while playing *Pokémon Go*. In other cases in England, players were nearly cut off from land by the rising tide while playing at the seashore, and some players got lost in a network of caves while hunting for Pokémon. One intensive analysis of news reports from July 2016—at the height of the *Pokémon Go* craze—in England found 14 different car crashes attributed to *Pokémon Go* and 113,993 incidents of distraction while driving due to the game in a 10-day period. Eighteen percent of the *Pokémon Go*-related tweets evaluated during that period indicated that a person was playing the game while driving (e.g., "omg I'm catching Pokémon and driving" [Ayers, Leas, Dredze, Allem, Grabowski, & Hill, 2016]). Niantic has a list of safety tips on their website for using the game in the real world. These are among the tips for keeping players safe:

- When you're out and about playing *Pokémon Go*, stay aware of your surroundings at all times—especially when traveling alone or in areas you're not familiar with. Whenever you start the app, you'll see a reminder to help you keep this precaution in mind.

- To make sure you and those around you are safe, do not play *Pokémon Go* while riding a bike, driving a vehicle, operating heavy machinery, or doing anything else that requires your full attention.

- If a Pokémon appears in an inaccessible location, or in a place where it might not be safe to approach it (for example, on a construction site or on private property), do not try to catch it. (www.pokemongo.com, 2016)

Another interesting potential negative outcome of playing the game is players venturing into mosquito-infested areas. The Zika scare of 2016 brought heightened attention to this mosquito-borne virus, especially in the city of Miami, Florida. When researchers overlaid maps of *Pokémon Go* locations (PokéStores and Pokémon gyms) and Zika virus activity (both known infections and known high concentrations of the Ae. *aegypti* mosquito that carries the virus), they found that there were two spots at the edge of an infected neighborhood where the game was asking people to go. Other potentially dangerous spots existed in the maps overlay, as well, in different parts of the city.

INTRODUCTION

What people are not doing while they are using their technological devices—that is, the activities that are displaced—poses a significant risk for physical health; however, at the same time, modern computer-based tools can allow people to take charge of their personal health, for example by increasing their physical activity.

Another major concern—this time for mental health—is the addictive qualities of technology, with Internet addiction and other technology addictions having been identified.

SEDENTARY BEHAVIOR AND SLEEP

While your devices make you happy and enrich your life, they also may make you sedentary due to how they work and the effects they have on your activity levels and eating. Sitting around and doing no physical activity is of great concern for children, teenagers, and young adults, who should be in a stage of life that involves a lot of physical movement. Sitting down for long periods of time is not normal for children and young adults like it is for older individuals. Therefore, a lot of the research examining how technology impacts physical activity is focused on the younger set.

A whole set of technologies has been linked to sedentary activity. Research on the topic has clearly shown that more time spent on technology activities is linked to less time spent in physical activity, although, for gaming, not all types of gaming operate in the same way. When large groups of people are asked to report on their technology use and also their health, research studies find that there is a negative relationship, such that more hours of technology use are associated with lower health or less activity. This is true for the use of passive technologies, like television watching, where the user has no or little interaction with the device or software. It also is true for the use of interactive technologies, like using the Internet. Sometimes, researchers do not measure physical activity directly; rather, they may measure the outcomes of physical activity, such as a person's body mass index (BMI), with higher values being bad and the highest values indicating obesity. Data show links between technology use and BMI, and these links—when television viewing is involved—have been interpreted as revealing that exposure to ads selling unhealthy food increases poor eating behaviors. Heavy Internet users are not only less likely to exercise than other Internet users, but they are also less likely to engage in other health-related behaviors, such as seeking medical care. There is a range of explanations of what causes this relationship.

Because of the ways that certain technologies work, there appear to be some ways of spending your time that discourage physical movement. Some personal technologies involve devices that are large and hard to move, such as televisions, while other technologies are smaller and more portable, like cell phones. Thus, the technical aspects of the devices can influence how much physical activity you can do while you are using the device. A study of more than 600 young people in the United Kingdom, aged 11 to 18 years old, found that video gaming was linked to their physical health—in this case, their BMIs—but that mobile phone usage was not. Psychologists say that different technologies afford different actions and behaviors; in this case, one of the affordances of the mobile phone is that it allows the user to move around while using it.

In the UK study, adolescents who were "always engaged" with video gaming had higher BMIs (and thus worse health) than adolescents who were "never-users." The scientists interpreted the results as showing how technology use can displace active behaviors in adolescence. When it comes to gaming, sports gaming rules as the healthiest form of video gaming. Also, online gaming, such as playing role-playing games where users take the personalities of characters in an immersive virtual environment, may be worse for people than console gaming where users connect a device to their TV set and stand or sit in front of the television to play. By the time young people get to college, their video game playing may be having a negative impact upon their exercise-related behaviors: BMIs are worse, exercising and walking is less frequent, and exercise is shorter, for people who spend more time playing video games. Massively multiplayer online role-playing games (MMORPGs) had the most negative effect on exercise and health in one study. The link between sports gaming and physical health seems to have two parts to it. On the one hand, research shows that young people who play sports video games are then more likely than others to play real sports; on the other hand, adolescents who play real sports then become more likely than others to play sports games.

When considering the explanations of how technology makes a person sedentary, the most obvious connection is that when you are doing one thing—such as watching television—you cannot simultaneously be doing another thing—such as playing dodgeball; this is called displacement. One research report has provided a concise statement of the displacement hypothesis: "each 'dose' of screen time takes the place of alternative pursuits that might be more satisfying [i.e., healthful]" (Przybylski & Weinstein, 2017, p. 2). While much research supports the process of displacement, the research also reveals subtleties in how displacement works. For one, it should be noted that exercise can be displaced by other activities—not just technology use—especially if those activities last a relatively long time. For example, reading would be expected to displace exercise, whether the reading is online or via printed texts. Also, displacement does not explain the negative effect of technology use on all health-related behaviors. Health-related activities such as taking vitamins are impacted by technology use, even though they do not take much time at all to carry out. Another explanation is a lack of parental engagement when using technology. If parents of young people are not engaged in monitoring, setting rules for, or discussing use of technology, then they might also fail to monitor, set rules, and discuss health-related and exercise behaviors.

If you watch television, or if you watch videos on a streaming video service such as YouTube.com, then there is a real chance that food-related advertising is affecting your eating habits. So exposure to advertising through technology use presents a double whammy of lack of exercise and increased eating when you are not really hungry. Traditional activities for kids, adolescents, and young adults do not have the problem of exposure to advertisements designed to get you to eat more food. Doing homework (not on the computer) and reading (in print) are good examples. Even the type of hardware used to play games may matter, with gamers being less able to snack while playing games on a console. Eating despite not being hungry causes an increase in energy intake in the body thus requiring additional physical activity later to burn off the energy. When playing online games, users typically sit at a computer and mainly use one hand to control the action on the screen. So it's easy to use the other hand to snack. Snacking when not hungry may contribute to weight, and thus BMI, if it is not offset by physical activity.

However, there may be some actions that you can take to lessen the impact that these technologies have on you. Experts have made these basic recommendations to help people get around the negative effects of technology use on physical activity and eating. For one, reduce your screen time. Reducing screen time is especially important for children, in order to take advantage of their natural proclivity for physical activity. Second, use personal sensors (e.g., exercise wristwatches) to improve physical activity. In one study of using personal sensors to track physical activity—in this case, a pedometer—there was a 32% reduction of sedentary behavior in people who were the least active. Finally, replace stationary gaming with physically interactive gaming. Interactive gaming includes console games that require physical movement, sometimes requiring special devices that are held in the user's hands.

Technology is also displacing the important act of sleeping. Scientists have measured the quality of sleep that teenagers and emerging adults are getting recently. A commonly used measure of sleep quality is the Pittsburgh Sleep Quality Index (PSQI). It is an English-language questionnaire that assesses several areas of sleep functioning, and it is able to classify people as poor sleepers or good sleepers. One of the items on the questionnaire asks how many hours of sleep a person gets at night. It is generally accepted that 7 to 9 hours is normal, while having less than 7 or more than 9 is abnormal. Good sleep includes elements of quality (lack of problems), latency (time to fall asleep), duration (length of sleep), efficiency (feeling well rested after sleep), lack of disturbances, no need for medication, and no daytime sleepiness. Perhaps not surprisingly, scientists have found that sleep quality in Americans is poor. Many teenagers have an evening circadian preference that clashes with the need to wake up early in the morning to go to school. This preference leads to teens selecting relatively late bedtimes, reducing sleep duration, and impacting performance on mental tasks done in the morning (like class performance). Approximately 40% of teenagers in the United States show the evening circadian preference. High school students are said to be experiencing an epidemic of insufficient sleep.

A significant portion of college students have also been classified as poor sleepers. Significant numbers of college students, or emerging adults, are getting poor sleep either as measured with the PSQI or as determined by sleep duration. In one large study done in the United States, more than 60% of college students were found to be poor sleepers, with 75% of the students reporting that they feel "dragged out, tired, or sleepy" once a week or more. A portion of the sleep problems was caused by tension and stress that are high for college students, generally. In the same study, the average bedtime was 12:21 a.m. and the mean risetime was 8:05 a.m., resulting in about 7 hours of average sleep. This number is at the extreme low end of the recommended range of 7 to 9 hours of sleep per night. Another study of college students in the United States found that nearly half were poor sleepers. In this case, poor sleep quality was associated with depression and anxiety. Finally, another study in the United States found that college students' average score on the PSQI was in the poor sleep range. Further, this is a pattern not particular to the United States, as it has been found in other countries as well, for example, in Australia. In Australia, one study found that 32.9% of college students were poor sleepers.

It is abundantly clear that adequate sleep is necessary to be a good thinker. The general ability to think—scientists refer to this as cognition—is linked to good sleep. There is evidence that optimal mental and emotional functioning requires sufficient sleep. When it comes to memory, sleep performs amazing functions. Sleep can determine which memories from the day should be remembered and which should be forgotten; sleep can integrate new information into our existing memory networks; and, sleep can generate new memories based on information already stored in our memories. Sleep helps some memories get stronger so that they are more easily remembered, and sleep helps sleep enhances weak memories so that they can be recalled later on. Additionally, sleep benefits the brain generally, as well as other areas of performance, such as mood and physical health. Good sleep helps to prevent physical sickness and is said to restore the brain. And the importance of sleep starts early on in life. Performance on mental tasks is linked to getting sleep in young children and preteens. Good sleep helps young minds develop thinking and other skills in a healthy way.

While some mental tasks, such as intelligence tests, have not shown the effects of poor sleep, many other mental tasks have. A lack of sleep—sometimes called sleep deprivation—impairs functioning in most cases. Cognition is negatively affected by a lack of sleep for children, teens, and emerging adults. Elementary school students aged 8 to 11 years old were asked to perform a memory task on a smartphone regularly throughout the day for a month. When researchers examined the kids' sleep patterns, the results showed that sleep quality, the duration of sleep, and feeling tired all predicted the fluctuations in memory performance. Daytime sleepiness also affects performance on mental tasks for adolescents. Inattention and impaired memory contribute to poor academic performance. Getting insufficient sleep causes people to do mental tasks more slowly and to make more errors. Problems with executive function occur due to lack of sleep. Executive function includes mental skills that keep us focused and on track for completing our goals. Learning, problem solving, and creativity are impaired by lack of sleep, and concentration is affected.

Several studies have shown that using personal technology is associated with changes in sleep. The bulk of the research has been done with U.S. college students, because that is a group of people who are easily accessible to the researchers; the researchers tend to be college professors. In a typical study, students are asked to complete questionnaires—possibly more than once—that ask about their sleep habits, their technology use, and other variables like academic performance, emotional status, and physical status. In several cases, texting stands out as an activity that is linked to poor sleep. While the exact reasons are not known for sure, several possibilities exist: people who text a lot may be more likely to be texting when they are supposed to be sleeping (i.e., displacement), people who text a lot may have higher levels of exposure to the blue light that comes from device screens (i.e., a biological mechanism), and people who text a lot may be sleeping near their phones which wake them up during the night (i.e., nighttime awakenings). Different types of technologies, but mostly texting, have been linked to sleep problems. College students with higher PSQI scores—and thus worse sleep—are more likely than others to have texting dependence and iPod dependence, two conditions where people have difficulty regulating their amounts of texting and music device usage. The poor sleepers also had higher levels of depression, higher levels of anxiety, and poorer executive function than the good sleepers. What is the reason behind all of the late-night and sleep-time texting? Some researchers have pointed a finger at social media—that is, wanting to stay connected to others—as the culprit. Some scientists have likened the mobile phone problem to a mother who can sleep through the sound of a train but awakens instantly at the sound of her baby crying. People's hypervigilant attachment to their phones might make them easily awoken and unlikely to get good sleep. The link between texting and sleep problems appears to be universal. One study in Egypt found not only that texting at night was linked to sleep quality, but also that two-thirds of the adolescent participants slept with the TV on.

Video gaming might interfere with sleep as well. Compared to 50 minutes of gaming prior to sleep, a study with Australian adolescents found that doing 150 minutes of gaming led to less time asleep, more problems sleeping, and a delay in falling asleep by 17 minutes on average. And being online for any reason is associated with sleep and other health-related problems. In a very large study of Chinese college students, it was found that students who used the Internet the most were the ones who tended to oversleep and were more likely than others to have long sleeping bouts. With most of these studies, one must keep in mind, however, that much of the research uses a correlational approach to research design; therefore, those results do not prove that personal technology causes sleep changes. Also, one of the problems with using questionnaires to assess sleep is that people may forgot their actual sleep details, but a study in the northeastern United States asked students to keep sleep diaries in order to get around this problem. The results showed that 47% of college students are subject to nighttime awakenings, with 40% of the students actually answering phone calls during sleep hours; further, people who used their devices during sleep hours got worse sleep.

The biological explanation of the effect of technology use is through an effect on the normal biochemical process that regulates sleep. Scientists know that sleep is modulated biologically by a chemical called melatonin. Released at the right time of day, melatonin induces sleepiness and leads to sleep. Laboratory studies show that short wavelength light, or blue light, can suppress our body's natural tendency to release melatonin. It is known that the blue light from electronic displays can cause melatonin suppression under certain conditions. Reading an electronic book, or e-book, for 4 hours before bedtime, for 5 nights, caused adults to release less melatonin, take longer to fall asleep, be less drowsy at bedtime, and have reduced morning alertness compared to reading a printed copy of a book. In fact, this much reading of an e-book, rather than reading the print copy of the book, shifted the adults' sleep cycle by 1.5 hours. Yet the issue of melatonin suppression might not be of practical consequence with short uses of devices before bedtime, or with relatively dim screens. Using an iPad for one hour before bedtime did not affect the sleep of Australian adolescents.

The effects of technology use might be different for people of different ages and circumstances. School-aged children, adolescents, and college students may be most at risk for sleep problems related to technology use. For example, fourth and seventh graders in the United States who sleep near a device with a small screen—for example, a smartphone—get 21 minutes less sleep than other students, and they are more likely to report having insufficient sleep. Sleeping in a room with a television is related to getting 18 fewer minutes of sleep. Adults appear to have more flexibility in adjusting their sleep schedules in order to compensate for bad sleep caused by technology use. In a nationally representative sample of participants in Belgium, residents who had Internet access in their bedrooms, used the Internet more than others, and viewed more TV than others, went to bed later—the authors called this time shifting—but were able to make up the sleep at a later time.

TAKING CHARGE OF PERSONAL HEALTH

There are different kinds of devices that fit into the category of personal health technologies. Wearable devices, smartphones, and healthcare "apps" take advantage of certain modern principles of electronic technology, and already present themselves as lucrative industries in the technology marketplace. The devices have become popular because the sizes of the sensors and computers have diminished greatly, and the costs of electronics have been reduced significantly. Some devices are designed to fit onto your body directly, while other technologies depend upon a smartphone being used. Examples of devices that fit directly onto the body—the so-called wearable technology—include smartwatches (wristwatches that have smartphone capabilities along with built-in sensors), earbuds that can measure heart rate, and jackets that contain multiple sensors and tracking technology. A person might also wear a fitness tracker or activity tracker that comes in the form of a wristband or bracelet. Applications on smartphones, while not directly attached to a person's body, can already track the number of steps a person takes, as well as tracking movement using a built-in accelerometer, a device that determines motion. Many of these products are featured each year at one of the world's largest conventions for new personal technologies, the International Consumer Electronics Show. Driving the industry is a theory of how people will incorporate personal healthcare technology into their lives, and a consumer base that is willing to spend billions on the devices and the technologies. Starting with healthcare applications on smartphones and tablet computers, the market has moved in a large way to wearable devices. The market for medical/healthcare applications on smartphones was about $150 million in 2011. The market surged with the advent of wearable devices, reaching into the billions of dollars. Estimates for future sales vary, but one estimate is as high as $53 billion in sales by 2019.

Mainly, companies that market the products see a typical consumer as a relatively passive player in their own health care, but one who can benefit greatly from the features of the devices. One researcher who visited multiple conventions of the

Consumer Electronics Show, carefully observing and tracking the products that were being pitched, cleverly called the viewpoint of the industry "data for life." The data-for-life approach argues that personal data tracking must become habitual, but must not overwhelm a consumer with numbers and figures that are hard to interpret. Instead, the devices should "nudge" consumers into making changes to their lifestyle by analyzing the flow of data and interrupting consumers when necessary. For example, you may wake up in the morning to an alert on your sleep tracking bracelet telling you that you achieved poor sleep quality the night before. The device can then offer suggestions for how you can improve your sleep the coming night. As the researcher wrote, a user will

> not only trust her suite of devices and software to remotely *track* her but also to keep her *on track*, interrupting the flow of her experience to prompt her—when an algorithmic analysis of her own real-time data deems it necessary—to eat, drink, or rest. . (Schüll, 2016)

The essence of the data-for-life viewpoint is captured in an advertisement from Fitbit, one of the major manufacturers of wearable tracking technology. In a promotional video for one of its products, a woman is shown looking at a small device and there is a caption that reads, "small daily decisions = BIG RESULTS."

It is possible that such personalized health care will extend effective health monitoring to people with little money, and to those who live in remote regions not served well by traditional medical facilities. These technologies make the promise to provide personalized health care to the masses, but there is not much scientific research done on the topic yet. For personal healthcare technology to work effectively, it must use some of the characteristics of contemporary electronics. For one, the devices must not interfere with day-to-day activities. There are many devices that can do this. Wristwatches can be worn throughout the day and during sleep. Bluetooth headsets and earpieces can be worn while at work or while driving. Google Glass—a technology that is worn like glasses and allows for recording visual information—can be worn without interfering with many other activities. Another important characteristic of cutting edge devices is permanence: the devices are always on, even when we sleep, thus collecting data around the clock. Also, the technologies collect information about ourselves that we cannot detect with our own five senses; this is called extensibility. Finally, connectivity is an important characteristic of wearable technology and other personal healthcare technologies. Devices collect data and transmit the data to a personal database via wireless technology or the Internet. They may also share this information with a larger organization such as the product manufacturer. Connectively applies to social media, too, when devices from different users can be linked in such a way to provide group updates on each person's status.

Research with wearable technology and healthcare apps shows that they are useful for some purposes, but not for others. Devices used to improve physical activity have appealing features, as well as some drawbacks, and do not always achieve their purpose. People wearing the devices report being motivated to move, being appreciative of the social aspect of the using the system (e.g., sharing and comparing results), and finding the devices easy to use. However, at the same time, people also find that the devices make mistakes in tracking, can be difficult to keep charged, and are easily forgotten and not worn when they should be. Although some studies have found that the devices increase physical activity, others have not. For identifying specific health conditions, the devices have proven effective in research. One study asked participants to wear seven different devices simultaneously, and was able to track personal circadian rhythms (sleep-wake cycles), early signs of Lyme disease (a bacterial infection picked up from tick bites), and insulin dependence (a key factor in diabetes).

Tracking one's health might also include tracking stress. Stress in your life has a mental component and a bodily component. It can be caused by everyday problems, and also by the technologies that you use. When a person encounters an event, either at the moment or when thinking about future events, she evaluates the event and determines whether the demands of the event will exceed her mental and physical resources for responding. When preparing for final examinations at school, for example, students must judge whether they feel prepared to be successful on the exams. If there is an imbalance in the resources needed to succeed at the event, then coping mechanisms must be used to reduce stress. Problem-focused coping attempts to deal directly with the stressor, while emotion-focused coping attempts to reduce the negative emotions associated with stress. Escapism is an emotion-based coping mechanism that reduces stress but does not adequately solve the problems that are causing stress. If a young man reduces his stress by viewing online pornography, he is not directly addressing the stressor that caused the stress in the first place and he might be creating new problems for himself related to problematic pornography use.

The bodily component of stress involves a set of physiological reactions that include an elevated heart rate, sweating, and changes in blood pressure. Extreme stressors—events that trigger stress and require coping mechanisms—might include, for instance, being forced to participate in sexting with your romantic partner even when you don't want to. Unwanted sexting happens with about 20% of U.S. college students, and is often brought about through subtle tactics like repeated asking and being made to feel obligated to participate by a partner. Signs of trauma and stress are significantly related to unwanted sexting in both men and women, but the relationship between these are twice as strong in female college students as in male college students. More mundane stressors could be feeling overwhelmed with the number of messages in your email inbox or worrying about whether your smartwatch is tracking your daily steps properly. For people who use email a lot, the hassles of daily emails—having to continuously monitor one's email messages—can lead to a feeling of being out of control, although in many cases messages can be deleted easily and quickly (e.g., spam messages) and are not technically stressful. But for the high cost of monitoring messages, some researchers have referred to email as a tyrant. A study of U.S. consumers showed that people who wear smart devices have worries related directly to their devices, like whether the devices are accurately measuring their health. Consumers who actively tried to address their worries, either by problem-focused coping or by emotion-focused coping, were more likely to keep using the devices.

Technology may play role in stress detection and in stress reduction, sometimes in positive and sometimes in negative ways. Devices and software tools are available that attempt to assess a person's current stress levels, and possibly correct them. While some people have been known to monitor their own electronic messages for signs of stress, the promise of automatic detection of stress lies in wearable devices and in mobile phone apps. An app called mycompass for students in India has shown positive results for assessing stress—and also depression and anxiety. Not only might devices and apps be able to detect stress, but they might also be able to provide feedback to help reduce stress. To identify stress, your smart devices and apps can either monitor your physiological changes like an increased heart rate, or they can prompt you to answer questions about your stress levels. Once identified, software can suggest that you refrain from making important decisions or can provide soothing—and hence stress reducing—stimuli such as pleasant music or sounds in a process known as digital nudge technology.

While these technology-based approaches to monitoring stress might not be for everyone, they have certainly taken a hold of a certain segment of society. A group of individuals known as the Quantified Self (QS) have committed themselves to tracking as much information about themselves as they can. However, experts in the wearable devices industry recognize that regular people might not be as interested in quantification as the QS group is. The QS members have shown that it is possible to detect stress by carefully evaluating daily email correspondence. In the future, the behaviors of the QS members may become normal for everyone. However, most people currently perceive the quantification effort as narcissistic and obsessive—in other words, abnormal.

For people with chronic illnesses or disabilities, technology—in the form Internet-based groups—can provide a safe place for building community with others, and participation in these communities has increased rapidly. A person's online presence provides few clues as to her real identity, and this online anonymity could make people more comfortable and less socially anxious, lowering the barriers to participation in a health community. Such online health communities provide empathy, support, and friendship. Starting with email communications in the 1990s, online communities have become diverse in how they are constructed and the media that are used. In some cases, the communities are specific to a particular disease or related diseases and run on a website dedicated for that purpose. Research shows that participants in these health communities are seeking information about the illness or disability in question, as well as social support. In other cases, the community can be a subgroup of users in a larger social networking system, such as Facebook, where the users communicate and interact with each other within the more general world provided by the system. When community members are satisfied with the social support that they receive online, then they also show lower scores on measures of mental health, such as depression. Women who participated in a breast cancer support group showed improved emotional and psychological outcomes. So just like in the case of physical, face-to-face social networks, social support online has positive benefits to one's mental health.

Online health communities are rife with empathic responses. In one study that analyzed over 400 messages posted in a depression community for teenagers, a substantial number of the messages contained empathic messages. For example, "deep [empathic] support" was defined as reassurance, giving help, and deep emotional support; more than 80% of the messages contained such support. In another study of over 500 postings in diabetes, cancer, and infertility online communities, empathic discussion was the most frequent type of post, with 45% of the postings being empathic in nature. Another study of 2,000 messages from over 100 online health communities found that 81% of the communities contained some empathic content. One of the factors that drives people to use and continue to use a particular health community is the level of perceived empathy, defined in one study as "an individual member's perception regarding other members' feelings of compassion, warmth, sincerity, and sensitiveness towards oneself and towards the problems one has narrated or posted" (Nambisan, 2011). It turns out that one's level of perceived empathy is impacted by how similar one judges the other users to be to herself. This type of similarity, called homophily by researchers, can be measured with questionnaire items given to a user. An example item on a questionnaire would ask a user to what degree members of the online community "behave like/do not behave like" herself. Aside from the empathy that is perceived to exist in an online health community, other aspects of the experience of participating are the practical value of participation (the pragmatic dimension), how well the members socialize (the sociability dimension), and how easy it is to navigate the website (the usability aspect).

Another potential way to take charge of one's health is to get fit by playing games. While the vast majority of computer and video games require no more physical effort than moving one or two hands or fingers at a time, there is a subset of games starting decades ago that were designed to require that the player moves her body. The unique features of innovations in gaming over time have included extending the input features of arcade gaming, adding devices to home video gaming platforms, and incorporating locomotion into phone-based games. These innovations are well exemplified by *Dance Dance Revolution*, the Nintendo Wii, and *Pokémon Go. Dance Dance Revolution*, perhaps the first game to incorporate serious physical movement into its gameplay, was heavily featured in video game arcades. Players copied increasingly complex dance patterns by dancing on a pressure-sensitive mat. Enormously popular in the early 2000s, up to 45% of all 8- to 18-year-olds in the United States had played it. Later, boosts to home video gaming platforms allowed the in-home platforms to incorporate hand, arm, head, and other movements. Various mechanisms beyond the traditional handheld gaming controllers are used by the video game platform manufacturers to allow physical interaction with the gaming system. These include accelerometers placed into controllers that measure the speed of device movement, optical sensors that use light to detect movement, and systems that use cameras to detect body movement directly without controllers. The first generation of these at-home platforms included the Wii, the Xbox 360, and the PS3. The Nintendo Wii came out in 2006. Exergames—the games that use these features of home platforms—require physical activity to control a game, such as in running place to make a computer figure run on the screen as in *Marathon* on the Nintendo Wii platform, or moving your hands and arms in a particular way to simulate rock climbing as in *Active Life: Outdoor Challenge*. As the hardware behind gaming became more sophisticated and the processor speeds increased, the games were capable of adding an improved psychological dimension as well: the games became more realistic and captured the player's attention better in processes referred to as immersion and presence by scientists. The Nintendo Wii, with its Wii Play and Wii Sports lineup of games, stood out as an at-home gaming platform featuring physically interactive video games. By 2010, 64% of American youth aged 8 to 18 years old had played physically interactive games on this platform. The Nintendo Wii was heralded as providing a new sense of interaction that simulated real-life. Involving the whole body in the gameplay was so lifelike that some scientists raised the possibility that the player could feel like she was actually in the game.

Traditional games require so little energy to play that they are often considered a sedentary activity; yet the clever modifications of the hardware integrated with software design can demand greater physical activity from players, and thus increased energy expenditure. But if one expected millions of game players to get fit from playing exergames, then surely the phenomenon has not been a success. Nonetheless, research over this time period shows that these types of games do actually increase physical activity and exertion, as well as affect players' cognition in a positive way. Research shows that games like *Dance Dance Revolution* and those on the Nintendo Wii platform cause greater energy expenditure than other games, and they affect the body in ways that normal exercise does, for instance, elevating one's heart rate. The games are not as good at this as real physical activities, but playing them might make people more likely than not to go out and get some real exercise. Players of exergames can reach moderate and sometimes vigorous exercise levels, and may even increase their desire to engage in real exercise. Playing physically interactive video games also can have an indirect, long-term effect on people, at least for sports-related video games. Playing sports-related games causes youths to become more involved in real-life sports; the opposite is true, as well. Studies show that there is not only greater energy expenditure, but also greater oxygen consumption and increased heart rate for exergame players compared to sedentary games. Not surprisingly, the level of physical intensity achieved by a player depends upon the activity simulated in the game; in one study, Wii Golf raised energy expenditure levels no higher than being sedentary. In another study, Wii Sports Boxing showed the greatest physical reaction in adolescent players compared to Wii Sports Tennis and Wii Sports Bowling. An interesting effect of playing exergames occurs when a person's avatar—his or her in-game appearance—is changed. Making an avatar appear fat causes players to expend less energy than they normally would. In children, exergames can cause short-term improvements in mental skills like inhibition—the ability to ignore irrelevant information.

MENTAL HEALTH

Technology not only affects people's physical health; it also affects mental health. A key issue in this regard is Internet addiction. All around the world, addiction to technologies is taking its toll. It's fairly common to hear about gaming addicts wearing diapers while they play so that they do not have to leave their game to relieve themselves. Extreme cases have involved death and/or dismemberment. Reports exist of addicts depriving themselves of essential factors for living, neglecting their dependents with extreme consequences, trying to take control of their addictions using violent means, and carrying out vicious and brutal acts. In one case, a young couple neglected their three-month-old baby daughter while they raised a virtual baby together. The (real) baby eventually died of malnutrition. Some startling outcomes are the stories of three cases in South Korea: in one, a young gaming addict was driven to kill himself but killed his mother first; in another, a 23-year-old addict was successfully treated, then, overwhelmed by the loss of his former gaming friendships, committed suicide. And in another story, a young man addicted to gaming played continuously without eating or sleeping. When he finished his game, he died. A case in China revealed that a 19-year-old Internet addict tried to savagely end his addiction—not by taking his life—but by cutting off one of his hands, with the idea that he would no longer be able to use the Internet. Using a kitchen knife from home, he chopped off his left hand, leaving it on a bench in the city; doctors were able to reattach the hand after it was retrieved.

Some Asian countries have already set up networks of Internet addiction treatment centers and, in certain cases, have passed laws that might reduce the incidence of addiction. The hordes of Internet addicts among youth in Asian countries is often attributed to the high number of cybercafes that are open all night long, seven days a week. Additionally, countries like South Korea have fantastically well-developed Internet infrastructures, with over 90% of homes having high-speed Internet access. One treatment center in South Korea, is known as the Easy Brain Center. Electric shock therapy is used there, under the assumption that it stimulates the brain's frontal lobe; one physician describes the frontal lobe as the part of the brain that makes people act like humans. Some treatments have gone too far, ending in death. After the deaths of several teenagers due to the use of the therapy, the technique was banned in China. To prevent these adolescents from sneaking out on therapy, Chinese treatment centers have been known to top their outer walls with barbed wire. South Koreans knew the problem was serious when youngsters begin breaking the law as part of their gaming addiction. For example, although tattoos are banned in that country, young gamers have been known to get tattoos representing their favorite games, such as *League of Legends*. In response to increased awareness of gaming addiction problems in youth in South Korea, the country passed a law known as the Cinderella law. It bans kids younger than 16 years old from playing Internet games between the hours of midnight and 6 a.m.

While Asian countries are ahead of the rest of the world in identifying and treating this type of addiction, North America has also started to see and address the problem. Noteworthy cases of Internet addiction have cropped up in North America, and formal treatment is starting to be provided here. One such case is that of Marshall Carpenter, who was playing video games up to 15 hours a day, getting his nutrients from soda, and barricading himself in his room. He lost his sports scholarship at his university and dropped out of college. Eventually, his father literally broke down his son's door and instigated a long process of recovery at a treatment center. Carpenter moved into one of the first live-in rehabilitation centers in North America, reSTART Life, located outside of Seattle, Washington. reSTART has been operating for eight years, treating more than 150 men, but only 6 women.

The pattern of vastly more men becoming addicted to the Internet than women is found in countries around the world. Another one of the first U.S. inpatient treatment centers was run by Dr. Young (of the Internet Addiction Test fame) in Pennsylvania.

In the rehabilitation program at reSTART, recovering addicts first get 45 days of residential treatment and then move offsite as long as they agree to continue psychotherapy and attend addiction meetings. They also agree to some rules of living, such as staying away from the Internet for six months and putting effort into finding a job. In the program, Carpenter eventually graduated to living on his own with a group of other young recuperating addicts. One roommate got addicted to gaming at age nine; as an adult, his gaming led to the loss of his job and then intentions to commit suicide. Another roommate became homeless for six months due to Internet addiction and found himself living in his car. In the car, he would spend all day on his computer tablet connected to the Internet, addicted to Internet pornography. He masturbated 6 to 10 times per day to the point of bleeding, but wouldn't stop.

Another case is that of Andrew Fulton; he spent two stints at reSTART. His story started as young man, addicted to gaming. In college, he once went on a three-week gaming binge that he planned in advance. He bought a case of caffeinated soda, stocked up on simple food items, and left his room only to use the restroom. He bathed two times. Mr. Fulton's family tricked him into getting help for his problem by having his grandparents ask him to stop by and look at some vacation photos. Instead of looking at photos, the whole family was there to do an intervention. They took him to reSTART. There also is the story of Cam Adair, from Canada. His gaming addiction started in elementary school. His parents did an experiment where they let him play for as long as he wanted. They decided to see how much gaming that he would do. After 15 hours, his mother stopped the experiment; Adair had got up from the computer only to go to the bathroom during that time. After serious battles with his parents, he eventually reached a low point when he planned to commit suicide, and even drafted a suicide note for this family and few friends. His plans were interrupted by a call from friends who asked him to go the movies. He went, had a great time, he says, and realized the depth of his problem. Later, he told his father about the suicide note, a step that led to rehabilitation. However, Adair relapsed and started gaming again, up to 16 hours per day. In a crucial moment in time, he decided that he could only solve his problem by going "cold turkey," voluntarily putting an end to his gaming. It worked for him, and now he makes a living by speaking about video game addiction, and specifically about how to quit it forever.

Internet addiction is more than just spending too much time online. Some significant problems can occur, including online romantic or sexual affairs that devastate existing relationships, student Internet abuse that impairs academic performance, and employee Internet abuse that affects business outcomes such as productivity. One person has had so much influence in the field of Internet addiction that she might be said to be the originator of the field; this person is Dr. Kimberly Young. Dr. Young was not the first to address the problem of getting addicted to computer technology; other researchers had identified addictions to technology, computers, and video gaming prior to the widespread use of the Internet. However, her research focused on the qualities of the Internet that were becoming part of more and more people's everyday lives. After providing the initial tools and concepts for the rest of the world, her ideas have been both contradicted and confirmed by others, leading to a significant evolution of what it means to be addicted to the Internet. Is Internet addiction a solitary, holistic, phenomenon where people become hooked on the Internet itself? Young has been said to be advocating this view, while dissenters have advocated the view that people become addicted to very specific aspects of the Internet or that people use the Internet to fuel their other addictions.

As early as the 1980s, it was clear that people going online wanted to interact with other people, even strangers, in electronic spaces known as chat rooms. Early stories emerged about regular people overusing the Internet and suffering significant problems by doing so. Dr. Young published a famous case about a 43-year-old homemaker who, Dr. Young said, broke the stereotype about addicts being heavily involved in technology and having other addiction problems. Dr. Young noted that many of the Internet addicts spent their time using these and other interactive, Internet-based applications. Young's original notion of Internet addiction was holistic, with the idea being that the Internet itself provides opportunities for overuse or addiction. However, she did make a distinction between more interactive forms of Internet use and ones that were not, and later, she identified subtypes of Internet addiction.

Two of the key measurement tools developed by Dr. Young include the Diagnostic Questionnaire and the Internet Addiction Test (IAT). Based on the idea that Internet addiction could be similar to other addictive behaviors like gambling, she generated a short list of questions—the Diagnostic Questionnaire—that were given to people approaching her with signs that they might have problems from overuse of the Internet. People who answered five or more of the eight questions with a "yes" answer were potential addicts (e.g., "Have you repeatedly made unsuccessful efforts to control, cut back, or stop Internet use?"). As she learned more and more about these addicts, Dr. Young refined her measurement tool; this resulted in one of the current gold standards of measuring Internet addiction—the Internet Addiction Test (IAT). The IAT contains 20+ questions in a multiple-choice format that give clinical psychologists a tool for evaluating the degree to which people might be addicted to the Internet. When she compared people who were dependent on the Internet—dependent being another word for addicted—to people who were non-dependent, Dr. Young found several interesting differences. The dependent persons spent 38.5 hours per week online while the non-dependents spent 4.9 hours per week online; the dependent people engaged in two-way communication when online while the non-dependent people mostly did information gathering; and the dependents reported personal, family, and occupational problems due to Internet use when the non-dependents had no problems.

Can you get a high from using the Internet in the way that drug addicts might get high from using illicit or illegal substances? Dr. Young suggested that indeed a person could get high from using the Internet; further, this high might serve as a reward that drives Internet addiction. On the front lines of dealing with potential Internet addicts, therapists and psychologists might be the best people to know what Internet addiction is like in people's lives. Dr. Young and her colleagues surveyed a group of therapists; the results showed the existence of five subtypes of Internet addiction: cyber-sexual addiction, cyber-relationship addiction, net compulsions (gambling, shopping, and trading), information overload (compulsive information gathering), and computer addiction (game playing).

A wholly different approach is to think of the Internet as a tool that addicts use to fuel their existing addictions. Someone who is addicted to shopping—that is, he spends an inordinate amount of time and money buying apparently unnecessary items—can use the web to feed the addiction; or, someone who is addicted to gambling can spend time and money gambling online. Still other researchers have proposed that a general form of Internet addiction might exist alongside a set of very specific addictions tied to particular uses of the Internet. According to these researchers, problematic Internet use (PIU)—often used as a synonym for Internet addiction without using the word "addiction"—of the general type (GPIU) has different origins and causes than the specific type (SPIU). Perhaps an approach that acknowledges all of these types of addiction will prevail.

The original, clinical concept of Internet addiction was based on existing mental disorders defined in the *Diagnostic and Statistical Manual* (DSM) of the American Psychiatric Association (APA). The DSM is known as the bible of American psychiatric medicine; it tells the research and therapeutic communities what mental health problems officially count and can be diagnosed. The current version of the DSM is DSM-5. In the DSM, substance abuse and problem gambling are clearly defined in a way that allows clinicians to identify and diagnose the disorders. Dr. Young used these definitions—known as criteria—to formulate her idea of Internet addiction; she borrowed and altered the original criteria to create new ones. Internet addiction was defined by Dr. Young using the DSM-IV criteria as a base. Dr. Young chose substance dependence as a model for Internet addiction because the word "addiction" does not appear in the DSM. The seven criteria for substance dependence that appeared relevant to Internet addiction are withdrawal, tolerance (needing higher and higher doses), preoccupation with the substance, greater use than intended, activities to procure more of the substance, loss of other interests, and disregard for negative consequences. The Diagnostic Questionnaire was based on these DSM-IV criteria.

To make Internet addiction an official mental health diagnosis, the next step would either be to add it to the DSM as a possible disorder of interest, or to outright add it as a diagnosis. Before a diagnosis of a mental illness is placed into the DSM, the illness is sometimes characterized as an issue of interest to the psychiatric community. When a potential disorder has been identified in the research community, but there is not yet enough scientific data to characterize the disorder, it will be included in the DSM with the goal of bringing attention to the problem and possibly including it in the next version of the DSM. The APA does this formally by placing the issue into the Appendix of the DSM. While the members of the APA were deliberating over the next version of the DSM (DSM-5), there was speculation in the research community that Internet addiction would be listed as an issue for further study. This was based on the perception that most experts who had studied PIU believed that there were, in fact, individuals who could become dependent upon the Internet. At the same time, a fair number of researchers have called for the disorder to be placed directly into the list of diagnoses in the DSM, possibly as a type of illness related to compulsions and impulsivity. As the DSM-IV was being evaluated and revised, researchers into the area of Internet addiction advocated that Internet addiction be considered an impulse-control disorder. Impulse-control disorders occur when a person has difficulty resisting behaviors that are ultimately destructive. Aware of the high levels of Internet addiction being recorded in Asian countries, some researchers became concerned that Internet addiction was very prevalent in the United States as well, but underreported.

However, complications with the scientific understanding of the construct of Internet addiction have hampered these possible next steps. As mentioned earlier, not all researchers agree that Internet addiction is real in the way that it was originally conceptualized. One of the major criticisms of the concept of Internet addiction is that people do not become addicted to the Internet; rather, people are addicted to specific activities on the Internet, like gambling. Quite possibly, this disagreement in the research literature has prevented the APA from including Internet addiction at all in the DSM in its most recent editions. With the concept of addiction in flux, there might not be enough agreement among scientists to allow the disorder to be identified in the DSM. The DSM-5 does not contain Internet addiction as a disorder, nor as an issue of interest. (The manual of disorders used internationally—the International Classification of Diseases—does not include Internet addiction, either.) The newest DSM does, however, include Internet Gaming Disorder as an area of interest.

Despite not being formally recognized as a clinical diagnosis, some of the research on Internet addiction has revealed how it takes place in the brain. As an analogy, consider hunger and food. When you are very hungry and begin to crave your favorite foods, your brain begins to plan and execute behaviors that culminate in getting those foods. This appetitive system also encourages us to take actions to satisfy our sexual, nurturing and other urges. This system of seeking out ways to satisfy our urges—also known as approach—exists alongside a system that steers us away from actions that would disgust us, make us feel badly, or negatively affect our mood (also known as avoidance). For example, for many people, a marshmallow has "hot" features that make it desirable: it is a sweet, rewarding treat. On the other hand, imagining the marshmallow as a little white cloud "cools" the stimulus and reduces activation of the appetitive and reward systems. Romantic infatuation, sexual attraction, and personal attachment are other states that can drive the appetitive system. These appetitive states can activate the same reward areas of the brain that are activated in drug addictions. This appetitive system of the brain, in a similar way, can also make you take actions that lead to satisfying less biological cravings, such as a gambling addict having a craving to use a casino slot machine or a teenager having an urge to find out what his friends are up to on Facebook. In addicts, the craving or urge is a precursor to engaging in the problematic behavior.

For an addict, encounters with computers or computer-related objects can be triggers for cravings. These addiction cues are even known to activate the brain's reward center in Internet addicts. The allure of using the Internet engages parts of the brain that want to seek out and use the Internet; when these urges and cravings are satisfied, they produce internal satisfaction through the brain's reward system. Stimuli that activate our reward center—those things that we find rewarding—activate the appetitive system; stimuli that have the opposite value to us activate a behavioral inhibition system that supports avoidance. At the same time, knowing that addictive behaviors can be destructive, the brain's cognitive control system, located in an area known as prefrontal cortex (PFC), battles the other systems in a struggle to prevent the destructive behaviors from being carried out. Many parts of the PFC work together to organize, plan, and restrict our behaviors in a way that helps us achieve our rational goals. The logical, cold aspect of the cognitive control system often is contradicted by the emotionally charged reward system that feeds into the PFC. In fact, brain imaging research has shown that people with serious problems associated with misuse of technology can have deficits in parts of the PFC. This supports the idea that the cognitive control system is working to reduce Internet- or technology-related behaviors that are problematic, like neglecting one's family because of spending too much time online. In one study investigating cybersexual addiction, people who showed more signs of cybersexual addiction were less able to effectively sort a set of pornographic pictures compared to those without those signs. This indicated to the researchers that cybersexual addiction is associated with reduced cognitive control when addiction cues, such as the pornographic pictures, are present.

While the whole world has been affected by personal computer technology and the explosion of the Internet, Asian countries have been identified as being ahead of other regions of the world in addiction problems. And within Asia, some countries have higher rates of technology-related problems than others. People in Asia, Europe, and North America appear to be using personal technology more than in other regions of the world. While there are significant rates of Internet addiction in all of these regions, rates in Asian countries are sometimes higher than in the other regions. In some of these Asian countries, scientists have worked to identify the rates of Internet addiction, especially among children and adolescents. Countries that have found significant, and occasionally relatively high, rates of Internet addiction include South Korea, Taiwan, and urban areas in China. Rates of Internet addiction in adolescents have been found to range from 6% to 15% across Asian countries. In one study, China had a rate of 14% Internet addiction among students while the United States had a 4% rate. A study that compared six Asian countries on Internet addiction prevalence found that the Philippines had the highest prevalence rates, with 5% of adolescents being classified as addicts according to the IAT. South Korea stands out as a country featuring high rates of Internet addiction. In South Korea, Internet gaming addiction is especially problematic for adolescents. Actually, there is considerable uncertainty about the rates of Internet addiction in various regions and countries, as different countries have used different measures of Internet addiction and varying levels of concern over its existence. It is possible, for instance, that PIU in the United States is as common as it is in Asian countries, except that the effort to measure it and to diagnose it has not been made in this country. Going hand in hand with the potentially very high rates of Internet addiction in Asian countries, certain nations have outspent American and European nations on addressing Internet addiction. South Korea and Taiwan have put forward more resources toward research and treatment of Internet addiction than the United States, for example.

It is possible that the unique circumstances of Asian culture and particular Asian countries have contributed to higher rates of Internet addiction in those places than in American and European countries. There are possibly several aspects of Asian culture that contribute to Internet addiction, especially in youth. In some Asian countries, such as Singapore, computer/Internet centers are much more widespread and popular than in Western countries. This could be a factor in the development of addictive behaviors like pathological gaming in those countries. Only a few years ago, Singapore and Hong Kong had some of the highest rates of smartphone usage in the world. The availability and ownership of personal technology in Asian countries was higher than other parts of the world for many years, which, when combined with relatively strong pressures on youths to perform in school, may have led to technology overuse as a form of ineffective coping. The pressure that students place on themselves to do well in school can be fairly intense; but what if parents, family, and the school system were also all placing intense pressure on students? This could negatively affect teenagers' satisfaction in life, making them look to online and virtual worlds for escape (an unhealthy coping strategy). Just like youths in other parts of the world, Asian youths who have trouble with people in everyday life—for instance, getting along with family members and relatives—will look for ways to lessen their stress by coping. One possible coping mechanism is to go online, a behavior that might contribute to PIU. Not having supportive friends can be a significant negative impact in a young person's life. This might also push young people into online activities. Another aspect of Asian culture noted by Western researchers is the tendency for Asian societies to treat any time taken away from family or education as pathological (in other words, disordered). Parents may especially be driving the widespread interest in Internet addiction among youths, affecting not only how their own children are treated, but also governmental policies.

Different types of treatment have been proposed for Internet addiction, along with various strategies for working with people who are afflicted. Early on, Dr. Young provided clinicians with several strategies for working with patients who might have Internet addiction. These strategies included "practicing the opposite" (disrupting normal routine in order to break the online habit), external stoppers (schedule being online in a way that it is ended after a short period of time by a natural activity, like having to leave for work), setting goals, abstinence, reminder cards (making small lists of reasons to not use the Internet or good reasons to use the Internet), personal inventory (assess what activities are missed due to Internet use), support groups, and family therapy. An interesting dimension in the treatment of Internet addiction is the use of drugs to alter mood and/or behavior, though not all treatments involve drugs. A further aspect is that the different subtypes of Internet addiction—e.g., cybersexual addiction—might need different therapies. However, it has been found that most treatments work on Internet addiction. These treatments improve the symptoms of Internet addiction, reduce the amount of time spent online, lift depression, and reduce anxiety. Some have positive effects on people's thinking processes, with the results helping scientists understand a little more about Internet addiction than was known before. In one study, researchers used brain monitoring to examine the electrical activity associated with memory and attention. Internet addicts typically show deficiencies in these electrical markers, but after a three-month program of therapy, the markers returned to normal levels. In another study, not only did the electrical markers of memory and attention return to normal, but so did people's short-term memories. The fact that treatments can return a person's thinking back to normal suggest that Internet addiction caused the problems in cognition in the first place.

Other technology addictions include gaming addiction. Under the name of Internet Gaming Disorder (IGD), it has been officially warranted as a condition for further study in the DSM-5. There is a key distinction made between gaming addicts and gaming enthusiasts: both spend a lot of hours gaming, but only the addicts develop problems because of their game playing. Further, brain imaging and brain activations show that the brains of these two types of people do not function in the same way. The section of the DSM that contains conditions for further study is Section 3 (the appendix), meaning that IGD is not yet an official diagnosis of a mental health problem. Including IGD in this part of the DSM implies that the disorder is not yet seen as a potent problem. Only very little is known about the development and maintenance of a gaming addiction; the bits and pieces that are known suggest that gaming addiction involves several different psychological and neural systems. One part of the frontal cortex—the orbitofrontal cortex—has less volume in gaming addicts than in non-addicts, meaning that there is less neural tissue to perform tasks. As described earlier, the frontal cortex is linked to executive function and cognitive control; indeed, gaming addicts are worse at cognitive control than non-addicts. More research supports the implication of executive function and the frontal brain areas in IGD. A broad pattern of research data—brain activation and performance on tasks—in gaming addicts suggests impaired cognitive control compared to healthy control (HC) participants (people who are similar in all other ways to the addicts but do not have an addiction). Another possible angle on understanding the development of gaming addiction is that it comes about when people, in response to life's stressors, seek a way of coping with their problems. Because video game addiction is much more common in men than in women, this unhealthy coping might be a particular coping mechanisms for guys. The brain's reward system has also been implicated in IGD. One possibility is that addicts respond differently than HCs to cues in the environment that trigger cravings for video gaming.

As more and more research is conducted on the condition, including identifying the factors associated with gaming addiction, there is the possibility that IGD will become an official diagnosis of a mental health problem according to the APA. Scientists have noted the particular type of diagnosis that IGD might have in the DSM, including how it might be similar to pathological gambling and involve problems with impulse control. Originally, researchers suggested that Internet-based addictions would be classified as impulse-control disorders in the DSM; this is where other non-substance-related disorders were placed, such as pathological gambling in the DSM-IV. Since gambling disorder is in many ways like a sub-stance addiction, it is now listed as one of the "Substance-Related and Addictive Disorders" in the DSM-5, suggesting that IGD would be classified in the same category of mental illness.

Another possible technology addiction, cell phone addiction, may encompass a range of behaviors and devices. The modern cell phone (aka, the smartphone) per-forms so many functions that it's not clear whether people get overly attached to the phone itself, or to a particular function on the phone, like texting. Even so, some researchers are so concerned about cell phone addiction that they have called it a public health concern. The phrase Wireless Mobile Device (WMD) has been used to describe it—a play on the phrase Weapon of Mass Destruction. There are certain features of the devices themselves that make people want to use them. Functionality, design, and novelty are features of smartphones that make people want to acquire them and use them. Noticing the intensely attractive qualities of smartphones, a few researchers have projected that smartphone addiction will become a top addiction over time. A good example of how cell phones have taken a hold of people is students in the classroom; this is a setting where people can't help themselves from using their phones, despite there normally being rules against its use and even penalties for doing so. The phrase CPUse is a term that has been used to describe student cell phone use; in this case, it applies to students' use of cell phones in the classroom. (CPU also stands for Central Processing Unit, the main part of a computer responsible for running all of the computer programs.) CPUse is just using the device, while CPUse addiction is having problems associated with using the device. What do students do on their phones? The study of CPUse found that texting was the most common behavior on the phone. Being one of the top uses of cell phones, especially by adolescents, texting has been implicated in why people appear to be addicted to their devices. In at least one study looking at the motives behind frequent cell phone use, student use of phones in the classroom was driven by the students' desires to connect with other people.

Certain people are more likely to want to use WMDs, although it's not clear whether men or women are more likely to be addicts. In middle schoolers and high schoolers in the United States, girls were found to be more likely than boys to be compulsive texters, and, at the same time, compulsive texting was related to hav-ing worse school grades and other outcomes. In this case, the authors said that girls may feel the need to communicate with peers more than boys do, and this may lead them to compulsive texting. This pattern of higher cell phone addiction among females than males was found in another study of American college students. In contrast, males in Saudi Arabia show more smartphone addiction than females, at least among college students, but this research used a different addiction scale than other studies. However, it is true that being relatively young is a factor in addiction to cell phones. Adolescents tend to be more likely to be addicted to smartphones than other age groups. Among the Saudi Arabian college students, younger students—who also are less likely to be married—scored higher on cell phone addiction than other students. This might be due to the fact that younger people have fewer responsibilities and more free time for smartphone use than older individuals.

Scientists have been trying to measure cell phone addiction around the world. Worldwide interest in measuring smartphone addiction reveals the breadth of the problem as perceived by scientists. Learning about what predicts cell phone addiction, what other variables are associated with cell phone addiction, and what outcomes occur due to its presence will help scientists discern the underlying nature of the disorder. When researchers study cell phone addiction, they have to create very specific definitions of problematic behaviors and thoughts; they then create measurement tools based on these definitions. Typically, the measures focus on what are called problematic behaviors—actions that would likely cause a disruption to person's life in some way. The most frequent approach has been to take Dr. Young's IAT and adapt it to smartphones. This approach has resulted in the Smartphone Addiction Test. Another measurement tool is the Mobile Phone Problem Usage Scale. Aside from the United States, there are scales for measuring smartphone addiction in Great Britain, Italy, Korea, Spain, and Taiwan.

Psychological variables could either cause or be caused by cell phone addiction, or both. There is some evidence to link anxiety and stress with cell phone addiction. Many emotional reactions have been found to occur in addicts when they are not allowed to or can't use their phones. Distress, anxiety, depression, and anger all have been documented in adolescent smartphone addicts. A study in Lebanon found that people who had higher smartphone addiction scores also had higher levels of perceived stress than others. Other variables, such as self-esteem, also might be involved. Certain negative outcomes, such as poor academic performance, give insight into the disorder and how it affects people. When the researchers in Lebanon assessed smartphone addiction in college students, they found that students with more symptoms of addiction had worse academic performance than other students. The relationship between cell phone addiction and sleep shows that there is no way out of sleep problems for cell phone addicts. On one hand, turning off the cell phone can cause a person to get bad sleep due to anxiety and stress. On the other hand, leaving the phone on during the night can disrupt sleep (and cause daytime sleepiness) because the phone owner is accessible during the night. Other addictive behaviors, like substance abuse, have not been found to correlate with smartphone addiction.

There is debate over whether addiction to cell phones exists at all. It has not been resolutely established as an addiction, although researchers often have characterized it that way. And not everyone agrees that problematic texting is problematic enough to qualify as an addiction or a serious mental health problem. Abuse of texting has been characterized as a compulsion—a behavior that satisfies obsessive thoughts—rather than as an addiction. Sometimes, problematic texting is referred to as a checking habit. An alternative interpretation of problematic cell phone use is that it's a compulsion, or an impulse disorder. Another possibility is that some people have an addiction tendency that applies to many different behaviors and can include cell phone use. Within the addiction way of viewing things, students who become addicted—that is, they show habitual use of the phone—may have started out using the phone as a simple amusement tool. An interesting alternative view of problematic cell phone use is that it has more to do with the reinforcement that a person receives from the phone that it does from an addiction;

some messages and information received from the phone are very rewarding (e.g., interacting with a best friend), while others are not. Scientists who study the power of reinforcement on behavior have long known that such partial reinforcement schedules create habits that are difficult to break. Whether problematic cell phone use is characterized as an addiction or not, it is clear that the phone itself serves as a constant cue to users to access their friends, look at social media, and find information using the device. Some measures of the rate of smartphone addiction have been extraordinarily high, as in the case of a 48% prevalence rate in college students in Saudi Arabia. What makes Saudi Arabia special perhaps, and other Arab countries, is a voracity for keeping up with modern technology, but this love of new technology is surely a worldwide phenomenon.

Two additional addictions that have been proposed and studied are email addiction and social networking site (SNS) addiction. (Addiction to online pornography and cybersexual addiction were described in Chapter 4.) More detail about email addiction has been provided by recent studies. The occasional reward received from checking emails could be creating an interval reinforcement schedule that increases a person's email checking behavior by reinforcing it every once in a while. In one study of workers in the UK, 12% were identified as email addicts based on their responses to a questionnaire based on concepts similar to those underlying Dr. Young's description of Internet addiction. Several suggestions have been made by experts to reduce the negative impact of a potential email addiction. People who find themselves overusing their email might consider making an email schedule, a process that involves carefully selecting the number of times to check email each day, the specific hours to check email, the duration of each email session, and the tasks to be performed in each session (for example, read only or read and reply). This could help to control the anxiety over not being able to check email and help to manage the rewards associated with constant email checking.

SNS addiction includes overuse of Facebook and may involve several of the same characteristics as substance abuse addictions. In some cases, researchers of Facebook use have uncovered the features of salience (ever present in one's mind and behavior), tolerance (needing ever increasing doses of Facebook), and conflict (with other activities). These features, similar to aspects of other addictions, may drive a compulsion to check Facebook, high frequency Facebook use, and use of Facebook to avoid responsibilities in the real world. Unlike substance abuse addictions, treatment for SNS addiction cannot be abstinence (stopping the use of the Internet); Internet use is an integral part of work and life in contemporary society. Some researchers have suggested that SNS addiction be treated with cognitive-behavioral therapy, a system of treatment designed around changes to a person's belief system. Two key goals of treatment for SNS addiction—and, really, any technology addiction—would be gaining control over Internet use and preventing relapse into damaging behaviors. Further, treatment is complicated by the fact that SNS addiction—if it exists and is like other addictions—is usually present alongside one or more other mental health problems, a situation known as co-morbidity. An additional complication that might arise from any technology addiction is increased media multitasking. Media multitasking is when you are trying to get too many tasks done at one time and find yourself juggling between different applications on a computer or between your cell phone and your laptop. In Taiwan, being addicted to technology is one of the reasons behind media multitasking; this not so much a problem for Americans (who say that they media multitask in order to manage their tasks).

CONCLUSION

The health-related aspects of technology use represent a diverse set of effects where technologies can degrade health in some cases and improve health in other cases. There is sufficient evidence to conclude that technology use, such as television and video gaming, can promote sedentary behavior and contribute to sleep loss. At the same time, wearable technologies and online health communities both can provide ways of improving a person's health, although the former may be helpful only to people who are comfortable with quantitative tracking and monitoring of their own health statistics. While exergames and other active games and devices can provide a temporary exercise experience, they have not provided users as a whole with long-term improvements in health. Finally, when it comes to mental health, scientists believe that there are several ways in which people can become addicted to technology use. Technology addictions lead to impairments of mood, social relationships, school performance, and work performance. While the most studied form of technology addiction, Internet addiction, has not been formally recognized as a psychiatric diagnosis, another form of addiction, Internet Gaming Disorder, is the condition that is poised to become a formal diagnosis. Other addictions that are currently being studied by researchers include smartphone addiction, social networking addiction, and email addiction.

The relationship between our health and our technologies is rapidly evolving. It seems like a new hardware product with potentially healthful, harmful, or addictive qualities is released by technology manufacturers almost weekly. Also, new software products—such as apps on our smartphones—are released even faster. Researchers continue to study the impact of personal technology upon health and mental health, but the pace of scientific research is slow and does not match the frenzied pace of technological innovation. This is true of all of the research areas covered in this book. Nevertheless, as scientists carefully unravel the nature of our relationship with computer-based technologies, more will be learned about both the positive and negative impacts of technology use upon our physical, emotional, and cognitive states.

Interview with an Expert: Dr. Kimberly Young

As a psychology professional, Dr. Kimberly Young does extensive public speaking, engages in important scientific research, and develops programs related to technology overuse and abuse. Her work provides therapy and counseling for Internet addicts, as well as parenting guidelines. Dr. Young is the founder and director of the Center for Internet Addiction and Netaddiction.com. The Center offers specialized treatment for Internet Addiction, a form of cognitive-behavioral therapy known as CBT-IA. Dr. Young also founded the first

U.S.-based inpatient hospital clinic for Internet Addiction at the Bradford Regional Center (Pennsylvania). For parents, she has offered a screening guide to help prevent technology-related problems in youth: the 3-6-9-12 Screen Smart Parenting Guidelines. For 12- to 18-year-olds, for example, Dr. Young defines what is normal behavior so that parents can recognize when youth are deviating from it. She says, "Teenagers should do the things they have always done: They should see friends, get jobs, complete chores, stay involved with school activities and friends, and test the boundaries of their independence" (*New York Times*, July 16, 2015). Dr. Young has an academic faculty appointment at St. Bonaventure University (New York) and has published more than 50 scientific articles. In addition, she consults with business firms dealing with problems related to employee Internet misuse and abuse.

Q: What got you involved in Internet addiction when computers and the Internet were hardly as omnipresent as they are now, and smartphones did not exist?

A: I get asked this question a lot. Basically, in 1994 my friend's husband was spending too much time on AOL chat rooms and she was very concerned. He was spending 40, 50, 60 hours a week online at a time when it was still $2.95 an hour. Not only did this create a financial burden, but their marriage ended in divorce as it became clear that he was meeting women in online chat rooms.

This episode prompted me to question if people could get addicted to the Internet the same way we talked about getting addicted to drugs, alcohol and sex. I posted a small survey online, taking the same clinical criteria for pathological gambling, and converted it to the Internet. The next morning, I had over 40 emails at a time when I might've gotten two emails a month talking about problems such as job loss, divorce, and school failure due to excessive Internet use. I start hearing from parents and spouses who had loved ones that they felt were addicted to the Internet. It was a small pet project of mine that grew into international news as reporters started talking about this phenomenon, and apparently I was the only researcher studying and talking about Internet addiction. I continue to hear from those who either had an addiction or felt they knew somebody who had an addiction. It was then that an entirely new field was born.

Q: What are your thoughts about how much of a problem Internet addiction is, particularly among younger people in their teens and early twenties?

A: Early on, I spoke that Internet addiction is an umbrella term used to describe a multitude of application problems experienced by the end user. That is, we might talk about pornography addiction, online gaming addiction, social media addiction, and compulsive Internet gambling which are definite subtypes of the problem under the umbrella term Internet addiction.

I think it's a problem for anyone with access to the Internet. In the olden days, the question used to be how much time is too much. Now the question is how young is too young to be allowed to use the Internet due to its potential addictive qualities that young minds might not be able to resist. In a TEDx talk that I gave, I outlined the difference between chronic checkers, who constantly check their phones but most likely out of compulsion and addiction, which carries with it a clear symptomology.

The issue is the level of consequence, as many users of technology, regardless of age, check their phone all the time. Oftentimes it might be email from work and text messages from friends. Then there are those who suffer very specific consequences in their job or at school or in their marriage because of the amount of time they spend on devices and technology. There is a large difference between productive use of the Internet and recreational use. For someone making reservations for a future trip, it's likely not problematic. For someone playing multiuser role-playing games 15 hours a day at the exclusion of other relationships or activities, it is not fine. While time is not a specific factor of addiction, I think in the extreme we can see that that's a problem.

Q: Why do you think that Asian countries are ahead of the Western world in treating Internet and other technological addictions? What can we learn from them?

A: I've been fortunate to speak with representatives in various Asian countries about their motivation to prevent and treat Internet addiction. I think one specific factor is that they have government-run health care, so when they saw a problem with Internet addiction they were able to mobilize rather quickly to treat it from the government level. For example, in South Korea they have several ministries or arms of their government that have collaborated to put together a master plan for the prevention and treatment of Internet smartphone addiction. They have prevention programs in schools and a variety of treatment centers to address this problem. In America, we are lagging behind because we haven't put any effort into prevention models and/or treatment. In America we have private insurance companies that certainly would not want to reimburse for such treatment and I think there's a political issue with how technology is viewed in terms of the productive uses of it rather than anything that might prove problematic.

With Internet addiction, we must look at the extreme behavior but the totality of using technology isn't patently positive. This makes it more difficult to formalize Internet addiction as a condition, yet there really is a segment of the population having significant problems with moderating their use of technology.

Q: What do you foresee in the future about Internet addiction?

A: In recent literature over the past decade, more attention has been paid to the neurobiological basis of Internet addiction. Several studies and books have been written addressing the role of the prefrontal cortex of the brain in Internet addiction. This is consistent with other addiction disorders. Studies have also shown dopamine to be a significant factor in Internet addiction. Again, this is consistent with other addiction disorders. It may be that addiction is not triggered by the specific activity, but something problematic in our brains, and it manifests itself in various ways including Internet, gambling, sex, or alcohol. I think it's a growing body of research that also shows that with very young children the most common side effects, cognitively, are attention and concentration problems. There is also new research on physical concerns such as obesity in children who are sedentary in front of screens for a good portion of their days.

Since I began studying Internet addiction I have seen the research develop rather quickly. It has become an entire field with good quality studies showing that it does exist and that it is treatable. I think in a short time Internet addiction will become its own disorder in the psychiatric literature in America. It is already endorsed in several other countries as well as the World Health Organization. I can't imagine that it wouldn't, in time, be considered a diagnosis in our psychiatric literature. There are just too many studies showing that it is also preventable not to do anything about it.

Glossary

Affordances
Thoughts and actions that are linked directly to the hardware and software characteristics of a device, such as pull-down menus.

Amygdala
A brain area associated with processing emotions; it is part of the limbic system.

Blended Courses
School courses that mix together offline meetings and online activities or resources.

Cognitive Control
A set of mental processes that people use to stay on track when performing a task.

Cognitive Load
The theory that tasks of different complexities require different amounts of mental and brain resources.

Cognitive Processes
The psychological processes that are used to analyze information gathered from the world, such as memorization.

Computer Literacy
The set of skills that people use to effectively interact with computer-based devices, such as using web browsers.

Correlational Research
A research method that determines whether two variables or psychological characteristics are associated with each other.

Cortex
The part of the brain that surrounds the rest of the brain; it contains many of the brain areas that are involved in higher-order processes.

Cyberpsychology
The scientific field that investigates how the psyche and the Internet are related to each other.

Cybersex
The set of behaviors that people use to engage in sexual activity over the Internet or by using computer-related technologies; an example is sexting.

Disinhibition
The state of mind that occurs when people feel free to behave or speak in a way that they normally would not.

Displacement Hypothesis
The scientific hypothesis that engaging in technology-related activities reduces or prevents other behaviors.

DSM (*Diagnostic and Statistical Manual*)
A scientific publication that is used by psychiatrists and psychologists to diagnose individuals with mental illness.

Evolution
The scientific theory that explains how physical and psychological characteristics of humans change over time.

Executive Functions
The set of mental processes that people use to exert influence over other mental processes, such as inhibition of unwanted thoughts.

External Distractions
Stimuli from the environment that grab a person's attention and direct it away from the task at hand, such as a phone notification.

Flipped Classrooms
School courses in which lectures take place online, outside of classroom time.

FOMO (Fear of Missing Out)
Purported to be a psychological state of anxiety associated with wanting to know what one's friends are up to at the moment.

Frontal Cortex
The part of the brain heavily involved in thinking and planning; it is a large area located in the anterior of the brain.

Generation X
The group of people born after the Baby Boomers, starting approximately in the year 1965.

Generation Y (millennials, digital natives)
The group of people who grew up with everyday use of computer-related technologies, born roughly in 1989 and later.

Generation Z (aka, iGeneration, iGen)
The group of people born after personalized technology became widely available, roughly in 1999 and later.

High-Level Processes
Mental processes that perform deep and insightful analysis of information gathered from the environment, such as reading comprehension.

ICT (Information and Communication Technology)
The set of computer-enabled devices, as well as software, that allows people to exchange information and messages, such as mobile phones.

Identity Development (Identity Formation)
The set of psychological processes that help people shape their perceptions of who they are and what their place in society is.

Impulse Disorder
A mental health problem in which people cannot stop themselves from carrying out certain behaviors.

Internal Distractions
Thoughts that are not related to the task that a person is supposed to be working on.

Internet Gaming Disorder
A mental health problem that may occur when gaming activities interfere with other key aspects of life.

JOMO (Joy of Missing Out)
The state of mind that may occur when people refrain from using their computer-enabled devices for an appreciable period of time.

Limbic System
A set of brain areas that process emotions and the events in the environment that give rise to emotions.

Longitudinal Research
A research method in which a group of individuals is tracked over time.

Low-Level Processes
Mental processes that collect and analyze information from the environment, such as identifying a letter on a computer screen.

Mediators
Psychological variables that influence attitudes, thoughts, or behaviors.

Melatonin
A brain chemical that signals sleepiness.

Meta-Analysis
A research method in which a scientist gathers together the data from other research studies and uses statistical tools to look for patterns in the aggregated data.

Moderators
Psychological variables that change how technology and behavior relate to each other.

Neuroplasticity
A brain process in which the structure or function of brain areas changes over time.

Nomophobia
The psychological state of being afraid of losing access to one's smartphone.

Peer Review
A set of behaviors that scientists use to evaluate each other's work.

Phatic Communication
Exchanging messages in order to maintain one's relationships.

Phonological Sensitivity
The set of psychological processes that allow infants and young children to learn the common speech sounds of their own language.

Prefrontal Cortex (PFC)
The part of the brain that contains the neural networks for planning, organizing, evaluating, and multitasking; it is part of the frontal cortex.

Prosocial Behaviors
Behaviors that help other people or promote positive attitudes, such as offering to help someone in need.

Reward Areas
The parts of the brain involved in directing people's thoughts and actions toward pleasing stimuli.

Scripts
Mental processes that guide people through typical, recurring situations.

Self-Regulation
The set of psychological processes that help people stay focused and emotionally stable, such as knowing to take breaks during a long task.

Sensory Processing
The set of mental processes that collect information from the outside world through the five basic senses.

Sexual Identity
A psychological concept that reflects a person's sexual preferences and self-image.

Short Message System (SMS)
A set of hardware and software that allows people to exchange brief messages, usually text-based, using telephone communications systems.

Social Augmentation
The scientific hypothesis that people who form relationships online are expanding their social networks.

Social Displacement Hypothesis
The scientific hypothesis that people who form relationships online are losing their offline relationships.

Text-Speak (Textese)
A style of language with shortenings and abbreviations that is suited for the exchange of brief messages between people; an example is LOL.

Tolerance
The psychological process of needing to have increasing levels of technology use in order to feel satisfied.

Valence

The property of an emotion that describes whether it is positive and pleasing or negative and uncomfortable.

Working Memory

The mental process that lets people hold small amounts of information in mind while performing a complex task.

Directory of Resources

ARTICLES AND BOOKS

Adams, R. (April 23, 2013). Sal Khan: The man who tutored his cousin—and started a revolution. *The Guardian*.

Alter, A. (2017). *Irresistible: The Rise of Addictive Technology and the Business of Keeping Us Hooked*. New York, NY: Penguin Press.

Apple, Inc. (June 19, 2013). Apple awarded $30 million iPad deal from LA Unified School District.

Araujo, T., Wonneberger, A., Neijens, P., and de Vreese, C. (2017). "How Much Time Do You Spend Online? Understanding and Improving the Accuracy of Self-Reported Measures of Internet Use." *Communication Methods and Measures*, 11(3), 173–190.

Atchley, P., and Strayer, D. L. (2017). "Small Screen Use and Driving Safety." *Pediatrics*, 140(s2), s107–s111.

Ayers, J. W., Leas, E. C., Dredze, M., Allem, J.-P., Grabowski, J. G., and Hill, L. (2016). "Pokémon GO—A New Distraction for Drivers and Pedestrians." *JAMA Internal Medicine*, 176(12), 1865–1866.

Baron, N. S. (2008). Adjusting the Volume: Technology and Multitasking in Discourse Control. In J. E. Katz (Ed.), *Handbook of Mobile Communication Studies* (177–193). Cambridge, MA: MIT Press.

Baron, N. S. (2015). *Words on Screen: The Fate of Reading in a Digital World*. New York, NY: Oxford University Press.

Barraket, J., and Henry-Waring, M. S. (2008). "Getting It On(line): Sociological Perspectives on E-dating." *Journal of Sociology*, 44(2), 149–165.

Bayer, J. B., Ellison, N. B., Schoenebeck, S. Y., and Falk, E. B. (2016). "Sharing the Small Moments: Ephemeral Social Interaction on Snapchat." *Information, Communication and Society*, 19(7), 956–977.

Bilton, N. (June 15, 2014). Looking at link between violent video games and lack of empathy. *The New York Times*.

Boulton, M., Lloyd, J., Down, J., and Marx, H. (2012). "Predicting Undergraduates' Self-Reported Engagement in Traditional and Cyberbullying from Attitudes." *Cyberpsychology, Behavior, and Social Networking*, 15(3), 141–147.

Bowman, L. L., Waite, B. M., and Levine, L. E. (2014). "A Cross-Cultural Comparison of Media Multitasking in American and Malaysian College Students." *International Journal of Cyber Behavior, Psychology and Learning*, 4(3), 1–17.

Brown, J. D., and Witherspoon, E. M. (2002). "The Mass Media and American Adolescents' Health." *Journal of Adolescent Health*, 31, 153–170.

Browne, M. N., Freeman, K. E., and Williamson, C. L. (2000). "The Importance of Critical Thinking for Student Use of the Internet." *College Student Journal*, 34(3), 1–5.

Calvert, S. L., Appelbaum, M., Dodge, K. A., Graham, S., Nagayama Hall, G. C., Hamby, S., et al. (2017). "The American Psychological Association Task Force Assessment of Violent Video Games: Science in the Service of Public Interest." *American Psychologist*, 72(2), 126–143.

Carr, N. (2010). *The Shallows: What the Internet Is Doing to Our Brains*. New York, NY: W. W. Norton.

Carrier, L. M., Spradlin, A., Bunce, J. P., and Rosen, L. D. (2015). "Virtual Empathy: Positive and Negative Impacts of Going Online upon Empathy in Young Adults." *Computers in Human Behavior, 52,* 39–48.

Collyns, D. (May 9, 2004). How text messages changed by life. *BBC News*.

Crompton, H. (2013). Mobile Learning: New Approach, New Theory. In Z. L. Berge and L. Y. Muilenburg (Eds.), *Handbook of Mobile Learning* (47–57). Florence, KY: Routledge.

Cutino, C. M., and Nees, M. A. (2016). "Restricting Mobile Phone Access during Homework Increases Attainment of Study Goals." *Mobile Media and Communication*, 5(1), 1–17.

Davis, M. J., Powell, A., Gordon, D., and Kershaw, T. (2016). "I Want Your Sext: Sexting and Sexual Risk in Emerging Adult Minority Men." *AIDS Education and Prevention*, 28(2), 138–152.

de Bertodano, H. (September 28, 2012). Khan Academy: The man who wants to teach the world. *The Telegraph*.

Dill, K. E. (2013). *The Oxford Handbook of Media Psychology*. New York, NY: Oxford University Press.

Döring, N. (2014). "Consensual Sexting among Adolescents: Risk Prevention through Abstinence Education or Safer Sexting?" *Cyberpsychology: Journal of Psychosocial Research on Cyberspace*, 8(1), article 9 .

Duggan, G. B., and Payne, S. J. (2009). "Text Skimming: The Process and Effectiveness of Foraging through Text under Time Pressure." *Journal of Experimental Psychology: Applied*, 15(3), 228–242.

Ellison, N. B., Vitak, J., Gray, R., and Lampe, C. (2014). "Cultivating Social Resources on Social Network Sites: Facebook Relationship Maintenance Behaviors and Their Role in Social Capital Processes." *Journal of Computer-Mediated Communication*, 19, 855–870.

Elson, M., and Ferguson, C. J. (2014). "Does Doing Media Violence Research Make One Aggressive?" *European Psychologist*, 19(1), 68–75.

Ferguson, C. J., and Kilburn, J. (2010). "Much Ado about Nothing: The Misestimation and Overinterpretation of Violent Video Game Effects in Eastern and Western Nations: Comment on Anderson et al. (2010)." *Psychological Bulletin*, 136(2), 174–178.

Gazzaley, A., and Rosen, L. D. (2016). *The Distracted Mind: Ancient Brains in a High-Tech World*. Cambridge, MA: MIT Press.

Gentile, D. A., Bailey, K., Bavelier, D., Brockmyer, J. F., Cash, H., Coyne, S., et al. (2017). "Internet Gaming Disorder in Children and Adolescents." *Pediatrics*, 140(s2), s81–s85.

Gentile, D. A., and Gentile, J. R. (2008). "Video Games as Exemplary Teachers: A Conceptual Analysis." *Journal of Youth and Adolescents*, 37, 127–141.

Giles, D. (2003). *Media Psychology.* Mahwah, NJ: Lawrence Erlbaum.

Greenfield, D. N. (1999). *Virtual Addiction.* Oakland, CA: New Harbinger.

Hacker, D. J., Dunlosky, J., and Graesser, A. C. (1998). *Metacognition in Educational Theory and Practice.* Mahwah, NJ: Erlbaum.

Hald, G. M., and Malamuth, N. (2008). "Self-Perceived Effects of Pornography Consumption." *Archives of Sexual Behavior*, 37, 614–625.

Hasan, Y., Bègue, L., and Bushman, B. J. (2012). "Viewing the World through 'Blood-Red Tinted Glasses': The Hostile Expectation Bias Mediates the Link between Violent Video Game Exposure and Aggression." *Journal of Experimental Social Psychology*, 48, 953–956.

Hollnagel, E. (2011). When Things Go Wrong: Failures as the Flip Side of Successes. In D. A. Hoffman and M. Frese (Eds.), *Errors in Organization* (225–244). New York, NY: Routledge.

Hughes, D. M. (2004). "Prostitution Online." *Journal of Trauma Practice,* 2(3–4), 115–131.

Ibrahim, Y. (2008). "The New Risk Communities: Social Networking Sites and Risk." *International Journal of Media and Cultural Politics*, 4(2), 245–253.

Jagatic, T. N., Johnson, N. A., Jakobsson, M., and Menczer, F. (2007). "Social Phishing." *Communications of the ACM*, 50(10), 94–100.

Just, M. A., Keller, T. A., and Cynkar, J. (2008). "A Decrease in Brain Activation associated with Driving When Listening to Someone Speak." *Brain Research*, 1205, 70–80.

Khan, K. S., and Chaudhry, S. (2015). "An Evidence-Based Approach to an Ancient Pursuit: Systematic Review on Converting Online Contact into a First Date." *BMJ Evidence-Based Medicine,* 20(2), 48–56.

Lapidot-Lefler, N., and Barak, A. (2012). "Effects of Anonymity, Invisibility, and Lack of Eye-Contact on Toxic Online Disinhibition." *Computers in Human Behavior*, 28, 434–443.

Lee, S., Kim, M. W., McDonough, I. M., Mendoza, J. S., and Kim, M. S. (2017). "The Effects of Cell Phone Use and Emotion-Regulation Style on College Students' Learning." *Applied Cognitive Psychology*, 31(3), 360–366.

Ling, R. (2005). The Socio-Linguistics of SMS: An Analysis of SMS Use by a Random Sample of Norwegians. In R. Ling and P. Pedersen (Eds.), *Mobile Communications: Renegotiation of the Social Sphere* (335–349), London: Springer.

McKiernan, A., Ryan, P., McMahon, E., and Butler, E. (2017). "Qualitative Analysis of Interactions on an Online Discussion Forum for Young People with Experience of Romantic Relationship Breakup." *Cyberpsychology, Behavior, and Social Networking*, 20(2), 78–82.

Mills, K. L. (2016). "Possible Effects of Internet Use on Cognitive Development in Adolescence." *Media and Communication*, 4(3), 4–12.

Mouton, F., Leenen, L., Malan, M. M., and Venter, H. (July 30–August 1, 2014). Towards an Ontological Model Defining the Social Engineering Domain. In *ICT and society* (266–279). Springer Berlin Heidelberg.

Mueller, P. A., and Oppenheimer, D. M. (2014). "The Pen Is Mightier Than the Keyboard: Advantages of Longhand over Laptop Note Taking." *Psychological Science*, 25(6), 1159–1168.

Müller, K. W., Dreier, M., Beutel, M. E., Duven, E., Giralt, S., and Wölfling, K. (2016). "A Hidden Type of Internet Addiction? Intense and Addictive Use of Social Networking Sites in Adolescents." *Computers in Human Behavior*, 55, 172–177.

Nambisan, P. (2011). "Information Seeking and Social Support in Online Health Communities: Impact on Patients' Perceived Empathy." *Journal of the American Medical Informatics Association*, 18, 298–304.

Paul, R. (1995). *Critical Thinking: How to Prepare Students for a Rapidly Changing World*. Santa Rosa, CA: Foundation for Critical Thinking.

Przybylski, A. K., and Weinstein, N. (2017). "A Large-Scale Test of the Goldilocks Hypothesis: Quantifying the Relations between Digital-Screen Use and the Mental Well-Being of Adolescents." *Psychological Science*, 28(2), 204–215.

Rosen, L., Cheever, N. A., and Carrier, L. M. (Eds.) (2015). *Handbook of Psychology, Technology and Society*. Hoboken, NJ: Wiley-Blackwell.

Rosenbloom, S. (August 23, 2014). Dealing with digital cruelty. *The New York Times*.

Rothman, E. F., Kaczmarsky, C., Burke, N., Jansen, E., and Baughman, A. (2015). "'Without Porn . . . I Wouldn't Know Half the Things I Know Now': A Qualitative Study of Pornography Use among a Sample of Urban, Low-Income, Black and Hispanic Youth." *Journal of Sex Research*, 52(7), 736–746.

Ryder, R. J., and Graves, M. F. (1994). *Reading and Learning in Content Areas*. Columbus, OH: Merrill.

Schüll, N. D. (2016). "Data for Life: Wearable Technology and the Design of Self-Care." *BioSocieties*, 11(3), 317–333.

Scriven, L., and Paul, K. (Summer 1987). A Statement on Critical Thinking. Presented at the 8th International Conference on Critical Thinking and Education Reform.

Smith, A. (September 11, 2006). Texting slang aiding children's language skills. *The Guardian*.

Smith, H. J., Milberg, S. J., and Burke, S. J. (1996). "Information Privacy: Measuring Individuals' Concerns about Organizational Practices." *MIS Quarterly*, 20(2), 167–196.

Stone, E. F., Gardner, D. G., Gueutal, H. G., and McClure, S. A (1983). "A Field Experiment Comparing Information-Privacy Values, Beliefs, and Attitudes across Several Types of Organizations." *Journal of Applied Psychology*, 68(3), 459–468.

Sutherland-Smith, W. (2015). Authorship, Ownership, and Plagiarism in the Digital Age. In T. Bretag (Ed.), *Handbook of Academic Integrity* (575–589). Singapore: Springer Nature.

Temple, J. R., and Choi, H. (2014). "Longitudinal Association between Teen Sexting and Sexual Behavior." *Pediatrics*, 134(5), 1–8.

Texts "do not hinder literacy" (September 8, 2006). *BBC News*.

Thornton, B., Faires, A., Robbins, M., and Rollins, E. (2014). "The Mere Presence of a Cell Phone May Be Distracting." *Social Psychology*, 45(6), 479–488.

Turkle, S. (2015). *Reclaiming Conversation: The Power of Talk in a Digital Age.* New York, NY: Penguin Press.

Twenge, J. M. (2017). *iGen: Why Today's Super-Connected Kids Are Growing Up Less Rebellious, More Tolerant, Less Happy—and Completely Unprepared for Adulthood—and What That Means for the Rest of Us.* New York, NY: Atria Books.

Uncapher, M. R., Lin, L., Rosen, L. D., Kirkorian, H. L., Baron, N. S., Bailey, K., et al. (2017). "Media Multitasking and Cognitive, Psychological, Neural, and Learning Differences." *Pediatrics*, 140(s2), s62–s66.

Underwood, M. K., and Ehrenreich, S. E. (2017). "The Power and the Pain of Adolescents' Digital Communication: Cyber Victimization and the Perils of Lurking." *American Psychologist*, 72(2), 144–158.

Westin, A. (1967). *Privacy and Freedom* (1st ed.). New York: Atheneum.

Wheeless, L. R., and Grotz, J. (1976). "Conceptualization and Measurement of Self-Reported Disclosure." *Human Communication Research*, 2, 338–346.

Williams, A. (February 10, 2010). The new math on campus. *The New York Times*.

Williams, E. J., Morgan, P. L., and Joinson, A. N. (2017). "Press Accept to Update Now: Individual Differences in Susceptibility to Malevolent Interruptions." *Decision Support Systems*, 96, 119–129.

Young, K., Pistner, M., O'Mara, J., and Buchanan, J. (1999). "Cyber Disorders: The Mental Health Concern for the New Millennium." *Cyberpsychology and Behavior*, 3(5), 475–479.

Young, K. S. (2008). "Internet Sex Addiction." *American Behavioral Scientist*, 52(1), 21–37.

ORGANIZATIONS AND WEBSITES

American Academy of Pediatrics (Family Life & Media). www.healthychildren.org/english/family-life/media/pages/default.aspx
This professional organization posts summaries of research about digital media, as well as tools to help parents plan and organize their children's online activities.

Center for Internet Addiction. netaddiction.com
Founded by Dr. Kimberly Young, this organization provides information and resources for people who are concerned about their addictions to technology.

Common Sense Media. www.commonsensemedia.org
> This nonprofit organization provides reviews and insights into the appropriateness of movies, television shows, and other media for children.

CyberBullyHelp. cyberbullyhelp.com
> A website maintained by three cyberbullying experts that contains information and resources related to online aggression.

Entertainment Software Rating Board (ESRB). www.esrb.org
> This nonprofit organization gives ratings to video games and apps that help parents and youth make informed decisions about using them.

Institute of Digital Media and Child Development. www.childrenandscreens.com
> This is a nonprofit organization started by Dr. Pamela Hurst-Della Pietra to investigate the long-term effects of technology use upon children and adolescents.

reSTART. netaddictionrecovery.com
> This organization provides treatment to individuals who are suffering from various technology addictions.

SCIENTIFIC JOURNALS

Computers in Human Behavior. www.journals.elsevier.com/computers-in-human-behavior
> This journal publishes original research into the role and impact of technology from the perspective of psychology and psychiatry.

Cyberpsychology, Behavior, and Social Networking. www.liebertpub.com/overview/cyberpsychology-behavior-and-social-networking/10/
> This journal is the official journal of the International Association of Cyber-Psychology, Training & Rehabilitation (iACToR).

Cyberpsychology: Journal of Psychosocial Research on Cyberspace. cyberpsychology.eu
> This interdisciplinary journal publishes social sciences research about cyberspace.

Journal of Computer-Mediated Communication. academic.oup.com/jcmc
> This journal is one of the official journals of the International Communication Association and publishes work from social scientists on how people communicate with computer-based media devices.

Index

About the Author

Mark Carrier, PhD, is professor of psychology at California State University, Dominguez Hills. He is coeditor of the *Handbook of Psychology, Technology and Society*, and contributor to *iDisorder: Understanding Our Obsession with Technology and Overcoming Its Hold on Us* and *Rewired: Understanding the iGeneration and the Way They Learn*. He is a member of the American Psychological Association.